Deserving and Entitled

SUNY series in Public Policy

Anne L. Schneider/Helen M. Ingram, editors

Deserving and Entitled

Social Constructions and Public Policy

Edited by
Anne L. Schneider
and
Helen M. Ingram

State University of New York Press

Published by
State University of New York Press, Albany

For information, contact State University of New York Press, Albany, NY
www.sunypress.edu

Production by Judith Block
Marketing by Michael Campochiaro

Library of Congress Cataloging-in-Publication Data

Deserving and entitled : social constructions and public policy / edited by Anne L.
  Schneider & Helen M. Ingram.
     p. cm. — (SUNY series in public policy)
  Includes bibliographical references and index.
    ISBN 0-7914-6341-9 (alk. paper) — (ISBN 0-7914-6342-7 (pbk. : alk. paper)
    1. Social groups—Political aspects—United States. 2. United States—Politics and
government. I. Schneider, Anne L. II. Ingram, Helen M., 1937– III. Series.

HN90.S6D47 2004
320.6'0973—dc22

                                                                    2004044245

10 9 8 7 6 5 4 3 2 1

Contents

PART V
Social Constructions, Identity, Citizenship, and Participation

Foreword

Deborah Stone

If social scientists ever discover the molecule of governance, surely it will be the category. The vote may be the smallest indivisible bit of government *formation,* although chads—the pieces of cardboard that are meant to be removed to indicate a voter's preference—make even that proposition debatable. But if we care about *governance*—what government does and what kind of society it makes— then we need to attend to the social construction of categories.

Governance is conducted through rules, and rules are composed of categories. Every rule divides people by their identity, their behavior, or their situations, and then specifies how members of different categories are treated differently. In some deep sense, what we mean by "policy" is precisely this deliberate ordering of the world according to the principle of "different treatment for different categories." This is the idea behind the notion of target groups.

Helen Ingram and Anne Schneider are now the foremost theorists of target groups. In their earlier work, they explored and mapped this essential aspect of public policy, and they provided a framework the richness of which is proven by the chapters in this new book. With their concept of target populations, they have hit on the essence of policy making and policy politics.

Rules and laws necessarily treat people differently. Such differences aren't troubling in and of themselves. In fact, "different treatment for different categories" might be the very definition of intelligent behavior. Any creature, human or legal, that doesn't make distinctions and act on them is an automaton, a prisoner of instinct. But in a society founded on the right of all citizens to equal treatment under the law, different treatment for different categories can be troubling to say the least.

The essays in *Deserving and Entitled* all grapple with this fundamental paradox of democratic governance: How to reconcile the equality and universalism of democratic ideals with the differentiation required by policy practice? The U.S. Supreme Court has formulated one shaky answer to this question. So long as a categorical distinction embodied in a rule bears a rational relationship to the government's purpose for making the rule, all is fair. The categories behind rules rise to the level of troubling inequalities when they dovetail with pervasive stereotypes and prejudices and when they rest on distinctions that have nothing to do with government's real goals. As Stephanie DiAlto notes in her chapter, the detention of Japanese Americans during World War II confused identity (Japanese) with political behavior (loyalty). "Detention for reasonable cause is one thing. Detention on account of ancestry is another," one Supreme Court justice noted wryly (*Hirabayashi v. United States* 1943).

Over decades of constitutional jurisprudence, the Supreme Court has offered special protection to groups who have been victims of particularly harsh stereotyping and prejudice. The Court has recognized a few classifications—race, national origin, and religion—as "suspect classes." Any rule that rests on one of these categories is automatically subject to a higher level of scrutiny than courts would normally apply in evaluating a law's fairness.

The essays in this book explode this pat legal resolution. Negative social construction of target groups is an amorphous and complex process that can generate powerful legal and political inequalities, but because it is so amorphous, it isn't detected by law's doctrinal radar. Moreover, political efforts to remedy damaging and unjust social constructions sometimes inadvertently sustain them or create even more harmful ones.

For example, to fight racial discrimination in housing, advocates emphasized the good and worthy black middle class, so that they might be the vanguard of equality. Once segregation was broken by these "better" blacks (the strategy hoped), whites would see goodness in more and more black people and more doors would open. As Mara Sydney points out, however, the strategy was a double-edged sword, because the social construction of some blacks as good entailed dividing blacks into deserving and undeserving, and reinforced racist stereotypes. Advocates for immigrants, Lina Newton shows, used a similar strategy to obtain better treatment, this time dividing immigrants according to their supposed motives. Some were good, hardworking, and legal, in contrast to others who were free loaders, lazy, and illegal. Together, these chapters show that even advocates for inclusion and equal treatment sometimes divide their constituency into more and less deserving parts.

To fight the degenerative politics of derogatory social constructions, well-meaning citizens attempt a politics of integration, community building, and inclusion. But sometimes this new politics is disintegrating, fragmenting, and exclusionary. Sanford Schram's analysis of welfare politics is a case in point. Advocates for the poor sought to bolster popular support for public assistance by countering the myth that welfare recipients are mostly black. They put out reams of data saying that the rolls were predominantly white. For the last few years, however, the rolls have indeed been more than half black (depending, of course, on how we count, but that's another story). Statistical inaccuracy and getting caught on the facts is the least dangerous outcome of this defensive strategy, Schram notes. By taking pains to construct recipients of Aid to Fami-

lies with Dependent Children (AFDC) as a mostly white population in order
to save the program, advocates subtly bought into the larger cultural notion that
whites are more deserving of public aid. They failed to confront the prejudice
behind the myth. In rendering poor black people less visible than poor white
people in the welfare world, advocates failed to reveal the kind of information
that *should* drive policy, namely how systematic economic and social forces
make blacks more likely than whites to be poor and reliant on welfare.

Together, these essays develop a sophisticated understanding of how social
construction of target population "works." How does a difference between
groups go from being a neutral description to an engine of hierarchical ordering? All the chapters address this question in one way or another, but Sean
Nicholson-Crotty and Kenneth Meier highlight the role of moral and political
entrepreneurs. Why do some social constructions endure while others are more
plastic? Stephanie DiAlto compares the case of Japanese Americans with
African Americans to find some answers. And, of course, the chapters by Sidney, Newton, and Schram (mentioned above) all show how efforts to change
social constructions sometimes harden and perpetuate them instead. Why do
some categories seem natural and obvious even though they are artifacts of politics and law? Kay Schriner challenges the obvious when she questions the
assumption that people with mental illness or disability should not be allowed
to vote, and shows how legal and political disabilities were manufactured out of
intellectual and emotional ones.

What does social construction of target populations mean for democracy?
Every chapter in this book engages this question. Schriner's chapter on suffrage
hits hard at the core act of democratic participation. Laura Jensen addresses
another important way citizens engage with government—as beneficiaries of
government assistance, rather than as voters. Perhaps the beneficiary role is the
more important one, for voting is only a process to reach an end: establishing a
government that fosters citizens' well-being. Drawing on her recent book,
Jensen finds the "founding moment" for categorical entitlement programs in
the 1818 Revolutionary War veterans' pension program. The first categorical
entitlement program is so crucial to American political development, Jensen
argues, because it transformed Congress from governing by petition to governing by legislation. Instead of citizens petitioning Congress as individual sup-
plicants and Congress acting as a jury, the citizen now faced Congress as a
member of a group with common needs, and Congress responded as a deliberative body, deliberating about problems, not specific people. Jensen's chapter
rightly leads off the book, for the categorical structure of entitlement that she
identifies sets in motion the social construction of categories that the rest of the
book explores.

In depicting the earliest categorical entitlement politics, Jensen also illuminates another paradox of American democracy: a state that professes equality
among citizens creates a loyal citizenry, one group at a time, through selective

rewards. The state's *modus operandi* is "divide, distribute, bind." As Ingram and Schneider note in their introduction, the United States professes equality and universalism, while governing with a system that creates and maintains privilege.

Does spinning off government functions to private organizations and not-for profit entities escape the dilemmas of divisiveness and denigration? No. Nancy Jurik and Julie Cowgill probe into a microenterprise development program that offers loans to low-income clients to help them start businesses and become economically self-sufficient. In pursuit of organizational survival, donor funds, and accountability, these organizations, Jurik and Cowgill find, cream the most educated and financially stable clients to generate a success record for themselves. They seek grantees who are compliant with the agencies' training programs and the views of staff on how to run a business. Hence, they replicate the screening and sorting processes used by government welfare agencies and reverse their own priorities, helping the least disadvantaged, most promising clients, instead of the most needy.

Michelle Camou finds something similar in neighborhood associations. They, too, tend to pursue their nominal goals of economic development and neighborhood community building by examining and reforming the individuals in their target population. They lean to causal theories that make "individual lifestyles" the source of community problems, and they therefore offer services and programs aimed at reconstructing their target population, instead of the economic and social infrastructures of the community.

A destructive dynamic operates through all the policies and social constructions examined in this book, and Dionne Bensonsmith captures it perfectly in her chapter on welfare politics. She states that the Moynihan Report "helped provide justification for shifting government intervention from the public (institutional structures that cause poverty and disenfranchisement) to the personal (namely the family and the individual." (p. 335[Verify page number]). This shift is one of the most serious consequences of policy making for target populations. Too often, target-group thinking generates causal stories that blame *people* for problems. Politics and policy shift their focus from reforming infrastructures and institutions to reforming people and their behavior.

Policy designs that focus on types of people, in turn, shape citizens' political beliefs about the nature of government and their role as participants. Joe Soss compares clients of AFDC and Social Security Disability Insurance (SSDI), two government income-maintenance programs that rest on very different policy designs. AFDC teaches its clients that they are dependent on the whims of their caseworkers, and that the only way to interact with government is to comply with "summons" and "directives" they receive but cannot challenge. SSDI teaches its clients that the government operates by rules, and that the same rules will apply no matter which government employee handles their case. It provides them with a sense of "standing" to question and challenge the way they are treated by government.

Soss's portrait of the civic effects of AFDC brings us full circle to Jensen's portrait of government in the post-Colonial era. Governance through personal discretion of street-level bureaucrats—the Immigration and Naturalization Service (INS), police, welfare workers, neighborhood associations, microenterprise agencies—comes close to the old petition system, where the citizen addresses government as a needy supplicant instead of as a voting, participating equal. In the chapters, we see the full range of possibility of how social construction of target groups shapes political identity and behavior. Jensen's war pension beneficiaries and Soss's disability insurance beneficiaries occupy a much nicer political universe than Bensonsmith's and Schram's welfare recipients, or Schreiner's mentally disabled, or DiAlto's Japanese Americans during World War II.

But if Soss's chapter holds out the promise of policy designs that foster democratic culture, it also carries a sobering analysis of the profoundly individualistic assumptions of even some of the better entitlement programs. *Both* AFDC and SSDI, he points out, require applicants to "prove they have specific characteristics that set them apart from normal citizens. . . . They pay benefits to deviating *types of people* rather than offering compensation based on problems arising from social structure. The basis of payment is not that some groups are systematically more likely to suffer discrimination, develop injuries and health problems, or be disadvantaged by the lack of workplace accommodations for children or impairments. . . . In this manner, the welfare state atomizes individual claims" (p. 416[Verify page number]).

Old-age insurance, Medicare, and the G.I. Bill of Rights are entitlement programs that don't atomize individual claims; people prove their entitlement by pointing to their membership in a large and normal class of citizens, not by parading their personal inadequacy and neediness before a human arbiter. Such programs are not covered in this text (the early veterans' pensions excepted), but the book gives readers the tools and the impetus to reconstruct entitlements and laws on a more democratic footing.

"At bottom," Ingram and Schneider observe (p. 42[Verify page number]), "the power of the state rests as much upon the nobility of its professed ideals as upon its monopoly over the power of coercion." This book holds the mirror of American democratic ideals to policy practice—and what a powerful mirror it is.

INTRODUCTION

Public Policy and the Social Construction of Deservedness

HELEN M. INGRAM AND ANNE L. SCHNEIDER

Since time immemorial, human societies have constructed differences between people like themselves and the unfamiliar "others," who often are viewed with distrust, dislike, and even hatred. Primitive tribes all over the world have considered themselves people chosen by God(s), while others are not so privileged and, perhaps, are not really human beings. In First American languages, a number of indigenous peoples before the European conquest chose names for themselves meaning *the people,* implying that others were less than people. Similarly, although the roles were reversed, missionaries who accompanied the conquistadors in their mastery of the New World debated whether or not the Indians had souls.

A fundamental notion of the Declaration of Independence, the Articles of Confederation, and the Constitution is that all *citizens* are equal, albeit with citizenship closely circumscribed. Nevertheless, the notion of privileged classes was viewed with disdain, an outmoded custom of Great Britain and Continental Europe that the new nation forever intended to reject. America would have no aristocracy, no nobility, and no ruling class. There would be no standing army, with associated ranks affording civilian or military privileges, and there would be no overbearing bureaucracy, with officials trained for lifelong public service with public salaries. Viewed from a contemporary vantage point, the first constitution fell far short of its radically democratic ideals in that it restricted voting to white, male property owners, tolerated the inhumanity of human slavery, and engraved into law the idea that persons of African descent were to be counted as three-fifths of a white person.

In spite of the many shortcomings of the early constitution, the principle of equality remained deeply ingrained in the American consciousness. Great progress was made in the nineteenth century in ending slavery, providing equal protection of the law as a constitutional right, and granting equal opportunity to some of the previously disadvantaged persons through policies such as the

1

Homestead Act, free public education, the system of land grant colleges and universities, and recognition of the right of labor to organize and strike. In the twentieth century legal barriers to voting for women were removed, the franchise extended to the eighteen- to twenty-one-year-old age group, citizenship status was awarded to Native Americans, and equal protection of the law extended to more people in more contexts. Yet, democracy in the United States scarcely can be considered a finished project. Public policy—and the laws that policy produces—are the principal tools in securing the democratic promise for all people. Public policy is able to insure that all people—not just the select few—are considered deserving and entitled. Yet, policy also has been the primary means of legitimating, extending, and even creating distinctive populations—some of whom are extolled as deserving and entitled and others who are demonized as undeserving and ineligible. These groups have been treated very differently in the governance process.

The purpose of this book is to explain, examine, and criticize the social construction of deservedness and entitlement in public policy. The editors and authors contend that in the governance process, groups are identified and constructed as deserving and undeserving. These constructions (whether or not they already are part of popular culture) gain legitimacy. Differences become amplified and, perhaps, institutionalized into permanent lines of social, economic, and political cleavage. Unless challenged by social movements and countervailing public policies, social constructions of deservedness and entitlement result in an "other"—an underclass of marginalized and disadvantaged people who are widely viewed as undeserving and incapable. Marginalized people become alienated from the society as well as from one another. Often, they are unable to recognize their legitimate political interests or take political action that would protect their interests. In the remainder of this Introduction we will provide the groundwork for understanding how social constructions of deservedness came to play such an important part in the governance process.

SOCIAL CONSTRUCTIONS OF GROUP DESERVEDNESS

While they may differ as to the reasons, observers of human behavior agree that "there is a fundamental human desire to view one's own group as positive and occupying higher social status than other relevant groups" (Monroe, Hanking, and Van Vechten 2000). This may be the result of genetics that favor loyalty to the kinship group or perhaps because authoritarian family structures produce personalities predisposed to this type of separation. Some evolutionary theories contend that competition for survival results in individuals cooperating among themselves against common enemies. Still others believe that a bias toward in-group superiority is simply rational behavior in the face of natural resources scarcities.

Regardless of the reason, many different sociological, psychological, and biological theories acknowledge a process called *maximizing the difference* through which people attempt to distinguish their group from others, whether or not there is personal gain (Tajfel 1970). People strongly identify with their own group and exaggerate positive traits, especially at the expense of the lesser-regarded others. Groups and societies create myths and rationales that justify the dominance of some groups over others. Such stories and myths undergird beliefs that differences are fundamental, natural, and beyond human invention or social convention. Race, ethnicity, and gender are particularly good examples of socially constructed differences, greatly magnified and encrusted with mythology and custom. Whatever differences in genetic and biological endowments that exist among these groups are exceedingly small and by no means support the vast differences in social roles and treatment.

By asserting that group traits are socially constructed, we do not suggest that no real differences exist between groups and that factual distinctions are somehow made up. Almost always there are real distinctions, as in differences in skin color. Yet, neutral observation of facts, especially the very small variations in skin coloring that separate races, would suggest no factual basis for the very large differences in social constructions of deservedness, trustworthiness, honesty, and proclivity toward criminality that distinguish popular racist constructions. The facts of group characteristics may be real, but the evaluative component that makes them positive or negative is the product of social and political processes.

GROUP DESERVEDNESS AND GOVERNANCE

From the beginning, the United States espoused a system of limited government in which a great deal of power remained with individual citizens and, when ceded to governments, resided primarily in states and localities rather than the federal government. The gradual accretion of national power was the consequence of events, economic changes and, importantly for our argument, federal actions to cement the allegiance of important constituencies or groups to the nation.

Governments want to bind powerful groups to the state by providing a stake or permanent entitlements to those whose support is most needed (Skocpol 1992). Thus, governments have exploited peoples' tendency toward group categorization, positive group identification, and willingness to accept negative perceptions of undeserving groups. Entitlements, provided to those whose support is most needed and who are most easy to justify as deserving, need not be equitably distributed to serve the state-building function. As Laura Jensen argues in the first chapter, early American entitlements to Revolutionary War veterans constitute an example of social construction of deservedness through governance. As she notes, the Continental Army was recruited and maintained through the long years of war through promises of entitlements to soldiers whose stay in service until the end of enlistment was critical to victory. After the war, the Continental Congress was strapped for funds and reneged on many of its promises. Ultimately, as Jensen explains, justifications were marshaled to separate the most deserving veterans from the less deserving, and pensions were afforded to some, but not all, veterans and certainly to only a small portion of those suffering from the ravages of war. Such special treatment was justified by the social construction of deservedness, which magnified small differences in the characteristics and experiences of revolutionary soldiers and made those differences the basis of vast variability in their treatment by the government.

Of course, in designating categories of deservedness, government exploited values deeply held and widely shared among citizens. The liberal bias in favor of property holders was variously exploited in the nation-building enterprise. As already noted, voting eligibility was originally restricted to men with property. The inability to manage property, except under guardianship, was considered a basis for voter disqualification (see chapter 2). The virtue of the "yeoman farmer" who owned his own land was extolled by Thomas Jefferson—who used the argument of lands for the landless as a rationale for the Louisiana Purchase, a prime example of an exercise in state-building. The American West was settled by persons mainly of European descent through the Homestead Act, which gave tracts of land to those who could prove themselves deserving simply by their willingness to live on and work the land. Other settlement policies provided land to railroads, schools, and some "others" who were constructed as essential to establishing civilization and democracy. In providing these lands to those deemed deserving, Congress reinforced the values of land ownership and the strength of railroad companies. These initial entitlements were permanent and have been expanded throughout U.S. history as the federal government has been pressured to provide crop price supports, crop retirement programs, funding to purchase and store crop surpluses, and infrastructure support for irrigation projects on lands that many would argue ought never to have been farmed.

Property ownership and good citizenship are closely associated in American governance. Not only has the government awarded property to help create the kinds of citizens it wants, it has withheld property from those constructed as undesirable. As Stephanie DiAlto (this volume) explains in chapter 3, Asians were prohibited from holding land in California in the nineteenth and early twentieth centuries. Native Americans were stripped of much of their homelands and, when reservations were created for them, individual property ownership—the hallmark of the being a "real American"—was long withheld. While foreigners are allowed to own property within the United States, this too has been contested when foreign groups are viewed as a threat.

In the early 1990s, there was great concern that Japanese groups had too much property, especially on the West Coast, and laws were introduced to restrict their access to real estate markets (see chapter 3).

With urbanization and industrialization, land ownership (if not property ownership) might have faded from the popular image of what is required to be truly American were it not for the positive reinforcement of public policy, which provided new categories of the deserving. The Federal Home Loan Banking System supported Savings and Loan Associations throughout America to provide home loans within neighborhoods. Besides rescuing many home-owners in default during the Depression, the federal government also provided federally insured low-interest loans to home buyers and subsidized interest rates on home loans for veterans of World War II. The social construction of the homeowner is positive and well entrenched through policies regulating public and private banking and real estate institutions. Politically, it is virtually impossible to remove the income tax deduction for home mortgages, even though home purchases have become more of a financial investment than a commitment to citizenship within stable neighborhoods, as it was originally intended.

Public policy is the primary tool through which government acts to exploit, inscribe, entrench, institutionalize, perpetuate, or change social constructions. It is fair to observe that there are many different sources of social constructions besides policy and that, overall, policies are not the most important tools constructing groups (Lieberman 1995; Schneider and Ingram 1995). The role of governance in social construction probably is smaller than the combined influence of market advertisements, music, film, and other aspects of historical custom and popular culture. Yet, policy is the dynamic element through which governments anchor, legitimize, or change social constructions. It is the means used by government to powerfully support or undercut widespread practices of social separation, such as racial segregation in schools and housing. It is also the tool through which government can raise up previously disadvantaged groups, as it has done with the aged through the Social Security system and the disabled through the *Americans with Disabilities Act*. Alternatively, it can create categories—such as drunk drivers—which without the force of law would not have existed or at least would not have borne any real stigma.

PERSISTENCE IN SOCIAL CONSTRUCTIONS

Some social constructions seldom, if ever, change and are accepted as the natural order of things. Surely the sanctity of property and the positive construction of property owners fits in this category. "Idiots," the "mentally retarded" or, in contemporary parlance, the "intellectually challenged" were long imprisoned either in their own homes or with debtors and criminals. Schriner (see chapter 2) describes how "idiots" were lumped together with the "insane" and sometimes with "criminals" in the wording of state constitutions, with all three groups negatively constructed as unfit for the right to vote. While they are objects of pity and sympathy, at least in childhood, "village idiots" have essentially the same status today that they had in the Middle Ages. There are enormous differences in the degree of mental retardation, and some otherwise "incompetent" minds are capable of beautiful art and incredible acts of generosity and love; yet, the mentally disabled tend to be lumped together as a group. Adult persons of low intelligence are often viewed as dangerous, and it has proven very difficult to secure special rights for these negatively constructed groups. Generally, it has required courts to intervene to protect the retarded from the death penalty when it is not at all clear that these individuals comprehended the full meaning of their acts. Even under these circumstances, courts more often than not are unsupportive. Although it would seem reasonable that the parents of retarded children might have both the incentive and the political power to mobilize for change, the stigma of having a retarded family member remains strong. Consider the widespread practice of prenatal screening, a technological advance fueled by the desire to abort fetuses that are at high risk of retardation. Clearly, there are exceptions—such as the Kennedy family, which has advocated for including the mentally retarded with other more positively constructed disabled groups. Yet, the negative social construction is persistently predominant. Even though it ought not to be a crime or even a stigma to be "stupid" or "dumb," it has certainly been treated as such. Additionally, contemporary parents who give birth to retarded children are quietly stigmatized as genetically deficient or careless.

The persistently negative social construction of African Americans is a well-recognized, lingering injustice in America. A century and a half after the abolition of slavery, African Americans still are more likely than other groups to be perceived as lazy and more apt than others to engage in crime. The persistently negative social construction of African-American women as Jezebels and welfare queens is very strong and has, arguably, been reinforced by policy and social science analysis (see chapters 9–11). Entitlements have been difficult to either grant or sustain for African-American welfare recipients who are negatively constructed. As Mara Sidney argues in chapter 4, it was necessary to separate some blacks from other African Americans and to construct them more positively, as the "New Black Middle Class," in order for them to become legally entitled to enter the housing market on the same terms as whites.

Path dependency theory sheds some light upon the persistence of social constructions (Pierson 2000a). Once a course has been set in a positive or negative direction in relation to the construction of some group or idea, the difficulties of change accumulate over time. As Paul Pierson observes:

Policies, grounded in law, and backed by the coercive power of the state, signal to actors what has to be done and what cannot be done, and they establish many rewards and penalties associated with particular activities. Most policies are remarkably durable. Especially in modern societies, extensive policy arrangements fundamentally shape the incentives and resources of political actors. (2000a, 259)

The ways by which public policy can set a path-dependent direction in motion and protect it from change are nicely illustrated by the national parks and forests systems. The product of the conservation movement during the Theodore Roosevelt Administration, public land ownership might well have been defeated or reversed under the more conservative Harding, Coolidge, and Hoover administrations. We have already observed that the positive social construction of private property ownership is more American than apple pie. In addition, the nation had a long tradition of giving land away rather than managing public lands itself. Yet, with the passage of laws by Congress, the U.S. Forest Service and the National Park Service came into being with very strong, positive images as defenders of nature. Smokey the Bear and Ranger Rick came to be heroes immediately recognizable by any American child. The early creation of the great National Parks, like Yellowstone and Yosemite, fed into a construction of the American West as a playground for millions of urban Easterners. Concessionaires at National Parks and the lumber and grazing interests that profited from multiple-use National Forests were strong forces against privatization, but the stronger impediment was symbolic and emotional. The Grand Canyon, and its Park Service protectors, came to rival the Statue of Liberty and Ellis Island in terms of representing true American values. Institutions such as the federal management agencies and their constituencies—including conservation and resource extraction interest groups—worked in tandem with positive social constructions of these places to perpetuate the national forests and parks and to rebuff any serious challenge.

Policy persistence is more common than policy change. Shifts in party control of the executive or legislative branches of government and changes in court justices alter access to and distribution of power among interests. Nevertheless, the strengths of governing institutions and interest groups and the power of discourse have legitimized existing policy work and protected it from sudden or dramatic change (Baumgartner and Jones 1993). A kind of punctuated equilibrium exists in many policy areas whereby long periods of policy stability are interrupted by a short burst of innovation which, in turn, becomes entrenched into another long-lasting regime (Baumgartner and Jones 1993). Change is also resisted by policy networks—constellations of elected officials, agency representatives, interest groups, scientists, and policy analysts—which share the core beliefs that undergird the policy philosophy (Sabatier and Jenkins-Smith 1993). The core beliefs of policy networks often are grounded as much in ideology as in science, and sometimes are impervious to unsettling influences like new scientific evidence. The stability of long-term social constructions of deservedness and entitlement are among the policy ideas that cause inertia in policy change.

A key factor contributing to persistent social constructions of deservedness and entitlement is that not only do the deserving and entitled get stronger over time (as they are institutionally reinforced), but also the undeserving and unentitled may unwittingly collude with the powerful and positively constructed to perpetuate their own subordination. As Gaventa (1980) has argued, the powerless may be deprived of even the capacity to know their own interest. They sometimes come to identify with their oppressors in that they believe the maldistribution of resources is simply the way things are or that the entitled are truly more deserving than themselves. The deserving too often build positive identity by exaggerating their own worthiness and amplifying the differences between themselves and others.

Overcoming negative identity is difficult and often unsuccessful because of actions that may make sense to individuals but harm the collective cause. In some instances, individuals within a negatively constructed group will leave the group if they can or hide their membership, as many gays and lesbians did for years. Instead of building on the virtues and strengths of the group as worthy people, they abandon the group or hide, thereby failing to challenge the dominant perspectives. In other instances, members of negatively constructed groups may actually agree with the unfavorable characterizations assigned to them, but distinguish themselves by parsing the construction so that "others" in the group actually are undeserving, but they, personally, are different (see chapter 11). Some of these strategies allow dominant groups to continue to believe that the less advantaged are responsible for their own plight. Negatively constructed groups, however, sometimes are able to convert negative identities to positive identities, to mobilize, and to participate in changing their own social construction—a topic we will explore.

POLICY CHANGE AND CHANGES IN SOCIAL CONSTRUCTIONS

Reputations for deservedness are not always permanent, and entitlements do change. Circumstances may change, thereby discrediting previous ways of thinking about issues. Many social constructions are contestable, so that one or another perspective can become dominant. Some groups exist without any noticeable social construction until events or entrepreneurs recognize political opportunities and create positive or negative constructions of them. Public policies and social constructions of groups interact in a reciprocal manner so that they mutually affect each other. A changed social construction of deservedness can precipitate change in policy and, alternatively, public policy change can alter constructions.

External events may create opportunities for new constructions, which subsequently lead to policy change that inscribes the changed construction and lends it legitimacy. Prior to September 11, 2001, Arab Americans and the religion of Islam did not have a widespread dominant construction in the United States. In contrast with many other minority groups, persons of Arabic descent (or those who practice the Islamic religion) were not granted "protected minority" status and were, with some exceptions, overt examples of discrimination were far less common. (Exceptions include the "Owned by Americans" signs throughout the United States, indicating motels that are not owned by Arabs.) The suicide hijacking of four commercial jet airliners and the subsequent attack on the World Trade Center and the Pentagon that killed 2,800 people brought about a dramatic change. "Islamic," "Arab," or "Middle Eastern" became common prefixes to "terrorist." Persons who "looked" Arabic were removed from airplanes, even though they had legitimate tickets and had done nothing to warrant their removal. Racial profiling took on an entirely new meaning as hundreds of persons from Middle Eastern countries or of Arabic descent were questioned and were required to register with the federal government if they were not citizens. Many were incarcerated on suspicion of minor violations of immigration policy. The negative construction of Arab Americans expanded to greatly damage the construction of all immigrants, who subsequently were denied employment in airline terminals without any evidence that they had been or might be involved in sabotage. Policy proposals that would have granted legal status to thousands of Mexican Americans who have lived in the United States for many years were suddenly postponed as unthinkable. These events occurred even though no one suggested that Mexican Americans had any greater likelihood of involvement in terrorism than "homegrown" terrorists such as Timothy McVeigh.

Events also may bring about significant changes in existing constructions. Prior to 1983, the social construction of persons with AIDS was as undeserving. Gay men, who were believed to be the only carriers of the disease, were viewed as the cause of their own problems through their own risky behavior and lifestyles. After AIDS was found to occur in babies, women, and individuals who had received transfusions of infected blood, the group began to be constructed more positively. The story of Ryan White, a thirteen-year-old schoolboy in Indiana who was banned from his classroom, added a civil rights dimension to the story that helped transform public opinion and resulted in more positive media coverage. The identification of admired sports figures—like Arthur Ashe and Magic Johnson—with the disease also contributed to revising the prevailing social construction. Movies like *Philadelphia* portrayed gay men more positively than before, and the cohesion and bravery of gays themselves in face of the health threat did much to reconstruct their image.

In response to the changing image of persons with AIDS, federal, state, and local governments extended greater entitlements, including greater access to social services and job protection (Schneider and Ingram 1997). Among the effects, however, was a differentiation among the more deserving and less deserving types of persons with AIDS, as reflected in the funding allocation patterns mandated by the *Ryan White Act of 1990* (Donovan 1994). Moreover, the most affective policy tool in preventing the spread of AIDS among drug users—needle exchange programs for intravenous users—was repeatedly rejected because of the undeserving construction of these people (Donovan 1994).

Social movements have become a powerful force for social change. History has shown repeatedly that even the powerless have power when they are able to come together and resist dominant constructions, oppose oppressive policies, mobilize, and associate themselves with widespread fundamental values of fairness and justice. All of the great social movements of the twentieth century produced fundamental, long-lasting policy changes. The women's movement first produced the right to vote, and though the equal rights amendment failed by the smallest of margins, women's rights have been continually expanding in the United States as a result of inclusion in the *Civil Rights Act of 1964*. The social movements of African Americans produced impressive gains, as did the peace movement (that eventually helped end the Vietnam War), the environmental movement, the gay and lesbian movement, and numerous others actions within state and local politics.

Contested social constructions are inherently unstable and are ripe for policy change that subdivides populations into more deserving and less deserving categories. Lina Newton (chapter 5) shows that Mexican-American immigrants are commonly constructed both positively and negatively. They are seen as natural residents of the American Southwest, which was ruled by Spain and Mexico for more than four centuries. They are also recognized as hardworking, brave, and ambitious—willing to suffer the deprivations of dangerous, illegal border crossings to get to this country and then accept low wages and undesirable jobs that nonetheless are a means to get ahead and support a family. Alternatively, they can also be constructed quite negatively as illegal aliens, since there are millions of undocumented Mexicans living in this country. They can also be constructed as unentitled freeloaders on the grounds that they "wrongfully" receive welfare, health, and education benefits while not paying taxes—even though they all pay sales taxes and, in some cases, property taxes. Political entrepreneurs like Governor Pete Wilson of California were able to capitalize on the negative side of the contested construction of Mexican Americans in backing ballot propositions such as Proposition 187 in California that prohibited Mexican immigrants from receiving a wide range of state and local benefits, including education for their children. As Newton (chapter 5) asserts, the backlash against immigrants extended to the elimination of federal payments for immigrant health care of undocumented persons.

The immigrant examples illustrate that entrepreneurship is another important force for change in policy and change in social constructions of deservedness. Economic, political, social, and moral entrepreneurs have the ability to tap into the language and interests of diverse groups to create a common frame of reference, or a unifying social construction or vision, that bridges previous differences. Entrepreneurs facilitate "consensus formation," or a convergence of meaning in social networks and subcultures (Tarrow 1998, 21). Thus, groups that may have thought they had nothing in common find themselves working together. Mintrom (2000) argues that such entrepreneurs have been able to marshall the discontent of various groups about public schools and to offer charter schools as an alternative to alleviate many problems that previously were viewed as disconnected. Part of the unifying vision was a negative construction that public school bureaucracy is more interested in teacher and administrator entitlements than in educating children. Another important negative social construction was that immigrant pupils who did not speak English would be unable to perform up to any reasonable standard. Public policy facilitates entrepreneurship by creating opportunities that invite entrepreneurs to exercise their talents. It might be argued that busing and immigration policies created conditions in public schools which led to widespread discontent among white parents, who became receptive to entrepreneurs with new visions and alternatives that struck a responsive chord.

While entrepreneurship can be a very positive force in American politics in that it facilitates policy change, some entrepreneurship builds upon and amplifies the xenophobic and racist sentiments that continue to be undesirable undercurrents in the imperfect U.S. democracy. A number of the chapters in this volume (see particularly chapters 3, 5, and 9) illustrate how political capital is made by exploiting racist divisions and amplifying differences along racial fault lines. In our previous work we have termed this *degenerative politics,* which is characterized by its exploitation of derogatory social constructions, manipulation of symbols or logic, and deceptive communication that masks the true purpose of policy. We are concerned that degenerative politics has become more common as other means for solidifying public support become increasingly scarce. Governments that face severe budget constraints are less able to attract and bind people to a common understanding of the public interest through the provision of costly public services and entitlements. Therefore, the capacity to include almost everyone as part of "deserving" constituencies does not occur so regularly when budgets are tightly constrained. Moreover, the erosion of allegiance to political parties among the populace means that coalitions that support policies must be built one individual policy at a time, rather than depending on a large base of partisan support that continues across many issues. This affects the ability of parties to hold their core constituency together. In the absence of a partisan base built on positive constructions and the allocation of policy benefits, scapegoating is an easy alternative way to gain allegiance from the party constituency and to distinguish itself from other parties. Increasingly, campaigns focus on "negative campaigning" in which party entrepreneurs find subgroups that can be blamed for prevailing problems. Rather than focusing on the systematic biases within our economic and social system—which constitute the best explanations for the very different rates of economic, social, and political success—the victims are blamed for their own problems (see Schram, chapter 10; Ingram and Schneider 1991).

Constructing groups as undeserving and then inflicting punishment on them as a means of gaining political advantage is most evident in criminal justice policy. Sean Nicholson–Crotty and Kenneth Meier (chapter 8) demonstrate the construction of a "dangerous class" responsible for violence, insecurity, and the corruption of youth. This kind of extremely negative construction under certain circumstances can lead to draconian policies aimed against deviant targets. Moral entrepreneurs are most likely to emerge and succeed when the deviant group is readily identifiable to both the mass public and political elites and is portrayed as "out of control." All too often in America the "dangerous class" has been strongly associated with negative racial stereotyping as Chinese Americans were in the 1909 law banning the smoking of opium, and African Americans in the 1984 *Comprehensive Crime Control Act*. While the existence of a "dangerous class" is often associated with the culture and lifestyles of whole racial and ethnic groups, punishment is leveled against individuals who are held responsible for their own acts.

The ability of entrepreneurs to exploit the undeserving "other" is exacerbated by the highly individualistic culture in the United States and the belief of many American citizens in the absolute power of individual agency. Consequently, the causes of underweight and unhealthy babies at birth are traced to mothers who smoke or drink, not to the unavailability of prenatal care—which might have monitored and regulated pregnant women's behavior through medical advice and treated other causes of fetal health problems. The high arrest rate of black men is explained by black culture, not by racial profiling, joblessness, loitering, vagrancy, or gang laws that unfairly target gatherings of men of color. Sandford Schram (chapter 10) maintains that analysts too often overlook or mask the racial composition of welfare populations for fear that minority groups will be blamed for their own poverty, but that this is a mistake. It is better, he maintains, to recognize the overrepresentation of blacks in the welfare system and then to explore the root causes.

Policy has the capacity to create opportunities for change in social constructions, and it is possible for leaders to successfully advocate on behalf of disadvantaged populations that can be portrayed as powerless as well as not dangerous. Entrepreneurs have created advocacy groups on behalf of the physically disabled and others, using arguments that not all individuals begin from the level playing field assumed by those who believe that failure mainly is the fault of the individual. Not all persons begin with the same educational, income, cultural, racial, or gender advantages as others.

Sometimes policy helps overcome divisive social constructions by combining groups into a single target population when passing out entitlements (or punishments), thereby mixing persons who previously might have been divided into more privileged and less privileged groups. Also, policy may subdivide an existing group into classes of more deserving or less deserving and this, too, contributes to changes in the social constructions within what previously might have been a more homogenous group. As Mara Sidney concludes (chapter 4), the efforts of a Democratic-controlled Congress to eliminate housing discrimination in the 1960s—discrimination that had long been practiced against African Americans—met with considerable resistance. Much of the opposition was justified on the grounds that people who participated in the urban riots of the 1960s should not be rewarded for their unlawful and unruly behavior. This resistance was overcome by a policy strategy that subdivided African Americans into middle-class blacks, who had earned a right to escape from the ghetto, and the poor urban underclass of (implied) urban rioters, who were stuck in inner cities. The consequence for more positive social constructions of some but not all African Americans, therefore, was mixed. The African Americans who were most economically advantaged and, presumably, best able to organize were to be treated as if they were white. This construction leaves poorer, inner city residents without benefits and without the leadership that middle class blacks might have provided.

Policy is often its own cause, in the sense that feedback from previous policies can create the structural opportunities for social mobilization and change of social constructions (Wildavsky 1987). As Laura Jensen explains in chapter 1, when the policy and rationale that afforded pensions to soldiers and officers of the Revolutionary War became widely accepted, it was impossible not to extend the benefits to all veterans regardless of their economic status. The line between deserving and undeserving veterans was simply too difficult to maintain once veterans realized that some veterans, not including themselves, were receiving federal aid.

Public policies can be shaped in ways that encourage or impede feedback, and this, in turn, impacts the likelihood that social mobilization will occur to demand policy change. Information feedback, openness, and transparency favor mobilization. Secrecy has the opposite effect. Consider the tax codes, for example, that grant tax exemptions to various interest groups at the local, state, and national levels. Tax exemptions often occur without drawing attention, objection, or counter-mobilization because of the opaqueness and Byzantine complexity of the tax code (Smith and Ingram 2002). Only individuals who are able to hire tax accountants, lawyers as watchdogs, and lobbyists have an opportunity to challenge tax breaks. Tax exemptions have the same effects on the budget as do direct payments—like welfare checks—but the latter are much more likely to be noticed and to prompt political reaction.

Policy feedback is especially likely to prompt mobilization when it negatively affects well regarded and more powerful individuals. Opposition to the Vietnam War, for example, gained considerable attention—but made almost no policy progress—when it was concentrated among college students who were able to use their student status to gain draft exemptions. The opposition was easily constructed as scraggly, long-haired radicals with communist leanings. The change in the draft policy, so that student exemptions were eliminated in favor of a lottery that applied to all young men in relevant age groups who met physical requirements, provided an opportunity for a changed social construction. Opposition gained enormous ground and much greater respectability when all male college students, knowledgeable and vocal themselves and the sons of middle-income and upper-income parents, received their lottery numbers and knew that a draft notice was close behind.

The architecture of policy is important in understanding mobilization, as David Meyer explains in his analysis of draft policy:

> The nature of American draft policy gave antiwar organizations a vehicle for servicing their constituents: draft counseling. It also forced young men to confront the policy concretely as well as abstractly, making personal decisions about their own draft status and strategies (e.g., whether or not to pursue "conscientious objector" status). Both opposition to the draft in general, and concern about one's individual fate, pushed young men—and those who cared about them—into the full range of American political institutions including Selective Service bureaucracy, local draft boards, the courts, and electoral campaigns. (2002, 6)

The process set in motion by the draft policy had another, perhaps more profound effect. At the time, the policy allowed participants in protests to escape the stigma of being draft dodgers and unpatriotic. Through draft counseling, teach-ins, and protests, resisting an unjust war became a just cause. The ability of draft resisters to find a positive identity grounded in a moral cause was fundamental to mobilization. This is a type of effect that policy has on identity, which is central to social mobilization. We will address this concept further in this introduction.

Some negative social constructions are so uncontested and so accepted that mobilization does not occur even when policy would seem to offer an opportunity. While state constitutional debates over the franchise appeared to offer a platform to contest the disenfranchisement of persons designated as "idiots" and "insane," there was no real objection to their disqualification (chapter 2). Today there still are virtually no advocacy groups working to gain the right to vote for several groups who clearly have political interests that should be represented and who are capable of participating. This includes many of the "insane," some of the developmentally disabled, and persons convicted of felonies.

Even though, as we have noted, it is possible for negatively constructed groups to mobilize for social and policy change, the costs may be very high. Gays, lesbians, bisexual, and transgendered (GLBT) people have struggled to find effective strategies, just as African Americans, women, and other social movements have done. As Bernstein (1997) has pointed out, effective strategies depend on the context. Some gays and lesbians, for example, may choose to work quietly with legislative and administrative groups—largely behind the scenes—to argue that they deserve the same rights and protections as others under the constitutional guarantee of equal protection of the law. This signals that GLBTs are not different than other people. A "soft" strategy such as this may be effective in bringing about policy inclusion and, perhaps, in the long run—through association of gays and lesbians with all other people in terms of political rights—break down the perceptions that only certain kinds of sexuality are normal. On the other hand, as Bernstein argues, GLBTs may be disappointed in policy as an engine of change because strategies that focus on changing policy may not directly challenge prevailing values that afford privilege to heterosexuals. Other strategies that convert the negative identity associated with GLBTs into a positive identity through direct challenges to dominant values may be more effective. Some GLBT groups prefer explicit and vivid portrayals of homosexuality, bisexuality, and transgendered behavior, such as gay pride events and gay rights parades. Portrayals that some people describe as "flaunting" homosexuality are embraced by those attempting fundamental change in values and social constructions.

Another impetus for change can be found in science and technology advances. Scientific evidence of the biological basis of different forms of sexuality provides a rationale for arguing that no one type of sexual orientation has a special claim on normalcy and, therefore, no one type of sexuality should be more privileged than another. The implications for policy may seem promising, although some observers have argued that this line of reasoning is a slippery slope and is unlikely to deliver on the promise of equal rights for lesbians and gays (Brookey 2001).

Developments in weaponry that permit individuals with brainpower and other skills unrelated to physical strength to excel has contributed to the inclusion of women in the military, including participation among the fighting forces from which most promotions emerge. The social construction of the membership of fighting forces gradually is changing from one that emphasizes only physical hardship and strength to one with characteristics that more comfortably include women.

The negative construction of industries as polluters and the development of regulatory policies were made possible by the ability of environmental scientists to identify very small trace amounts of toxic and hazardous substances in air, water, or soils and the improved ability of health scientists to link illness to human exposure to such substances. We have previously argued (Schneider and Ingram 1997) that science, by itself, usually is not enough to instigate policy change. For real effectiveness, not only must there be a virtual consensus among relevant scientists about the facts (and often there is no consensus) but scientists also usually need to be aligned with interest groups and social movements, like environmentalism, that are able to capitalize on their findings.

While the alignment of scientific evidence with the interests of powerful and well-regarded groups is important in understanding policy change and change in social constructions, such analysis does not give sufficient weight to the power of science in framing issues that reinforce some constructions and undercut others. Try as they might, powerful nations have been unable to escape the stigma of being to blame for global warming. Scientific findings have made clear the large contributions of industrialized countries to greenhouse gasses. Science put global warming and greenhouse gasses on the agenda by tracing its causes to high energy use in industrialized nations. Despite the power of large, industrialized nations, they have been unable to escape the onus of being the greatest greenhouse gasses polluters.

Greater medical understanding of the brain's chemistry has affected the social construction of mental illness and behavioral problems. For example, the classification of attention deficit disorder has largely transformed the unruly child into a patient in need of medication. Parents are admonished not for their lack of discipline, but for their failure to get appropriate medical care for their children.

Social science also has an effect on public policies and social constructions. The poverty line below which families are deserving of aid is, for example, the product of policy analysis. Social indicators of all sorts—including consumer confidence, the unemployment rate, the crime rate, the inflation rate, and trust in government indices—are all social science inventions that carry real policy and societal consequences. Dionne Bensonsmith (chapter 9) maintains that the Moynihan Report on the pathology of black families exemplifies the way in which social science can have unintended, but very negative consequences. Nicholson-Crotty and Meier (chapter 8) note that the U.S Commission on Opium Use, convened in 1909, helped to legitimize the crackdown on opium use by the Chinese, while other narcotics went unregulated.

Finally, change in social constructions and policies sometimes occurs through incremental change in the demographic characteristics of a long-standing target population. Welfare mothers offer one of the best examples (Lieberman 1995; Schneider and Ingram 1995). From 1935 through the mid 1950s, most recipients of Aid to Dependent Children (ADC) were mainly young, white widows whose husbands had been killed in war. The predominant social construction of ADC was that of a humane program intended to permit mothers to stay home with their young children and provide them with a living wage and a loving home. As the proportion of white, war widows declined and minority single mothers increased, the social construction of "welfare mother" changed gradually to that of the irresponsible, immoral "Jezebel" or "welfare queen" (chapter 9) that eventually ended this entitlement to children in an effort to discipline or punish their mothers (chapters 10, 11).

DYNAMICS OF SOCIAL CONSTRUCTIONS

The social construction of deservedness has serious and long-term implications for allocating benefits and burdens in society. There is nothing benign about the tendency people have to construct divisive, value-laden differences between themselves and the "other"—who becomes the object of disdain. The damage is especially acute when these differences become embedded in public policies. Once embedded in policies, the differences take on the power of the state and its legitimacy.

In our previous work (Schneider and Ingram 1993; 1997), we have discussed how positive and negative constructions interact with political power to produce several different types of target populations. *Advantaged target populations* have significant political power resources and also enjoy positive social constructions as deserving people. Contemporary examples include business, science, the military, the middle class, and white people (that is, persons of European descent). *Contenders* have ample political power resources that generally equal those of advantaged groups, but contenders are not viewed as deserving. Instead, contenders such as "Wall Street bankers," "the rich," "big labor," or the "gun lobby" are recognized as quite powerful but have the negative social construction as unworthy because they are too "greedy," or they are "getting more than their share," or they are "morally bankrupt." *Dependents* are groups with few political power resources who are socially constructed as deserving in a moral sense, although helpless and usually in need of discipline. *Deviants* are in the worst situation. These are persons—such as terrorists, gang members, and criminals—who have few, if any, legitimate political power resources and who are constructed as undeserving because they are viewed as dangerous and of no value to the society.

Many policy-making arenas may become degenerative, as explained previously, in that government does not treat all people equally, but instead falls into a pattern of allocating benefits mainly to the advantaged populations and punishments to the deviants. Both of these policy arenas offer enormous political opportunity to political leaders and entrepreneurs even if they do not produce effective or efficient public policies. The powerful and well regarded are expected to reward governments, political parties, and others who advocate greater benefits and fewer burdens. Advantaged groups resent government spending on dependents, even though they recognize the importance of caring for children and others. They believe the needs of dependents should be met by local governments, families, and nonprofit organizations. Even more resented are funds allocated to deviants, except those funds necessary to inflict punishment.

The result of these policy-making dynamics—if they continue through a path-dependent process—is that policies become inefficient, ineffective, and unfair. Policies that are beneficial to advantaged populations increase as all levels of government and political parties compete with one another to provide benefits and benign regulations for the advantaged. Policies directed to the advantaged becomes oversubscribed (there is more of it than needed to meet actual societal needs), overfunded (more is spent on it than necessary), undertaxed, and underregulated. Although burdens are inflicted on advantaged populations, these tend to occur only when needed to regulate matters among competing powerful groups. Punishment policies may become very popular as they can generate tremendous political payoffs by advocating "get tough" policies, such as longer prison sentences without much initial impact on costs. Dependents tend to be ignored as much as possible. Policies for contenders take a somewhat different path because it is important to provide benefits to these groups—due to their political power—but to do so secretly so that others (the general public) that view them as undeserving will not know that contenders are receiving so much government largesse. Thus, policies may become very deceptive, complex, and opaque so that it is almost impossible to figure out what effects they may have. Similarly, it may become necessary to hide the true extent of government aid to advantaged groups, because a full revelation would produce the perception that they are getting more than they deserve. Thus, secrecy, complexity, deception, and opaqueness may come to be found throughout the policy-making system.

Even though governments have the power to produce policies without explanations, this is uncommon, especially in democracies, where legitimacy is a constant concern. Policies are almost always justified on logical grounds—as contributing to important ends—or in terms of fairness and justice. In degenerative policy-making systems, however, policies are not so much the result of rational analysis of problems and the crafting of solutions as they are the product of target populations seeking to frame problems in such a way that they become the obvious solution.

The rationale given for allocating benefits to advantaged populations typically involves claims that benefits must be provided because of important national interests, not because of the group's power or even their deservedness. The favorable treatment of business, industry, and science in the United States was justified originally as a way to escape the Depression and win World War II and later as a means to win the Cold War and defeat communism. When the Cold War ended, the rationale shifted to the need for economic success in a global economy, and more recently as the way to win the war against terrorism. Regardless of the rationale, the allocation pattern stayed very much the same.

The rationale for delivering burdens to deviants is that they deserve to be punished due to their irresponsible and immoral activities, or that punishment is essential to deterring such behavior. Dependents learn from policies that the lack of attention to their needs is because there are other, higher, priorities, and that others are more central to the nation's success as a whole. Rules of behavior are "for their own good," and it is unfortunate that the application of universal principles sometimes disadvantages them. When benefits are provided to dependents or to deviants—and policies sometimes do provide benefits—these are usually explained as being necessary to protect basic constitutional rights or to comply with court orders that seek to maintain rights and meet basic human needs. Occasionally, beneficial policies are provided to deviants when social science studies indicate that beneficial policies are effective, but this is usually accompanied by mandatory evaluations and demonstrated effectiveness.

TARGET GROUP CONSTRUCTIONS AND INSTITUTIONS

New institutional research—a broad revival of interest in institutions that has swept through law, economics, sociology, and political science—provides important insights into how social constructions come to be matters of habit and taken for granted. DiMaggio and Powell (1991) focus on the cognitive, cultural explanations of how certain patterns of action emerge and persist that would seem to be irrational from a strictly utilitarian, self-interest perspective. When broad fields or subject matters are framed by social construction of target populations, material resources and social status are consistently distributed through institutions to deepen the cleavages between advantaged and other target populations. For example, the land entitlements made available to white, male veterans lifted them above others, including women, Native Americans and former Confederate soldiers of the Civil War, and allowed these beneficiaries to be entitled to a wide range of agricultural, water, and other governmental aid (Jensen 2003). Just as important, cognitive elements, such as practical consciousness and shared typification of social categories experienced as "people like us," are continually reproduced by institutions (Bourdieu 1981, cited in DiMaggio and Powell 1991). Standardized cultural forms and accounts are diffused and reproduced by institutions across time and space. Thus, the paternalistic orientation toward women and children that reformers like Francis Perkins espoused was infused into the networks of social workers in the New Deal, diffused to the states, and perpetuated into welfare policies up to the present (Mettler 1998). Through institutions, the social constructions of target groups become semipermanent dispositions that are rarely questioned, even by those harmed by such constructions.

The social constructions of target groups through public policies stimulate and advance the typifications, or cognitive models, carried along by institutions and convey powerful messages about who matters in our society and who does not and what kinds of people get served by government and who is ignored or punished. This institutionalization of bias has enormous influence upon citizenship roles, group mobilization, and civic participation.

Citizenship, Mobilization, and Participation

Institutionalized differences in treatment by government and through experience with public policies carries strong messages to people that impact their orientations, identity, capacity for mobilization, participation level, and type of participation (Soss 2000). These messages are strikingly different depending upon the target group. Advantaged populations receive signals that their success is central to the nation's success as a whole, and that they deserve the favorable way they are treated. Understandably, advantaged groups have a very strong positive identity—one which seldom even recognizes the advantages they and their ancestors have received over the years. Contenders, on the other hand, realize that they commonly are feared and mistrusted. Thus, their policy benefits must come through subterfuge in which others, rather than themselves, appear to profit. Contenders come to believe that politics is a corrupt game that requires cunning strategies to be successful. They learn to look for opportunities when no one is watching, to carefully craft opaque policy with complicated provisions, through which government will insure their continued success. Dependents learn that they are not very important, they need to be disciplined, and they must look to families, faith-based institutions, nonprofits, and local government to meet their needs. The lessons that institutions (including public policies) teach to dependents disempowers them, even as it convinces them of their lack of importance. Often, they are treated rudely and inefficiently. They may discover that they have little recourse. Deviants learn that their problems are their own fault and that they deserve nothing but disrespect, hatred, incarceration, and isolation from society. They, too, are disempowered through public policy and other institutions. They tend to view government as corrupt.

Social identity is a central ingredient for the propensity to become active and for the success or failure of social movements (Brown 2000). It is interesting to note the dramatically different lessons that policy teaches about social identity. Advantaged populations identify with others like themselves—white people, businessmen or businesswomen, the middle class, scientists—and never doubt their ability to mobilize together for effective action. However, they seldom need grassroots social movements, because their access to policy is insured through lobbying efforts, as well as through the responsiveness that government officials at all levels grant to them by virtue of their political power resources and their image as good, hardworking, loyal Americans. Contenders also have a strong positive identity that resists negative labels and has enabled them, over time, to gain considerable political strength even when they are not well regarded. Labor unions offer a strong example of intense group loyalty compared with the far less positive image outside of it. Gays and lesbians, too, have gained considerable political power, but first a common, positive identity—that reconstructed the negative to a positive—had to be developed. "Black power" and the pride of being black that emerged most clearly in the 1960s, was a central motivating factor in the civil rights movement of African Americans.

Dependents may have a positive *personal* identity, but little connection with others that would serve as a strong *social* identity. The feminist movement transformed women's sense of personal worth into a social identity, for example, through consciousness-raising small groups that forged bonds among women and ingrained the legitimacy of women's place in the political world. Some persons viewed as deviants have a negative personal and social identity. It is very difficult, for example, for prostitutes, ex-convicts, or others who are stigmatized as part of the "dangerous class" (chapter 8) with a negative identity to organize themselves into effective political groups. It has happened, however. Gang members have come to embrace the very features that others disrespect—their special language, music, dress, and propensity for violence have become central to a shared social identity. In some instances, people labeled as deviants attempt to reframe their identity. For example, welfare mothers may begin to develop a strong, positive social identity if they can reframe their image from that of the "freeloader, immoral, irresponsible woman" to a "caring mother who would do almost anything to help her children" (chapter 11).

Policies may have unintended or counterintuitive (or both) impacts on identity. When policies—backed by the full authority of the state—embrace negative constructions of groups, they legitimate these constructions and help spread them throughout society. But policies also may be positive agents of change for marginalized groups when they challenge institutionalized negative constructions; for example, by including a negatively viewed group in policies that benefit much more positively viewed groups. Such challenges are difficult and risky for policy makers who seek public approval of their actions and must seek reelection on a regular basis. In addition, policies can provide specific points of mobilization and attack, particularly if the negative constructions are firmly ingrained in policy documents at high and visible levels. Such documents make explicit and, therefore, make vulnerable institutionalized bias that is largely invisible and taken for granted. By focusing attention on a specific policy, negatively constructed groups may use the perceived unfairness or inaccuracy to mobilize people and to change the policy that has offended them. Identity, however, is a fundamental precursor for social mobilization. Unless a negatively viewed group can either resist the construction and reframe it into something more positive, or adopt the negative frame as a status symbol of its own, mobilization is not likely to occur.

The politics of race, class, gender, and sexuality are, in general, an attempt by previously disadvantaged groups and their advocates to reconstruct themselves as more deserving or to gain sufficient political power so that image will become less important. The resistance from established or privileged groups—either to a change in the social construction or to the increased political clout of previously marginalized groups—creates intense divisiveness around such issues. Policy makers may exploit these divisions for political gain.

Although institutions differ in many important ways, there is a striking homogeneity of practices and arrangements in organizational life. This sameness extends to patterns that appear across different policy areas. Groups advantaged in housing policy, for example, also make out well in tax policy, economic development policy, and other areas. Similarly, dependents and deviants in welfare and criminal justice policy are less likely to be beneficiaries of educational opportunities and student loans. The systematic reinforcement of messages about who is deserving and entitled and who is not greatly amplifies policy messages. Public policy, of course, is not the only element in the institutionalized pattern of bias that impacts participation but, over time, its contribution is significant in terms of both the type and amount of participation. There is great irony in political participation patterns in the United States. The nation that holds itself up as a model of democratic governance in fact suffers from low and declining levels of political participation and vastly unequal access to the many different avenues of participation. Even though the nation has now achieved almost universal suffrage for adults who are legal citizens (see chapter 2 for exceptions), only 71 percent of those eligible to vote were even registered for the 2000 election. As a rule, fewer than half of the registered voters actually cast ballots. What is perhaps most tragic is that the dependent and deviant populations most likely to profit from policy change are by far the least likely to vote. The lowest levels of participation are recorded by the eighteen- to twenty-one year-old age group, persons with less than high school education, those in the lowest income brackets, and those of African-American, Native-American, or Latin-American heritage. They appear to have embraced the message that they do not matter—a message that they repeatedly experience in their association with institutions, their interactions with agents of the state, and the rationale surrounding public policy issues.

There are many other avenues of participation in public and civic life beyond voting. For example, people may belong to neighborhood associations that act as advocates on behalf of their community, or they may serve as volunteers with nonprofit organizations that actively provide support and services to persons who need them. People participate by giving to charitable organizations, working with their local schools to improve educational opportunities, participating in neighborhood cleanup campaigns, or getting involved in social movements on behalf of disadvantaged groups. People participate by expressing their opinions or requesting assistance from elected representatives or government agencies staffed by professional public servants. As noted earlier, entrepreneurs create social movements, neighborhood associations, nonprofits, and interest groups that become vehicles for political action. The level of participation in all these forms of civic and political work appears to be low, declining, and vastly uneven depending upon different race, ethnicity, social class, and educational level. Robert Putnam (2000) argues that each generation since those born before World War II has participated at a lower level than the generation before. The title of his well-known book (*Bowling Alone: The Collapse and Revival of American Community*) notes the irony that more Americans than ever are engaged in bowling as an activity, but fewer than ever belong to bowling teams.

The reasons for low and declining civic participation in the second half of the twentieth century are multifaceted and contested. What is important to our discussion is that the likelihood of participation varies consistently among the socially constructed groups—advantaged, disadvantaged, contenders, and deviants—that we have identified. The highest rates of participation are recorded by the groups that already benefit the most from public policies. At the same time, people who are most *disadvantaged* by public policies—and who would seem to have the most to gain from active, vigorous political participation—participate much less. *True*

The messages sent by public policies and other institutions is reflected in how people perform their role as citizens. Participation is higher among those with greater trust in government and those who believe that their participation will make a difference—that is, they have higher levels of efficacy in their relationship with government (Verba et al. 1993). Additionally, participation is greater among those with a highly developed sense of their own interests, who recognize that they are part of a group that has common interests and that they (and their group) have much to gain (or lose) from government action. Those who believe that their cause is worthy, that there are many others just like themselves who are mobilized for effective action, and who see their cause as being beneficial to the entire nation are more apt to participate than those who have a poorly developed sense of their own interests or who do not identify with others who have common interests.

The privileges of wealth are everywhere evident in American society, particularly in politics. Wealth is an important aspect of participation. Those who are better off may feel that they have more to protect, and wealth provides both an incentive and a means of political influence. Some forms of participation, in fact, have dramatically increased over the last half-century, and most of these are tied directly or indirectly to the role of wealth in politics. Organized interest groups, with paid lobbyists, are far more common today than at the beginning of the twentieth century. Initiative petitions—which allow important public policy issues to be placed on the ballot for a vote by the citizenry—have become a far more common method of participation. Originally intended to serve grass-roots movements and thwart the power of legislatures, initiative petitions are now often the tool of wealthy interests or individuals who are able to hire persons to gain the signatures and launch massive media campaigns against a (typically) unorganized and underfunded group. On the other hand, advocacy groups that are funded by philanthropic foundations and led by elites who work on behalf of dependents or deviants are far more common than in the past.

The opportunity structure for mobilizing social movements is greatly affected by policies—and public policies clearly favor mobilizing some kinds of groups over others (Meyer 2002). As Mara Sidney (chapter 4) illustrates, fair housing laws were designed to impede the mobilization of mino... Policies send messages about identity, as we have argued. Some that recognition of a common *positive* identity is central to the movements. Several of the great social movements of the twen the civil rights movement, the women's movement, and the gay/lesbian movement—all engaged previously disadvantaged people into a potent political force. First the movements raised the consciousness of these group members as worthy people who, if they worked together, could make a difference in the way they were treated by government. The importance of identity also can be seen in the exceptionally low participation rates and lack of organization among the homeless, prostitutes, ex-convicts, gang members, and welfare recipients. These groups suffer from a negative identity that must first be overcome before sufficient trust and motivation is found for political participation.

Policies also impact participation because they determine the rules of participation and the value of various kinds of resources in the political game. Again, policies tend to grant maximum participatory capacity to advantaged populations and the least capacity to dependents and deviants. We have already noted that suffrage was extended first to white, male property owners—clearly an advantaged population—and then gradually to others based on their moral qualities and their competence to exercise the vote. Only reluctantly was the vote extended to nonwhite persons, women, and the eighteen- to twenty-one year-old age group. For many years, the rules governing voter registration excluded people through the use of poll taxes and literacy tests that were administered locally, with local officials holding complete discretion for determining whether or not someone had paid for or had passed the literacy test. Even as late as the 1960s, some states permitted poll challengers to ask those standing in line to vote to read a section of the U.S. Constitution; if they were unable to do so, their right to vote would be challenged (Dean 2001).

Persons convicted of felonies, or those under guardianship due to mental or physical disability, are still unable to vote in most parts of the United States (chapter 2). Even though court decisions have been constructed around the principle of "one person, one vote," this principle is not extended to persons under the age of eighteen, even if they could show they were individually competent to vote. Interestingly, no one seems to make the argument that children, or others considered incompetent to vote, should be represented anyway. After all, they clearly have interests in the polity and could be represented through their parents' or guardians' vote. In this as in other cases, standardized social constructions of these groups as helpless dependents are so thoroughly institutionalized that bias continues unexamined.

Policies also grant an advantage to some groups when they permit money to play such a large role in elections and influence. In general, courts have been reluctant to allow effective regulation of contributions to political causes and have viewed money donations as a form of speech. Even when Congress passes campaign finance reform legislation, as it did in 2002, implementation through established structures is problematic. Money has fueled the dramatic increase in the use of initiative petitions, and it undergirds the massive lobbying efforts of powerful groups.

In addition to structuring the rules for voting and for the use of wealth, policies also establishes rules of participation during the implementation phase of the policy process. Policies that direct regulations toward advantaged populations, for example, almost always require public hearings that permit members of these groups to influence how the policies will actually be applied. To help mask the unpopularity of regulations, the impacted groups may be granted little-noticed points of access and the ability to challenge implementation processes through the courts. Even when policies require public hearings, these sometimes are dominated by experts to the virtual exclusion of ordinary citizens. Sidney (chapter 4) explains how housing legislation permitted voluntary compliance by banks—with no sanctions for violating the law—and granted no role for community-based organizations in challenging the lack of compliance by local banks.

In addition to these direct effects, policy allocations of benefit and burdens have profound impacts over a long period of time. Mettler (2002b) demonstrates the long-term effects that the GI bill has had on the participation patterns of World War II veterans. By providing grants for higher education to all World War II veterans, this policy provided higher education to an entire generation of persons, many of whom would not ever have attended college due to racial and financial barriers. Mettler's account, however, also documents that the design and implementation of this policy was one of inclusiveness. It was easy to establish one's eligibility: colleges and universities welcomed the veterans. They were treated with respect and as valuable members of the society. In contrast, policies that permitted slavery and later discrimination in the private sector—that denied property, home ownership, and loans to establish small businesses—have depressed the generation of wealth by African Americans and other minorities through many successive generations (Lipsitz 1995).

Soss (chapter 11) demonstrates differences in participation patterns between persons receiving AFDC and those receiving SSDI. AFDC policy is designed in a way that sends negative messages to recipients—they are untrustworthy, they ought to be working rather than staying home, they are irresponsible and immoral in having so many children, and they are receiving benefits only due to the government's generosity. SSDI, on the other hand, treats recipients with respect and does not engage them in morality arguments or difficulties in establishing eligibility. SSDI recipients have no case workers who counsel them about how they should live. The results are predictable—AFDC clients have exceptionally low participation rates and negative identity. Recipients often attempt to escape the negative identity by dividing the group into those who, in fact, fit the negative construction, but do not include themselves in this group. SSDI recipients, on the other hand, do not separate themselves into positive and negative recipients, have a stronger positive identity, and have markedly higher participation rates. Lieberman and Ingram and Schneider (1995) have argued that the *Social Security Act of 1935*, which designed one kind of policy for the elderly and a very different kind for mothers of young children, actually contributed significantly to the current power of the retired persons' lobby.

Across a wide variety of policy areas, the delivery of policy has been taken over by third parties, usually nonprofit or even for-profit contractors. Whether these contractors exhibit the same level of commitment to public service as government agencies can be questioned. Nongovernmental agents may follow the same pattern of institutionalized incentives that leads to biased service among government agencies, but they do not experience the same kinds of corrective governmental checks and balances (Posner 2002). Much has been written about the lack of accountability in policy designs with long implementation chains involving many levels of government (Pressman and Wildavsky 1973; Mazmanian and Sabatier 1983). The problem of accountability is greatly aggravated when services are contracted out. Recipients of benefits are often unaware that government, not the private contractors, should get credit for the help it is providing. Even more serious, recipients of inadequate services often do not know which agency should be held accountable and to whom to complain when performance falls short. As Jurik and Cowgil (chapter 6) indicate, implementation of policies for dependent groups by nonprofit organizations can fall far short of the stated policy goals. Complexity of structure in third-party government generally raises the costs of participation due to the increased efforts required of citizens to unravel lines of authority and accountability. Consequently, third-party policy designs that were supported because they brought government closer to the people may, in fact, lead to confusion and alienation (Smith and Ingram 2002).

To sum up, we are concerned that public policy often sends messages harmful to democracy. We are further alarmed that so many of the policy-making contexts in the United States today fit this discouraging model of degenerative politics that exacerbates inequality, injustice, and inefficiency in solving problems while eroding ethics of public involvement. In contrast, however, there are other models guided by other values, such as pragmatic problem solving, efficiency, responsiveness to all interests, ethical communication, fairness, and justice (Schneider and Ingram 1999). There are governing institutions that create an ethics quite different from those in degenerative systems.

CONSEQUENCES OF SOCIAL CONSTRUCTIONS FOR CITIZENSHIP

Most democratic theorists contend that democracy requires a knowledgeable, active, and engaged citizenry. We and others have argued that successful governance also requires an empathic citizenry that is capable of understanding and pursuing its own interests, but that also acknowledges and respects the interests of others (Ingram and Schneider 1993; Ingram and Smith 1993; Schneider and

Ingram 1997; Landy 1993). What is required of a "good citizen" includes participation, empathy, and recognition of both public and private interests. Citizenship is first of all a legal category; but beyond that, it is a sense of belonging to the broader society—a standing within the polity that demands respect (Shklar 1991). Citizenship is about membership in a society where one is respected, included, involved, and important to the success of the society. Thomas H. Marshall (1964) conceptualized citizenship as a series of phases beginning with rights that are extended by the state and, eventually, leading to full social, economic, and political equality.

We have explained how policies create different levels of participation through their direct effects on voting, their requirements for involvement, and through the differential messages they send to people. Policies impact citizenship because they encourage and facilitate participation by some, but discourage or exclude participation by others. Policies impact citizenship when they directly or indirectly create inequalities in political participation and when they contribute to the social construction of some persons as deserving and others as undeserving members of the society. Policy designs play an important role in dividing people into those who should and should not be fully participating citizens of the society. The social constructions of target populations become deeply embedded in the characteristics of public policies. People's experiences with these policies actually impact and help shape their identity, their orientation to government, their capacity for mobilization, their direct access to policy making, and their understanding of what people "like me" can and should expect from government. Policies send powerful messages about the role of citizens that make a difference in people's sense of efficacy, trust, and what others believe they deserve from government.

Policies impact people's ability to fulfill the role expected of knowledgeable, engaged, empathic citizens of the society. Public policies teach lessons— sometimes they attempt to teach the lessons of citizenship to everyone, but often they teach different lessons to advantaged, contender, dependent, and deviant populations. Sometimes they provide the means and motivation for active engagement to all segments of the population; but other times they disempower the disadvantaged. Policies often fail in their role of teaching the importance of public as well as private interests. To dependent populations, however, policies fail because they teach them only about public interests and to defer to others who are more important. Policies sometimes contribute to the construction of the "other" and exacerbate divisiveness around differences in race, ethnicity, gender, class, and sexuality. In other cases, policies actively seek to overcome divisiveness and bring about greater understanding and equality.

Finally, policies impact citizenship in the most inclusive sense articulated by Marshall through differential allocation of benefits and burdens. These allocations produce inequalities that last through many generations (Lipsitz 1995). On the other hand, when policies lead to actions that protect rights, reverse discriminatory practices, and meet the promise of political equality and equality of opportunity, then they become a positive force for more inclusive citizenship.

The chapters in this book continue the examination we have begun of the social construction of deservedness through public policies. Some authors trace the historical development of the positive (or negative) construction of groups; others examine how social constructions of deservedness plays out in nonprofit arenas and during the policy implementation process. Still others examine the roles of elected leaders, social science, policy analysis, and moral or policy entrepreneurs in constructing groups and embedding constructions into policy designs and institutions. The enormous significance of the social construction of deservedness is illustrated in the final chapter, in which Joseph Soss systematically compares the policy design of SSDI with the design of AFDC. This evidence shows that it is possible for public policies to either strengthen or disempower the groups of citizens those policies serve.

PART I

Historical Roots of Constructions of Deservedness and Entitlement

HELEN M. INGRAM AND ANNE L. SCHNEIDER

Human equality is among the enduring myths of American democracy. The Declaration of Independence is unequivocal in its claim that "all men are created equal and are endowed by their creator with certain unalienable rights." Such universal themes play an important role in nation building and in maintaining the legitimacy of the state in the eyes of its residents; but so also do much more specific rights and benefits that target some groups whose allegiance is especially important. David Easton's (1965) systematic approach to politics focused the attention of scholars upon the systemic need of the political system to attract support from the larger society. Such support, even in long-standing democracies, requires constant reinforcement through appeals to historic ideals, symbols, and myths and the distribution of favors and benefits that connect citizens to their government. At bottom, the power of the state rests as much upon the nobility of its professed ideals as upon its monopoly over the power of coercion. The chapters in this part illustrate the ways in which constructions of deservedness and entitlement through public policy are among the ties that bind.

Chapter 1 by Laura Jensen, "Constructing and Entitling America's Original Veterans," explains how early Congresses chose to allocate benefits to veterans of the Revolutionary War. It was not a foregone conclusion that allocation of rewards to deserving people would become a central function of government. Today, entitlements of all sorts are so much a part of governance in the United States that they seem a "natural" part of the public policy landscape. Yet, programmatic entitlements for particular groups of people were neither necessary nor easily established. Justifications had to be invented. The long-standing Congressional practice of dealing with claims on an individual basis had to be replaced with a *programmatic* entitlement to an entire *group* of people. There were extraordinary difficulties in crafting a coherent rationale and working out the details of who would be eligible and who would not. The original policy, which excluded many categories of veterans, provided a point of attack and prompted the emergence of organized interest groups that successfully expanded the benefit program until, in 1820, seventeen percent of the entire federal budget went to veterans (Dewey 1915, 169).

The institutional context was a critical factor in this policy design because the military was neither unified nor closely bound to the nation-state. Congress needed more authority at the center and more assurance that it could maintain the loyalty of a national army. Military leaders needed assurance that their soldiers would not simply vanish into the landscape. Providing selected benefits, however, to selected groups violated principles of equality and raised concern about creating a privileged standing army. Jensen shows that this original American entitlement program not only taught lessons about who was deserving and who was not, but also shaped the future policy discourse so that arguments became centered on the criteria for defining deservedness, rather than on whether targeting programmatic entitlements to selected target groups should be a proper function of the new national government.

Veterans' entitlements also have implications for citizenship and participation. Studies of recipients of the G.I. Bill have found that veterans who took advantage of educational and other benefits are significantly more likely to vote and engage in political and other public service activities (Mettler, 2002b). Being chosen by government as deserving and entitled had the effect of altering citizen identity so that the citizenship role was taken more seriously and its privileges and obligations exercised more frequently.

Being entitled and deserving of citizenship is one of the larger themes running throughout this book and is introduced in the next two chapters of this part. Citizenship and its associated rights and freedoms are tools that government wields to maintain the allegiance of established groups and interests by affording them a privilege that is not universal. While equality is a basic American principle, access to citizenship is unequal. Voting rights are restricted to those who qualify for them. The compelling logic behind the restrictions appears to be two fold: for citizenship to be cherished, it cannot be afforded to just anyone; and the state must be protected against the damage that might be done by the participation of unworthy and, therefore, excluded groups. Full citizenship is reserved for those who can fulfill certain qualifications thought to be "American," including the intellectual capacity and moral rectitude necessary for self government.

Kay Schriner's historical analysis (chapter 2) shows the dynamic process of change in suffrage laws in the nineteenth century that extended the vote to new populations, while at the same time adopting exclusions that deprived others of this right. Schriner's chapter, "Constructing the Democratic Citizen: Idiocy and Insanity in American Suffrage Law," explains how states came to deny voting privileges to individuals identified as "idiots and insane persons" and to other groups such as criminals, paupers, women, and blacks. Policy makers abandoned the property-holding requirements of the Colonial and Revolutionary War periods as being too restrictive and as not granting an appropriate role to wage earners. Instead, the states used a series of categorical exclusions based on gender, race, religion, criminal status, and alien status, some of which were removed over the years. However, in searching for reliable replacement symbols of unworthy persons, legislators settled upon disenfranchisement of people with disabilities, using terms such as "idiots," "insane persons," and "imbeciles." Beginning in 1819, one state after another excluded much of the mentally disabled population from voting, until today, all but six states deny disabled populations the right to vote, usually on grounds of either intellectual or moral incompetence. Schriner illustrates how conceptions of disability, deviancy, and dependency are used to justify the disfranchisement.

Like the preceding chapter on state building through entitlements to veterans, Schriner's chapter illustrates a preoccupation with supporting the polity, in this case by protecting it from damaging franchises of the morally and intellectually inferior. The chapter also emphasizes the association of the state and its welfare with the "rational"—capable and productive people who are the backbone of American enterprise and whose service undergirds the liberal, capitalist order. Government, it would seem by this view, rests upon the shoulders of the advantaged, and the rights of the advantaged deserve constitutional protection by disenfranchising mentally and morally inferior.

In chapter 2, and in the following chapter about Japanese Americans, the roots of negative social constructions based on long-standing cultural norms and prejudice are apparent. In this case, state constitutions were only inscribing into law something that "everyone knows" about the obvious incapacity of mentally and emotionally disabled people to vote sensibly. Further, the chapter emphasizes an association in social constructions between weakness, incapacity, and moral depravity that is observed by most of the authors in this book. Very often, mental and emotional disqualifications were addressed within the same sections of state constitutions that also covered disenfranchisement of criminals and were treated in the same language during legislative discourse. Neither population could be governed by consent, since neither had consent to give. The involvement of both categories in political activity could threaten democracy. This constructed association, especially when legitimated in state constitutional law, clearly imposed stigmas that amplified political marginalization of the disabled, along with more negatively portrayed criminals. We will see this same association of lack of capacity with moral inferiority portrayed in other chapters.

Among the most interesting findings in Schriner's chapter is the total lack of interest state legislators showed in defining the limits of the categories established in law. Unlike Congressional concern with detailing the characteristics of veterans that rendered them entitled, scant attention was paid to defining mental illness or incapacity. Instead, "insane" and "idiot" persons were often categorized by falling back upon the legal, property-based notion that anyone "under guardianship"—and therefore not competent to attend to financial matters—was also incapable of voting. That so little care was paid to clear classification is testimony of the political weakness and the negative construction of this group. Interestingly, no professional association of experts materialized to protect the interests of the mentally and emotionally disabled. In so far as educators and physicians were at all relevant, they tended to magnify the pitiable characteristics of these populations, a construction clearly at odds with asserting qualifications for franchise.

The institutionalization of negative social constructions by depriving these populations the franchise would seem to put these groups at such disadvantage that it would be virtually impossible to recover a positive identity and civil rights. Yet, the third chapter in this part, "From 'Problem Minority' to 'Model Minority': The Changing Social Construction of Japanese Americans," traces the processes through which the Japanese, who began the twentieth century constructed very negatively, managed to become reconstructed much more positively. Like the mentally and emotionally incapacitated, Japanese were initially thought to lack the necessary requisites for citizenship. They were portrayed as incurably "Mongolian" and culturally incompatible. Race, immigrant status, and the social construction of the culture of their nation of origin are the distinguishing features of the Japanese "otherness." These same characteristics are also important in the discussion of Mexican immigrants in chapter 5. Similar, too, is the popular propensity to ignore distinctions between legal and illegal residents. While these characteristics burden the Japanese Americans in the early 1900s, by the end of the century several of these characteristics turn out to be advantages in reconstruction of their social image.

Stephanie DiAlto goes further, in chapter 3, than previous authors in specifying the roles of interest groups—the media, legislatures, courts, and proponents of state ballot initiatives—in creating, perpetuating, and changing social constructions. White farmers, resentful of successful Japanese enterprise, were initially instrumental in pressuring state legislatures on the West coast to deprive persons of Japanese origin of property ownership, citizenship, and the franchise. The media reflected the preponderantly negative social construction, especially during World War II when Japanese Americans were incarcerated in internment camps. At that time, the construction of Japanese Americans was a direct opposite to the favorable social constructions of Japanese American soldiers, presented in the chapter by Laura Jensen that leads off this part. Most Japanese Americans were constructed as an enemy within that threatening security. Interestingly, however, Japanese Americans who served in the U.S. armed forces were excepted. Japanese-American veterans benefitted from the more general positive social construction of veterans, and their exemplary service was invoked later as part of the justification for more positive construction of the entire class.

Courts acted at first to institutionalize the negative social constructions that prevailed in the media and the state legislatures, thereby legitimizing very restrictive policies. By 1922, however, courts established an alternative line of precedent to protect the rights of American-born citizens of Japanese descent, giving jurists a great deal of latitude. The Supreme Court would later bend with prevailing negative public sentiment against Japanese Americans when political fervor ran high, as in the case legitimizing World War II internment. When such public pressures were less forceful, the Court acted as an arena in which Japanese Americans could press for rights. The availability of somewhat impartial courts helped to moderate and channel protest into accepted forums.

What is particularly instructive for the larger themes of the book, and a key to Japanese-American success at reconstructing a more favorable image, is strong and positive group identity. Japanese Americans never accepted the negative portrayal thrust upon them, and they resisted the temptation to divide themselves into those who were "truly" deserving and those who were not. Also, they did not attempt to "change American values." Instead, throughout their ordeal, they remained almost unified in their insistence that they embodied basic American values of industry, integrity, honesty, and that they had earned their citizenship. They lobbied on their own behalf, and once they achieved the franchise they exercised it.

Chapter 3 reinforces the larger message of this part of the book—that social constructions are manipulated to build support for the state and to continue the prevailing social structure. Reconstruction of Japanese Americans into the "model minority" is a mixed blessing, since it perpetuates the image of Japanese Americans as different and elevates their social position at the expense of African Americans, with whom they are compared. The "good" model can exist only so long as there is a "bad" model. Such constructions reinforce the degenerative racial politics that is so frustrating to the democratic promise of America.

1

Constructing and Entitling America's Original Veterans

LAURA S. JENSEN

Of all of the public policies involved in the social construction of citizens, entitlements are undoubtedly the most overt. Such policies deliberately and overtly invoke state authority to categorize groups of citizens as deserving of public benefits. They embed carefully crafted rationales for the allocation of public benefits and burdens in powerful legal discourses that render particular citizens worthy of the state's attention at particular moments in history. Individually and collectively, a nation's entitlements specify which people, personal situations, and behaviors deserve tangible, public recognition at a given time, while the entitlements' qualifying criteria and their silences describe those who are not deserving.

This chapter explores the ways in which American entitlements first constructed military veterans as deserving citizens by analyzing the program of pensions for veterans of the American Revolution enacted by the Fifteenth Congress in 1818. Members of the U.S. military forces have been considered deserving of public benefits for so long that veterans' entitlements seem an almost natural part of the American social policy landscape. Yet, benefits for nondisabled military veterans were neither foreordained nor easily established. Indeed, they originally were quite controversial. The establishment of Federal military service pensions required the formulation of a rationale that could legitimize the redistribution of public monies to a particular portion of "the people." Beyond the creation of a culturally resonant and acceptable definition of "veteran" for national policy purposes (a deceptively difficult task in the new republic), justifications had to be invented for endowing a subset of the populace with programmatic rights in a putatively egalitarian, constitutional democracy. Statutes proactively entitling *groups* of citizens to Federal benefits via public benefit *programs* embodied a new policy device that deviated radically from the tenets of representation and fiscal responsibility enshrined in the political and constitutional culture of early America, which obligated legislators to respond directly to the petitions and claims of citizens on an individual, case-by-case basis. The question of whether to pension veterans of the Revolution engaged state actors and ordinary citizens alike in a novel conversation about the appropriate limits of public policy—one that helped to establish selective, legal entitlement as a legitimate Federal practice in the United States and sanctioned future policies and programs that either implicitly or explicitly categorized citizens as deserving or undeserving of the nation's beneficence.

The idea that Federal entitlements of enduring significance were enacted during the early national period may come as a surprise to some readers, for entitlements commonly are considered to be contemporary phenomena, as are "welfare states," constructed around an array of national social programs. According to many scholars, there was no meaningful Federal social role before the late nineteenth century, when patronage-oriented Congresses established and expanded a massive system of pensions for Union veterans of the Civil War (Skocpol 1992). By the terms of preeminent accounts of American state formation, the limited, underdeveloped, frail shell that was the American state before the Civil War would not have been capable of enacting and implementing major Federal social policies on behalf of the nation (Skowronek 1982; Bensel 1990).

Nonetheless, the pre-Civil War state did precisely that, establishing national programs of care for military veterans and their survivors and for other classes of citizens who served the diverse purposes of the Federal government. Early American entitlements are critically important subjects for study, not only because we need to rethink early American governance and the trajectory of American state building, but moreover, because they furnish original examples of the social construction of citizens in American public policy (Jensen 1996, 2003). Analysis of the enactment and implementation of the 1818 pension law reveals how institutions, events, ideas, social structures, policy feedback, and the beliefs and ambitions of national policy makers shaped the definition and perception of veterans as a social group and worked to make that group politically and culturally relevant. It also illuminates how target populations, or the particular categories of citizens that come to be designated in public policy initiatives (Ingram and Schneider 1991; Schneider and Ingram 1993), may not be contiguous with associated social groups. In distinguishing both *between* and *among* particular groups of military men as it entitled only some veterans to Federal pensions, the 1818 pension legislation sent messages about which "types" of citizens and claims mattered, giving birth to new civic identities and mobilizing citizens socially and politically. Pressure along the pension program's statutory boundaries of inclusion shifted concern from the validity of entitlement as a policy practice to the details of program expansion and contraction. As a result, public policies allocating benefits and burdens on the basis of ascriptively determined group identity effectively were legitimized, enshrining "deservedness" as a central component of U.S. public policy.

PENSIONS FOR REVOLUTIONARY PATRIOTS

In his first annual message to Congress in December 1817, President James Monroe proposed the creation of a pension program for the surviving patriots of the American Revolution. The condition of the United States, Monroe informed the newly assembled Fifteenth Congress, was exceptional. Americans had never had so much to congratulate themselves about. The "abundant fruits of the earth" had filled the nation with plenty, an "extensive and profitable commerce" had expanded national revenues, and public credit had "attained an extraordinary elevation." Moreover, the nation's "free Government, founded on the interest and affections of the people," had "gained, and [was] daily gaining strength"; and "local jealousies" were "rapidly yielding to more generous, enlarged, and enlightened view of national policy." The nation owed its establishment to the service of the Revolution's veterans, yet some of them were "reduced to indigence, and even to real distress." It would "do honor to their country to provide for them," for these "very meritorious citizens" had "a claim on the gratitude of their country." Monroe urged Congress to enact a pension program immediately, before the opportunity to aid America's original veterans was lost. So much time had already passed, he argued, that the number of veterans to benefit from any provision would not be large (*Annals of Congress* 1817–18, 12, 19). After all, the war for independence had ended some three-and-a-half decades earlier.

The House of Representatives moved upon the president's proposal immediately, referring it to a select committee (all but one of whose members had, like Monroe, been Revolutionary officers) that reported back with a bill in a mere ten days. It proposed that every commissioned and noncommissioned officer, musician, or soldier who had "served in the revolutionary war," before the September 1783 treaty of peace with Great Britain, and who was "reduced to indigence," or "by age, sickness, or other cause rendered incapable to procure subsistence by manual labor," should become entitled to receive half of the monthly pay allowed to his grade for the remainder of his life from the U.S. Government. (U.S. House 1964; *Annals of Congress* 1817–18, 446).[1] The bill was essentially universal in its plan to entitle virtually all of the men who had served in the Revolution to benefits—provided that they were *also* poor or unable to work for a living.

Most of the House deliberations concerned the scope of the pension plan rather than the root concept of Federal veterans' pensions, which seemed an almost forgone conclusion as the nation's original patriots were lauded by their representatives. The introduction of the bill alone was hailed as "gratifying evidence of the re-connexion of public feeling with the principles of the Revolution" (Strother 1817–18, 497); and it was widely agreed that the war's "heroes of liberty, from whose fortitude and valor the present blessings of our country have, in a great measure, resulted, [we]re really entitled to the gratitude and consideration of the Government" (Johnson 1817–18, 510). Though a few members felt that pensions should be conferred only upon veterans who had fought in the war for a significant length of time, most others maintained that a more "liberal spirit should prevail." Some even advocated pensions for all Revolutionary veterans based upon service alone, rather than service coupled with poverty. As Representative George Strother of Virginia put it, "all who contributed to build up our magnificent political fabric" should be "embraced in the wide circle of gratitude" (*Annals of Congress* 1817–18, 491–99). Poverty nonetheless was retained among the House bill's criteria of deservedness. The bill passed unanimously just three weeks after Monroe's address, having been amended to provide a pension of eight dollars per month to every soldier and twenty dollars per month to every officer who had served in the Revolution- ary War in any of the regiments or navies raised by either Congress or the states, who were "reduced to indigence and incapable of procuring subsistence."[2]

The idea of creating Revolutionary veterans' pensions also enjoyed wide- spread support in the Senate. Pointing to the large Treasury surplus, Senator Robert Goldsborough of Maryland reasoned that because the nation was "opu- lent, powerful, and prosperous," it had the ability and the obligation to uphold the principles of justice and gratitude by remunerating the few remaining "worthy and indigent men" who had fought to establish American indepen- dence. While none of the Revolutionary veterans had "any strict claim in law" to government benefits, Goldsborough, on February 12, 1818, insisted that a case could be made to authorize the nation to reward those "justly entitled to [its] grateful remembrance." Moreover, they should be entitled to receive pen- sion benefits without having to submit to the humiliation of a means test, which would attach the stigma of pauperism to service pensions and transform the nation's intended benevolence into "polluted bounty." Beyond the "high and solemn duty" incumbent upon Congress to aid the veterans, there were motives of "national feeling and national character" involved that could not be disregarded. Would the Senate allow the history of the United States to "add another instance for those with whom the 'ingratitude of Republics' is a maxim?" (*Annals of Congress* 1817–18, 191–98).

Rhetoric about gratitude and justice aside, the Senate pension bill differed significantly from its House counterpart. Drawn up by the Committee on Mil- itary Affairs, it restricted pension eligibility to veterans of Continental forces *only*—and among them, to men who had served for a minimum of three years or until the end of the Revolution. There was no doubt that many veterans of the war were aged, poverty-stricken, and in need of assistance. The issue, how- ever, was whether the nation should provide pensions for all of them, or prof- fer benefits only to those veterans who, in Congress's opinion, were most deserving. Arguing for the Senate bill, Goldsborough maintained that it was not his purpose "to detract from the merits of any." It was simply that, if there was "any one definite class of men *more* meritorious than another . . . who, by their services and sufferings, ha[d] rendered themselves *most* dear to our recollections, and *most* worthy of our gratitude, they were the officers and soldiers of the Revolutionary Army." There was simply "no comparison between the sufferings of these men" and those of the militia, who had served close to home, where they were "plentifully fed and comfortably lodged at night," and able to attend to family and domestic concerns while not occupied with defending their neighborhoods. The Continental Army had traveled widely and fought and bled for the nation at large. "It was for the country they encountered all their hardships," Goldsborough argued, "and it is from the nation Treasury they ought to be reimbursed" (*Annals of Congress* 1817–18, 191, 196).

Clearly, the broad consensus that existed among congressional pension advocates with respect to the idea of Federal military pensions did not represent accord regarding the specific criteria that rendered veterans deserving of public largesse. Military service alone should have sufficed to qualify the Revolution's veterans for benefits if, as some members believed, the policy initiative was intended to create veterans' pensions *per se*. To a majority of Congress, however, mere service did not justify the establishment of a Federal pension program. Hence, they urged the establishment of qualifying criteria variously combining war service with poverty, the inability to work, military rank, length of military service, and service in particular military units (notably, Continental forces rather than "provincial" ones). Age was understood as a criterion of deservedness, but it essentially was taken for granted, given that the war had ended in 1783. So, too, was gender, since veterans were assumed to be men who had engaged in military service during the war for independence.

The pension advocates' inability to agree upon the definition of the veterans' deservedness for public policy purposes was complicated by the fact that a small group of senators objected vehemently to both the idea of Federal service pensions and the justifications offered for their creation. Though obviously in the minority, Nathaniel Macon of North Carolina and William Smith of South Carolina meticulously condemned every aspect of the proposed legislation. Their arguments registered deep concern over programmatic entitlement, particularly selective entitlement, as a policy practice. Macon and Smith understood that inequities and societal divisions would result from the government's creation of socially constructed legal boundaries separating deserving and undeserving citizens. The redistributive obligations to be imposed by the pension bill were ominous not simply for fiscal reasons. Macon and Smith could not comprehend how the distribution of national revenues to a select group of citizens could be justified, particularly when some of those who were to be excluded from receiving pensions seemed essentially similar to the citizens who were cast as deserving and who were slated to become entitled. As the House debate had suggested, the proposed exclusion of militia members from the bill's benefits was both incomprehensible and unprincipled if military service or "veteran" status was to be the statutory basis of desert. So was the bill's omission of the nation's nonmilitary poor if poverty or the inability to work was to be the criterion triggering congressional generosity. The motion to amend the already exclusive Senate version of the pension bill to benefit Army *officers only* was "language not known to our Constitution . . . repugnant to the principles of our Government, and at war with good sense and public justice." How, Smith asked, could the "benevolence, sympathy, and gratitude" ostensibly inspiring the pension bill "draw a line between the offi-cer and the soldier, when both ha[d] served their country, and both [we]re indigent?" And how could Congress "believe the public mind [wa]s prepared to pay a tax to maintain a pension system, because it [wa]s said that those offi-cers cannot submit to any industrious pursuits for a living?" There existed "thousands of poor" who were unable to work who demanded their repre-sentatives' attention "in an equal degree." Was Congress prepared to put all of the nation's poor citizens on the pension list? Smith declared himself "opposed to both the bill and [the] amendment in any form in which they could be pre-sented," because "no particular merit could be ascribed to any particular por-tion of the people of the United States, for services rendered during the Rev-olutionary war, in exclusion to any other portion who espoused that cause." Given the vital efforts and sacrifices of the militia and of other men, widows, and orphans north and south, Smith, on January 29, 1818, said the idea that the nation was "exclusively" indebted to the Continental Army was patently false (*Annals of Congress* 1817–18, 140–47).

Smith and Macon found their colleagues' arguments eliding benevolence and justice similarly specious. Contemporary theoretical and legal under-standings of justice made the notion of a "debt of gratitude" preposterous. Macon pointed out that "if justice required that the bill should pass, [then] neither the condition of the Treasury nor the [small] number [of veterans] to be provided for"—policy analysis "facts" repeatedly offered in support of the bill—"ought to be taken into consideration." Macon, like Smith also, found justice completely lacking in the Senate's elitist intent to benefit only veter-ans of Continental forces at the expense of other citizens of arguably equal merit. To "tax th[o]se people to give a pension to any, because they were in the regular army," he said on January 29, 1918, seemed like "taxing the bones of the brave and the ashes of distress." At the end of the war, the officers had received five years of full pay, and both officers and soldiers had obtained land from the United States. Even if the Continental troops had been paid in cer-tificates that had depreciated, so had the currency depreciated, which was "a national calamity, from which no one was exempt" (*Annals of Congress* 1817–18, 159, 155–56, 141–42, 148). In addition to their pay and land boun-ties, "there ha[d] not been an office of honor or profit in the gift of the United States, or any individual State, which ha[d] not been filled by a Con-tinental officer, if he asked for it." Additionally, the government had given to "every officer and soldier who ha[d] applied, a pension for life, if he had been wounded or disabled in the public service." Smith dismissed concern over the potential charge of "ingratitude" by European nations by asking, "what is it that they have not said to reproach us?" America did not suffer by comparison with Europe in its treatment of its veterans. It was the pensioner who complained of ingratitude and not the farmer and mechanic who paid the tax (*Annals of Congress* 1817–18, 147–48).

Finally, Smith and Macon expressed fear about the pension bill's impact as a policy precedent. If Congress could circumvent constitutional limits upon its authority to choose *one* subset of citizens, identify them as uniquely deserving, and endow them with rights to public benefits, it surely could do the same for others. Smith objected to Congress's proposed use of the spending power to create pension entitlements by noting that one of America's primary reasons for ridding itself of the British government was precisely "to get rid of pensions and placemen, and the power of their Parliament." Of "what avail is the Constitution," Smith asked, "if [legislative] precedent is to govern? Once establish a precedent, and you have no control over Congress but the discretion of its members; and, like the British Parliament, it will soon become omnipotent." To Smith, there was simply "one fact not to be controverted:" if Congress could give a pension to one man, it could give one to another, "without regard to his character" (*Annals of Congress* 1817–18, 148–49). Establishing a pension program inevitably would lead to new expectations. Opponents of the current bill might be told that the country could never have another Revolutionary war, but, as Macon charged, it did "not require the gift of prophecy to foretel that thirty or forty years hence, as much may be said in favor of the army engaged in the second war for independence, as we have now heard about the first" (*Annals of Congress* 1817–18, 157).[3]

These arguments for and against the Revolutionary veterans' pension bill convey a strong sense of how members of the Fifteenth Congress understood the deservedness of military veterans and how some imagined that they might translate those understandings into legitimate rationales for allocating tangible benefits and costs through public policy. Yet, there is much more to the story of the pension proposal. How and why did the Revolution's veterans come to be politically relevant and constructed as deserving and entitled in 1818, to the extent that Congress actively considered the enactment of a Federal pension program for some or all of them? How would Congress construct Revolutionary veterans in the final version of the pension bill that would be signed into law by President Monroe on March 18, 1818? What would happen when that law was implemented? How would the discourses of deservedness contained in the *1818 Pension Act* influence future political action and policy design? The answers to these questions lie in a complex interplay of early American institutions, policy feedback, ideas, interests, events, social structures, and political and fiscal opportunities and constraints.

From Colony to Confederation

The origins of the Act of 1818 lie in the origins of the American nation. In the first few years of its existence, the United States faced fundamental problems of institutional design and governance. It required a central state apparatus capable of waging war effectively against Great Britain and of governing at the center and the periphery. A key aspect of that state building was establishing and maintaining military forces, capable of winning the war for independence, then consolidating and expanding the nation. This was a thorny problem in a country philosophically opposed to "standing" or permanent armies, where the only military force believed to be appropriate was one comprised of citizen-soldiers contributing selflessly to the common defense as members of the polity. This was the militia: a free army of free men who were willing, because of their stake in society and belief in liberty, to fight to protect home and family and to preserve self-government.

Although the militia figured importantly in the minds of Americans and in the war effort itself, the demands of the conflict pushed the Continental Congress to augment the militia with a national land force in the form of the Continental Army, relying upon promises of salary and land entitlements to entice men into the nation's service (Jensen 2003). As the war dragged on, Army recruits were killed or left the service, enlistments lagged, and U.S. efforts faltered, Congress was forced to heed Commander George Washington's warning that "without some better provision for binding the officers by the tie of interest to the service," he would no longer be able to hold the army together (cited in Glasson 1918, 24–25). In May 1778, Congress reluctantly voted to establish service pensions of half pay for seven years for Army officers serving until the end of the war and lump-sum bonuses of eighty dollars for noncommissioned officers and soldiers (Ford et al. 1904–1937, vol. XI [1778], 502–03). The officers, who had expected more substantial recognition of their contribution to independence, immediately deemed the measure insufficient, and demanded that Congress both grant them pensions for life and enact pension legislation for their widows and orphans. The necessity of assuaging the Army's discontents eventually prevailed. Pensions for officers' widows and orphans were established in August 1780, and in October of that year—almost two-and-a-half years after the original half-pay legislation—a bitterly divided Continental Congress finally gave in to the concept of open-ended, pension benefits for life for the officers of the Continental line (Glasson 1918, 30–35; Burnett 1941; Kaplan 1951; Ford et al. 1904–1937, vol. XVII [1780], 772–73, vol. XVIII [1780] 958–61).

These benefits were enormously controversial. It was widely agreed that the nation should provide "invalid" pensions to those injured in combat, as the colonies previously had done. In 1776, the Continental Congress had enacted legislation granting pensions of half pay for life, or during disability, for those who lost limbs in combat or who otherwise were rendered incapable of earning a livelihood. Officers' service pensions were an entirely different concept, however: one that violated core American ideals. Beyond the long-term financial commitment that they represented—a commitment the Continental Congress did not quite have the authority to make—they signaled a rejection of the political, moral, and evangelical calls thought to motivate the citizen soldier in favor of the standing Army's corrupt association with patronage, rank, and pensions. Some members of the Continental Congress argued that it was only fair to compensate the Army's officers with pensions, who sacrificed their time and property while those they protected were at home amassing fortunes. Many others, however, were outraged by the pension plan, for in their view, the hardships that the officers endured were also suffered, perhaps to an even greater degree, by the Army's *soldiers* and the militia. Henry Laurens, president of the Continental Congress, bluntly asserted that while "necessity m[ight] be submitted to, . . . Republicans w[ould] at a proper time withdraw a Grant which sh[ould] appear to have been extorted" (Burnett 1921, vol. 3, 221).

In the short run, Laurens's prediction was essentially accurate. Congressional efforts to persuade the states to fund the service pensions in 1782 failed. As the end of the war approached, the Army's officers worried that their life pensions would never materialize and threatened that they would not lay down their arms unless some effort was made to guarantee them. When the officers declared themselves willing to have their life pensions commuted into an equivalent lump-sum payment at the conclusion of the war, Congress quickly passed a *Commutation Act* on March 22, 1783, two days before news spread of the signing of the preliminary peace agreement. It provided that the Continental officers would receive five years of full pay in money or securities bearing six percent interest per year in lieu of half-pay for life. Lacking the resources required to implement the act, Congress was forced to ask the states to approve the establishment of a new impost duty in order to meet the nation's extraordinary financial obligations, which included approximately $5,000,000 for the commutation of half-pay plus $300,000 per year in interest. The states' response in the face of such an onerous fiscal burden was slow at best and, at worst, extremely hostile (Kohn 1975, 33–35; Ferguson 1961, 164–67, 220–21; Glasson 1918, 41–42).

Though a major portion of the Continental Army came from New England, popular opposition toward the officers' pensions and their commutation there raged to such a degree that it produced, in James Madison's view, "almost a general anarchy." The protest was fueled by a staggering postwar economic downturn, high taxes, and antinationalist sentiment, but nonetheless focused squarely upon Congress's abandonment of republican, egalitarian principles. Northern newspapers were filled with vehement indictments of the Continental officers and their newly established hereditary Society of the Cincinnati, the formation of which seemed to substantiate the charge that officers' pensions would create an American aristocracy living off of the labors of others. The Massachusetts assembly replaced its representatives in Congress as a penalty for their agreement to the *Commutation Act* and formally censured Congress in July 1783 for enacting a law that was "inconsistent with that equality which ought to subsist among citizens of free and republican States" and "calculated to raise and exalt some citizens in wealth and grandeur, to the injury and oppression of others." Citizens were even more outraged in Connecticut, which in 1778 had proposed to amend the Articles of Confederation specifically to prohibit post-war pensions. Town meetings and state conventions passed hostile resolutions denouncing commutation as "unjust, impolitic, oppressive to the people, subservient of the principles of a republican government, and exceedingly dangerous when drawn into precedent." Half pay for life for nondisabled officers not only capitulated to self interest, but moreover, provided government authorities with a corrupt tool—the economic dependency of a select group of citizens—with which to expand its political influence, undermining the very ideals and institutions for which the Revolution had been fought (Hutchinson and Rachal 1962, vol. 7, 307–08; see also Royster 1979, 345–47; Buel 1980, 304–11; Kaplan 1952, 34–41).[4]

The bitter controversy over the officers' pensions and their commutation evaporated by the spring of 1784, as the prospect of peace became apparent and those who had fought in the war began to go home. The perception that Congress had acted appropriately and within its authority in order to maintain a disciplined Army spread. As it became clear that the officers would not be granted social distinction based upon superior revolutionary merit, concern over the pensions that were to substantiate that merit diminished significantly (Royster 1979, 348–68; Glasson 1918, 47, 52–53). When the Army was formally disbanded by Congress in November 1783, Continentals entitled to benefits were forced to return home with little more than promises in hand. Commutation certificates drawing six percent interest were distributed in lieu of cash in early 1784, but because the Confederation lacked the funds either to pay the interest on them or to redeem them, the Army veterans' treatment by the state could be seen by their fellow citizens to be essentially no better than that accorded others who had sought to create the new nation.

These institutional, ideational, and policy developments were part of the legacy inherited by the Fifteenth Congress when it assembled to consider the creation of pensions for Revolutionary patriots. American independence had been secured in a war of unprecedented intensity and magnitude, not through the efforts of a European-style, professional military, but by mobilizing a fluid hybrid of state and national forces and the citizens who supported them. This clouded what it meant to be a "veteran" in the new nation, as did ideological distinctions between citizen-soldiers and mercenaries and social and class differences between officers and soldiers. The Continental Congress's original promise of pensions only to Army officers and their survivors further divided military veterans even as the social group "veterans" was forming. That only disability pensions enjoyed widespread public approval did not prevent the Army's officers and other nondisabled veterans from feeling ill-used when their benefits were commuted at the end of the war and paid in scrip. They also continued to hope and expect that the government somehow would act to provide the compensation they believed they deserved.

FROM CONFEDERATION TO CONSTITUTIONAL DEMOCRACY

The issue of the Revolutionary War pension benefits lingered unresolved for decades after the ratification of the U.S. Constitution and its creation of a federal system of government. The Confederation government was in default between 1784 and 1789. Many Continentals sold their certificates for a fraction of their value, before the newly established U.S. Congress enacted a law providing for their redemption in 1790, and complained bitterly that they had been cheated twice: first by the government when it reneged on its promise of benefits for life and then by speculators who took advantage of them (Resch 2000). Believing that the fiscal incapacity of the Confederation had caused them to suffer great injustice, they formed a group of untiring claimants who would press their demands before Congress for decades. As Washington had argued upon disbanding the Army, half-pay for life was the "price of their blood and of [American] Independency." More than "a common debt," it was a debt of honor which could "never be considered as a Pension or gratuity, nor be cancelled until it [wa]s fairly discharged" (Fitzpatrick 1931–1944, vol. 26, 483–96, 492; Glasson 1918, 49–50).[5]

These were powerful arguments in the late eighteenth century, when relationships between debtors and creditors were viewed as social and moral bonds far stronger than mere legal obligation. Because such bonds depended ultimately upon personal faith and trust, defaulting debtors were not simply unfortunate victims of bad times. They were understood to be moral failures, "violators of a code of trust and friendship who deserved to [be] punished and imprisoned" (Wood 1987, 106–07). To citizens accustomed to this code of debtor–creditor relationships, the U.S. government's refusal to satisfy the veterans' claims must have been startling.

Indeed, the government's inattention likely appeared little short of astonishing, for during this period of time, political representation in the United States was rooted in an unmediated, personal politics of reciprocal obligation. Citizens were obligated to bring their concerns to their legislators and legislators were obligated to hear and act upon them. The ratification of the Constitution and Congress's subsequent creation of an independent Federal judiciary did not disrupt Americans' historic practice of taking their concerns directly to their elected representatives. Nor did it bring an end to the determination of citizens' claims as a *legislative* practice involving judgment about debt and legal obligation, a practice that linked representatives and their constituents directly and intimately over matters of right and remedy. From the early colonial era until at least the 1860s, monetary claims brought against the government were fiscal questions that were the province of the legislative bodies that maintained control over public funds under their powers of appropriation, not legal questions for the courts (Desan 1998a, 1998b; Shinomura 1985; Jensen 2003, 44–48, 67–69). Claims for relief from debts, taxes, poverty, and disaster were also issues properly brought to legislators.

The mechanism for conveying citizens' claims of need and right to Congress was the petition, a form of political speech that was vitally important during the early years of the United States' existence, both as an expression of the will of the people and as a device that structured politics and the processes of government (Mark 1998; Higginson 1986; U.S. House 1986). The right of citizens to petition their assemblies had evolved during the colonial period into an affirmative right that mandated legislative attention to the claims of the governed in ways that no other mechanism of political participation could. Although enfranchised, property-owning, adult white men seem to have exercised that right most vigorously, people with little if any formal political power—disenfranchised white men, women, African Americans, and Native Americans—also made use of the petition process to articulate social, political, and economic concerns (Bailey 1979; Olson 1992; Mark 1998, 2175–187). In the political and constitutional culture of the early Republic, constituents were expected to communicate their concerns and grievances and suggest remedies for them, even in the form of proposed legislation. Their representatives, in turn, were obliged to be receptive and responsive (Mark 1998, 2154, 2191–2212; Higginson 1986, 155; U.S. House 1986, 6).

All things considered, the nation's veterans had good reason to believe that their representatives should be attentive to their demands. After the close of the Revolution, however, the Continental Congress was involved in many larger issues of nation-building, including western land policy, foreign relations, the location of a permanent seat for the U.S. government, and the revision of the Articles of Confederation. Military policies remained a vital concern, but to the dismay of veterans petitioning for relief from poverty or for the resolution of pension claims, the question of what kind of military establishment was appropriate for the Republic in peacetime was far higher on the congressional agenda than the problem of how to live up to past promises to military men. The image of the citizen soldier was resurgent in the minds of many Americans, who viewed the end of the war as a victory of popular rather than military virtue, and continued to associate militarism with the inevitable rise of corruption and tyranny (Royster 1979, 327–68; Kohn 1975, 282–83). As Sarah Livingston Jay put it as she toasted the official treaty of peace between Britain and the newly independent United States of America, "May all our Citizens be Soldiers, and all our Soldiers Citizens!" (cited in Kerber 1990, 89–90).

Not surprisingly, Congress initially turned to the states and their militias for the nation's defense, resolving on June 2, 1784, that standing armies were "inconsistent with the principles of republican Governments, dangerous to the liberties of a free people, and generally converted into destructive engines for establishing despotism" (Ford et al. 1904–1937, vol. XXVII, 518–24). Yet, it was becoming increasingly clear to most Americans that some sort of regular, professional force was required to ensure internal order, vanquish hostile Native Americans, prevent foreign encroachments, and affirm the United States' position as a respectable member of the emerging international order. The dual "system" of national and state troops that finally was confirmed by the U.S. Constitution and the Bill of Rights embodied an ambiguous compromise between ideology and institutional necessity. Because the Constitution failed to spell out mechanisms for enlistment or conscription, the Federal government was left to rely solely upon its fiscal powers to "raise and support Armies." Military service thus was linked with compensation, rather than defined as a (male) obligation of citizenship, until the conscription legislation of the Civil War and beyond (Chambers 1987, 23–29; Kohn 1975, 40–88; Cress 1982, 75–109, 116–21).

In the early years of the nineteenth century, compensation in the form of one-time enlistment bounties or wages paid to military personnel, or pensions provided to men disabled in combat, remained conceptually distinct from pensions granted simply as a consequence of service. Petitions and claims from the Revolution's veterans nonetheless showered early U.S. Congresses. Some aging veterans pleaded for Federal assistance on the grounds of illness and infirmity, describing deprivation and mental anguish resulting from deepening poverty and inadequate disability pensions. Other individuals requested the establishment of a pension program on the grounds that their wartime sacrifices had either caused them to be poor or impaired their ability to be self-sufficient (Resch 2000, 85–86). Still others asked for remuneration as an expression of national honor and gratitude. Their petitions and accompanying testimony revealed how veterans perceived their own deservedness and attested to their expectation that Congress would attend to their pleas for assistance. As Rawleigh Christian of Northumberland County, Virginia, age sixty-three, wrote to Congress in December 1817:

> Your petitioner, having thus devoted the prime of his life to the service of his country and being now incapable from the effects of his wounds received in that service and his advanced age from procuring the means of supporting himself, and his aged wife, throws himself on the justice and bounty of the Congress of the United States under the most thorough assurance that they will not suffer the worn out Soldier of the Revolution to pine in want for that pittance which would be like a drop from the ocean when taken from the coffers of a great and wealthy country. Your petitioner therefore prays that your honorable body will grant him something for his immediate support and also such an annual pension as you may think just taking into consideration his services and situation.[6]

Nathaniel Kinnard of Portsmouth, New Hampshire, sent Congress a petition in January 1818 detailing his many years of Revolutionary service at sea (some under John Paul Jones), including five years spent as a prisoner of war, and his subsequent command of a cutter for the duration of the War of 1812. Compelled at the age of sixty-three to "throw himself on the bounty, or the justice of his Government" for subsistence, Kinnard prayed that his name might:

> be added to the Pension list, or that such other provision may be made for him, that the few remaining days, or years, which may be allotted him, may not be embittered with the reflection, that while he has devoted the best period of his life to his country, his services & sufferings should have resulted in the Poverty of himself and his family.[7]

Still another Revolutionary veteran, sixty-six-year-old George McBeth of the Pendleton District of South Carolina, informed Congress in early 1818 that he had "received no wound, while in the service of his country, to entitle him to obtain a pension from the bounty of his government, nor would he have even asked for the charity of that government, had not age and infirmities . . . fast hurrying him to the grave, rendered him incapable of making a support for himself and an aged wife." Thrown "on the cold charity of a careless world," McBeth had "no resources of happiness and comfort left but in the mercy of his god and the benevolence of his country." He therefore:

> appeal[ed] in the hour of distress, and beg[ged], that the hand that has so often bestowed food and raiment on the hungry and naked, [might] be extended to him, to shelter him from the pitiless storms of adversity that beat keen and heavy on his aged and defenseless head.[8]

As early as 1808–1809, disgruntled Army officers launched the legalistic argument that their loss of pension benefits through commutation in 1783 had constituted an unfulfilled contractual obligation of the government. They began to send memorials and petitions asking Congress to recognize not only that some of them were poor and in need of aid, but, more importantly, that their claims rested upon "such a very different ground from all other public creditors" that the sympathy and justice of their country simply had to be aroused. Believing themselves to be "legally and equitably entitled" to pensions "predicated upon services, sufferings, and privations, which have established the freedom of a Country, and the Independence of a people, subjected to despotic Rules and Regulations, and groaning under the Iron hand of oppression," they appealed "to the justice and magnanimity" of Congress for remuneration. Some officers even went so far as to assert that Congress's *discussion* of their claims in a previous session had "disclosed a tacit recognition of obligations" on the part of the nation. Although not all of the veteran officers were "equally urged by necessitous circumstances to present themselves as objects of the public generosity," the situation required them "to advance a demand upon the public equity and honor."[9]

Revolutionary veterans believed themselves to be worthy of, and entitled to, public largesse. They understood Congress to have the obligation to listen to their claims and to possess the authority necessary to create pension benefits. Some even thought that Congress was legally *obligated* to establish Federal veterans' pensions. There was, after all, a code of honor governing debtor-creditor relations, a legacy of congressional support for veterans, and a lingering policy precedent. The United States was dependent upon the efforts of citizen soldiers and upon compensation as its sole means of raising national forces. In addition, members of Congress were becoming increasingly dependent upon the good will of an expanding male electorate. Weren't the men who had spent the prime of their lives establishing the United States deserving of some form of support in their old age, when many were poor, perhaps as a result of their service to the nation?

THE ACT OF 1818

Public support for Revolutionary veterans' pensions was broad and bipartisan by early 1818. The passage of the inclusive pension bill in the House in the first session of the Fifteenth Congress was celebrated widely. Newspaper editorials observed that it was more than time to provide for America's aging veterans, whose exertions had secured the nation's very existence. "If a patriot when dead deserves a marble monument at the expense of his country," argued the *Federal Republican and Baltimore Telegraph,* "how much more does he deserve during life?" The "paltry panegyrics" of Fourth of July remembrances, however festive, were a grossly inadequate expression of gratitude to the "poor, emaciated, hoary veterans" who had braved death in the battlefield. The hour had come for the United States to demonstrate some "timely benevolence," so that history would attest that the nation had "not entirely lost [its] sense of justice, honor and humanity" (cited in Resch 2000, 101, 102, 106).

The urge to grant Federal service pensions to veterans in 1817–1818 was emblematic of an age in which Americans anxiously struggled to reconcile the values of their Revolutionary heritage and to devise ways to shore up civic virtue against the erosion of rapid societal change. As early as 1789, historian David Ramsay had felt compelled to conclude his pioneering account of the Revolution and the establishment of constitutional government with the exhortation: that his fellow citizens should "cherish and reward" the men who had left their private lives to work in the public interest, so as to "rescue citizens and rulers of republics, from the common and too often merited charge of ingratitude" (cited in Somkin 1967, 137). By the War of 1812, society's expansion and commercialization had elicited patterns of behavior at odds with an ideology of "disinterestedness" emphasizing the subordination of individual preferences to the public good (see Wood 1987). Many had begun to doubt the viability of the American experiment as citizens scrambled for material prosperity in a developing market economy. America's decisive victory over British power in the second war for independence, however, stimulated a resurgence of national self-confidence. This allayed fears that the United States could not survive as a virtuous commercial republic (Matthews 1991, 5–6; Somkin 1967, 11–54) and caused an awakening of historical consciousness (Maier 1997, 175–78; Cunningham 1996, 186–87).[10] Presidential and congressional reconsideration of the fate of America's surviving revolutionary patriots was almost natural in a society where an outpouring of paintings, historical tracts, public monuments, and literary works (like Parson Weems's best-selling biography of George Washington) revived the potent symbolism of the founding, and "held up Revolutionary heroes as models of selflessness and public spirit" (Matthews 1991, 21). Facilitated by an extraordinary Treasury surplus, the establishment of Federal pensions for the nation's original patriots would constitute tangible evidence of an enlightened, effectively governed people.

The pension idea also emerged at a time when the idea of public aid for the poor had become deeply ingrained in American culture (though opponents of public assistance worried that it could foster the attitude that relief was a right). Many encouraged a shift in public provision away from local aid toward more "efficient" institutional arrangements at the county and state levels of government. Additionally, some public and private welfare institutions had begun to appeal to the national government for support (Trattner 1984, 53–59). Backed by local officials who attested to the veracity of their claims, and relying upon military service to distinguish their situations from those of other poor Americans, aging Revolutionary veterans urged the creation of Federal pensions. That way, they would not be dependent upon their towns, almshouses, or other forms of local charity. In effect, they framed their poverty as a form of service-related disability and pressed Congress to recognize the similarity between their need for assistance and that of veterans physically disabled in combat.

All things considered, the time was ripe in 1817–1818 for the establishment of Revolutionary veterans' pensions. In the words of John Kingdon (1984), the policy, political, and problem streams had converged, and a window of opportunity had opened for creating new Federal policy. The Fifteenth Congress nonetheless had to reach consensus upon the choice of an appropriate target group of veterans and then construct their deservedness in law.

The amended enacted on March 18, 1818 entitled veterans of national forces only to pension benefits, as had been proposed in the Senate, but shortened the time of service required for eligibility. All men who had served in the Continental Army or Navy until the end of the Revolutionary War, or for at least nine months at any period during the war, who were still resident citizens of the United States and who were (or thereafter would become) by reason of their "reduced circumstances in life . . . in need of assistance from [their] country for support," became eligible to receive a Federal pension for life of either twenty dollars per month (for officers) or eight dollars per month (for non-commissioned officers, musicians, mariners, marines, or soldiers). Benefits were contingent upon a veteran's making a declaration of need to a district judge of the United States or before any judge or court of record of the state, county, or territory in which he resided. The judge would certify and transmit the record of each veteran's testimony and related proceedings to the Secretary of War, to whom Congress delegated final authority in determining pension claims. No one would be entitled to the provisions of the act until he had relinquished his claim to any pension benefits previously allowed him by the United States, but otherwise Federal benefits would commence payment from the date of the applicant's declaration of need (*Annals of Congress* 1817–18, 2518–519).

The *Pension Act of 1818* was a vitally important act of Federal domestic policy making. Most obviously, it established the precedent from which an enormous system of military service-related benefits directly evolved. Less than a month after the law was enacted, a resolution was introduced in the House of Representatives urging a supplementary act to grant pensions to the officers and soldiers of the Army and the militia not covered by the 1818 law, because many "were illy paid; and many, though not reduced in their circumstances, ha[d] strong claims on the justice and gratitude of their country" (*Annals of Congress* 1817–18, 1698). House members said they had concurred in a restricted definition of deservedness in order to make sure that the Act of 1818 passed, anticipating problems in implementation that would lead to the pension program's expansion. It took until 1832 for Congress to grant service pensions to almost all Revolutionary veterans regardless of their financial status and until 1836 to enactment the Revolutionary widows' pensions. Congress had, however, set forth in 1818 on the path to establishing benefits for those citizens serving in, or related to those serving in, the nation's future military forces.

The 1818 pension law also influenced the shape of American social benefits provision by establishing programmatic, statutory entitlements for groups of "like" citizens as the type of policy solution that eventually would be utilized to address a wide variety of issues of citizen well-being. As Senators Smith and Macon and their colleagues clearly comprehended, such policies operate by creating legal categories of citizens based upon their possession of chosen—not intrinsic—criteria of "deservedness." The 1818 pension law attributed deservedness to a select category of individuals combining nine months' service in the Continental Army or Navy, old age, gender, financial need, and U.S. citizenship and residency. However, as the debate in both the House and the Senate amply demonstrated, many other criteria or combinations of criteria might have been utilized to construct the virtuous citizen-soldier in law. The choices made by the Fifteenth Congress illustrated that selecting target groups for policy purposes has much to do with the exercise of political power. It is anything but a simple, technocratic exercise in logic (Ingram and Schneider 1991). As Senator Smith argued, militia service should have counted if military service was to be the basis for entitlement, for it was the militia who fought the war at Lexington and Concord before the nation even had a Continental Army. They also comprised the troops that provided essential military forces in the South. Citizens "engaged in other spheres, and employed in other occupations" also had been as essential and indispensable to victory as the Army. The distance between Smith's and his colleagues' construction of the Revolutionary veterans, coupled with the clear potential for more seemingly arbitrary categories of desert, was what led Smith to declare that he was unalterably opposed as a matter of principle to the selective privileging of a "particular portion" or category of U.S. citizens of "particular merit" or deservedness, no matter how such a category was defined (*Annals of Congress* 1817–18, 142–47).

What would happen when the pension program was implemented and only some veterans of the Revolution began to receive Federal benefits remained to be seen. Even advocates of the pension bill had recognized that the creation of formal, administrative categories identifying those deserving of government benefits necessarily involves the creation of *de facto* categories of "others" who are defined implicitly or explicitly as undeserving and excluded from civic consideration. When the 1818 law was enacted, it necessarily created an out-group of undeserving Americans, because it selectively qualified some, but not all, citizens for pensions. Those "other," excluded citizens ranged from men who served for fewer than nine months in the Continental Army or Navy to members of the militia to, at the extreme end of the spectrum, American women. Since the daughters of the republic were barred from formal military service, they could not be considered Revolutionary "veterans" of any kind (Stickley 1972).[11]

Yet they, too, had survived the conflict and many considered themselves patriotic. Revolutionary women indeed were critical to victory, their ostensibly "noncombative" role, "natural" weakness, and essentially invisible status under common law notwithstanding. They provided essential physical support to American forces by cooking, cleaning, sewing, and nursing; kept family farms and businesses in operation while men were away from home; sustained colonial boycotts of British goods; raised funds for the war effort; and protected children and property against squatters and marauding soldiers. At least some women believed that their contributions to independence were as worthy of recognition as those made by the war's official (male) patriots.[12] Petitioning the "Honnorabell" Continental Congress in 1786 in an effort to recover the loss of interest payments on money that she had loaned the state of New Jersey during the Revolution, Rachel Wells, a self-described "Sitisen" and widow "far advanced in years," argued:

I have Don as much to Carrey on the Warr as maney that Sett now at ye healm of government . . . ye poor Sogers has got Sum Crumbs That fall from their masters tabel. . . . Why Not Rachel Wells have a Littel intrust?

if She did not fight She threw in all her mite which bought ye Sogers food & Clothing & Let Them have Blankets & Since that She has bin obliged to Lay upon Straw & glad of that.[13]

Even when fifty-three years after the war Congress granted pensions to many women of the Republic, it was only by virtue of their relationships with men deemed deserving by the state. Those who were not widows of Revolutionary veterans, no matter what their situation, were not citizens who qualified to be placed among the nation's entitled.

CHALLENGING THE *PENSION ACT*'S CATEGORIES OF DESERVEDNESS

Male citizens who had fought in the war, but who did not meet the statutory criteria targeting "deserving" Revolutionary patriots, began to agitate for inclusion in the pension program as soon as the Act of 1818 was passed. That militiamen did not qualify for benefits particularly rankled them, and many tried to persuade Congress to expand the program to include men who had spent the requisite nine months fighting in state-level forces. One such veteran, Phineas Cole of New Hampshire, sent Congress a petition in 1819 in which he complained about the Act's construction of deservedness for policy purposes:

If the liberality of the Country is intended, as a reward to those who fought its battles, and sacrificed their property to secure its liberty, why surely then, no one has a stronger claim than your petitioner. He envies no one his good fortune, but he deems it a hard case, to see his companions in arms enjoying the country's bounty, while he, whose claim is as strong as anyone's, is compelled, at his advanced age, to earn a scanty pittance by the sweat of his brow.

Cole also told Congress that while he envied no person legitimately drawing a pension, he believed that there were many who did not rightly do so. "I wish well to Every honest man," he wrote, "but I think it my Duty as a Loyal Subject to give Some hints. . . . If a Person that is worth 3 or 4 thousand Dollars after his debt is paid comes under the provision of the act of Congress I confess I Do not understand the act."[14]

Others veterans urged Congress to extend benefits to all who had served, even if it required lowering pension rates across the board. Writing on behalf of themselves and all of the "war worn soldiers" who had fought for independence, Ebenezer Cousens and six other Revolutionary veterans observed that what had been legislated was perfectly agreeable—to every officer and soldier who met the description in the statute. Yet, they had not been paid for performing the same public services that the entitled men had, as no gentleman could "deny without a Blush." Why should their just dues continue to be withheld from them now? The passage of time never discharged a debt. So "Respecttable a body of men who compose[d] the general government" should respect the people and their claims. "If the sum first given was too much," Cousens and his colleagues told Congress, "set the compensation less, but let all share in the pension."[15]

The first pension applications under the Act of 1818 were filed within days of its passage and, after only six months, the War Department was so inundated that it could not act upon the applications as fast as they arrived. In December 1819, Secretary of War John Calhoun informed Congress that he had received approximately 28,555 claims and issued 16,270 pension certificates. It appeared that "impositions or mistakes" had occurred to a "considerable extent" despite the vigilance of Calhoun's department. Pension expenditures reached an alarming $1,811,329 dollars, or some 11.2 percent of all Federal spending in 1819, a year of national economic panic, then soared to more than seventeen percent of the U.S. budget in 1820.[16] The total cost of the pension program was estimated to be more than $75 million dollars, a figure exceeding the cost of fighting the Revolution (Resch 2000, 129, 143).

For a government staggering from financial reverses, pension costs alone were a serious concern and matters were exacerbated by widespread reports of benefits paid to applicants who were not truly needy. Stories and negative commentary about extraordinary numbers of claims, expenditures, and frauds were printed and reprinted in newspapers around the country from mid-1818 through late 1819, when the Sixteenth Congress assembled to consider the subject.[17] With the pension program already in operation, though, and with much larger problems occupying Congress's attention (including slavery and the admission of Missouri), the issue was no longer the wisdom of Federal veterans' pensions. Rather, the issue was pension *eligibility* and the accuracy of the pension program's criteria of deservedness. Finding it neither expedient nor in comportment with "the honor and dignity of the American nation" to repeal the pension act (*Annals of Congress* 1819–20, 851–52), the House Committee on Revolutionary Claims asked Secretary of War Calhoun to determine whether it could be refined to better effect its purpose.

Calhoun had long been worried about the potential for pension fraud because Congress had not precisely defined what it meant to be a veteran in "reduced circumstances" in the 1818 statute. He was also concerned that the Federal government was too dependent upon local actors for the verification of veterans' service records and financial need. His recommendation that only the criterion of absolute indigence would render the pension act's implementation free from "a latitude of construction"[18] led to a heated, protracted Congressional debate. It revived original arguments about the law's inegalitarian treatment of officers and soldiers, its exclusion of the militia, and the limits of the nation's obligations to its veterans. A divided Sixteenth Congress finally enacted legislation suspending pension benefits until recipients appeared before a court of record to produce proof of their poverty and testify that they had neither disposed of property nor hidden assets in order to qualify for benefits. The law empowered the Secretary of War to remove those veterans from the pension list who, in his opinion, were able to support themselves, with the caveat that anyone stricken from the list who had relinquished disability pensions in order to receive the benefits of the Act of 1818 would have their pension restored (*Annals of Congress* 1819–20, 2582–583).

As the solvency of the Federal government continued to deteriorate, requiring the Secretary of the Treasury to report that additional loans would be required to meet projected budget deficits, the Sixteenth Congress was forced to look for ways to reduce expenditures. Veterans' pensions posed clear potential for retrenchment, but the notion was rejected almost immediately. By the time the Seventeenth Congress assembled in December 1820, a majority of the House had not only abandoned the idea of pension cuts, but favored reviving the original provisions of the 1818 Act to restore the benefits of veterans stricken from the pension rolls. A bill for that purpose eventually passed in 1823 (*Annals of Congress* 1822–23, 1409–410).

The struggles of the Sixteenth and the Seventeenth Congress over the fate of the pension program provide an original example of the pressures for expansion and contraction that occur along the sociopolitical boundaries that entitlements create. Beset by fiscal distress and accusations of fraud and abuse on one side and by claimants outraged by their loss of benefits and status on the other, the state actors charged with the guardianship of both the public purse and morality had to grapple with the dual sense of national honor and purpose that had inspired them to enact the pension legislation in the first place. An economic upturn, coupled with a fine-tuning of pension eligibility criteria, allowed most members of the Seventeenth Congress to believe that they had achieved a proper balance in dividing deserving and undeserving veterans. Because many men not entitled to benefits under the 1818 law were actively and ever more stridently petitioning for inclusion in the program, however, Congress's respite from political pressure was brief.

Powerful arguments could be made in favor of expanded coverage. The pension program's overt exclusion of certain veterans from the nation's beneficence, whether members of the militia or regulars who had served for fewer than nine months, had sat uneasily with many members of the public and of Congress since the passage of the 1818 law. Such an exclusion, it was argued, was inappropriate in a democratic society. So, too, was the original pension law's two-tiered system of benefits which, in paying former officers and soldiers pensions of twenty dollars and eight dollars per month, respectively, effectively rendered the wartime services of the officers more valuable than those of the soldiers, embedding class lines in public policy. Allowing the nation's original patriots to suffer was also considered inhumane and unpatriotic. Sentimental appeals for the nation's gratitude, invoking the image of old, suffering soldiers, were quite persuasive, especially because they diverted debate from divisive issues of class and privilege toward the unifying ideals of national honor, patriotism, and America's mission (Resch 2000, 138).

Of course, there were alternative perspectives. Some critics believed that the officers' contributions had been more valuable to the war effort than the soldiers, or viewed veterans' length of military service to be a vitally important criterion of desert. Others believed that service alone should not suffice to distinguish military men from their fellow citizens. Still others thought that all pensions except those granted to veterans disabled in combat violated the ideology of the citizen-soldier, the terms of the Constitution, or both. But the idea that the nation owed a debt of gratitude to all veterans for their service in the Revolution ran deep, and some people were convinced that the veterans' deservedness had a legal, contractual basis. Americans were also uncomfortably aware of the classical charge that republics were ungrateful to their benefactors: part of a larger argument that magnanimous virtues belonged only to an aristocracy, whereas popular rule meant control by the mean-spirited. When the Revolutionary veteran the Marquis de Lafayette returned to the United States in 1824 at the invitation of President Monroe to travel as "The Nation's Guest" after an absence of forty years, Americans were primed and ready to welcome his reappearance "as a heaven-sent opportunity for such a clear-cut display of national gratitude as would vindicate republican government from [that] ancient aspersion" (Somkin 1967, 137).

Southerners increasingly argued that the expansion of the pension program was nothing more than an excuse to maintain tariff levels, but to little avail. In 1828, after forty-five years' worth of petitions, claims, and lobbying, the Continental Army's surviving officers and soldiers finally were compensated for their alleged losses due to commutation. A sharply divided Twentieth Congress granted *full* pay for life both to the surviving officers, entitled to half pay for life by the Continental Congress in 1780, and to the noncommissioned officers and soldiers, entitled to eighty dollars in 1778, *without* the requirement that they be poor.[19] Members of Congress were still unable to agree upon whether the new legislation was meant to fulfill a "debt of gratitude" or a "debt of justice"— that is, whether the law rendered the veterans it benefitted deserving of the nation's charity or rendered payment on a legal obligation (Jensen 1996, 393–95; 2000, 108–09).

Less than a year later, President Andrew Jackson proposed that pensions be extended to every Revolutionary soldier "unable to maintain himself in comfort."[20] Opponents stalled the idea for a time, but could not prevent the passage of legislation in 1832 providing full pay for life to surviving officers, noncommissioned officers, musicians, soldiers, Indian spies, mariners, and marines who had served during the Revolution for a total of two years in the Continental line or state troops, volunteers, militia, or naval service who were not already entitled to benefits. The new law originally required applicants to relinquish all other Federal pensions to claim its benefits, but was amended in 1833 to exempt disabled veterans from that restriction.

The passage of the 1832 law resulted in another explosion of claims and expenditures. John Quincy Adams, who as President had called for the act of 1828, noted in 1834 that Revolutionary claimants not only seemed immortal, but appeared to multiply with the passage of time (Adams 1876, vol. 9, 124). Even after pension frauds led to well-publicized exposés and indictments for forgery and perjury in 1834 and 1835, however, Congress declined to reform the Revolutionary pension program (Glasson 1918, 87–91). Blessed with another hefty Treasury surplus, it instead expanded the program in 1836, entitling the widows and orphans of men who had died (or would die) from wounds received in the nation's service to half pay for life. Rather than subject itself to "the charge of injustice or ingratitude towards its faithful sustainers," the Twenty-Fourth Congress admitted more of America's "most meritorious" citizens to the pension rolls.[21]

The Act of 1836 was by no means the last Federal pension legislation to recognize the deservedness of the Revolution's veterans and their dependents. In the wake of its enactment, Congress gradually entitled more widows of Revolutionary veterans to benefits of increasingly greater value, until the last pension legislation specifically enacted for the survivors of the nation's original patriots was enacted in 1878. In 1864, with the Civil War raging, the Union Congress decided to reward the "small band of revolutionary patriots, all that [we]re left of those brave and gallant men who acquired our independence,"[22] granting the twelve Revolutionary veterans remaining on the pension list an extra one hundred dollars annually as a sign of special national recognition. With only five of the Revolutionary patriots still living in early 1865, Congress increased their benefits to three hundred dollars per year. By June 1867, the last of the soldiers on the Revolutionary pension rolls had died. In 1868, however, the Reconstruction Congress discovered and pensioned two new men as Revolutionary soldiers at $500 per year, until the last known survivor of the nation's original war, Daniel Bakeman, passed away on April 5, 1869, at the age of 109 years, six months, and eight days (Glasson 1918, 92–93).

The Reconstruction Congress also finally recognized the deservedness of the veterans of the nation's *second* war for independence and their survivors. In 1871 they voted to establish a new pension program for all surviving soldiers and sailors who had served in the War of 1812 for at least sixty days and were honorably discharged (or had received personal mention by Congress for specific services during the war) and for their widows (provided that they had been married prior to the treaty of peace and had not remarried). Without a means test, the new program jettisoned poverty as a criterion of deservedness to grant pensions to War of 1812 veterans and their survivors simply upon the basis of service. There was, however, a catch: applicants were entitled to Federal pensions only if they had been loyal to the United States during the Civil War and were willing to swear an oath to support the Constitution. This exclusion of aged southerners, whose efforts had preserved the nation over five decades earlier, once again recast the meaning of patriotism and veterans' deservedness. While military service might be meritorious, only those veterans who demonstrated *sustained* loyalty to the state were deserving of recognition in the form of public benefits. As one member of Congress put it, the Federal government could "afford to be just and generous to its defenders," but it could not afford "to pension men who fought for its destruction."[23]

CONCLUSION: SOCIAL CONSTRUCTIONS AND PUBLIC POLICY

The record of the categorical veterans' pensions established during the first hundred years of the United States' existence tells us a great deal about the role of social constructions in politics and public policy. First and foremost, it reveals the complex, contingent, and changeable nature of attributions of deservedness in policy, even when the groups of citizens involved are viewed positively. The constructions that become translated into formal rationales for the allocation of public benefits and burdens in public policy are not simply derived from political culture or public opinion. Nor are they static, even in the case of historically well-regarded groups. Instead, they result from a complex interplay of multiple forces and factors that change over time.

The evolution of the early American veterans' pensions illustrates the fact that institutions play a key role in the production of social constructions, both by regulating access to public authority and by influencing the formation and expression of ideas and political beliefs. The ways in which social groups are defined, perceived, and made relevant at particular junctures are indeed an integral part of the historical institutional process (Lieberman 1995, 438). That the officers and soldiers of the Continental Army were constructed as deserving and entitled to public benefits in the 1770s and 1780s had everything to do with the government's need to create a stronger military. Service pensions could be justified by arguments about the national interest. Yet, their creation was also open to challenge, both within the Continental Congress and without, for the Army could not take sole credit for winning the war. Openings for protest emanated from the unique hybrid structure of the state and national forces that constituted America's military and from the vital conceptual link between militia service and male, martial citizenship. For years after the Revolution ended, and even after the *Pension Act of 1818* revived the superiority of the Army in public law, excluded veterans refused to remain a disadvantaged "other" and pushed Congress to recognize their deservedness.

write in notes

The *1818 Pension Act* demonstrated the influence that ideas, events, social structures, policy feedback, political and fiscal opportunities, and the beliefs and ambitions of policy makers have on the constructions that serve to target social benefits. Victory in the War of 1812, a resurgent nationalism, sympathy for aging soldiers, favorable public opinion, a new historical consciousness, cultural anxiety over the virtue of the Republic, and notions about debt and legal obligation all encouraged the establishment of a pension program. So, too, did the policy leadership of the veterans in Congress and a veteran president, whose habit of dressing in the old-fashioned, buff and blue dress of the Revolutionary period reminded all who saw him of the nation's original war. The Pension Act also was shaped by the social structures of gender and class; the rise of a male, mass electorate; a local urge to shift responsibility for poverty to higher governmental jurisdictions; a large Federal surplus; the politics of interest; and by the terms of previously established entitlements (including disability pensions and the officers' pensions legislated and commuted by the Continental Congress). It was the intersection of these factors and forces with institutional structures and requirements that led to the Fifteenth Congress's decision to target aged, poor, citizen-resident veterans of nine or more months' service in the Continental Army or Navy and entitle them to pensions in the Act of 1818.

Enacted retrospectively, some thirty-five years after the war, this was not legislation aimed primarily at sustaining the military. Its passage, nonetheless, encouraged veterans of past wars, whether financially self-sufficient or not, to expect service pensions, to be disappointed when they were not forthcoming from a grateful Congress, and to petition and lobby almost incessantly for their enactment. The law also encouraged men enlisting in the armed forces in subsequent conflicts to believe that they should be entitled to pensions, whether or not they were promised in advance of service. This example suggests that policy makers sometimes select target groups in policy initiatives in an effort not only to alter the behavior of members of those particular groups, but moreover, to induce other citizens to engage in behavior that might render them eligible to become targets advantaged by public policy in the future. The discourses of deservedness in the 1818 pension law sent potent messages about the nature of military service and citizenship both to American men and women and to future policy makers.

This process raises the question of how new discourses of deservedness emerge, or how groups may or may not come to be reconstructed as deserving or undeserving for public policy purposes. The history of the *Pension Act of 1818* demonstrates that one way groups come to be reconstructed as deserving is through the attribution of similarity between them and advantaged target groups. The composite character of the Pension Act's qualifying criteria invited comparisons and analogical thinking—in other words, invited particular forms of voice instead of exit—and created multiple potential pathways for policy change. Veterans not originally entitled to pensions (and their advocates) could and did argue that they were enough "like" those receiving benefits that they, too, should be considered deserving. Thus, the eventual extension of the pension program to veterans who had served in any military unit during the Revolution for a minimum of only fourteen days, regardless of means, and to their survivors as well as to the last living soldiers of the Revolution; and the retrospective enactment of pension programs for veterans of the War of 1812, certain Indian Wars, the Mexican War, and the Civil War. This is not to say that the successful attribution of similarity alone caused these developments; other factors and forces played important roles. Nonetheless, the existence of a formal discourse establishing the deservedness of the Revolution's veterans played a vital part in facilitating the positive social construction of additional military men.

Finally, the messages about deservedness contained in the 1818 pension law and subsequent amendments contributed to understandings about the kind of political claims that could and should be articulated and by whom, and encouraged certain behaviors while constraining others. From statutes entitling groups of Americans to pensions, land entitlements, disaster relief, and other forms of Federal aid (Jensen 2003), people in and out of Congress learned to argue over what reasons or criteria of deservedness were adequate for winning particular entitlements. Over time, they grew less and less concerned about whether fighting for programmatic rights was the best use of their energies, or whether an array of selective, categorical entitlements was the best foundation for a national system of care for veterans and other citizens. This realization profoundly affected the character of American democracy and citizenship, in ways and with consequences still discernible in the twenty-first century.

NOTES

1. The bill contained the caveat that no pension given to a commissioned officer would exceed the half pay of a lieutenant-colonel.

2. "H.R. 8" *Records of the U.S. Senate, 15th and 16th Congress: Amendments to H.R. Bills and Committee Papers for the Military Affairs Committee,* National Archives.

3. Veterans of the War of 1812 were already beginning to lobby for benefits when the act of 1818 was passed, but Congress did not establish pensions for them until 1871.

4. James Madison to Edmund Randolph, September 8, 1783 (cited in Hutchinson and Rachal 1962, vol. 7, 307–08); "Massachusetts Legislature to Congress," Ford et al. 1904–1937, vol. XXV [1783], 607–09; Resolution of the Town of Farmington, August 4, 1783, *Connecticut Courant,* August 12, 1783, 2.

5. George Washington, "Circular Letter to the States" [sent to the 13 state governors], June 8, 1783.

6. "Rawleigh C. Christian's Petition," December 1817, SEN 16A-G10, Center for Legislative Archives, National Archives.

7. "Petition of Nathaniel Kinnard," January 2, 1818, HR15A-G10.1, Center for Legislative Archives, National Archives.

8. "Petition of George McBeth," January 30, 1818, HR15A-G10. 1, Center for Legislative Archives, National Archives.

9. "Petition of a number of the surviving Officers in the Pennsylvania Line of the Army of the United States," December 7, 1808; "Petition of the late officers in the Virginia Continental line of the revolutionary army," January 10, 1809; "Petition of sundry officers of the revolutionary army now residing in the state of Tennessee," December 7, 1808; and "Memorial of sundry surviving officers of the late revolutionary army, residing within the State of Maryland," January 13, 1809, Center for Legislative Archives, National Archives.

10. Congress initiated the systematic publication of its records (beyond the two chambers' journals) in 1817 and, in 1818, authorized printing one thousand copies of the journal of the Constitutional Convention of 1787, which had previously been held secret. Congress also, in the last weeks of the Madison administration in early 1817, authorized the president to commission four paintings from John Trumbull commemorating the most important events of the Revolution.

11. Some women actually engaged in combat in the army by disguising themselves as men. The most famous of them was Deborah Sampson, who fought and was wounded in multiple battles before her identity as a woman was discovered. After leaving the Army, she married Benjamin Gannett in 1784, with whom she had three children; she died in 1827. Sampson Gannett's applications for state and federal veterans' pensions undoubtedly confounded legislators, who had few if any precedents to rely upon. The Commonwealth of Massachusetts granted her a pension in 1792 by constructing her deservedness in a manner simply not applicable to men: "said Deborah exhibited an extraordinary instance of female heroism by discharging the duties of a faithful gallant Soldier, *and at the same time preserving the virtue & chastity of her Sex unsuspected & unblemished,* & was discharged from the service with a fair & honorable character" (Resolve of the General Court of Massachusetts, January 20, 1792, Archives Division, Commonwealth of Massachusetts [emphasis added]). In 1804, Paul Revere similarly told Congress that Sampson Gannett deserved a veterans' pension because she was not tall, masculine, illiterate, and mean as he had expected, but rather, small, feminine, educated, and pleasant (Paul Revere to William Eustis, Member of Congress, February 20, 1804, Massachusetts Historical Society, photostatic copies in Stickley 1972, 240). Not until 1837, ten years after her death, did Congress recognize Sampson Gannett's claims—by granting her *husband* a pension as a Revolutionary soldier's *widower* (236).

12. Abigail Adams wrote: "Patriotism in the female Sex is the most disinterested of all virtues. Excluded from honours and from offices, we cannot attach ourselves to the State of Government from having held a place of Eminence. Even in freest countrys our property is subject to the controul and disposal of our partners, to whom the Laws have given a sovereign Authority. Deprived of a voice in Legislation, obliged to submit to those Laws which are imposed upon us, is it not sufficient to make us indifferent to the publick Welfare? Yet all History and every age exhibit Instances of patriotic virtue in the female Sex; which considering our situation equals the most Heroick" (Abigail Adams to John Adams, June 17, 1782, cited in Kerber 1980, 35).

13. Rachel Wells, Petition to Congress, May 18, 1776 (cited in Kerber and De Hart 1991, 87). Similar petitions for relief flooded both the Continental and U.S. Congresses during the war and afterward. As Linda Kerber and Jane De Hart have documented, however, the litany of women's petitions fell on unresponsive ears, leaving the women of the republic to beg or turn to the states for assistance. State legislatures, already burdened with heavy war debts, only occasionally granted pensions and then on a case-by-case rather than comprehensive (programmatic) basis (cited in Kerber 1980, 92–93; see also Mark 1998, 2183–185, 2227).

14. "Petition of Phineas Cole praying a pension," October 20, 1819, SEN 16A-G10, Center for Legislative Archives, National Archives.

15. "Petition of Ebenezer Cousens and others, praying compensation for services during the revolutionary war," December 18, 1820, Center for Legislative Archives, National Archives.

16. *Niles' Weekly Register,* September 19, 1818, pp. 63–64; John C. Calhoun to Joseph Bloomfield, Chairman, Committee on Revolutionary Pensions, December 22, 1819, *American State Papers, Class IX, Claims* [hereafter, *ASP, Claims*], pp. 682–83; Calhoun to James Noble, Chairman, Senate Committee on Pensions, February 8, 1823, *ASP, Claims,* p. 885. Pension expenditures as a percentage of all federal expenditures calculated from figures in Dewey 1915, p. 169.

17. See, e.g., *Middlesex Gazette* (Middletown, Connecticut), 16 July 1818, p. 3, citing an article in the *National Intelligencer* regarding claims so numerous that they might reach 50,000, subjecting the government to an expenditure of $5,000,000 dollars per year; and *Niles' Weekly Register,* December 12, 1818 and October 16, 1819.

18. Calhoun to Bloomfield, December 22, 1819, *ASP, Claims,* pp. 682–83; John C. Calhoun to Heman Allen, May 11, 1818 (Meriwether and Hemphill et al. 1959, vol. 2, 288, see also li–lii).

19. May 15, 1828, *Register of the Debates in Congress* [hereafter, *RD*] (20/1), Appendix, p. xv.

20. "Message of the President to Both Houses of Congress," December 8, 1829, *RD* (21/1), Appendix, p. 14.

21. July 4, 1836, *RD* (24/1), Appendix, p. xlvii; *RD* (24/1), p. 4285.

22. *Congressional Globe* [hereafter, *CG*] (38/1), March 4, 1864, p. 939. The bill passed swiftly and unanimously in both House and Senate. A list of the Revolutionary patriots—notably, all northerners—was printed in the *Congressional Record* (p. 939).

23. *CG* (41/2), May 28, 1870, p. 3926.

2

Constructing the Democratic Citizen: Idiocy and Insanity in American Suffrage Law

Kay Schriner

In struggling to create a lasting popular government, the founders of the American democratic experiment embraced the principle of equality among its citizens. At the same time, the new American states developed policies that defined citizenship in this new polity that constructed some groups as deserving of and entitled to full participation and other groups as not deserving or entitled.

This is especially apparent in the history of suffrage law. The American colonies generally followed the English practice of granting the privilege of voting only to men who held the required amount of real property. The property-holding qualification loosened with the emergence of more egalitarian economic conditions in the colonies, where land ownership was more widespread, and a market economy in which a man could support his family by earning wages rather than farming or renting his property. Eventually, taxpaying qualifications replaced or supplemented the property-holding qualification in most states. But these qualifications, too, were relinquished, and by the middle of the nineteenth century, only Rhode Island and New York had any form of property requirement (Keyssar, 2000, 29).

Abandoning economic distinctions, whether property-holding or taxpaying, did not mean that states instituted universal suffrage—quite the contrary. During the nineteenth century, states adopted a number of categorical exclusions based on gender, race, religion, and alien status (Keyssar 2000). They also began disfranchising some people with disabilities, using such terms as "idiots," "insane persons," persons "under guardianship" or "non compos mentis," "lunatics," and so on.[1]

The first state to adopt such a provision was Maine, which, in 1819, excluded "persons under guardianship" from voting. Massachusetts followed suit in 1821 with an identical provision. In 1830, Virginia disqualified "persons of unsound mind" and Delaware excluded any "idiot or insane person" in 1831. In the next several decades, the trend picked up speed. Many more states adopted such provisions, either when joining the Union or by constitutional amendment. By 1850, California, Iowa, Louisiana, Maryland, Minnesota, New Jersey, Ohio, Oregon, Rhode Island, and Wisconsin had joined in excluding some persons from voting because they were idiots, insane, lunatics, non compos mentis, or under guardianship. By 1880, eleven more states (Alabama, Arkansas, Florida, Georgia, Kansas, Mississippi, Nebraska, Nevada, South Carolina, Texas, and West Virginia) adopted constitutional provisions prohibiting voting by some disabled individuals. By the end of the century, Idaho, Montana, North Dakota, South Dakota, Utah, Washington, and Wyoming had entered the Union with constitutions disfranchising people on the basis of disability. After 1900, most of the new states joining the Union also had such provisions. Arizona and New Mexico did when they joined the Union in 1912; and Alaska and Hawaii did in 1959. Missouri, which joined the Union in 1821 without an exclusion, adopted one in 1945 (Schriner and Ochs 2000). Thus the percentage of states in the union with disfranchising provisions increased from less than 10 percent in 1820 to a high of 81 percent in 1940. The percentage of states with constitutional exclusions now stands at 72 percent.

Unlike the exclusions based on gender and race, disfranchisement based on disability has persisted. The constitutions of the states still include provisions excluding individuals labeled "idiots and insane persons," "lunatics," "persons of unsound mind," and "persons under guardianship." In many states, the legislatures have recently interpreted or refined constitutional provisions by, for example, specifying that persons may be disfranchised if declared legally incompetent or by ensuring due process in the disfranchisement procedure.

Today all but six states continue to prevent some individuals from voting either by constitutional provision or by statute (Schriner, Ochs, and Shields 2000). Generally, these laws are of little public interest. When they do become a part of the public debate, it is evident that many members of the public support them and believe they are necessary to ensure the intelligence of the electorate and the integrity of elections—as was the case in Maine in 1997 and again in 2000, when voters rejected proposals to repeal the constitutional exclusion of persons under guardianship for mental illness. Only rarely does a state repeal its prohibition.

In hindsight, it seems almost inevitable that states would disfranchise individuals labeled in this way. The break from property-holding and taxpaying requirements was a move toward a more democratic arrangement, but states replaced earlier qualifications with categorical exclusions out of concern for the intellectual and moral inferiority of idiots and insane persons as well as other groups. The delegates to the constitutional conventions in which these exclusions emerged believed they were doing what was required to perfect the schematic of representative government. They thought that adopting these exclusions was the proper—and necessary—action.

But the apparent ease with which exclusions could be justified is deceptive. Underlying the adoption process are myriad social, economic, and political factors that structured and gave meaning to the deliberations. It was *not* inevitable that individuals would be labeled as "idiotic" or "insane;" that "idiots" and "insane" individuals would be thought of as morally and intellectually unfit for democratic citizenship; or that formal exclusion of a generally discrete group of individuals (with intellectual or emotional impairments) would be the only or best alternative for protecting the integrity of the electoral process and ensuring the intelligence of the electorate. Instead, the adoption process demonstrates how new suffrage laws both reflected the social constructions of mental illness and intellectual impairment that were emerging in the nineteenth century and shaped these constructions—resulting in the political marginalization and stigmatization of persons with these impairments. The history of the disability exclusion thus illustrates the relationship between public policy and the social construction of certain groups as deserving and entitled (Schneider and Ingram this volume). Indeed, it tells us as much about the nature of American political thought and public policy as it does about the nature of disabled Americans.

WRITING THE DOCUMENTS OF DEMOCRACY

In this chapter, I draw on the debates of delegates at the nineteenth century state constitutional conventions to examine this process. Most of the states that currently have disability exclusions first adopted them during the nineteenth century, a period of extraordinary development in constitutional law. Among the most contentious topics was the qualifications of electors who would elect official representatives, reflecting the historical interest in the "democratic" elements of government. The history of the states' suffrage laws thus provides a fascinating glimpse of the interconnectedness and dual causality of public policy and social constructions of people with cognitive impairments and mental illness.

Constructing the Democratic Citizen

Having turned their back on the prior reliance on property-holding and tax-paying qualifications to sort the worthy from the unworthy, but still unable to provide for true universal adult suffrage, the nineteenth-century writers of the state constitutions debated the necessary competencies of the electorate, framing much of the discussion in terms of moral and intellectual qualities. The more liberal of the delegates recognized the undemocratic nature of economic qualifications and easily dismissed them as unnecessary and destructive, while conservatives clung to them for the stability they represented. Both groups, though, clearly believed that *some* restrictions on voting rights were required. Even when phrases like "universal suffrage" were used, they more often referred to *white manhood* suffrage than true universal adult suffrage.

In the delegates' search for a replacement of the old reliable symbol of property ownership (and, eventually, the taxpaying requirement as well), they tended to settle on the characteristics such as race and gender that are familiar to us today. But to these men in these times, it was also natural that idiots and insane persons be excluded from the electorate. The idea was so readily accepted that in some states it was barely discussed. At times, delegates simply accepted the recommendations of a committee addressing suffrage, or looked favorably on the proposal of a delegate to add a disability exclusion to a committee's work. Exclusions based on race or gender, or in the post-Civil War South the potential exclusion of Confederate rebels, produced the most contentious debates. For the most part, delegates were more inclined to adopt exclusions based on disability, criminality, and pauper status than those based on other characteristics and statuses.[2]

When delegates did address the disability exclusion, its necessity was rarely, if ever, questioned. Commenting on the proposal to keep idiots and insane persons from the polls, one Louisiana delegate said in 1845, "[a]s to the utility of this provision, it was apparent on its face.... It was manifest that they ought to be excluded from this right" (State of Louisiana 1845, 852). And the certainty with which such proclamations were made was matched only by the strength of the rationale. Intellectual competence was often the sole reason advanced for the disfranchisement of these individuals. A Nebraska delegate put it this way: "Why do not you permit them to vote ... ? Simply because, in the case of the child, of immature intellect; and in the case of the lunatic and idiot, because they have no intellect at all" (Nebraska State Historical Society 1871, 80).

Felon exclusions, also discussed during these conventions, usually were justified on different grounds. The distinction between the qualities of the felon and those of idiots and insane persons was worth noting, as in a Massachusetts delegate's contention that:

> We deprive an insane person of the right of voting, not as a punishment, but because he is unfit to take part in the affairs of government. He is intellectually disqualified. And the Committee propose to deprive the felon of the right of suffrage for the reason that he is *morally disqualified*. (State of Massachusetts 1853, 277)

But the distinction between idiots and insane persons and criminals was not always so clear, suggesting that criminality and disability were somehow related in that both made a person an imbecile. A Nebraska delegate indicated this confusion about the nature of "imbecility" in his observation that:

There are two classes—one deemed competent and proper to exercise the rights of power; the other class, sir, are those among the outcasts under the system we are organizing. And who are they that are among those individuals that walk forth proudly in the image, and boast the power to exercise the rights of complete citizenship? The individuals of the male sex of a certain age, certain qualifications. Who are they that are excommunicated, governed without their consent, taxed without being represented, deemed, sir, to be so imbecile as not to have the right to participate in the affairs of govt? They are the lunatic, the idiot and the person accused of crime. (Nebraska State Historical Society 1871, 298)

Deviancy and insanity were firmly connected in the minds of some. In Massachusetts, it was said that "there are those who deem it equally clear, that that man who has shown himself, in a sense, morally insane by the commission of flagrant crimes, ought also to be disfranchised" (State of Massachusetts 1853, 278).

To some delegates in these conventions, the legal tradition of excusing a person from some civil rights and responsibilities due to intellectual or moral incompetence (for instance, in contract law and property law) represented a sound basis for disfranchising them as well. The extension of a legal disability to the political realm was consistent with these practices and was based on the same premise. In this respect, the *liability* of idiocy and insanity was similar to that imposed on individuals who committed criminal acts. Just as criminals were driven to the fringe of civil society, so too were idiots and insane persons. With disfranchisement, the liability was newly applied to political citizenship. As a Nebraska delegate put it, the exclusion of some disabled individuals and criminals was justified because "[t]hey have no consent to give. A fool has no consent; the lunatic has none, and the child has none, and the man who is guilty of infamous crime, has forfeited his right, and hence we take it from him as a matter" (Nebraska State Historical Society 1871, 80). And in Massachusetts, a delegate said, "Idiots and insane, and those excluded from society by infamous crimes, are manifestly not a part of the acting society, and can make no contract" (State of Massachusetts 1853, 221).

The exclusion of idiots and insane persons thus was easily and quickly justified in the constitutional conventions of the nineteenth century. They were based, primarily, on the theory that these individuals did not possess the intellectual competence necessary for political participation. This was usually the top criterion for distinguishing between persons who were deserving of and entitled to political equality and those who were not. Above all, the citizen must be capable of rational thought and action. The democratic citizen was rational, reliable, and trustworthy, and these characteristics were considered beyond the scope of the idiot and insane person. The labels worn by these persons made them the antithesis of the democratic citizen.

There was also another kind of logic at work in these instances. Usually, the suffrage section of a state constitution consisted of a main clause indicating that white males with certain qualifications could vote. The disability disfranchisement was typically placed in a separate clause, often in the same clause with criminal or pauper exclusions. The 1831 Delaware constitution is a good example of this construction:

> Article IV. Section 1. All elections for governor, senators, representatives, sheriffs, and coroners shall be held on the second Tuesday of November, and be by ballot; and in such elections every free white male citizen of the age of twenty-two years or upwards, having resided in the State one year next before the election, and the last month thereof in the county where he offers to vote, and having within two years next before the election paid a county tax, which shall have been assessed at least six months before the election, shall enjoy the right of an elector; and every free white male of the age of twenty-one years, and under the age of twenty-two years, having resided as aforesaid, shall be entitled to vote without payment of any tax: *Provided,* That no person in the military, naval, or marine service in this State, by being stationed in any garrison, barrack, or military or naval place or station within this State; and no idiot, or insane person, or pauper, or person convicted of a crime deemed by law felony, shall enjoy the right of elector. [emphasis added].

In handling the disfranchisement of idiots and insane persons in this way, delegates were both implying their similarity to criminals and paupers and implying that these groups were different from women and blacks, who were excluded by the language of the main section of the article. The nature of the *similarities* to criminals and paupers was not always seen consistently; in Massachusetts, paupers and persons under guardianship were all first disfranchised because of their economic dependency (Schriner and Ochs 2001), while in other states it appears that idiots and insane persons were disfranchised, at least in part, because they, like criminals, were deviant.

In significant respects, though, the use of a separate article and the combining of groups within those articles indicates that idiots and insane persons (and criminals and paupers) were thought to be *different* from women and blacks. For one thing, the former groups were smaller. Even at the height of the frenzy about the "increasing" numbers of idiots and insane persons in the latter part of the nineteenth and early twentieth centuries (Trent 1994), few would have argued that there were as many idiots and insane people as women or blacks.

Second, the characteristics sometimes imputed to idiots and insane persons bore some similarities to those applied to African Americans, who were thought to be childlike and inherently intellectually inferior. Notably, though, while at least a few convention delegates usually were willing to argue that blacks possessed these essential qualifications, there is not a single instance of a delegate proposing that an idiot or insane person did. While some argued that education and economic advancement would prepare blacks for participation, there is scant evidence that delegates saw idiocy and insanity as other than permanently disqualifying conditions. Their etiology was unimportant and their prognosis largely irrelevant.[4]

Finally, the groups had different social constructions at that time. Gender and race were master statuses and obvious at birth. Idiocy, while often thought to be a congenital condition, and insanity, which usually developed during adulthood, were not (at least at that time) master statuses with the same characteristics as gender and race.[5] The evolution of disability into a master status would take some time; during the nineteenth century, the disfranchisement of women and blacks in the major clause of suffrage articles in state constitutions was consistent with the historical understanding that race and gender were essential categories. Idiocy and insanity were not, at least not yet.

The delegates' perspectives on representative government gave them little reason to doubt the ability of elected officials to represent the interests of persons who were labeled as idiotic or insane. Even though those individuals were unable to represent themselves, their interests would be protected, just as the interests of other disfranchised groups were. This protection also was a form of guardianship. In this formulation, elected officials would exercise *political* guardianship over the interests of persons who did not actually take part in elections, just as legal guardians looked after their business and personal affairs.

The idea of political guardianship was a comfortable notion that applied to many groups, not just to idiots and insane persons. Criticisms of the notion were sometimes met with incredulity. As one Massachusetts delegate asked, "Are we to represent only those who have a right to put a ballot into the ballot box? What becomes of one half of our laws, that are made for the interests of women, children, the insane and the paupers?" (State of Massachusetts 1853, 208). Another delegate, too, was disbelieving: "Are the women and children neglected in legislation? Are the insane and foreigners neglected in legislation? I apprehend not" (State of Massachusetts 1853, 226).[6]

In constructing the competence line, the delegates to the constitutional conventions were both responding to and contributing to changing constructions of idiocy and insanity. The delegates apparently believed that democracy had to be protected from the untrustworthiness of people with these impairments. Their willingness to disfranchise these groups suggests their understanding of what would happen if such persons were not disfranchised. Surely they did not believe that many individuals labeled insane or idiotic had ever voted, or that there were sufficient numbers of idiots and insane persons to swing an election. Their motivations almost certainly had more to do with the symbolic nature of the exclusion. If idiots and insane people could be excluded, then the electorate could be purified. If the electorate was pure—morally and intellectually competent—then democracy itself could be pure.

DRAWING BOUNDARIES OF WORTH AND ENTITLEMENT:
THE ACCURACY AND POTENTIAL MISUSE
OF THE COMPETENCE LINE

The difficulty of knowing who was and who was not competent to vote was seldom discussed; but when it was discussed the points made have an eerily contemporary feel. This concern, which is often expressed when contemporary disability exclusions are discussed, was also a prominent issue during the nineteenth century. It was well-stated by a Massachusetts delegate who noted that:

> Well, it will often be found equally difficult to ascertain who are insane persons, paupers, or idiots; and yet these several classes of persons are usually excluded, the difficulty of determination, not being regarded as a sufficient reason for making no disqualifying provision respecting them. The distinction or difference between an idiot and person with just enough of intellect to render him a responsible being and capable of exercising the civil rights of a citizen, is very slight. The dividing limit is an extremely narrow one. It is very difficult to tell exactly where daylight ends and where night and darkness begin. (State of Massachusetts 1853, 278)

Though it may be difficult to draw the line, the delegate reasoned that this did not, of course, provide a reason "why an idiot should be allowed the important and responsible right of suffrage. . . . Nor should insane persons be permitted to exercise this right" (State of Massachusetts 1853, 278). It was just sometimes difficult knowing, with certainty, who was worthy and entitled and who was not.

This uncertainty nonetheless did not deter the delegates from attempting to devise a foolproof scheme. Indeed, what little trouble the delegates had in adopting the disability exclusion arose primarily from the question of how exactly to do it. A simple reliance on the labels—no matter what they were or how firmly they were planted in the minds of some delegates—was bothersome. In reconsidering their "under guardianship" exclusion in 1853, Massachusetts' delegates debated the mechanism by which it would be implemented. The committee on suffrage had proposed that the original 1820–1821 language be changed to "no idiot or insane person," but the terms were objected to by a delegate, who said:

> My difficulty in reference to this resolve is, that the only criterion that I know of, or that any one can know of, by which to settle this question of insanity or idiocy, is the judgment of a tribunal that is [fit] to pass upon that matter. I would not, by any means, be willing to leave it to the selectmen, when the day of voting comes, to pass upon the question whether I was idiotic or insane. I should think that was a miserable tribunal to judge of this question, as regards myself, to say nothing about any other gentleman in reference to

this matter. . . . I would not deprive any person of the right to vote upon the judgment of the selectmen, and because they might believe a person to be idiotic or insane who was not so, and the only evidence that they should consider as sufficient to deprive any voter of his rights was a solemn adjudication, by a competent tribunal of law or probate, that the person was so, and that he was incompetent to vote. (State of Massachusetts 1853, 274)[7]

To some delegates, the use of a distinction such as "unsound mind" was preferable to terms such as "under guardianship" or "under interdiction," because it was uncertain whether everyone who fell in this category would be kept from voting. A broad term such as "unsound mind" would have the same advantage of "under guardianship" in its legal grounding, but would presumably disfranchise more of those who *should* be. As explained by a Louisiana delegate:

[T]he expression "of unsound mind" [is] a technical expression, and to be met with in the civil code. It [is] embodied in our jurisprudence. But in addition to that, the very same expression was used in a similar section in the constitution of Virginia. The framers of the constitution in Virginia found no difficulty in construing the meaning of the term, and they were certainly as intelligent as the members of this body. It was very plain to understand it: it obviously meant a person bereft of reason. Now, as to limiting the restrictions to persons under interdiction, that would not attain the object. Those only were placed under interdiction who had property to manage; other insane persons were not, because there was no motive why a decree of insanity should be pronounced against them. It was very evident that if the term insane persons under interdiction were used, it would apply to a very limited number of those who were bereft of reason. (State of Louisiana 1845, 853)

It was also the case that delegates were troubled by the potential for misusing the category for personal or political reasons. It would be unacceptable to permit the decision as to mental competency to be made by election officials or other voters. In comments that reflected the common usage of phrases such as "madness" and "insanity," a Louisiana delegate raised this possibility:

In times of high excitement, the voters of political parties would accuse each other reciprocally of unsound mind. Who was to decide? The commissioners of election? They would be influenced by like political feelings, and an election might be arrested, and great disorders prevail, arising out of this question of sanity. A man may deem another that differs with him in opinion insane. (State of Louisiana 1845, 852)

The use of the competence line thus presented the possibility that it could be inaccurately drawn, or used for nefarious purposes. Delegates seemed to understand that the competence line was an inherently difficult one to draw.

Part of the reason was the lack of consensus (then and now) on what constitutes competent voting. What did it mean for a voter to choose between candidates? Was it simply a selection based on some inchoate impression of the candidates' qualities and abilities—or was it based on a searching inquiry into candidates' standings on issues of personal importance to the voter or perhaps the general welfare? A further complication, also understood by the delegates, was that a line based on the intangible criterion of competence could be abused, especially if it rested on labels such as "idiocy" and "insanity."

In the end, these concerns were overcome by the delegates' apparent belief that (a) an exclusion was necessary, and (b) that the need for the exclusion outweighed any potential for inaccurate application or misuse. The concern was less for the individual who was being disfranchised than for the democratic whole. By establishing idiots and insane persons as undeserving and unentitled, the delegates were both reflecting widespread views about the competence of these individuals and further legitimizing their exclusion from the political mainstream of American society.

THE POLICY AND ATTITUDINAL ORIGINS OF THE COMPETENCE LINE

Delegates to the state constitutional conventions of the nineteenth century faced many uncertainties and difficulties in writing these constitutions, but disfranchising idiots and insane persons was not among them. Other than the technical concerns of how exactly to define the groups in reliable terms and how to guard against abuse of the disability exclusion, delegates did not much trouble themselves with it. The perfunctory nature of the adoption process, however, belies the complexity of the circumstances and attitudes that made the exclusions seem so natural. The disfranchisement was the culmination of various social, economic, and political forces that shaped the selection of certain individual differences for the attention of the public and policy makers. Idiocy and insanity had taken on identities that were largely discrete and distinctively negative.

One important basis for the emergence of the competence line in American suffrage law was its existence in law more generally. A long tradition in English law and a growing acceptance in American law allowed for individuals to be designated as incompetent based on insanity, idiocy, sickness, or drunkenness. Once so designated, the individual could then be placed under legal guardianship (Jimenez 1987). The purpose of this practice was clear. It was to "protect the property of a mentally incompetent person and to apply it primarily for his and his family's benefit and enjoyment, and incidentally to preserve it for his heirs" (Woerner 1897, 376). The reason for unsoundness of mind was of little importance; what mattered was the necessity of saving that person's financial resources from being squandered.

Legal traditions were part of the foundation on which the disability exclusions were built, but the nineteenth century also brought change that confounded and disturbed many people, especially those who occupied positions of social and political influence. Economic conditions were being transformed by the forces of capitalism, and many more men (and increasingly, women) earned their families' income in industrial settings through wage labor. Huge numbers of immigrants were arriving from Europe and elsewhere, and their social and religious habits met with the disapproval of many Protestant citizens. Immigrants were crowded into poor urban neighborhoods and residents from rural areas moved into the cities as well in search of work in the factories created by industrialization (Katz 1986).

Poverty was of increasing concern to the public, who saw in the poor a potential threat to the social order. In the view of some, the poor behaved badly and did little or nothing to improve their status or living conditions. They refused to take responsibility for themselves and were far too willing to accept the assistance of private and public charities. Their failure to embrace the dominant social values of diligence, frugality, and virtue made them suspect (Trattner 1999).

In fact, poverty itself came to be suspect. During colonial times, poverty was looked on as God's will, a perfect reflection of the natural order. Some were meant for a grand existence and some for a meaner one. Those ideas were changing, though, and poverty was beginning to be thought of as a moral failing. The work ethic insinuated that anyone who wanted to work could find employment and that work would bring a living wage. Submitting oneself to the discipline of the labor market was expected and would be rewarded. If there was poverty, it was due to the personal failings of the poor, not the unavailability of work or the inadequacy of wages (Trattner 1999).

For persons with mental and cognitive impairments, the events of the nineteenth century had profound effects. Increasing regimentation in industrial workplaces made their participation in the labor force more difficult. Concerns about their moral degeneracy, dependency, and crime made others view them with scorn. Thus, they maintained their positions at the bottom of the economic and social ladders, but with perhaps greater stigma than in earlier times. They were increasingly likely to be labeled as among the deserving poor, but at best such designation meant only that they were given easier access to public assistance and were blamed less than others for their absence from the labor force (Stone 1984).

The advent of science and nineteenth-century developments in education and medicine also influenced the status of people with emotional and intellectual impairments. The human condition was broken into parts and subjected to classification, study, and treatment. Insanity and idiocy were increasingly the province of educators and physicians, whose expertise was relied on by state legislatures as they struggled with the pressing problems of the day. Indeed, motivated both by altruistic intent and self-interest, these men became effective propagandists, seeking the attention of lawmakers and using strategies that seem second nature to us today.[8]

For the most part, legislators were convinced by the arguments that insane persons could be treated, and perhaps cured, and that idiots could be educated well enough that they could occupy a "respectable mediocrity" (quoted in Trent 1994, 58). Beginning in the first half of the century, insane asylums were built and, later, institutions for idiots were established (Grob 1994; Trent 1994). During a period of increasing state power and larger budgets, legislators found it relatively easy to fund programs that were sold to them on the basis of their effectiveness in dealing with serious social problems.

Having secured public funding, the superintendents of asylums and institutions formed national associations. The purposes of these associations included keeping, for themselves, the position of experts on whom policy makers and the public depended. Using proclamations, the publication of photographs and reports from their association meetings, and pleas for higher funding, they exercised considerable control over the language used to describe idiots and insane persons (McGovern 1985).

The superintendents were joined by a contingent of social reformers. Fueled by the horror of seeing insane persons and idiots housed with common criminals and paupers in jails and almshouses, reformers seconded the professionals' preference for separate institutions for these populations. Including notables such as Dorothea Dix, this group devoted great effort to describing to the public and to policy makers the deplorable conditions of the jails and almshouses, and they demanded that more attention be paid to the particular needs of individuals who were mad or idiotic.

Virtually all those who were voicing concern about insanity and idiocy appealed both to idealism and to fear to press their claims. Describing the insane and idiots in terms designed to provoke sympathy was a common tactic. Complementing these more pathetic portrayals were those emphasizing the pathology and deviancy of idiots and insane people (Trent 1994). But professionals made a difference. At least in the first half of the century insanity was believed to be curable before exploding populations and a more severely impaired clientele made the asylums' promises of cures seem unrealistic and ultimately unattainable (Grob 1994). Idiocy, too, had a good prognosis, especially in the heyday of educators' innovative experimentation. It was not until the latter half of the century that idiocy came to be seen as "hopeless degeneracy" (Trent 1994, 87).

These changing social constructions had profound political overtones. Indeed, these are evident in the early writings of men who strove to influence public opinion and public policy. Benjamin Rush, a Philadelphia doctor considered to be the founder of American psychiatry and a man of political importance (Carlson, Wollock, and Noel 1981), said boldly that "[c]ertain forms of government predispose to madness" (Rush 1830, 66). Republican government was especially likely to cause insanity. When men were more politically active, Rush believed, madness loomed as a real threat. "In a government in which all the power of a country is representative, and elective, a day of general suffrage, and free presses, serve, like chimnies in a house, to conduct from the individual and public mind, all the discontent, vexation, and resentment, which have been generated in the passions, by real or supposed evils, and thus to prevent the understanding being injured by them" (Rush 1830, 66–67). Once passions were thus inflamed, insanity could set in.

Rush's belief that democratic forms of government were threats to mental stability is notable because it describes one mechanism for relating government and insanity. The first could cause the second by exciting the passions, which in turn produced insanity. Rush's views were largely rejected by subsequent theorists, though, who tended to be more oblique in their treatment of political participation. Their speculations on the etiologies of insanity and idiocy did not typically lay blame at the door of representative government specifically, but instead were more suggestive about its possible role. Some argued that the complexities of advanced civilizations such as theirs, which included representative governments, might cause insanity. In implicating systems-level factors in the etiology of madness, they seemed to allow for the possibility that the demands of democracy could contribute to that condition. With respect to idiocy, the theorists were unlikely to discuss the issue at all.

There was widespread agreement on one idea, however. Almost without exception, those expressing opinions about the nature of insanity and idiocy portrayed them as rendering the affected individuals *incompetent*. Insane persons had lost their ability to reason and idiots had never had it in the first place. These notions had become integral to the construction of these impairments. Often phrased in terms of legal tradition and statuses, it was common to consider idiots and insane persons as inherently incapable of equality in civil affairs. Further, protecting them from the worries and stresses of modern-day entanglements was more important than protecting their equality. As Isaac Ray, an important figure in early and mid-century American psychiatry, wrote in *Treatise on the Medical Jurisprudence of Insanity*:

> [t]o incapacitate a person from making contracts, bequeathing property, and performing other civil acts, who has lost his natural power of discerning and judging, who mistakes one thing for another, and misapprehends his relations to those around him, is the greatest mercy he could receive, instead of being an arbitrary restriction of his rights. (Ray 1838, 237)

To Ray, disfranchisement was a logical extension of the long-held practice of restricting civil rights. Writing in 1838, he had observed that most states did not restrict voting rights at that time and the lack of attention to this detail concerned him:

It may be mentioned as a curious fact, however, that while the idiot is denied the enjoyment of most of the civil rights, he is quietly left by the constitutions of the several states of the union, in possession of one of those political rights, that of suffrage, the very essence of which is the deliberate and unbiased exercise of a rational will. How this anomaly has arisen, it is not easy to conceive. A natural jealousy of any attempt to encroach upon the popular right might apprehend evils to this institution in allowing the mental qualification of voters to be too closely scrutinized, but such fears could hardly have been expected in view of the unlimited control maintained by the law over the property and personal liberty of idiots. (96)

Assessing the Competence Line: (Un)worthy and (Un)entitled

The institution of the competence line in the suffrage laws of the various states was thus firmly rooted in the conditions of the time. The legal concepts of incompetence, dependency, and guardianship offered principles that could be readily adapted to the political sphere as nineteenth-century Americans shaped their evolving notions of political participation, representative government, and citizenship. In the context of suffrage, the increasingly distinct groups of idiots and insane persons were characterized as *politically* incompetent and untrustworthy. Like criminals and paupers, they were not equal.

The consequence was that persons with mental illness and intellectual impairments were forced to the margins of American political life. While they probably had never been involved in politics in large numbers before that time, neither had they specifically been told they could not participate. While the economic qualifications of earlier periods had undoubtedly kept many such individuals from taking part in electoral politics, it was not until the nineteenth century that they took on a social construction as the antithesis of the democratic citizen.

The exclusion of these groups confirmed the political philosophies of the emerging republican order. The logic of social-contract theory rested on assumptions that every man was rational and free. Those individuals who were not could not enter into this most fundamental arrangement. The natural incapacities of the idiotic and insane placed them outside the realm of political agreement.[9] The legal restrictions imposed on persons with such impairments were but one mark of their inferiority; they were now rendered politically disabled as well. Just as they could not enter into civil contracts, neither could they take part in the political contract.

The dependency of idiots and insane persons—always a political relationship as much as an economic one—remained important. In earlier times, they had been but two of the many groups who occupied the lower rungs of hierarchy, exchanging "allegiance and loyalty" for protection from economic and political threats (Steinfeld 1989). As republican values took hold, the shape of the alliance was transformed and the people's sovereignty replaced that of the monarchy; but still there were some who were not admitted to the sanctity of the popular reign. Those who were excluded included anyone who was unworthy and unentitled by virtue of dependency, deviancy, or incompetence. Idiots and insane persons were viewed as at least incompetent (sometimes morally as well as intellectually) and often dependent and deviant as well. They thus failed on two counts: they did *not* possess the qualities required for polit-ical equality and they *did* possess the qualities that threatened democracy and made the populace fearful. In a very real sense, democracy itself must be pro-tected from them.

Events and changing political philosophy also transformed the meaning of voting itself. Property-holding qualifications had affirmed hierarchical and dependent relationships because of the personal and political advantages that property ownership was believed to bestow on a man. But as electoral partici-pation came to be viewed as a right that allowed the expression of particular individual and group interests, it took on the mantle of virtue itself. Virtue was now a "man's capacity to look out for himself and his dependents" (Appleby 1984, 15). When cognitive and emotional impairments meant dependency, incompetency and, perhaps, deviancy, those persons identified as having such conditions could not be expected to look out for their own interests, much less the common good. Idiots and insane individuals, like the others disfranchised during the nineteenth century, thus were caught up in the procession of demo-cratic progress. The nation's optimism about the promise of democracy was tempered by fear and pessimism about true universal adult suffrage.

When a democracy decides that some citizens are worthy of participation and others are not, it says a great deal about the assumptions on which notions of citizenship rest. In the case of the American states deciding on the qualifica-tions for full democratic citizenship, the determination was rooted in long-held ideas about the purpose of political representation and the structural necessities for ensuring its realization. Legislatures made up of the people's representatives, elected fairly from qualified contenders for office, were of central concern. To ensure that these representatives were responsive both to the common good and to the particular interests of individuals and groups, they must be elected by those who possessed the intellectual competence and moral grounding on which sound political judgments were made.

Just as importantly, the people's legislators must know their place. The *peo-ple* were sovereign, not the legislatures or the governors or the judges. Recog-nizing the sovereignty of an entity as amorphous as "the people" required a great leap of faith. Given the historical fear of democracy—with its images of mob rule—this was no mean feat. It is understandable that men building this new people's government would feel the need to ensure for themselves and for all time that "the people" were competent to rule themselves.

The competence line thus must be understood as a part of the inexorable process by which public policy has established some groups of American citizens as unworthy and unentitled (Schneider and Ingram 1993). The disfranchisement of idiots and insane persons occupies a meaningful position in this process by institutionalizing political judgments that these persons were incapable of participating and, perhaps more importantly, that to survive, democracy must exclude them.[10]

This situating of "incompetent" individuals as being unworthy and unentitled to political citizenship illustrates how policies can create seemingly objective distinctions that affirm broader political values (Stone 1993). Once "insanity" and "idiocy" were defined as social problems, the forces of professionalism and politics added to the burden of "idiots" and "insane" persons by hardening the negative social constructions of their conditions. Based as much in political rhetoric and practicalities as in any verifiable knowledge about the necessary capacities of the democratic citizen or the (in)abilities of those targeted for disfranchisement, the suffrage laws of the nineteenth century both confirmed and shaped social constructions of these groups.

The proclaimed reasonableness and necessity of disfranchisement apparently were not subjected to searching scrutiny. The social constructions of idiocy and insanity, so evident in the terms themselves, were sufficient grounds for the exclusion. Inevitably, though, the exclusion of people labeled as mentally ill and those with intellectual impairments from the electorate also further stigmatized and marginalized these individuals. The policies that specifically identified these groups as undeserving and unentitled only made them seem more so.

NOTES

1. Several important histories of suffrage law have been written, none of which truly addresses the disability disfranchisements discussed here. Some texts ignore them altogether. The most notable works on suffrage law include Chute 1969, Keyssar 2000, Porter 1918, and Williamson 1960.

2. It is not always clear what happened during deliberations at the constitutional conventions. Not all states published their debates, and others published minutes of the proceedings with only sketchy information. Space considerations require me to focus here on a few states where the historical record strongly suggests the delegates' motivations for adopting the disability exclusion. Published debates from other state constitutional conventions generally support the findings discussed in this chapter.

3. This same delegate took issue with the logic of the argument, saying "This argument stands out in bold relief. It is as follows: 1. Insane people, idiots, traitors, and convicted criminals are not permitted to vote; 2. Women are not permitted to vote; therefore women are insane, fools, criminals, and traitors. What an argument, ye Gods

and little fishes! . . . Its equal I never heard, excepting once.'Sam,' a negro, says to Sambo, 'Sambo, can you tell me why a cow is like a hoss?' 'I dunno, I gibs it up. Why am she like a hoss?' 'Because a cow cannot climb a tree'" (Nebraska State Historical Society 1871, 292).

4. An exception is a part of Estabrook's lengthy speech on behalf of woman suffrage, in which he says "There may be cases when a lunatic has lucid intervals, that he is as much entitled to vote as you or I, but at no time has woman the right to exercise this privilege" (Nebraska State Historical Society 1871, 130).

5. Barnartt and Scotch (2001) argue that in contemporary America, disability is a master status, though with important differences from race and gender. It is not a fixed characteristic, but a process of interaction between a physical or mental impairment and the environment. The boundaries of disability are not as clear and distinct as those of race and gender, and the definitions of disability vary according to the purpose for which the definition is made. While Barnartt and Scotch acknowledge that race and gender are not the concrete categories that many think they are, disability is even less so. Also, the group of people who would be labeled as having a disability is highly heterogeneous, and individuals move in and out of the category.

6. Guardianship was not always believed to be the equal of actual representation. The difference was recognized by a Massachusetts delegate, who said: "The most that can be said of it is, that those persons who are elected exercise a sort of guardianship over the women and children and foreigners in their districts. They are not their representatives. They assume a guardianship, and perhaps it is their duty to exercise a guardianship over the interests of those who have no voice in the election; but this is not representation" (State of Massachusetts 1853, 208).

7. At times delegates considered allowing juries to make the determination. Maryland considered amending its provision denying the franchise to any "person under guardianship as a lunatic, or as a person non compos mentis" to also exclude any *"person under guardianship as a lunatic, or as a person non compos mentis, or found to be a lunatic or non compos mentis by the verdict of a jury"* [emphasis added]. The suggestion, however, was rebuffed.

8. For accounts of developments in disability policy affecting persons with mental illness and intellectual impairments, see generally Dain 1964; Davies 1959; Deutsch 1949; Fox 1978; Grob 1994; Scull 1989; Tomes 1984; Trent 1994.

9. In Locke's Second Treatise (1962), the relationship between reason and contract was clearly stated: "But if through defects that may happen out of the ordinary course of nature, anyone comes not to such a degree of reason wherein he might be supposed capable of knowing the law, and so living within the rules of it, he is never capable of being a free man, he is never let loose to the disposure of his own will, because he knows no bounds to it, has not understanding, its proper guide; but is continued under the tuition and government of others all the time his own understanding is incapable of that charge. And so lunatics and idiots are never free from the government of their parents: *Children who are not as yet come unto those years whereat they may have; and innocents, which are excluded by a natural defect from ever having*" [emphasis in original].

10. The reasonableness and necessity of these exclusions are addressed in Schriner, Ochs, and Shields 1997. The primary objections to the disfranchisements include (a) their potential violation of the constitutional guarantee to equal protection, (b) the availability of other means (such as statutes prohibiting various forms of electoral misconduct) to ensure the integrity of elections, and (c) the potential for education and training programs to ensure the intelligence of the electorate.

3

From "Problem Minority" to "Model Minority": The Changing Social Construction of Japanese Americans

STEPHANIE J. DIALTO

INTRODUCTION

Always has to be something worse [handwritten annotation]

T he social construction of "deservedness" and "entitlement" that is the focus of this volume has powerful consequences for racial and ethnic minorities in the United States. For the positive construction to exist, it must be constructed against a negative one—neither can exist without the other. Historically, racial and ethnic minorities in the United States have all taken their turn as targets of the "undeserving" and "unentitled" constructions at the hands of the dominant group.[1] Not all targets, however, have successfully overcome their negative construction to join the ranks of the positively constructed. Japanese immigrants and their Japanese-American children have so far proven to be an exception.

Today Japanese Americans are valorized by the media and by policy makers alike as members of the "model minority." William Petersen, the scholar who first promulgated the model minority construction, held up Japanese Americans as the standard bearer that other minority groups should emulate and said that "by any criterion of good citizenship that we choose, the Japanese Americans are better than any other group in our society, including native-born whites" (*The New York Times* 1966, 3). But this was not always the case. Japanese immigrants began the twentieth century constructed as a "problem minority," in sharp contrast to their current construction. Japanese immigrants and their citizen children were initially described by detractors as "different in color; different in ideals; different in race; different in ambitions; different in their theory of political economy and government. They speak a different language; they worship a different God. They had

not in common with the Caucasian a single trait" (Smith 1995, 49). In a 1942
Gallup poll, at the height of their negative construction, Americans characterized
the group as "treacherous, sly, cruel, and warlike." By 1961, however, the Gallup
poll revealed that Americans positively constructed the group as "hardworking,
artistic, intelligent, and progressive." How does a group, once thought to be so
dangerous that its members had to be rounded up and sent to internment camps,
come to be constructed as the hallmark of good citizenship less than twenty years
later? How can we account for the shift from a patently negative social construction to a seemingly positive one?

Many scholars have written on the historical experience of Japanese immigrants and their citizen children in the United States and have examined their
changing construction. Two areas make the focus of this chapter different from
previous work. First, it provides a more explicit examination of how policy, discourse, and the courts worked in concert to advance first a negative construction of the group and then, later, a more positive one. I demonstrate how policy, discourse, and the courts—each powerful agents of social constructions in
their own right—overlapped and combined in such a way as to produce constructions much stronger than each could have done independently. I argue that
policy, the media, and the courts each has particular strengths in creating social
constructions of group identity, but that their power is especially magnified in
areas where their functions overlap. Second, I simultaneously examine how the
agency of Japanese immigrants, and later their citizen children, intersected with
policy, discourse, and legal decisions to mitigate the effects of negative constructions and to bring about change in the way they were constructed. Group
members were far from passive targets of the negative constructions that were
imposed upon them, and their actions played a critical role in changing their
externally imposed construction.

Finally, I provide a longitudinal look at the Japanese and Japanese-American experience in the United States from the 1890s to the present and their
changing construction from "problem" minority to "model" minority within
the context of my earlier discussion.

POLICY, DISCOURSE, AND THE COURTS

Public policies are significant in socially constructing group identities because
they often establish the boundaries within which social constructions are formulated and then institutionalized. Schram notes that "the politics of identity
is pervasive in analyzing and making public policy" (1993, 250). The goals of
the policy, the means available to achieve it, the interests the policy serves, and
the political climate all help to determine how target groups are constructed.
Politicians and policy makers are important agents of social constructions
because "they not only make the most consequential decisions in the lives of

ethnic minorities or about minority-majority relations, they also crucially influence the agenda for public debate and the political and ideological boundaries of consent and dissent" (van Dijk 1993, 285). In shaping the boundaries for public debate about group identity, public policies often constrain the way citizens think about groups other than their own.

Constructions embedded in policies rely heavily on context—they are not created out of thin air. Therefore, the social, historical, economic, political, religious, and legal contexts all shape the construction of group identities built into policy designs. Policies and the social constructions embedded in their designs, in turn, shape the contexts in which they are developed. By "transforming the political, social, economic, and legal settings in which groups exist" (Schneider and Ingram 1995, 445), policies transform what social constructions are politically relevant in a given moment. Constructions that are relevant at one moment in time may not be appropriate as the context in which they were created changes.

Policies are powerful generators of social constructions because they "are the mechanisms through which values are authoritatively allocated for the society" (Schneider and Ingram 1997, 2). Because they are approved by the people through a vote or by representatives for whom they have voted, policies are at some level representative of public opinion, if not directly the voice of the people itself. This approval is biased, however, in favor of those groups with political access and power. "In politics, meanings are made concrete when we pass a law or adopt a policy. At that moment, state action can institutionalize certain constructions and inhibit others" (Lieberman 1995, 440). In this sense, public policy lends authority to social constructions of group identity by officially categorizing groups as "winners" or "losers."

Public policies serve an important learning function for their targets. Ingram and Schneider contend that "experiences with public policy affect citizen orientations and influence attitudes toward government and self-images, as well as images of other groups" (1993, 72). The content of policies has powerfully felt consequences and sends important messages about whose problems matter and whose do not, whose interests will be served and whose will not, who has political power and a meaningful voice and who does not, and which groups should exercise the full range of citizenship benefits and which should not. These messages, in turn, have significant effects on the perceived agency that groups have to challenge and change the constructions embedded in the policies that affect them and can also impact the degree to which groups might align with one another in their challenges.

Finally, public policies are revealing for what they tell us about the powerful. Grodzins writes that "policy decisions are made by men, and men inevitably, if not consciously filter program objectives through their own values, their own aggressions, their own struggles for status and prestige" (1949, viii). Policies, therefore, reflect the concerns of the powerful and tell us how the

dominant group in society constructs itself and its interests in addition to how
it constructs those groups that it identifies as a challenge or a threat to the
preservation and maintenance of its power.

Legal mandates alone, however, are not sufficiently powerful on their own
to create and maintain social constructions of group identity. Constructions of
deservedness and entitlement must also be accompanied by a rationale that
lends support to their authority. This rationale is supplied by discourse, perhaps
most powerfully by the mass media. The media often act as a "moral entrepreneur" that places constructions of groups on the public radar which are then
often taken up and institutionalized within public policies. Blankenship and
Kang contend that the "media . . . are among those who have both the initial
power to characterize and the power to diffuse those characteristics" (1991,
313). These media constructions of groups are then adopted by "political entrepreneurs," such as policy makers, and embedded in policy designs. Nicholson-
Crotty and Meier (this volume, chapter 8, 299–300) draw the distinction
between moral entrepreneurs and political entrepreneurs in this way:

> moral entrepreneurs use typifying and stereotyping behaviors to generate
> anxiety about a particular group and place the actions of that group on the
> public agenda. Political entrepreneurs, or policy champions, rely on different
> tools and motivations to translate those concerns into public policy.

Social constructions of group identity that are generated and transmitted by the
media in its capacity as a moral entrepreneur lend powerful support for public
policies created by the political entrepreneurs who institutionalize these constructions, thereby giving them additional credence and legitimacy.

Media discourse shapes our beliefs about the world around us—especially
about phenomena, events, and groups of which we have no direct knowledge.
Gamson et al. note that "media imagery provides many of the essential tools"
(1992, 389) for making sense of what is going on around us. They argue that
"media messages can act as teachers of values, ideologies, and beliefs and . . .
they can provide images for interpreting the world" (374). Holzner further
contends that "we are quite willing to accept the reality of things which we
have never seen when they are communicated to us through socially and culturally defined channels" (1968, 8) such as the mass media. For this reason, discourse in the media powerfully shapes our perceptions of group identities and
the position of our own group in society relative to others.

The lens through which media images of the world are constructed is
"not neutral but evinces the power and point of view of the political and economic elites who operate and focus it" (Gamson et al. 1992, 374). As major
media outlets have become concentrated into fewer and fewer hands, this construction becomes especially problematic for minorities. The domination of
mass media by the majority group allows for the exclusion of minority groups,

already disadvantaged in power generally, to challenge the status quo and reinforces existing power relations and the creation and perpetuation of damaging social constructions.

Discourse in the media is especially important in shaping social constructions of groups during critical historical moments and offers valuable insight into public opinion. Chiasson's examination of the media found that "numerous studies indicated that during times of crisis, people turn more to their newspapers for guidance than they would normally" (1991, 263). As a result, citizens are exposed to a more narrow range of constructions of groups transmitted through authoritative channels. Social constructions of groups during critical moments are therefore often more rigid and harder to challenge than those constructed during quieter times. Some observers contend that during critical moments the press better reflects public opinion than during other moments. Harding writes that:

> the press is less like a weathercock than one is tempted to think, and more like a dog on a lead; while things are quiet the lead is long and slack and the dog makes excursions some distance from its master's path, but at moments of danger it is bound to come closer, and by watching the press at these times we can see with more accuracy the path that the public is taking. (1937, 390)

Social constructions, therefore, may resonate more effectively at these critical moments because they accurately reflect public opinion compared with those created at other times, which more closely reflect the perspective of the powerful elements of society.

The courts also play an important role in the process of socially constructing group identities. Courts are an influential agent of social constructions because they extend or deny legitimacy to legislative and executive acts. The courts have been charged with the power and duty of determining what are legitimate interpretations of policies and their application within the context of the Constitution. "Legitimacy is established by showing that the decisions accomplish appropriate objectives or by showing that they are made in appropriate ways" (March and Olsen 1989, 49). Courts, therefore, are capable of challenging and changing damaging social constructions and then subsequently recommending how policies should be understood and enforced. This does not always occur, however. There are many instances in which the courts have upheld the legitimacy of laws and policies that are based on negative constructions of minorities, as we will see in the case study later in this chapter.

The significance of the courts in socially constructing group identities is especially evident when it comes to issues of race, as courts have been at the forefront of racially constructing groups for more than a century. Legal decisions have played a crucial role in defining and delineating racial categories that shape every aspect of life. In his study of the courts, Ian F. Haney López (1995) notes that initially the courts used two different criteria to socially construct individuals and groups as white or nonwhite: common knowledge and scientific evidence. For a number of years, the courts used both rationales in creating and maintaining racial constructions in their decision-making:

> However, after 1909, a schism appeared among the courts over whether common knowledge or scientific evidence was the appropriate standard. . . . In 1922 and 1923, the Supreme Court intervened in the prerequisite cases to resolve this impasse between science and popular knowledge, securing common sense as the appropriate legal meter of race. (544–45)

In so doing, the Court not only clearly demonstrated that race is a social construction rather than a biological reality[2] but also opened racial constructions up to further subjectivity by moving away from a "scientific" rationale in favor of common knowledge. Haney López argues that the courts constructed whiteness and its privileges through a two-step process. First, the courts defined who was not white. Second, they denigrated those deemed nonwhite. Haney López contends that "these cases show that Whites fashion an identity for themselves that is the positive mirror image of the negative identity imposed on people of color" (548). For the positive construction of deserving and entitled to exist, it must be constructed simultaneously against its diametric opposite.

Courts have a great deal of flexibility in determining the extent and timing of their action. Upper courts, for instance, can choose not to review the decisions of lower courts. Because federalism splits the power of the judicial branch between the local and federal levels, there often are contradictions in the decisions—and in the social constructions of identity embedded in them— handed down across localities at the state and local levels as well as between those of state and federal courts. State and local courts often lend legitimacy to state and local policies that create and maintain damaging constructions of group identity by handing down decisions supporting them in direct contradiction to federal laws. Depending on the political climate, the composition of the Supreme Court, economic conditions, and other factors, these decisions may or may not be heard or struck down (or both) at higher levels.

As much as we would like to think that courts are unbiased institutions and that judges make decisions in a political vacuum, "absolute judicial impartiality is a myth . . . judges have political biases just as most people do" (Irons 1989, 16). Personal political convictions and values, therefore, are not absent from judicial decision making and often shape the constructions of groups by the courts. Epstein and Walker (1998) argue that because judges are political appointees they will in some ways reinforce the opinions of the majority through their selection of particular cases ("judicial activism") as well as by the decisions they hand down. Furthermore, the courts are not as far removed from public opinion as many would believe. Epstein and Walker note that "there have been times when the Court seems to have embraced public opinion, especially under conditions of extreme national stress" (1996, 43). This has important implications for the social constructions of groups that are embedded in legal decisions handed down by the courts.

Courts have provided an opportunity structure for minorities to challenge and reconstruct their negative social constructions. The forum afforded by courts provides an impetus for mobilization as well as a target for groups that have been negatively constructed by public policies. Minorities and "interest groups have used trial courts for the express purpose of defining issues, arguing their cause, formulating solutions, and working generally toward a change in public policy" (Mather 1995, 183). The courts provide politically powerless groups with a voice that often cannot be expressed through more traditional political channels such as the franchise. The power of courts is found not in the ability to enforce decisions, since they lack this power, but in the ability to "change public opinion, which in turn can reset the priorities of the political institutions" (Epstein 1995, 348). In this way, courts can provide minorities and other negatively constructed groups with some agency and a meaningful avenue of mobilization and change.

While public policy, media discourse, and courts are each powerful agents of social constructions of group identity in their own right, their power is especially magnified when their functions overlap and mutually reinforce one another. In building a framework to describe the social construction of identity, if we were to connect policy, discourse, and institutions in a chain there would be no proximate order. It is not simply that policy authoritatively represents and articulates public opinion about groups while media discourse justifies and maintains social constructions by generating consent and courts provide social constructions with legitimacy. The process is much more flexible and dynamic than this. The social construction of identity "cannot be conceptualized as a mechanical sequence of events" (Holzner 1968, 15). Rather, policy, discourse, and courts intersect at particular points, creating areas in which they overlap. The process is better characterized as a set of concentric circles rather than a chain. While each of the three entities perform individualized functions in the social construction process, they work simultaneously in conjunction with one another in a dynamic process, producing social constructions that are far more powerful than each could create and maintain on its own.

For instance, the divisions between policy, media discourse, and the courts are not nearly as clearly delineated as I have depicted them here for the sake of clarity. Policy is "an ensemble of discursive practices" (Schram 1993, 253), and legal decisions are both the product of discursive contests and discursive products. Furthermore, public policies are the product of politicians and policy makers, but courts make policies as well. "Test cases sponsored by social reform organizations are a classic example of policy making in trial courts through the filing of legal claims" (Mather 1995, 183). We can think of many other instances in which functions overlap and are not mutually exclusive.

Policy, discourse in the media, and courts also frequently reinforce one another's actions. For instance, van Dijk argues that "due to the specific and nearly exclusive role of the mass media in communication and the production of public discourse, other elites [such as policy makers and jurists] need the media to inform both the public at large and each other, to exercise their power, to seek legitimation, and to manufacture consensus and consent" (1993, 243). According to van Dijk, the power of elites would be more vulnerable to challenge if it were not for the support of the mass media.

At the same time that each of these components influences the other, they also each shape themselves. Once policies are implemented, they are reshaped through the political and institutional context in which this occurred (Mettler 1998). Media discourse results in the formation of particular beliefs and "ideological beliefs have structural consequences, and social structures give rise to beliefs" (Omi and Winant 1994, 74). Finally, courts legitimate certain constructions, but institutional change (such as the composition of the Court) has the ability to change these constructions.

Policy, media discourse, and courts acted both independently and in concert in creating, articulating, rationalizing, and legitimating particular racial constructions of the Japanese in the United States which, in turn, influenced how they were constructed as citizens in relation to the dominant groups in society. In the prewar, World War II, and postwar periods the Japanese had both clear social constructions as a race and as citizens. Policy, the media, and courts played significant roles in generating and changing these constructions, as did group members themselves. The following section applies the previous discussion of the social construction of group identity to a longitudinal exploration of the changing construction of Japanese immigrants and their citizen children from "problem minority" to "model minority."

CONSTRUCTING THE "PROBLEM MINORITY": THE PREWAR PERIOD

In the pre-World War II period three contextual factors were significant in shaping the social construction of Japanese immigrants as a "problem minority." The first, and perhaps most influential, of these was their economic success as farmers in the United States. Although they owned very little land in comparison with whites, and much of this land was agriculturally marginal, the Japanese would become such successful farmers that "at the end of the nineteenth century, Japanese farm laborers, labor contractors, and small farmers became the next formidable challenge to the class opportunities that white Californians sought to retain for themselves" (Almaguer 1994, 183).

Special interest groups, including nativist and agricultural groups such as the Native Sons of the Golden West, the Western Growers Protective Association, and the California Joint Immigration Committee, organized early in opposition to the Japanese. White elite members of these groups constructed Japanese immigrants as a growing threat to white land ownership and economic prosperity.[3]

A second key element in building the negative construction of Japanese immigrants was the prevailing belief that culture and race were inseparable. Politicians and the media were prominent in shaping this perspective and the courts did not rule differently. By constructing the Japanese in nonwhite terms and subsequently positing them as unassimilable on account of their racial and cultural characteristics, elites were able to justify discrimination against them as necessary for racial preservation. Popular discourse portrayed the Japanese as immigrating with the intent of establishing an extension of the Japanese empire on American soil. Through the denial of citizenship, predicated on racial inferiority, the Japanese could more thoroughly and effectively be politically and economically excluded by whites.

The third factor influencing their negative construction was the perceived threat of the rising military prowess of Japan. In 1905, Japan defeated Russia in the Russo-Japanese War. In a historic first, a nonwhite nation had defeated a white one. In light of this event, the federal government moved to mediate restrictive and discriminatory policies targeting Japanese immigrants so as not to insult Japan. This had the effect of tempering, to some degree, the growth of discriminatory laws and policies enacted at the federal, state, and local levels prior to World War II which might otherwise have grown unchecked.

Japanese immigration to the United States began as a slow trickle in 1886 and quickly grew from there. Initially, they were positively constructed by whites in contrast to the Chinese, a negatively constructed group. Before long, however, their industriousness and economic success rendered them a threat and they became the targets of negative constructions that had the effect of elevating the status of the Chinese. By 1905, the transition was complete, with the *San Francisco Chronicle* making clear the distinction between Chinese and Japanese immigrants: "the Chinese are faithful laborers and do not buy land . . . the Japanese are unfaithful laborers and do buy land" (Ogawa 1971, 13–14). As their perceived threat to whites grew, the Japanese came to be constructed in ways similar to the previous constructions held by the Chinese—primarily as nonwhite and as noncitizens. In constructing identities oftentimes "designers rely heavily on previous experiences; many times the designing dynamic involves little more than tinkering" (Schneider and Ingram 1997, 78) and this is reflected in the description of prejudice against the Japanese being "a tail to the anti-Chinese kite" (Daniels 1977, 21).

Although politicians and the media were important in laying the groundwork for the negative construction of the Japanese in this period, it was the courts that institutionalized discrimination at the highest levels. In a number of important decisions the courts successfully constructed the Japanese as non-white and, therefore, ineligible for citizenship based on the *Naturalization Act of 1790,* which stipulated that only "free white persons" (later amended to include blacks) were eligible for citizenship. On the basis of these rulings, the courts and the federal and state legislatures had a legitimate basis upon which to discriminate against the Japanese.

In 1894, in the case of *In Re Saito* or *Saito v. United States,* a Massachusetts circuit court first legitimized anti-Japanese discrimination, ruling that the Japanese were not white, but rather were Mongolian and, therefore, were ineligible for citizenship based on the *Naturalization Act of 1790.* The decision in this case was significant because it provided a legitimate basis upon which future discriminatory policies targeting the Japanese on a racial basis could be enacted. Many of these policies would discriminate not against the Japanese explicitly but against "aliens ineligible for citizenship"—a racially coded term that would be used against the Japanese time and again with the support of the courts. Ultimately, there came to be "more than 500 national, state, and local laws and ordinances that circumscribed and restricted the lives and opportunities of those of Japanese ancestry directly or indirectly in the pre-World War II era" (Myer 1971, xxi). These policies would touch every facet of their lives.

Having successfully excluded Japanese immigrants from citizenship, whites next turned to preventing their immigration entirely. Although ultimately unsuccessful, their actions were credible enough that Japanese residents began importing "picture brides" to circumnavigate those restrictions on immigration that were successfully implemented. Ultimately, however, their own ingenuity unwittingly led to a strengthening of their negative construction. By the 1930s, Japanese-American children, with full citizenship rights, would come to outnumber their alien parents. The media began to herald the impending "Hawaiianization" of the Pacific Coast in earnest. Valentine Stuart McClatchy, an ardent anti-Japanese voice during the period and publisher of the *Sacramento Bee,* estimated in exaggerated terms that allowing for immigration and the Japanese birthrate in the United States, "forty years from 1923 the Japanese population of the United States . . . would be in round figures 2,000,000; in eighty years, 10,000,000; in 140 years, 100,000,000" (1978, 35). Politicians echoed the distress of the media and fervently spoke out in favor of further restrictions against the Japanese. In 1920, William D. Stephens, governor of California, told constituents that:

> "the fecundity of the Japanese race far exceed that of any other people that we have in our midst" and [he] urged Japanese exclusion from the United States "entirely on the principle of race self-preservation and the ethnological impossibility of successfully assimilating this . . . flow of Oriental blood." (Grodzins 1949, 7)

The agency of the Japanese provided their detractors with the very evidence needed to support and strengthen their negative construction.

In addition to beginning families, Japanese aliens were also leasing and purchasing land. The economic threat they posed to established whites sparked organization against them. Between 1913 and 1925, nine states passed legislation to keep the Japanese off of the land. Of these laws, perhaps the best known is the *Alien Land Law of 1913* (Webb-Heney bill), passed in California, which prevented "aliens ineligible for citizenship" from owning private property and restricted their ability to lease land. By carefully constructing its discrimination against the Japanese in racially coded terms, the state was able to argue "that the laws of the United States discriminated against Orientals, not the laws of California" (Daniels 1977, 51). While the law itself only implicitly hinted at discrimination against the Japanese, the author of the policy, California Attorney General Ulysses S. Webb, explicitly stated that the Japanese were its intended target. The law, according to Webb, was intended to "prevent ruinous competition by the Oriental farmer against the American farmer."

The primary construction at the heart of these alien land laws was the notion that the Japanese possessed huge land holdings that threatened to displace white land ownership. In fact, in 1910, just a few years before California's alien land law was passed, only "13,000 of 28,000,000 arable acres were owned by the Japanese, with one Japanese farmer to every 201 Caucasian" (Ogawa 1971, 40). In 1913, the year the land law was passed, "the Japanese in actuality owned only one acre out of every eight thousand acres in the state of California" (Le Pore 1994, 268–69). The land laws were merely a cover to shield the real problem—the Japanese could produce a higher yield and a better range and quality of crops with less land than whites could. In 1910, they produced roughly 20 percent of the agricultural output of California, and the value of their land came to exceed that of whites. By 1940, West Coast farmland was valued at about $37.94 per acre, compared with $279.96 per acre for that of Japanese farmers. These land laws were more the result of pressure from constituents (wealthy landowners and the working class) than from an active desire of lawmakers to exclude the Japanese from ownership. However, enough legislators shared the same sentiments to secure passage of the alien land laws.

Much as they had sought to circumnavigate restrictive immigration policy, the Japanese worked to circumvent the land laws. They did so by vesting their land in the hands of their citizen children and by forming land companies at the urging of Japanese-language newspapers. California responded with the *Land Law of 1920,* which specifically prohibited noncitizen parents from serving as guardians for their citizen children and forbade land companies with majority Japanese ownership from purchasing land. The law passed by a margin of three to one. In this instance, the new generation of land law emerged in response to the growing agency of the Japanese, rather than merely from demands of powerful voters.

Japanese agency also extended to legal strategy during this period. In 1922, in *Estate of Tetsubumi Yano* or *In re Estate and Guardianship of Yano,* the Supreme Court legitimized Japanese agency by ruling that noncitizen parents could act as guardians of their minor children. This action allowed them to continue to purchase land in their children's names. In 1928, a lower court further legitimized their agency when the Supreme Court of Sonoma County ruled that, in accordance with the Fourteenth Amendment, children born to Japanese immigrants in the United States were citizens and, thus, were entitled to all the accompanying rights and privileges of that status "irrespective of racial descent." Although the courts had been willing up until that time to discriminate against noncitizens, they made it clear that citizens, regardless of color, were protected under the law. The affirmative precedents established by the courts in these cases gave them great latitude in constructing the Japanese and Japanese Americans in future cases.

The courts, however, continued to discriminate against Japanese immigrants by perpetuating their construction as nonwhite and, therefore, ineligible for citizenship. In the 1922 case of *Takao Ogawa v. United States,* the Supreme Court ruled that the Japanese are "clearly of a race which is not Caucasian," being "yellow" and not white. In 1924, the Court again affirmed that only whites and blacks were eligible for naturalization in the case of *Hidemitsu Toyota v. United States* by striking down a 1918 and 1919 act of Congress that allowed aliens who had served in the armed forces during World War I to file for naturalization. Taking its cue from the courts, the Congress soon passed the *Immigration Act of 1924,* preventing Japanese immigration entirely.

The Supreme Court also upheld the validity of the California land acts in a series of 1923 decisions. In *Porterfield v. Webb,* the Court ruled that the farming of land by aliens ineligible for citizenship would "in effect amount to a deprivation of its use, enjoyment, and occupancy by the citizen." In *Webb v. O'Brien,* the Court ruled that sharecropping arrangements were not legal because "the allegiance of farmers to the State directly affects its strength and safety." In *Frick v. Webb,* the Court ruled that aliens ineligible for citizenship could not own interest in agricultural corporations because it was tantamount to having an economic interest in the land. The Court clearly established that having constructed the Japanese as nonwhite and, therefore, as aliens ineligible for citizenship, they would not be permitted to hold land in California if state law prohibited it, even if state law contradicted federal law.

Both Japanese immigrants and their Japanese-American children focused on the courts during this period in an effort to challenge their negative construction. It was their feeling that legal support and recognition, not disruptive protest, would be the most effective strategy in gaining acceptance into American society. In 1908, the Issei (Japanese immigrants) formed the Japanese Association of America, which hired white lawyers to challenge discriminatory laws in the courts and published pamphlets in an effort to positively influence public opinion toward the group. The Nisei (first-generation Japanese Americans) formed the Japanese American Citizens League (JACL) in 1930, modeled after American interest groups, in response to discrimination. The JACL focused on constructing their membership as American first and Japanese second. Individualism, free enterprise, and private property ownership represented Americanism to the JACL. Group agency in this period focused on gaining inclusion within American society and the body politic.

The Japanese immigrant press reinforced this attitude by advocating "an ideology of 'racial responsibility' which encouraged Nisei to respond to racism by embracing life in America as loyal, hardworking citizens who would 'prove' their worth" (Yoo 1993, 74). Those of Japanese ancestry constructed citizenship as something to be earned and not simply claimed. They would demonstrate their worthiness through action. The negative constructions of the group so influenced the ways in which those of Japanese ancestry saw themselves that "virtually all Nisei journalists used the term 'American' to refer to white Americans and used racial qualifiers to denote other groups including themselves. Despite the fact that many Nisei saw themselves as 'Americans,' they rarely referred to themselves as such" (Yoo 1993, 74). They had so internalized their negative construction that it not only affected their perception of themselves but also the strategies that they believed were necessary to order to challenge it.

THE JAPANESE AS "ENEMY ALIENS": WORLD WAR II

During World War II, the Japanese continued to be constructed as nonwhite, unassimilable and, therefore, unfit for citizenship (although it was done in explicit rather than implicit terms). Japanese immigrants and their Japanese-American children came to be constructed not as a "problem minority" but as "enemy aliens." This even more damaging construction would ultimately seal their fate for exclusion and then internment. The courts, having already expressed a willingness to discriminate against the group in support of white interests, continued to do so and thus effectively legitimized their second class status. Discriminatory policy and public discourse designed to exclude the Japanese built upon the negative constructions entrenched in legal decisions.

Two primary negative constructions prevailed during the wartime period. The first targeted those of Japanese ancestry as "disloyal." Japan's growing militancy in the 1930s and the attack on Pearl Harbor were evidence used to support this construction. Detractors held that the Japanese had not come to the United States to become citizens, but rather represented the forerunners of a people who sought to establish racial and economic domination. The second continued to focus on their racial characteristics. It was asserted primarily through policy and discourse and, subsequently, was not contradicted by judicial rulings that loyalty was a matter of race—despite efforts by individuals and groups to convince Americans otherwise.

The disloyalty construction did not arise immediately after the bombing of Pearl Harbor, as might be expected. General John DeWitt, commander of the Western Defense Command—who ultimately was in charge of evacuating and relocating those of Japanese ancestry and who was among the policy's most outspoken advocates—initially announced "an American citizen, after all, is an American citizen. And while they may not all be loyal, I think we can weed the disloyal out of the loyal and lock them up if necessary" (Smith 1995, 107). In the days and first weeks following Pearl Harbor, there were few outright attacks on the loyalty of persons of Japanese ancestry. Before long, however, longtime opponents of the Japanese began to gather steam and they swept up mainstream public opinion in their wake.

By January 1942, nativist groups and others had become a dominant voice in the press pushing for the evacuation of those of Japanese ancestry from the West Coast, although there was no plan by the federal government or military to do so at the time. In his examination of the press during that time, Grodzins found that:

> the ratio of editorials unfavorable to resident Japanese to those favorable was more than six to one in the period between January 26 and February 1. News favorable to Japanese in five California metropolitan newspapers was squeezed to less than 4 percent (from a high of 22 percent) of all news about Japanese by the end of January. (1949, 278)

News that was favorable to the Japanese did not have a fair chance in the press because it was commonly situated in newspapers alongside articles that negatively constructed their race and character. The eventual policy of evacuation and relocation reflected public demand and media pressure. The power of discourse in the media is such that "Army action was based on precisely the same type of reasoning (and partly justified in precisely the same words) that went into the public demands" (295). General DeWitt, who initially had drawn a distinction between the loyal and disloyal, soon reversed his position entirely and proclaimed the impossibility of separating the two groups.

Five days after DeWitt's declaration, President Roosevelt signed Executive Order 9066 authorizing the exclusion of Japanese aliens and citizens from the Pacific Coast region. This action was significant because "actions taken as a result of beliefs about an environment can, in fact, construct the environment" (March and Olson 1989, 47). In excluding the Japanese from the coastal areas on the premise that the loyal could not be distinguished from the disloyal, a rationale that in large part had been disseminated through the press, the government lent official support to popular fears. These fears, in turn, accelerated the racial construction disloyalty of the Japanese.

Not only were few distinctions drawn between the loyal and disloyal, there were few made between citizens and noncitizens. When citizens were referred to in the press, they were rarely described as such. Instead, "code terms like 'non-aliens' or 'other persons of Japanese ancestry' were substituted" (Okamura 1982, 102). This eased the policy of evacuation and relocation. In March 1942, public opinion surveys reflected this lack of distinction in that "93 percent of those questioned approved of the relocation of Japanese aliens and nearly three-fifths favored the same treatment for 'the Japanese who were born in this country and are United States citizens'" (Coombs 1991, 91).

Negative constructions were not discouraged during this period because they helped to justify the discriminatory policies of curfew, evacuation, and relocation. Politicians used negative constructions to generate support for their own offices, white agricultural interests utilized them to eliminate economic competition, and nativist groups found them useful in their campaigns for racial preservation.

Negative constructions embedded in policy designs at this time sent those of Japanese ancestry, alien and citizen alike, important messages that were internalized and that shaped their agency. Lieutenant Commander K. D. Ringle, of Naval Intelligence, noted at the time that "whether the younger and succeeding generations are truly American in thought, word, deed, and sentiment will depend on the way in which they are treated now, and on how they are helped to meet the test of this war" (Myer 1971, 70). Two of the three branches of the federal government had institutionalized the negative construction of Japanese aliens and citizens. The executive branch did so with Executive Order 9066 authorizing the internment of individuals of Japanese ancestry. The legislative branch supported this policy the following month by enacting a statute that carried criminal penalties for those who violated the order. This action left the judiciary in the position of determining whether policy makers and the media had appropriately constructed the group through their actions. Ultimately, the Supreme Court would side with the other branches of the federal government. They would have few cases in which to do so, however, because only one Japanese in ten thousand filed cases and the Supreme Court heard only four.

The two most definitive cases of the wartime period addressed the constitutionality of the curfew and the exclusion order. In *Hirabayashi v. United States* (1943) the first case heard by the Court, a Japanese American deliberately challenged the constitutionality of the curfew, arguing that it should apply to all citizens or to none at all. The Court narrowly constructed the issue by choosing to review only the curfew and not the evacuation or internment orders. Ultimately, the Court upheld the curfew, with Chief Justice Harlan Fiske Stone writing for the majority that "in time of war residents having ethnic affiliations with an invading enemy may be a greater source of danger than those of a different ancestry."

Although the decision was unanimous, only three justices wrote concurring opinions recognizing that by supporting the dominant racial construction that the Court was establishing a dangerous practice. In his concurring brief, Justice William O. Douglas declared "I think it is important to emphasize that we are dealing here with a problem of loyalty not assimilation. Loyalty is a matter of mind and of heart not of race.... Detention for reasonable cause is one thing. Detention on account of ancestry is another." Justice Frank Murphy declared that "to say that any group cannot be assimilated is to admit that the great American experiment has failed, that our way of life has failed when confronted with the normal attachment of certain groups to the lands of their forefathers." He further stated that "American citizens have been placed under a special ban and deprived of their liberty because of their particular racial inheritance . . . the result is the creation in this country of two classes of citizens." Instead of subjecting the curfew policy to strict scrutiny and striking it down due to its discriminatory nature, the Court chose not only to side with the executive and legislative branches but to institutionalize racial discrimination itself.

In *Korematsu v. United States* (1944), a Japanese American challenged the constitutionality of the exclusion order. Again, the Court narrowly constructed the questions it would evaluate. There was a division within the Court whereby the majority wanted to separate the exclusion order from the policy of relocation and a minority of justices argued that they should be heard together. In reviewing only the exclusion order, the Court demonstrated its reluctance to review the validity of the prevailing construction. By a 6 to 3 decision, the Court failed to strike down the exclusion order. Writing for the majority, Justice Hugo Black argued that "hardships are a part of war, and war is an aggregation of hardships. . . . Citizenship has its responsibilities as well as its privileges, and in time of war the burden is always heavier." He further contended that "Korematsu was not excluded from the Military Area because of hostility to him or his race" but rather because of military necessity. Military necessity, in turn, had relied heavily on popular discourse in the media. By failing to strike down the exclusion order, the Court accepted the predominant racial construction of the Japanese, which alleged that their concentration on the West Coast, their religion, language schools, membership in social and cultural organizations/associations, dual citizenship—or all of these factors—were evidence of racial characteristics that predisposed them to be disloyal.

In his dissenting brief, Justice Murphy challenged the majority's rationale, writing that "the exclusion order necessarily must rely for its reasonableness upon the assumption that *all* persons of Japanese ancestry may have a dangerous tendency" toward fifth-column activity. Murphy concluded "that this forced exclusion was the result in good measure of this erroneous assumption of racial guilt rather than bona fide military necessity." Murphy further charged that:

> to the extent that assimilation is a problem, it is largely the result of certain
> social customs and laws of the American general public. Studies demonstrate
> that persons of Japanese descent are readily susceptible to integration in our

society if given the opportunity. The failure to accomplish an ideal status of assimilation, therefore, cannot be charged to the refusal of these persons to become Americanized or to their loyalty to Japan. And the retention by some persons of certain customs and religious practices of their ancestors is no criterion of their loyalty to the United States.

Murphy's dissent went to the heart of the negative construction of race and citizenship that had long plagued those of Japanese descent.

In his dissenting brief, Justice Robert Jackson recognized the danger in institutionalizing negative constructions through judicial rulings. In his evaluation of the Court's role in reviewing military orders, Jackson argued:

> once a judicial opinion rationalizes such an order to show that it conforms to the Constitution, or rather rationalizes the Constitution to show that the Constitution sanctions such an order, the Court for all time has validated the principle of racial discrimination. . . . A military commander may overstep the bounds of constitutionality, and it is an incident. But if we review and approve, that passing incident becomes the doctrine of the Constitution. There it has a generative power of its own, and all that it creates will be in its own image.

Here, Jackson points to the mutually reinforcing power that public policy decisions and legal decisions have on one another.

What is perhaps most significant about the Court's decision in *Korematsu* is that it was handed down just hours after the War Department's announcement that the exclusion orders were to be revoked. The Court could have chosen to reject the negative racial construction of the Japanese and, in so doing, advanced a more positive one without compromising the actions of the other branches, but it failed to do so. Rostow argued that "the Supreme Court could afford to view the issues in perspective, giving full weight to its own judicial responsibilities for the development of constitutional law as a whole" (1945, 197). The Court could have subjected the curfew and exclusion laws to standards of strict scrutiny. It could have given further consideration to the powers of its decisions, which "can change the way Americans think and behave" (Epstein 1995, 247). But it did not. By not striking down the curfew and exclusion orders and, in fact, by supporting the argument of "military necessity," the Court legitimized the notion that the loyalty of those of Japanese ancestry might be suspect and, thus, institutionalized racism at the highest levels.

During the war, those of Japanese ancestry continued their activism to challenge their negative construction. Despite their widespread negative construction, Japanese Americans never stopped trying to become positively constructed as full-fledged "Americans." Harry H. L. Kitano (1986) noted that many Nisei looked to the future, believing that sacrifices would have to be made in the present so as to provide a better future for the next generation (Sansei).

Their desire to be accepted as Americans subsequently shaped the tactics that Japanese Americans thought necessary to achieve that goal. The JACL pushed for Japanese Americans to serve in the armed forces, lobbying for an all-Nisei unit. The editor of the *Minidoka Irrigator* argued that military service would be the best way to challenge their negative construction and the need for an all-Nisei unit was paramount for the "publicity value and potential," keeping in mind that "favorable publicity is our greatest need." In November 1942, their efforts culminated in the creation of the 442nd regiment, an all-Nisei unit, which ultimately became the most decorated unit in the U.S. Army. Upon their return at the end of the war, President Truman presented the unit with the Distinguished Unit Citation, telling them "you have fought not only the enemy but you fought prejudice and you have won." This moment signals a beginning of the shift to a seemingly more positive construction. The impetus for this shift was largely a result of sustained Japanese-American activism, culminating in their status as war heroes—much of the credit for their changing construction can be attributed to the actions of Japanese Americans themselves. However, the change also came about because the negative construction had outlived its utility. Due to the effects of internment, they no longer presented an economic, political, or social threat to white interests.

POST-WORLD WAR II: THE "MODEL MINORITY"

In the post-World War II era the negative construction of those of Japanese ancestry underwent a dramatic shift. Once constructed as "pagan in their philosophy, atheistic in their beliefs, alien in their allegiance, and antagonistic to everything for which we stand" (Smith 1991, 81), the common wisdom about them now has become "scratch a Japanese American and find a white Anglo-Saxon Protestant" (Kitano 1969, 3). Their construction shifted from that of "problem minority" to "enemy aliens" to "model minority."

Political and economic circumstances were significant in changing their construction. As the United States emerged from the war in its new role as hegemony, the American people could afford to be more generous in their treatment of the Japanese. Furthermore, relations with Japan shifted in the postwar years as the country became an important ally in helping to contain communism. Additionally, Japan represented an open market for the sale of U.S. goods. On the home front, the internment of those of Japanese ancestry left them economically devastated. In losing their land, they also lost their status as an economic threat to white interests.

However, Japanese-American agency also played a crucial role in their changing construction. The 442nd combat unit did more to help the Japanese earn their citizenship status and the respect of their fellow Americans than did perhaps any other factor. According to the War Relocation Agency (WRA):

> Their performance had the effect, not instantaneously, but gradually, of quieting the voices of all but the most rabid of the American racebaiters, and of enlarging materially the ranks of the forces of good will that were determined to see that the families of Nisei fighters were accepted as full Americans. (Smith 1995, 391–92)

In the postwar period, it became less acceptable to construct Japanese Americans and their alien parents negatively than it had been previously.

The shift in their construction first became apparent in the renewed efforts to restrict landholding in California. In 1946, California voters failed for the first time to garner enough support for an anti-Asian ballot proposal when the decision to incorporate the alien land laws into the state's Constitution did not pass. Discourse in the press was important in shaping the electoral outcome, this time helping to turn the tide away from anti-Japanese legislation. "In the areas in which the anti-Japanese press exerted considerable influence . . . a majority of voters supported Proposition 15. Where most of the newspaper publishers opposed the proposition, nearly two-thirds of the voters cast ballots against it" (Leonard 1990, 478). The vote, however, represented a limited victory because the laws remained on the books and could be enforced. The courts, rather than the voters, would ultimately invalidate the land laws.

In *Oyama v. United States* (1948) the Supreme Court upheld the right of alien parents to give their citizen children the gift of land, reiterating its earlier position that citizens (no matter what their racial background) were entitled to all the rights and protections of citizenship. In 1952, the Court finally struck down California's alien land laws in *Sei Fuji v. the State of California,* recognizing that the term "aliens ineligible for citizenship" was really a cover for racially motivated politics.

That same year, the federal government enacted the *Walter-McCarran Act,* also known as the *Immigration and Nationality Act of 1952,* thus removing race as a qualification for naturalization and allowing Japanese aliens to become citizens. This policy had several effects. First, it recognized the Japanese character to be congruent with white conceptions of citizenship. They were fit to be Americans. Second, it gave authority and legitimacy to the agency of Japanese Americans who had mobilized through the JACL to put the issue on the political agenda. Finally, and perhaps most importantly, it invalidated all laws that relied on ineligibility for citizenship for their power.

While the 1950s were an important period for the rejection of Japanese-American negative construction, the 1960s were the decade when their seemingly more positive construction as the "model minority" emerged. The construction was the product of the mainstream press and a handful of white academics, who used it to keep other minorities, such as blacks and Chicanos, in their place. The relative success of Japanese Americans in the face of hardship was held up as an example to which other minority groups should aspire. Once negatively constructed, Japanese Americans were now used to negatively construct other minority groups. Claire Jean Kim describes this process of racial triangulation as one in which "dominant group A (Whites) valorizes subordinate group B (Asian Americans) relative to subordinate group C (Blacks) in order to discipline C" (1999, 107). Their positive construction, therefore, was not without a price.

The "foreign" racial qualities that had previously been used against them were now touted as an asset. According to William Petersen, the scholar who initiated the model minority construction, "the Japanese . . . could climb over the highest barriers our racists were able to fashion in part because of their meaningful links with an alien culture. Pride in their heritage and shame for any reduction in its only partly legendary glory—these were sufficient to carry the group through its travail" (*The New York Times* 1966, 3). The group now earned praise for both their traditional values and their American ones. The very qualities that were used to build their former negative construction were now the foundation for their new, seemingly positive construction.

During the 1960s and 1970s, Japanese-American activism continued to grow as they discovered their voice. This culminated in their pursuit of redress from the federal government for the internment. On February 19, 1976, President Gerald R. Ford rescinded Executive Order 9066, the evacuation order. In his presidential proclamation, he stated "we know now what we should have known then—not only was the evacuation wrong, but Japanese Americans were and are loyal Americans." Symbolically, they had received an apology, but many desired substantive remedy. The JACL mobilized in favor of a federal commission that would study the circumstances and possibility of redress. The JACL carefully constructed their redress efforts to be in the interest of all Americans, not just Japanese Americans. Their efforts culminated in the creation of the Commission on Wartime Relocation and Internment of Civilians (CWRIC) by Congress in 1980. CWRIC held hearings across the country and received testimony from a range of groups, not restricted to Japanese Americans, including historians, scholars, government officials, and others. CWRIC released its report, "Personal Justice Denied," in mid-February 1983, in which it found no basis for "military necessity" and the policies that followed from it. The report had the effect of reconstructing Japanese Americans as a target of policy, transforming them into a "deserving" group in policies that would follow. In August 1988, as a result of CWRIC's recommendations, Congress enacted a redress bill that awarded a one-time, tax-free payment of $20,000 to each internment survivor. On August 10, 1988, President Ronald Reagan signed that bill and the national apology that accompanied it.

Building on the policy successes of the 1980s, Fred Korematsu and Gordon Hirabayashi, aided by the Asian Law Caucus, filed *coram nobis* cases asking federal judges to vacate their wartime convictions. *Coram nobis* requests are limited to those cases where it is believed some fundamental error or manifest injustice has occurred. The fundamental error that Korematsu and Hirabayashi wanted corrected was the Court's failure to acknowledge in its wartime decisions that military necessity was a racially coded term that masked racial prejudice during the war period—that there was, in fact, no evidence to prove that Japanese aliens or Japanese Americans were disloyal and, therefore, there was no need for the curfew or evacuation policies.

During Korematsu's proceedings, it was revealed that the War Department had destroyed or altered (or both) documents and evidence when presenting the government's case. Both the Justice Department and the Supreme Court had unknowingly relied on the statements of the War Department as fact. On November 10, 1983, Judge Marilyn Hall Patel vacated Fred Korematsu's conviction for violating the exclusion order. This ruling unmasked the former construction of the Japanese as an undeserving group and reconstructed them as deserving. The decision was significant because it represented the first time that a judge vacated a criminal conviction upheld by the Supreme Court in its final appeal.

Gordon Hirabayashi also successfully had his exclusion and curfew convictions vacated. The omission and destruction of evidence by the War Department played a prominent role in his case as well. The most glaring instance was that in which General DeWitt's final report was changed to lessen its racial prejudice. DeWitt reasoned in Chapter II of the final report, entitled "Need for Military Control and for Evacuation," that loyalty could not be determined even with unlimited time. The War Department, knowing the Supreme Court would not uphold the constitutionality of its actions on this reasoning, suggested that a total of 55 changes be made to DeWitt's final report, including one reconstructing DeWitt's racial prejudice as an issue of time—that there was insufficient time to determine the loyal from the disloyal. In light of the falsified findings of this report, the Ninth Circuit Court of Appeals vacated Hirabayashi's convictions in 1987 and ordered a lower court to carry out the order.

Although their current construction as a "model minority" has been firmly in place since the 1960s, Japanese Americans at times are still plagued by their former negative construction. During economic downturns, they often are the target of frustration expressed by other groups. As negative racial constructions flare up again, Japanese Americans (and other Asian groups) have been the targets of violence.

The model minority construction, while seemingly positive on its face, is damaging to Japanese Americans in a number of ways. First, by emphasizing their success as a group, its unitary nature overlooks differences within the group. The Japanese-American community is not a homogenous one, and not all Japanese Americans are successful. As a result, Japanese Americans are sometimes not targets of policies from which they could benefit. For instance, they often are lumped with whites as victims of affirmative action, rather than garnering the acknowledgment that they have members that could benefit from these policies (Ancheta 1998). Second, their model minority construction serves as a shield to disguise the fact that Japanese Americans, as members of the larger pan-ethnic umbrella of Asian Americans, are increasingly the targets of violence. Many Americans would be surprised that Japanese Americans, the model minority, are targets of the same violence that other minorities experience. Third, their elevation to a status closer to that of whites contributes to tensions with other Asian groups with more recent immigration histories that are not looked upon as favorably as Japanese Americans. It also creates tensions with minority groups that are compared to the model minority construction and fall short; for instance, the construction of African Americans as an urban underclass. Finally, Ancheta argues that the model minority construction is problematic because it provides "a false sense of security, as if the model minority stereotype could protect them [its targets] from racial discrimination . . . some Asian Americans come to believe that success can always be achieved through adherence to the model minority stereotype" (1998, 162). So, while the model minority construction in many ways represents an improvement over their former status—as a problem minority and then as enemy aliens—it is not without its drawbacks.

CONCLUSION

Public policy, media discourse, and institutions such as the courts each are powerful agents of social constructions of group identity in their own right. Policy often effectively sets the boundaries within which positive and negative constructions of groups are formulated. Discourse in the media shapes our conceptions of the world around us and helps us to better understand our position within it relative to other groups. Courts are often at the forefront of categorizing groups and legitimizing or challenging social constructions of identity brought before them.

While each agent of social constructions is important for the individualized functions that it serves, its power is magnified and enhanced when we consider the ways in which it overlaps and mutually reinforces the other agent. Social constructions of identity that are created at the intersection of policy, media discourse, and the courts have powerful consequences for their targets and send important messages to them about the extent and types of agency that groups have to challenge those constructions that have been externally imposed upon them without their consent.

The evolution of persons of Japanese descent from "problem minority" to "enemy alien" to "model minority" in the United States illustrates how the social construction process cannot be conceptualized in a linear fashion, but rather must be envisioned in a more dynamic and less mechanistic way. As policy, media discourse, and the courts each shaped the context and the environment within which they acted, their actions resulted in the environment reshaping the conditions under which future action would occur. The case also demonstrates that the agency of targets is not to be overlooked in the social construction process. Far from being passive targets of the negative constructions imposed upon them, Japanese aliens and their Japanese-American children played a critical role in changing their construction to one of "deserving" and "entitled."

NOTES

I would like to thank Claire Jean Kim, Helen Ingram, and Anne Schneider for their insightful comments on earlier drafts of this chapter.

1. For instance, African Americans have been characterized as "lazy," "violent," and as possessing a "culture of poverty." Native Americans historically have been constructed as "savages," "half-breeds," "uncivilized," and "inferior" relative to whites. Asian Americans were initially described as "pagan," "peculiar," and "unassimilable."

2. To say that race is a social construction is not to say that race has no social meaning or experienced consequences. Racial constructions are powerfully felt and shape every facet of an individual's life.

3. Not all white Americans or even white citizens of the West Coast held racist views of Japanese immigrants and the use of the term "whites" in this chapter is not intended to essentialize race. As with any racial group, whites did not speak or act in a unitary fashion. White Americans held a number of different perspectives and constructed Japanese immigrants differently. During World War II, many sympathetic whites supported Japanese aliens and citizens and opposed the government's treatment of the group. However, much of the opposition to the Japanese originated with whites in California and on the West Coast. The use of the term "white" encompasses the activity of these individuals and groups and it should be understood that it is not meant to be representative of the entire white race but rather of a particular subset of the group.

PART II

Congressional Discourse: Forging Lines of Division between Deserving and Undeserving

ANNE L. SCHNEIDER AND HELEN M. INGRAM

The history of the United States is filled with ironies and contradictions. How do policy makers and ordinary people reconcile the chasm between the ideals of equality and community inscribed in the minds of every school child with the real experiences of persons of color and the poor? Why, given the pervasive belief in equal opportunity for all, are there so many policies that, when examined in detail and in terms of their consequences, obviously confer unequal opportunities? At the same time, democracy has grown substantially. Given the long-standing cultural bias, prejudice, and even hatred directed at persons of non-European ancestry, how is it possible that laws were passed in the United States that ended slavery? Eliminated Jim Crow laws? Prohibited white-only schools? Overcome massive resistance from the private sector and prohibited preferences for whites in housing, loans, job applications, and public accommodations? Provided (at times) positive public policy for immigrants? If there actually is some deeply ingrained psychological or evolutionary reason for people to create an "other" group that is marginalized and hated, then why or how has the United States managed to overcome so much of the disadvantage once experienced by women, persons of non-European heritage, the disabled, and those with non-majoritarian sexual preferences?

Part of the answer lies in public policy, which has a role in forging a diverse and accepting society. In contrast with what some cultural theories seem to assume, public policies are not just a reflection of a dominant culture. Even in a democracy, there is no straightforward translation of prevailing beliefs and values into policy designs. Instead, policies emerge from a complex and often chaotic environment involving the social construction of knowledge, the social construction of social groups, power relationships, entrepreneurial leadership, and the rules of policy-making institutions. In the introductory chapter and in the first part of this book, we examined how policies allocate benefits in the ongoing effort to bind people to the nation and sustain the legitimacy of government. But we also recognize that policy making may become degenerative. In degenerative democracy, public officials create negative social constructions of unpopular groups and develop deceptive policy discourses that harm citizenship and democracy. Language confers positive and negative constructions. The language used in official contexts is especially important because it legitimates positive and negative identities. Laws are not just bundles of advantages or disadvantages, but are also messages about who matters and who does not. The American Congress is the primary voice for the American people and is particularly important in constructing identity. The public expressions of members of Congress are as important as the way they vote. Strategies are not just rational ways of appealing to reason, but contain emotional elements about who contributes to the general welfare and who does not.

Nation building can proceed not only by conferring benefits on the powerful and well regarded, but also by punishing unpopular and less powerful groups. Punishment of the "other" can be used to curry the favor of the advantaged. Policies allocate benefits to some and burdens to others, but policy also allocates prestige or stigma. Negative and divisive social constructions become embedded in the policy design itself, with subsequent long-term impacts on racial minorities, the poor, and other disadvantaged groups.

But not all policy-making contexts are degenerative. In fact, we have contended elsewhere that policy-making institutions typically engage in degenerative politics on some issues but not others (Schneider and Ingram 1997). At times, conditions come together in such a way that policy makers focus on issues of justice and injustice, and on pragmatic strategies to solve problems, that will extend the full benefits of citizenship to all people. Congress is a good example. This institution sometimes engages in manipulative, deceptive, and degenerative policy-making systems, but in other instances, its members take the lead in pursuing justice through federal policies designed to overcome centuries of discrimination.

The chapters in this part examine in detail the strategies used by Congressional advocates for racial minorities in federal policy-making contexts involving housing and immigration. These chapters illustrate how the boundaries of target populations are negotiated and constructed as part of the rhetoric and the strategies used in crafting legislation. In the housing legislation, racial minorities were subdivided into the deserving and the undeserving so that positive policy could be achieved for some even though it left others out. In immigration policy, those who might otherwise be considered deserving were grouped with persons who were not considered deserving as a strategy for denying benefits to both groups.

Chapter 4 by Mara Sidney, "Contested Images of Race and Place: The Politics of Housing Discrimination," examines two very different policy designs—

each intended to address racial inequality in housing. Her analysis of *Housing Act of 1968* and the *Community Reinvestment Act of 1977* involves a comparative examination of the issue contexts, the dynamics policy design process, the institutional culture, the characteristics of the policies that emerged, and the policy feedback systems that generated subsequent pressure for change. One of the great strengths of this chapter and chapter 5 by Lina Newton on immigration is in the detailed analysis of language used by advocates and opponents, along with the role that the social constructions of target populations played in the discourse. In the housing policy arena, each policy targeted discrimination—and in that sense offers insight into how legislators attempted to bring issues of justice into a policy arena more commonly characterized by injustice, racism, sexism, and class distinctions. Given the very different contexts, however, legislators crafted different discursive strategies.

Fair housing supporters initially used the urban riots of the 1960s as urgent justification for a fair housing law. By 1968, however, a conservative turn in Congress and public opinion against the "excesses" of the civil rights movement made this a problematic argument. Opponents countered with the narrative that federal legislation should not be used to reward black urban rioters for their illegal behavior. To do so would simply be caving in to their demands. Supporters of the 1968 law then found it necessary to create the idea of a professional black middle class who deserved to escape the ghetto and to separate them from the black urban rioter who did not deserve federal legislation that would address the conditions of the ghetto. Supporters created two narratives: one directed at blacks, which said that the new law would open up housing markets and eliminate discrimination in housing; the other, directed toward white opponents of the law, which said there were very few middle class blacks who could afford the high cost of housing in white suburban neighborhoods. Thus, they told the opponents, the law would have very little practical effect. Supporters of the CRA a decade later, also working during an era of backlash against the social policies of the 1960s, avoided discussing race but justified the policy through images of the kinds of places the law would benefit. The CRA was framed as only a small change in existing policy designed mainly to clarify existing law. This was almost a "stealth" law, passed without much scrutiny within or outside the legislative arena. Thus, both policies involved elements of deceptive narratives designed to overcome major resistance to integrating housing.

Race played an important role in the design, implementation, and future amendments of each of the housing acts. Both legislative acts succeeded in overcoming strong institutional bias that opposed regulations, and they insured the provision of affordable housing for minorities and the poor. Yet, the discursive strategies that were needed to navigate the political and institutional context resulted in modest policies with design limitations that greatly reduced the capacity of these laws to make a difference in minority access to housing.

This study illustrates that there is no best way to frame issues or design policies for the deeply disadvantaged, especially when race is involved. "Successful" strategies for allocating benefits to politically weak and negatively viewed groups must encompass very clever rhetoric and logical and coherent arguments that will work within a specific institutional context. The advocates must have some degree of political power within the institutional setting and must be able to carve out some segment of the negatively viewed group that can be reconstructed as deserving. Additionally, placing burdens on powerful people may be almost impossible, and it results in the development of weak policy tools, such as voluntary compliance with the law by banks.

Efforts to strengthen the *1968 Fair Housing Act* through amendments were unsuccessful for twenty years and then succeeded only when additional target groups were included and the discourse deracialized. CRA, deracialized from the start, was able to channel benefits to low-income minorities due to their income status, but was not able to generate enough support to impose strong regulations on banks to insure that they would eliminate their racially biased lending patterns. There were no sanctions for banks, and community advocates had no legitimate role in calling for accountability. In 1999, in a successful effort to weaken the CRA, opponents injected negative images of the community advocacy groups, who used this "place-based" law on behalf of poor and minority neighborhoods. Thus, a weak law at the outset, with few guidelines for regulators and no sanctions for violators, was further weakened over the next decade. In the case of housing discrimination, the power and positive images of advantaged populations opposed to reform were deeply entrenched, yet some progress was made in this arena against enormous odds. Sidney points out, however, that the institutional bias against racial minorities and fear of powerful opposing institutions (such as banks) produced weak policy designs that limited the potential for change. She argues that fair housing policies are held back by the dynamics of a degenerative policy-making system, but that clever rhetorical strategies occasionally permit positive policy that enables racial minorities to enjoy more of the benefits of citizenship than they had in the past. Overcoming racism in housing "once and for all," however, is something public policy has not yet been able to accomplish.

In chapter 5, "'It Is Not a Case of Being Anti-immigration': Categories of Deservedness in Immigration Policy Making," Lina Newton examines how modern immigration policies communicate—symbolically and through instrumental access or restrictions—who fits the "citizen ideal" and who does not. The history of immigration policy in the United States has been characterized by cycles of xenophobic and racist reactions to immigrants interspersed with more positive and accepting policies. Immigrants, she points out, have historically carried both positive and negative social constructions—providing an interesting opportunity for policy makers to choose which construction they wish to portray in any given context.

One construction of "immigrant" is as the building block of the nation and the people from whom the melting pot has been created. Members of Congress frequently take great pride in citing their own immigrant backgrounds. Most of those immigrants, of course, were of European ancestry and elicit visions of highly motivated, hard working people who pulled themselves up by their bootstraps, overcame initial discrimination (such as against Italians, the Irish, and Catholics), and earned their way into the American dream. The other construction is of immigrants from less positively viewed places, usually with darker skin, who are either stealing American jobs or are too lazy or too uneducated to perform well in the American economy. These people sometimes are viewed as culturally or genetically incapable of being truly "American." Immigration policy for many years was highly racialized, in that quota systems provided distinct advantages to European immigrants at the expense of persons from virtually everywhere else in the world, particularly Asia, Latin America, and Africa.

Yet, in 1965, during a period of considerable social reform, federal immigration policy changed fundamentally and eliminated race and national origin as the grounds for entry. Additionally, in 1985, under a Republican President and a Democratic-controlled Congress, immigration policy took still another positive turn as it granted amnesty to thousands of persons residing in the United States without proper documentation and, for the first time, focused on controlling illegal immigration by placing sanctions on employers who hired them. The policy logic was that jobs enticed people into the United States and that if employers were punished for hiring them, the jobs would dry up and immigrants without proper documentation would stop coming. Whether genuine or not, there was an expressed concern that illegal immigrants could easily be exploited by employers.

Only a decade later, under a Democratic President and a Republican Congress, immigration policy once again took a much more negative turn. In her intricately detailed discourse analysis of the *Congressional Immigration Act of 1996,* Newton shows how federal policy, even though it no longer singles out groups for exclusion on the explicit basis of national origin or race, actually distinguishes still between the "right" and the "wrong" kinds of immigrants with rather clear racial or origin implications. The 1996 act ostensibly was an attempt to "control the border" and reduce illegal immigration. The rationale put forth by anti-immigration proponents of the bill was that the availability of welfare services in the United States acted as a magnet to attract people from other countries (mainly Mexico). By taking away the lure of public services, the flow of immigrants to the United States could be curtailed.

One of the particularly amazing aspects of the 1996 act, however, is that it grouped legal and illegal immigrants into a common category for the purpose of denying certain public services, thereby lending support to the notion that *all* immigrants are damaging to the nation. Even though experts disagreed about the fiscal impacts of immigrants, the legal residents were singled out both in public opinion and public policy as "freeloaders" who did not deserve access to public benefits.

Newton's analysis is based on the language in policy debates. She points out that both the positive and negative images of immigrants are expressed in the legislation. The introduction of the bill, for example, extols the virtues of immigrants as hardworking, freedom-loving, patriotic Americans, many of whom bring special skills to the workplace. Congressional supporters of the legislation that would be very repressive toward immigrants argued that it was not "a question of being anti-immigration. This country was founded by immigrants. I am the son of one of them" (quoted in Newton this volume). The problem immigrant, however, was constructed as a freeloader. Citizens were constructed positively and contrasted with the noncitizen immigrant, even those who were in the United States legally. A second prominent narrative is that of the "criminal alien" who is "criminal" by virtue of being in the United States illegally.

Opponents of the 1996 act attempted to craft effective opposing narratives, Newton argues, but their objections to the bill did almost nothing to construct a more positive image of immigrants. Opponents were held together mainly by arguing that the policy went too far and that the "cure would be worse than the disease." Thus, even the opponents of the anti-immigrant legislation did not promote a positive social construction of this group.

Both of these chapters shows the importance of rhetorical strategies in framing the issues and the central role of socially constructed target populations. Constructions are created or reflected by policy makers and, through the policy arguments, shape the characteristics of policy designs and signal who really belongs to America and who does not.

4

Contested Images of Race and Place: The Politics of Housing Discrimination

MARA S. SIDNEY

Enacting public policies to address racial inequality is notoriously difficult. This is especially true in the case of housing discrimination. Such
proposals prompt resistance from the real estate and finance industries,
as they threaten to upset housing patterns. By extending government's reach
into the private sphere of family home and neighborhood, they also have
attracted opposition from white people. Respondents interviewed as part of
this research recognize that housing issues raise value conflicts, involve powerful industry and constituency interests and, thus, create dilemmas for political
actors. According to one state legislator, "Housing is the most visceral issue in
American politics. Particularly when the issue of race becomes involved, there's
nothing that even approaches it."

This research analyzes and compares two critical junctures when legislators successfully negotiated these obstacles to produce laws designed to reduce
and sanction discriminatory housing practices. The legislative processes that
culminated in the *Fair Housing Act of 1968* and the *Community Reinvestment Act
of 1977* (CRA) offer an ideal opportunity to examine the impact of social constructions on policy designs. Each law targets discrimination, but there the similarity ends. The legislators who crafted these laws responded to different political contexts by developing distinct discursive strategies. Specifically, fair
housing supporters offered positive images of racial groups to justify policy
adoption, whereas community reinvestment supporters avoided discussing race,
instead offering images of the places that would benefit from the law rather
than the people. These choices gave rise to quite different policy designs, both
of which continue to govern efforts to reduce housing discrimination in the
United States.

Using Schneider and Ingram's analytic framework and text analysis of Congressional debates, this chapter compares the rhetorical strategies legislators used
to advocate for fair housing and community reinvestment laws (Schneider and

Ingram, 1993; 1997). It links these strategies to features of the policy designs that emerged and considers their implications for subsequent political efforts to amend the laws. Ultimately, the analysis addresses the question of how racial inequalities can be politically addressed most effectively—how can benefits to racial minorities be secured? The CRA is a class-based policy the advocates of which initially avoided specifying that poor and minority people would benefit from the law. The CRA is not understood as a "special program" for minorities, although a significant portion of its advocates and beneficiaries are people of color. On the other hand, fair housing now specifically targets racial minorities, along with a range of other "protected classes," for benefits.

FAIR HOUSING: A RACE-CONSCIOUS APPROACH TO HOUSING INEQUALITY

The first national law to address racial discrimination in housing, the *Fair Housing Act of 1968,* truly was a landmark piece of legislation. It prohibited homeowners, real estate agents, lenders, and other housing professionals from engaging in a range of practices that commonly had been used to keep neighborhoods racially segregated, such as refusing to sell or rent to a person because of his or her race, lying about the availability of a dwelling, or "blockbusting"—inducing white owners to sell their homes by telling them that blacks were moving into the neighborhood (P.L. 90–284). The last of the 1960s-era civil rights laws, the *Fair Housing Act* tackled the arena long felt to be the most sensitive to white people.

Congressional proponents of a national fair housing law faced a particularly hostile political context in 1968, marked by urban riots and black militancy, by declining political power for blacks as a social group, and by a powerful conservative coalition in Congress. Social construction analysis helps identify how these legislators were able to transform political risk into opportunity.

Issue Context: A Hostile Environment for Fair Housing

In the late 1960s, the emergence of the Black Power movement, the proliferation of urban riots, and the shift of activism to the North changed understandings of civil rights issues. These developments conflicted with the rhetoric of civil rights that emphasized achieving integration through nonviolent means. Televised images of police officers and dogs attacking peacefully protesting black activists gave way to images of Black Power activists advocating pursuit of justice through separatist strategies and direct action tactics, violent ones if necessary (McAdam 1982). This shift coincided with the increasing incidence of riots in ghetto neighborhoods. Between 1966 and 1968, 290 "hostile outbursts" occurred in the United States, during which 169 people were killed,

7,000 wounded, and 40,000 arrested (182). Also, the attention of civil rights activists was shifting to the North as leaders began to decry the poor living conditions blacks experienced throughout the country. These changes within the civil rights movement led to changes in how whites perceived blacks, their demands, and their problems. By 1966, 70 percent of whites believed that "Negroes were trying to move too fast" (Sundquist 1968).

In addition to changing images and changing understandings of civil rights issues, black political power was declining. Their increasing loyalty to the Democratic party decreased their attractiveness as swing voters (Sundquist 1968). The civil rights movement was undergoing fragmentation, which under-cut its political influence (McAdam 1982). Although directors of the Leader-ship Conference on Civil Rights lobbied for fair housing law by testifying at hearings and negotiating behind the scenes, their presence paled in comparison to the large-scale mobilization efforts that had emerged around previous civil rights bills (Graham 1990).

White homeowners and the housing industry clearly held the most polit-ical power. Whites held it through their status as the majority population. The housing industry held it through its political mobilization against fair housing and its historic privileged status in federal housing policy dating from the Depression era. The real estate industry was the most vocal opponent. In 1966, the National Association of Real Estate Boards (NAREB), representing eighty-five thousand members of local real estate boards, mobilized real estate agents to send thousands of letters to members of Congress voicing their opposition to a fair housing bill. Because fair housing law would affect their constituents, the decision calculus of Northern legislators on fair housing proposals was likely to differ from that used on previous civil rights bills.

The institution of the U.S. Congress—its operating procedures and orga-nizational structure—was the arena in which proponents of fair housing strate-gized and struggled to win support. Party affiliation was less important on civil rights issues than ideology and regional identity. Coalitions of Northern Democrats and moderate Republicans had provided the votes to pass previous civil rights laws. In the 1966 elections, Republicans gained seats both in the Senate and in the House. Those elected in the House shifted the body toward a more conservative stance. New Republican senators actually were more mod-erate than the Democrats they had replaced and, therefore, their presence increased the pool of possible swing voters on the fair housing issue (Graham 1990). Nonetheless, the Senate minority leader Everett Dirksen, who had shown his ability to control the votes of many Republicans in past civil rights battles, strongly opposed fair housing (1990).

Attention to swing voters was especially important because on civil rights issues, the conservative coalition frequently took advantage of the Senate rule enabling filibusters. In 1966, Senator Dirksen had led a successful filibuster against a fair housing bill and he threatened to do so again. Fair housing supporters needed more than a majority to win passage, because they would first need two-thirds of the members to vote for cloture. Finally, 1968 was an election year, making discourse especially important to those legislators up for reelection, who would have to defend their votes to constituents.

Dynamics of the Design Process

Nearly all accounts of the legislative process leading to the *Fair Housing Act* emphasize that no one thought the bill had any chance of success. Analysis of the issue context shows why expectations were so low and why supporters, overjoyed at their success, called its passage "a miracle" (Graham 1990). Fair housing supporters had to develop a political strategy that could turn a political risk into an opportunity. Opponents in Congress skillfully exploited the risks, emphasizing during debate that a fair housing law would trample the rights of upstanding, "truly American," white homeowners. Additionally, it would subject the housing industry to frivolous claims and to the government's heavy hand. Supporters adapted their rhetorical strategy to the new context of civil rights described above, something they had not done in 1966 when a fair housing bill died in the Senate (Sidney 2001). They created a narrative about fair housing that helped secure passage, but they built into the policy design elements that would limit prospects for changing housing patterns and processes.

Table 4.1 summarizes the coded Senate debate on proposed fair housing legislation in 1968. Three aspects of the supporters' persuasive strategy reflect their adaptation to the issue context. First, they portrayed the urban riots as a window of opportunity, rather than allowing opponents to dominate discussion of them. Second, they constructed a new target group, middle-class blacks, who they presented as deserving better housing, as distinct from low-income blacks. Third, they used free-market rhetoric to weave together conflicting narratives about fair housing aimed at white and black constituencies. Each part of this rhetorical strategy shaped the policy design that the Senate adopted.

Riots: Creating a Sense of Urgency. Urban riots seemed to give fair housing opponents irrefutable evidence that fair housing should not become national law. In earlier debates, supporters portrayed blacks as noble victims of discrimination, trapped in ghettos by forces beyond their control. This was a typical image used in legislative struggles for civil rights, advancing the notion that blacks relied on the goodwill of whites to grant them dignity and freedom. But as riots erupted summer after summer across the country, civil rights opponents could depict blacks as violent and destructive, "deviants" rather than "dependents." They claimed that passing fair housing law would reward black lawlessness and endanger other Americans.

In 1968, supporters used the riots as a key component of their persuasive strategy, invoking them nearly twice as often as opponents (26 percent vs. 15

percent of statements). They used the riots to create a sense of urgency about addressing the problems of the ghettos, which they described as products of housing discrimination. Supporters also addressed fears aroused by Black Power activists by claiming that the riots symbolized a larger battle taking place between a group Senator Walter Mondale (D-Minn.) called "black racists" and the rest of society (including "moderate" blacks):

> There is a critical debate now under way in the ghetto. The issue is quite sim-
> ple—whether there is any basic decency in white America and whether white
> America ever really intends to permit equality and full opportunity to black
> Americans. . . . We believe that our continuing failure to put an end to segre-
> gated housing lends a powerful argument to the black separatists and black
> racists, and can only speed the process of separation and alienation. (*Congres-
> sional Record* 1968, 2274)

A Deserving Target Group: The Black Middle Class. Although they provided a sense of crisis, the riots created a problem of deservedness that fair housing support-ers solved by constructing a new target group. They distinguished blacks along class lines and described a small group of middle-class professionals who deserved to escape the ghettos and who, simultaneously, could afford to do so. While hardly anyone in previous fair housing debates had referred to middle-class blacks, nearly a quarter of advocates' statements in 1968 did so, often through references to witnesses who had testified in Senate hearings the previ-ous year. These stories brought individual faces into the debate. During the 1967 hearings, a black U.S. Navy lieutenant and a black college professor testi-fied about how discrimination thwarted their efforts to find decent housing for their families. The Lieutenant was turned down by 36 leasing agents while searching for housing in the Washington, D.C. area (U.S. Congress 1967, 194).

Other witnesses had reported the stories of two black sisters, a welfare worker and a nurse, who were prepared to offer the asking price for a two-fam-ily house when the owner raised the price (U.S. Congress 1967, 99); a black doctor, who read the real estate ads each week describing the pleasures of the suburbs, but knew he could not move there despite his income and education (116); and a black research technician, who found an apartment for his family in a suburb near his lab, had his application rejected despite the intervention of his company's directors, community leaders, and local religious organizations (377). Senators drew on these stories during floor debate to personalize the plight of the black middle class. We can see these accounts as conscious efforts to allay white fears that rioters would invade their neighborhoods if fair hous-ing became law. Supporters emphasized that fair housing would enable mem-bers of the black middle class to escape the ghetto, while low-income blacks would gain only the hope of escaping in the future; middle-class blacks could live the American dream, low-income blacks could dream it. Sen. Edward Brooke's remarks capture this line of reasoning:

TABLE 4.1

Fair Housing Debate 1968 (Senate): Target Group Images and Policy Rationales

(Percents are column percents)

Target Groups	Legislators	
	Supporters	Opponents
Blacks	**26% of statements** Victims of discrimination, trapped in ghettos *Valence: Positive*	**10% of statements** Rioters *Valence: Negative*
Middle-class blacks	**24%** Portraits of individual black professionals who can afford to leave ghetto, but face discrimination *Valence: Positive*	**2%** Law would give black soldiers returning from war privileges that discriminate against white soldiers. *Valence: Neutral*
Low-income blacks	**9%** Law would provide hope of upward mobility *Valence: Neutral/positive*	0
White Homeowners	**14%** Individual homeowners would be exempt *Valence: Positive*	**56%** Upstanding, worked hard to achieve home ownership; fair housing would rob them of property rights, freedom of choice; victimize them with false claims *Valence: Positive*

(continued on next page)

TABLE 4.1 *(continued)*

	Legislators	
Target Groups	**Supporters**	**Opponents**
Housing Industry	12% Most want to behave fairly; problems come from actions of unscrupulous few; law would "shield" good industry members *Valence: Mixed*	8% Law would burden industry members, making them subject to false claims and the heavy hand of government. *Valence: Positive*
Agent Federal Government (HUD)	3% Opponents overstate; federal power is needed to address problems of housing discrimination *Valence: Positive*	19% Too powerful, ready to usurp individual and states' rights, bureaucracy is eager to expand power. *Valence: Negative*
Rationale Riots	26% Riots prove fair housing is needed; battle between black moderates and extremists; government needs to show that moderates are right	15% Fair housing law would reward blacks for lawlessness and violence
Policy Logic (Causal Assumptions)	24% Free market frame: Law would allow equal opportunity to housing, but income inequality will prevent drastic change in residential patterns	0
Total Statements	58	48

Source: Congressional Record, February 6–March 11, 1968

r housing does not promise to end the ghetto; it promises only to nonstrate that the ghetto is not an immutable institution in America. It will scarcely lead to a mass dispersal of the ghetto population to the suburbs; but it will make it possible for those who have the resources to escape the stranglehold now suffocating the inner cities of America. It will make possible renewed hope for ghetto residents who have begun to believe that escape from their demeaning circumstances is impossible. (*Congressional Record* 1968, 2279)

Emphasizing Modesty: Reliance on the Free Market. Schneider and Ingram theorize that to succeed in promoting a policy, legislators must develop a rationale that links problem definition, target groups, and policy design. The rationale must explain how a particular policy design allocates benefits and burdens in a way congruent with target group images and in a way that will mitigate a particular social problem. Prior to 1968, civil rights opponents challenged the logic of fair housing proposals, which always exempted some housing. They called these bills hypocritical for stating opposition to discrimination, but enabling so many individuals, exempt from coverage, to practice it. They also noted that states and cities with fair housing laws still had ghettos, which challenged supporters to explain how the modest bills they proposed would begin to solve the problems of housing discrimination and deteriorated neighborhoods. In the past, supporters responded weakly by noting that the bills' exemptions were political compromises.

In 1968 when fair housing supporters constructed the target group of the black middle class, however, they were able to build a policy rationale using free-market rhetoric to weave together the elements of their argument and to encompass elements of the opposition argument. Using the free-market concept enabled advocates to tell two stories at once: that fair housing law would *and* would not bring social change. In particular, they could say (to blacks): Removing race from the housing transaction will make housing available to all. But they also could say (to whites): Economic inequality means that few black families will move into white neighborhoods.

In stating that fair housing law was insufficient to break up the urban ghettos, supporters answered the critique that fair housing law would not work: They made the proposal's promise of ineffectiveness a reason to support it. Senator Mondale articulates this story here:

the basic purpose of this legislation is to permit people who have the ability to do so to buy any house offered to the public if they can afford to buy it. It would not overcome the economic problem of those who could not afford to purchase the house of their choice. (*Congressional Record* 1968, 3421)

The notion of the free market thus pulled together two narratives into a plausible policy rationale. Indeed, Table 4.1 shows that about a quarter of supporters' statements articulated this logic. On the one hand, supporters could emphasize that fair housing law would correct the problems of segregation and discrimination by eliminating the dual housing market, enabling blacks and whites to have equal opportunity to all housing. They argued that this change in the terms of housing supply was a crucial step toward addressing the problems of the ghetto. On the other hand, supporters acknowledged that removing race from the housing transaction would leave in place the racial economic gap. Characteristics of housing demand would remain untouched and only those black families who could afford to leave the ghetto would be able to do so. Supporters claimed this was a small group, and opponents, in the meantime, proposed no alternative solution to the riots and the ghettos.

The Fair Housing Policy Design

Key elements of the policy design within the *Fair Housing Act* reflect the discourse supporters used to promote passage in a hostile political context. Burdens on powerful groups are undersubscribed, as are benefits to weaker groups. The statute focuses on the private housing market, reflecting the discourse on free market processes and middle-class blacks. The design also includes mechanisms that hinder the policy from reducing housing discrimination and segregation, supporting the story told by fair housing supporters that fair housing law would not lead to drastic change.

Table 4.2 outlines the framework of the Fair Housing policy design. Broadly, the law prohibits racial discrimination in housing transactions, from rental and sales to lending, insurance, and appraisals. It delineates a set of prohibited practices and directs the U.S. Department of Housing and Urban Development (HUD) to establish a process for taking, investigating, and conciliating claims. The law also establishes the right of private citizens to file suit in federal court.

Undersubscribed Burdens and Benefits. Schneider and Ingram predict that when legislators succeed in channeling benefits to weak groups, the benefits will be undersubscribed and provided at levels insufficient to remediate the group's problems. Similarly, burdens conferred on advantaged groups are likely to be undersubscribed and conferred at levels insufficient to change behavior to an extent that would remediate the problem. While supporters created the new target group of middle-class blacks to justify providing them benefits, they still faced the difficulty of imposing burdens on politically powerful, white homeowners and the housing industry (who tended to be portrayed in positive terms).

The *Fair Housing Act* covered all housing except small, owner-occupied multifamily dwellings and single-family homes sold without a real estate agent. This coverage was broader than that in an earlier bill, but unfolded in three stages. Blacks benefitted from the *Fair Housing Act*'s relatively broad coverage,

TABLE 4.2

1968 Fair Housing Policy Design and 1977 Community Reinvestment Design

Policy Type	Fair Housing	Community Reinvestment
	Civil Rights	Regulatory
Goals	1. To protect civil rights 2. To provide subsidized housing on a nondiscriminatory basis	To encourage banks to meet community credit needs (and to limit redlining)
Target Groups		
Benefits	Protected class of individuals: Race, national origin, religion	Places: Low- and moderate-income neighborhoods
Burdens	1. Housing industry (real estate agents, landlords, developers, leasing agents, lending institutions, insurance companies) 2. Most homeowners 3. Federal government (HUD and participants in federal housing programs)	Federally regulated banks and savings and loan associations
Enforcement Structure		
Agents	1. Department of Housing and Urban Development 2. Department of Justice (DOJ)	1. Federal Home Loan Bank Board 2. Comptroller of the Currency 3. Federal Reserve Board

(continued on next page)

TABLE 4.2 *(continued)*

Policy Type	Fair Housing Civil Rights	Community Reinvestment Regulatory
	3. State and Local Civil Rights Agencies (with substantially equivalent laws)	4. Federal Deposit Insurance Corporation
Rules	Prohibits specified discriminatory practices Covers most housing after three years Requires HUD to operate programs so as to "affirmatively further" fair housing	"Convenience and needs" means credit needs Lenders have "continuing, affirmative obligation to help meet the credit needs of local communities"
Tools	Complaint process, conciliation efforts (HUD) Work with housing industry (HUD) Private litigation (Individuals) Pattern and practice suits (DOJ)	CRA Examination (assess record of community reinvestment) (Home Mortgage Disclosure Act [HMDA] data available) Application review process
Discretion	Relatively low on Goal 1, high on Goal 2	High
Funding	Authorized, not guaranteed	None

Sources: P.L. 90–284, P.L. 95–128

but gradual implementation tempered the gain; only after three years would most housing be covered.

The *Fair Housing Act* assigned administrative enforcement authority to HUD, allowing the agency to investigate complaints received but not to initiate investigations. Agency officials had to rely on "conference, conciliation, and persuasion" with the guilty party. HUD's power to issue injunctions and restraining orders against offenders, and to use the courts to enforce them, had been removed from the bill in negotiations with Senator Everett Dirksen. Also in the final version, HUD was directed to convene with representatives of the housing industry to discuss implementation procedures and caps were placed on the level of damages that courts could award victorious plaintiffs. Stronger enforcement authority for HUD would have benefitted blacks by enabling government to find and sanction discriminatory behavior. Conversely, such mechanisms would have burdened whites by subjecting them to legal action and punishment. In a sense, blacks had the burden of enforcing the law themselves, because they had to bring claims to HUD or to the courts to set enforcement in motion.

Schneider and Ingram suggest that policy designs inform target groups of their status as citizens, telling them "whether they are atomized individuals who must deal directly with government and bureaucracy to press their own claims, or participants in a cooperative process joining with others to solve problems collectively" (1993, 341). The *Fair Housing Act* designates blacks as the former. Although designers wanted to address the problem of housing discrimination, they also took care not to overburden the people whose behavior they wanted to change.

Private-sector Housing and Middle-class Blacks. The fair housing policy design offers more resources to middle-class than to low-income minorities and it targets private-sector housing more directly than public-sector housing. This emphasis is consistent with the free-market rhetoric fair housing proponents used, as well as their construction of middle-class blacks as the target group who would benefit from fair housing law. The bulk of the statute consists of rules and tools designed to minimize racial discrimination against individual home seekers, by working to eliminate it from housing transactions in the private sector, such as agent-client relations and mortgage-lending decisions. It specifies which practices are prohibited, directs HUD to establish a process to receive complaints, and authorizes individuals to file lawsuits in federal, state, and local courts. Structurally, middle-class blacks stood to benefit more from these rules and tools than low-income blacks since they were likely to have the resources, both educational and financial, to engage in the complaint process or to file a civil lawsuit.

One short section of the statute addresses public-sector housing. Section 808 requires HUD to integrate "fair housing" into its existing housing pro-

grams "in a manner to affirmatively further the purposes of this title," direct-
ing attention to the operating procedures and outcomes of federal programs
(such as public housing and FHA loan guarantees). Whereas the fair housing
statute is quite detailed in its delineation of the enforcement process for the
private sector, it offers no guidance on how HUD is to incorporate fair
housing into its own housing programs. This higher level of discretion results
in more variation in how HUD defines the "affirmatively further" requirement. The degree to which fair housing law has benefitted low-income
blacks, who rely on subsidized housing, thus varies according to federal
commitment and leadership.

Ensuring Gradual (and Minimal) Change. Finally, the debate's double narrative of
stasis and change emerged in the policy design. On the one hand, the statute
asserted the message of equal opportunity by covering most housing and by
outlawing practices that obstructed access to housing. At the same time, the
degree to which burdens and benefits were undersubscribed worked to limit
change, because the policy offered neither severe sanctions to deter those
engaging in discriminatory practice nor adequate resources to blacks or to
HUD to enforce the provisions aggressively. The staged introduction of
dwellings to be covered under the law also prevented the law from immediately
increasing the housing supply for blacks. Finally, the law's judicial and administrative processes are complex and slow, thus the likelihood of solving a com-
plainant's immediate housing problem is low. This delay serves to slow the
degree to which the policy directly acts as a vehicle of achieving integrated living patterns.

COMMUNITY REINVESTMENT:
A PLACE-BASED APPROACH TO DISCRIMINATION

The *Community Reinvestment Act of 1977* is a regulatory policy aimed at
reducing lending discrimination against places ("redlining") by placing an
affirmative responsibility on banks to serve all portions of their markets,
including low-income neighborhoods. The context in which Congressional
supporters worked to secure its passage in 1977 was neither as hostile nor as
emotional as that of fair housing. By the late 1970s, Democratic supporters
held the positions of power in Congress that fair housing's opponents had
controlled ten years earlier. Sponsors used these positions to limit the visibility and controversy surrounding the community reinvestment measure. Legislators avoided the "degenerative politics" that had marked fair housing discourse by remaining silent about the people who would benefit from the
CRA, including the racial minorities who resided in many of the neighborhoods at stake.

Issue Context: Fertile Ground for Community Reinvestment

Community reinvestment policy was debated in the midst of profound changes in the American urban landscape, as Northeast and Midwest metropolitan areas lost population and jobs, while Southern, and especially Southwestern, cities grew. This trend was unsettling (especially to those in the declining areas) because it followed one hundred years of "consistent expansion" in urban areas (Mollenkopf 1983, 213). Accompanying these changes was continued and accelerated suburbanization within metro areas—Northern and Midwestern central cities especially suffered. During the 1970s, many central cities lost population. Those remaining tended to be poorer and less educated than their suburban counterparts. The recession of 1973–1975 compounded these problems. Uneven development deepened within central cities. Federal urban and housing policies, combined with local officials' desire to attract middle-class residents and business, resulted in demolition of low-income housing and its replacement with office complexes or luxury housing or both. In the 1970s, gentrification began to occur in some urban neighborhoods, also displacing poor people.

Federal urban and housing policy was in flux; a new role for the federal government was emerging that focused on local decision-making and public-private partnerships. The Nixon Administration had directed the consolidation of urban and housing programs into a block grant program that emphasized local discretion. President Jimmy Carter focused on community development and programs that encouraged partnerships between business and local government. Policy makers, scholars, and activists were beginning to emphasize the role of the private sector in shaping the urban landscape.

Passage of the *Home Mortgage Disclosure Act of 1975* (HMDA) had placed the issue of redlining on the federal agenda. The HMDA debate introduced the notion that lending patterns were linked to trajectories of neighborhood decline. Whereas legislators in the fair housing battle were trying to pass a bill that had failed repeatedly in Congress, legislators supporting community reinvestment policy were building on the success of the HMDA. This disclosure law was controversial and the votes were close (*Congressional Quarterly Almanac* 1975). At that time, legislators argued that consumers had a right to know a bank's lending patterns when deciding where to open an account. If a bank used the deposits of inner-city neighborhood residents to make loans in the suburbs, urban residents might choose to place their savings elsewhere, into a bank that "reinvested" in their community. While lenders denied that they redlined, by 1977 they were less able to make that claim, as the first rounds of disclosure data were showing uneven lending patterns (Christiano 1995).

The groups who would be affected by community reinvestment policy had different degrees of political power and different allies in government. Civil rights and neighborhood advocates had first raised the issue of redlining. The community reinvestment movement emerged in particular neighborhoods in a handful of states, when advocates began to protest banks at the local and state levels—several states adopted anti-redlining legislation. In 1975, these groups, led by National People's Action in Chicago, took the issue to Congress and found allies among Democratic legislators from urban districts. They convinced Senator William Proxmire (D-Wisc.), chair of the Senate committee on Banking, Housing, and Urban Affairs, to support anti-redlining proposals (Christiano 1995). He became the primary spokesperson for the CRA.

In contrast to grassroots activists, financial institutions enjoy a privileged structural position because they are understood as critical engines of the U.S. free-market economy. Bankers tend to view consumer regulation as burdensome and invasive (Khademian 1996). Federal regulators consider consumer compliance issues such as community reinvestment secondary to their mission of ensuring the economic viability of financial institutions (1996). Regulators opposed the CRA in letters and testimony to Congress (U.S. Senate 1977). The banking lobby did not spearhead a major campaign against the bill, although when it was debated on the Senate floor, senators received phone calls from their own bankers to express opposition.

In the mid-1970s, Democrats enjoyed strong majorities in both chambers of Congress. This was the peak of Democratic strength since backlash from the civil rights era had reduced Democratic ranks in the mid-1960s. More important for the CRA was the committee system, where specialization and norms of deference give small sets of senators and representatives control over policy arenas. Policies on banking regulation tends to have low visibility—it is perceived as technical and complex and relatively few congressional members are eager to work on the issue. Those members who do specialize thus have a high degree of influence. Ranking Democrats on the Senate Banking, Housing, and Urban Affairs Committee supported the CRA.

Leaders in Congress used rules to limit debate and participation. The CRA was debated only in the Senate, with very few legislators present. Committee members added the CRA to the 1977 Housing and Community Development bill, which included controversial changes in the allocation formula for the Community Development Block Grant (CDBG) program, directly affecting the amount of money flowing to members' districts. Conflict over the CDBG led to a deadlock in the Conference Committee that required Congress to pass two stopgap funding measures. By the time the Conference Committee reported the *Housing and Community Development Act,* there was little interest in further delay to reconsider the CRA provision, even though a handful of members continued to oppose it (Christiano 1995; U.S. House 1977).

Dynamics of the Design Process

While community reinvestment supporters in Congress faced the political challenge of channeling benefits to weak groups and burdens to strong ones,

the 1977 issue context held greater prospects for success than fair housing in
the late 1960s. Supporters could frame the policy to mesh with an emerging
concern about urban decline. The key positions of power they held in a Democratic Congress enabled them to use institutional rules to their advantage, off-
setting the systemic power enjoyed by the banking industry and by federal regulators. They were able to restrict the scope of conflict by limiting the proposal's
visibility. The Conference Committee reported the bill by a 7–7 vote, with four
senators appending additional views stating their opposition to the CRA (U.S.
Senate 1977); this suggests that if the CRA title had received more attention,
it may have attracted more opposition.

The following analysis of Senate debate on community reinvestment draws
from data summarized in Table 4.3. The issue did not draw attention from legislators outside the reporting committee. Only seven senators spoke—two in
favor of the CRA, five against it—and all were committee members. Most
remarks were made when Senator Robert Morgan (D-NC) introduced an
amendment to strike the CRA from the bill. Few legislators were present;
Morgan refers to three. Although limited, the debate does offer the chance to
examine the rhetorical strategy supporters used to promote the CRA and to
consider how the stories they told influenced the policy design that emerged.
Supporters nested the issue within the larger problem of urban decline and
portrayed the bill as a clarification of existing regulations. Most statements concerned the regulators or lenders, with less attention given to the neighborhoods
that would benefit from the law. Additionally, no attention was given to individual beneficiaries or to the advocacy organizations poised to use it as a tool
in their communities.

Focus on Regulators: Policy Clarification not Policy Change. Consistent with Schneider and Ingram's expectations, the politically powerful groups whom the law
would burden received the most attention. Speakers referred in nearly every
statement to the regulatory agencies that would enforce the law. A cornerstone
of the supporters' rhetorical strategy was the suggestion that the CRA was a
modest alteration of the existing framework of regulations governing financial
institutions. Also, it would require regulators to make only limited changes in
their examination and charter-approval procedures. Law dating from 1935 gov-
erns the bank charter approval and renewal processes, requiring regulators to
ensure that financial institutions meet "the convenience and needs" of local
communities. CRA supporters argued that their bill clarified rather than
changed this policy, by specifying that Congress defined "convenience and
needs" as credit needs, in addition to the depository needs that examiners routinely assessed. According to Senator Proxmire, the CRA would "reaffirm" that
"convenience and needs does not just mean drive-in teller windows and
Christmas Club accounts"—that is, diversified depository products and services—"It means loans" (U.S. Senate 1977, 17630).

Linking Banks to Neighborhood Decline. The supporters' rationale for the allocation of burdens and benefits by the CRA rested on a negative portrayal of
financial institutions ("contenders") and the depiction of urban neighborhoods
as victims that would benefit from the law—places are targets, not people. The
story drew on ideas and images of the emerging landscape of urban America,
with its declining Northern cities and the emerging paradigm of urban policy
that brought together the public and private sectors. Although supporters
blamed banks for neighborhood decline, they emphasized that the CRA remedy was meant to encourage change through incentives rather than to harshly
punish infractions. As Senator Proxmire said, "Bankers sit right at the heart of
our economic system . . . the record shows we have to do something *to nudge
them, influence them, persuade them* to invest in their community" (U.S. Senate
1977, 17630 [emphasis added]).

Supporters contrasted rich financial institutions with poor, older, urban
communities and claimed that banks caused urban blight by redlining these
neighborhoods. In 44 percent of their statements, supporters claimed that the
refusal of banks to make loans in old neighborhoods resulted in decay. Additionally, the willingness of banks to accept deposits from the same community
where they refused to extend credit was especially unjust. Supporters sometimes noted that U.S. banks loaned money in foreign countries. Senator Proxmire read a letter from a banker defending his institution's loans to developing
countries with "urgent economic development needs." "What about the urgent
economic development needs in Detroit, Philadelphia, Baltimore, and Boston?"
Proxmire asked. "The banking industry must be encouraged to reinvest in local
needs rather than continuing to favor speculative loans to shaky foreign
regimes." (U.S. Senate 1977, 17630). Focusing on lenders made sense from a
practical perspective as well; according to Proxmire, "The banks and savings and
loans have the funds. . . . If we are going to rebuild our cities, it will have to be
done with the private institutions" (17603).

Opponents focused on contesting the role financial institutions played
in urban decline and characterized the CRA as an unacceptable intervention in the free market. They described bank lending policies as rational
market responses to a complex set of forces. Senator John Tower blamed
local government for blight, noting that inner-city neighborhoods did not
receive adequate public services—such as schools, street maintenance,
garbage removal, and public transportation (U.S. Senate 1977, 17633).
Opponents charged that the CRA would chase banks out of urban neighborhoods. When forced to make risky loans, banks would choose to pull out
of the community altogether. The community reinvestment title smacked of
"credit allocation," opponents claimed—a practice antithetical and dangerous to the free market. But the solutions they preferred tended to depend
on government subsidy and, thus, were out of synch with new ideas about
solving urban problems.

TABLE 4.3
Community Reinvestment Debate 1977 (Senate): Target Group Images and Policy Rationales
(Percents are column percents)

Target Groups	Legislators	
	Supporters	Opponents
Financial Institutions	44% of statements Neglect local communities; take $ from community and invest elsewhere (engage in redlining). Resource-rich; ignore responsibility; need "encouragement." *Valence: Negative*	38% of statements Financial institutions reallocate $ from affluent neighborhoods to poor ones. Should not be forced to make risky loans. *Valence: Positive*
Neighborhoods	33% Older, urban neighborhoods suffer from denied credit; resource-poor. *Valence: Positive*	23% Older urban neighborhoods suffer from multiple problems emerging from complex process. *Valence: Neutral / Positive*
Agent Regulatory Agencies	89% CRA simply asks regulators to consider reinvestment as one part of application process. They do not do this now, despite "convenience and needs" requirement; reluctant to address redlining issues. *Valence: Negative*	69% Agencies already assess responsiveness to community ("convenience and needs"). CRA would overburden with more regulations & work. *Valence: Positive*

(continued on next page)

TABLE 4.3 *(continued)*

Target Groups	Legislators	
	Supporters	Opponents
Rationale	33%	69%
	Low-cost solution; govt. needs private sector to solve inner-city problems; govt. grants privileges to fin. inst. w/charter and fin. inst. have public responsibilities.	CRA would overburden financial institutions and regulatory agencies—"mountain of paperwork"; govt. should not undertake credit allocation; existing laws address issue; ambiguity of language is problematic.
Policy Logic	11%	31%
	Disinvestment by financial institutions causes neighborhood decline; reinvestment will lead to neighborhood revitalization.	CRA would further deprive neighborhoods by discouraging banking activity within them. Sanctions not severe enough to change behavior.
Number of Statements	9	13

Source: Congressional Record, June 6, 1977

A Strategy of Omission: Activists and Racial Minorities. As supporters and opponents of the CRA argued over the role of banks in urban decline and whether federal banking regulators were adequately assessing the banks' lending records and thrifts, they kept silent about two groups that would benefit from the proposed legislation: community activists and racial minorities. I suggest that this silence contributed to the proposal's low visibility. Neighborhood organizations and civil rights groups had put redlining on the political agenda, both at the local and national levels (Christiano 1995; Squires 1992). Grassroots activists had testified at Senate hearings on the proposal and had helped draft the bill. They anticipated using the law in their communities and offered suggestions to the Senate committee about how to make it more effective. They had been active in the legislative effort that led to the *Home Mortgage Disclosure Act of 1975.* Yet, nowhere in the Senate debate do legislators mention the work of community organizations, who were likely to challenge banks and regulators in communities across the country. Rather, legislators focused on the formal agents who would be charged with implementing the law—the federal regulators.

Discourse about the CRA focused on class rather then race. Activists understood the redlining problem to be motivated by racial and class bias (Squires 1992). Activists themselves were racially diverse. The CRA could not be categorized as exclusively a black or Latino issue, even though many racial minorities stood to benefit from it. Low and moderate incomes were what constituents had in common. In Senate hearings, activists talked about class and race. Their testimony described the neighborhoods suffering from redlining as racially diverse and their stories of struggles with banks in their cities described individuals—many of them black—who were denied loans by local banks (U.S. Senate 1977, e.g., statements by Ralph Nader, Gale Cincotta, Conrad Weiler, Ronald Grzywinski).

On the Senate floor, however, legislators refer to race only once. By framing the beneficiaries of the CRA as places rather than people, senators avoided discussion of the deservedness of individual beneficiaries that had marked fair housing debates. The CRA would contribute to revitalizing declining cities and neighborhoods, according to legislators; they did not speak of it as a special program that would channel loans to poor people and minorities. Nesting the CRA in an existing regulatory framework enabled this depersonalization, because the language of banking regulations required chartered financial institutions to meet the convenience and needs of *communities,* not explicitly of individual consumers. The *Home Mortgage Disclosure Act* similarly had required banks to report lending data by neighborhood (census tract), not by individual.

Community Reinvestment Policy Design

Features of the *Community Reinvestment Act* reflect the stories supporters told about the bill and, to some extent, address the concerns raised by opponents.

Like the debate itself, the community reinvestment statute lacks visibility; it is a short title in a long piece of legislation focused primarily on housing and community development programs (P.L. 95–128). As Table 4.2 shows, the CRA includes no funding authorization, no specific mandates or sanctions. It directs federal regulatory agencies to include in their bank examinations an assessment of how well an institution meets the credit needs of low-income neighborhoods. Additionally, the agencies would take this record into account when considering applications for branches, insurance, mergers, and acquisitions.

An Inherited Design: Implications for Agents and Targets. The *Community Reinvestment Act* mobilized a preexisting framework to address the problem of lending discrimination, or redlining. In doing so, it inherited several features of that framework, including the orientations and priorities of regulators and a set of target groups. As emphasized by supporters during debate, the CRA modified the regulations governing nationally chartered or insured financial institutions. The Act used the language of previous banking regulation, as it clarified the definition of "convenience and needs" to mean credit needs. It also directed regulatory agencies to encourage community lending "consistent with the safe and sound operation" of local banks.

The CRA assigned responsibility for implementation to the four agencies that already were responsible for banking regulation: the Comptroller of the Currency, the Federal Reserve Board, the Federal Deposit Insurance Corporation, and the Federal Home Loan Bank Board (now the Office of Thrift Supervision). These agencies examine banks regularly, assessing management practices and balance sheets, essentially judging whether banks are economically viable or whether they operate with too much risk. Banks must apply for permission to receive federal insurance, to add branches, and to merge with or acquire other banks. The CRA folded one more task into the regulatory process.

Across the agencies, regulators tend to view consumer compliance issues, such as community investment, as secondary to their missions and bothersome to enforce (Khademian 1996). Although the agencies share a basic mission— and a negative view of regulations—they vary greatly in management and oversight styles, in examination cycles, and in their autonomy from elected officials (1996). Assigning implementation of the CRA to four regulatory bodies meant the law would be enforced in four ways and that subsequent efforts to modify enforcement must change the behavior of four sets of civil servants. A final implication of using the existing regulatory system to address redlining was that only banks falling under the jurisdiction of these four agencies must comply with the law; the CRA thus applies to depository institutions, but not to other financial institutions, including mortgage companies and credit unions.

Undersubscribed Burdens and Benefits. The CRA can be understood as a victory for constituencies concerned about redlining, for the rhetorical strategy supporters used, and for the effort to limit the visibility of the title. It also entailed

a policy design that minimized burdens to financial institutions (and to regulators) and minimized benefits to poor neighborhoods. Rather than debating
how to ensure maximum benefits for deteriorating neighborhoods, legislators
argued about whether the law would impose unacceptably high burdens on
lenders and regulators. Supporters claimed that the CRA only clarified existing law without requiring additional reporting or regulatory procedures. With
each version of the bill, this argument became more true.

The original version had directed lenders to delineate a "primary savings
service area," analyze its credit and deposit needs, indicate the percentage of
deposits that would be reinvested in the area, and demonstrate what it was
already doing to meet credit needs. Lenders would have had to report period-
ically the amount of credit extended in the service area. Regulators were to use
these reports when considering applications from banks for opening new
branches, conducting mergers, and so forth.

In Senate hearings on this original bill, community advocates objected to
what they saw as a high level of regulatory discretion, asking for more specific
directions to regulators about what to look for and what to demand of banks.
But in the second version of the bill, lenders' reporting requirements were
eliminated, as was reference to calculating the portion of deposits that would
be reinvested. This latter deletion bolstered the supporters' claims that the CRA
would not allocate credit. In the final version, the regulators received the burden of assessing an institution's lending record and were directed to take the
record into account when evaluating applications. However, the CRA minimized this burden by leaving discretion to regulators. Nothing in the law's text
indicated what would constitute such an assessment, or the weight regulators
should give it when considering a bank's request to branch, merge, and so forth.
The CRA contained no funding authorization—regulators would receive no
special appropriations to carry out this new responsibility, confirming the supporters' assertions that this was neither new nor onerous, that regulators could
use data already disclosed by banks.

The CRA also minimized burdens on lenders and regulators by its lack of
explicit sanctions for noncompliance. The implicit threat to lenders was that
regulators could decide to deny an application for a merger if an institution had
a poor record of community lending, but the CRA did not include any specific rules about this. Rather, its language directed regulators to "encourage"
lenders to attend to the credit needs of low- and moderate-income neighborhoods. Indeed, Schneider and Ingram predict that powerful groups, when they
receive burdens, do so through the use of incentives rather than punishment.

Beneficiaries. During legislative debate, Congressional supporters made clear that
the CRA was intended to help deteriorated inner-city neighborhoods that
community advocates described as poor and working-class, racially diverse
communities. The initial version of the law identified the beneficiary as a "pri-

mary savings service area" defined by each lending institution. Opponents complained of this concept's vagueness. In the final version, as legislators reduced reporting requirements, they defined the beneficiary more explicitly. Regulators were required to consider banks' lending records to the low- and moderate-income neighborhoods within their communities.

Despite their awareness of the work of community organizations on redlining issues, CRA supporters chose to keep silent about these groups during Senate debate. The first version of the law directed regulators to encourage consumer organizations to testify on the lending records of local banks. During the Senate hearings, activists urged legislators to go further and to expand the role groups could play by giving them authority to sue lenders and regulators for failure to comply with the law. Instead, the mention of community groups was eliminated from subsequent versions of the bill. Regulations already required that a public comment period accompany bank application reviews, so groups would be able to intervene that way.

POLICY FEEDBACK: THE INFLUENCE OF POLICY DESIGNS ON POLITICS

The analysis thus far has shown that at two critical moments in history, legislators successfully navigated the obstacles to enacting laws to reduce housing discrimination. That is, they were able to channel significant benefits to politically weak groups. Faced with different political contexts, legislators developed different strategies for winning votes. These strategies shaped the policy designs that emerged. In different ways, the *Fair Housing Act* and the *Community Reinvestment Act* tempered benefits to racial minorities by limiting burdens on powerful industry groups.

Schneider and Ingram and other scholars argue that understanding the structure of policy designs matters because these designs channel subsequent politics and problem-solving efforts. Fair housing and community reinvestment policies set in motion a range of programs, as well as subsequent amendments, designed to reduce discrimination. Since 1968, we see signs of progress and signs of persistent problems. Most Americans now know about civil rights protections in the housing market, and HUD receives thousands of complaints every year. The Department of Justice's litigation in fair lending and fair housing has brought nearly $40 million in relief and civil penalties, while private lawsuits brought $115 million in relief between 1990 and 1998 (Lee 1999). Research, however, documents a lack of confidence in fair housing law, with most people who think they have been victims reporting that they do nothing about it (Abravanel and Cunningham 2002).

A recent national study found a lower incidence of discriminatory treatment than it had found ten years earlier, although it estimates that half of minority home seekers experience some form of adverse treatment (Turner et al. 2002). Home loans to minority and low-income borrowers are rising, as are home ownership rates, but disparities in lending persist between whites and people of color (Joint Center for Housing Studies 2002). Studies link the CRA to regulated banks' higher rates of lending and service to low- and moderate-income people and neighborhoods. Yet, growing proportions of mortgage loans are made by lenders not subject to the CRA and some banks have rolled back earlier CRA commitments (2002).

Fair housing and community reinvestment politics have taken divergent turns. Fair housing politics has become deracialized and "fair housing" is increasingly understood as an individual right, while attention to segregated housing patterns has declined. Community reinvestment politics has grown increasingly contentious and degenerative. These developments show that the political project of achieving racial justice faces persistent challenges, although the nature of these challenges varies across policies and issues.

Fair Housing Politics Post-1968: The Rise of New Target Groups

Advocates attempting to strengthen the 1968 law were successful twenty years later, when Congress passed the *Fair Housing Amendments Act of 1988*. In addition to granting HUD broader enforcement powers and removing caps on legal damages, the amendments added two new protected classes: the disabled and families with children. In 1968, target-group images were at the center of debate, as supporters and opponents offered contrasting images of white home-owners and black home seekers. In 1988, new target groups took center stage. In much of the debate, legislators struggled to define "disability." In the House, about 20 percent of legislators' statements and in the Senate nearly 50 percent of statements articulated categories of deserving and undeserving disabled people. Thus, the law exempted users of illegal drugs and transvestites from protection against housing discrimination. Legislators also debated the rights of the elderly vis-à-vis families with children. In about one-third of their statements, they questioned whether the preference of some elderly people to live with other seniors constituted discrimination against families with children. The final policy exempted senior housing.

Legislators used new target groups to bolster their argument for strengthening fair housing enforcement. They emphasized that these new targets needed protection from discrimination and that current law was ill-equipped to offer it. As the number of target groups grew, discussion of racial minorities declined. In the House, about 13 percent of legislators' statements mentioned these groups, though in the Senate about 30 percent of the statements included reference to minorities. Also striking was the nearly complete silence about segregation, which had been a focus of the 1968 debates, as legislators disputed the meaning of and response to urban ghettos. Although levels of racial segregation in housing remained high in 1988, only 3 percent of Representatives' statements and 1 percent of Senators' statements mentioned it as a rationale for strengthening fair housing law.

Fair housing debate thus became deracialized to some degree, as racial minorities became only one of a wider set of protected classes. The dominant definition of "fair housing" in the original design (nondiscrimination against individuals in private housing transactions) became more deeply entrenched, as discussion of segregation as a salient dimension of the problem fell away. Advocates for new target groups, primarily disability rights advocates, boosted the political power of civil rights groups lobbying to strengthen fair housing law. The amendments gave HUD much greater authority but did not increase its resources, thus necessarily diluting the amount of attention the agency could devote to racial discrimination, now that it also worked on ensuring that housing be accessible to the disabled. Consequently, undersubscription of benefits to target groups continues. More generally, the original policy design's parameters did place boundaries on subsequent legislative consideration of how to combat housing discrimination. Advocates and legislators debated how and whether to strengthen the existing mechanisms of investigating and punishing discrimination in individual transactions, rather than considering the many other causes of discrimination and segregation that drive housing inequality. The fair housing policy design has "locked in" a particular approach to the problem of housing discrimination.

Amending Community Reinvestment:
Toward Degenerative Target-group Politics

The initial debate on community reinvestment focused only in part on target-group images. Supporters and opponents offered conflicting images of banks as rich actors contributing to neighborhood decline or as rational free-marketeers contributing to the national economy. Legislators avoided discussion of who exactly would benefit from the CRA, focusing instead on the physical condition of neighborhoods—places, not people. But over time, the human beneficiaries have become visible. Supporters and opponents of the CRA now offer competing images of who wins. Supporters tell stories of families who have purchased homes, entrepreneurs who have started businesses, community organizations that have built affordable housing—adding up to the turnaround of declining urban neighborhoods and small towns. Opponents paint community groups as illegitimate beneficiaries of the CRA who threaten local banks until they are "bribed" with grants and loans. The CRA design created no explicit role for community groups or citizens in enforcement. This omission enabled opponents to question the legitimacy of such activity later on.

Debate and passage of the *Gramm-Leach-Bliley Financial Modernization Act of 1999* (GLBA) occurred in a political context hostile to the CRA and the law included measures that weakened it. The GLBA altered the regulatory framework for financial institutions by, as supporters noted, "tearing down the firewalls" established after the Depression between different sectors of the financial services industry—securities, banking, and insurance. It set the stage for companies to offer "one-stop shopping" for financial services. The CRA became relevant because legislators and advocates asked what the community reinvestment obligations would be of these new financial creatures, some of which engage in activities not covered by the CRA. The law's final version stated that before banks could acquire or affiliate with securities or insurance companies, they had to have a "satisfactory" CRA rating—the second highest of four ratings. This is a much weaker provision than community advocates sought and also weaker than provisions included in earlier versions of the bill.

But most relevant here is that the GLBA "shines sunlight" onto community groups who engage in CRA advocacy. Its sunshine provision requires public disclosure of agreements that groups have with banks and annual reporting of how they use these funds. Although regulators are forbidden from enforcing these agreements, they can declare them null and void if community groups do not comply with disclosure and they can compel groups to return any funds received. Note that the initial law made no mention of community groups at all; here, however, regulations are imposed upon them. Although CRA debate was nearly invisible in 1977, the opposite was true in 1999. Conflict over the CRA provision held up passage of the GLBA and involved top officials in the Clinton Administration.

Whether these new regulations will prove onerous to community groups or discourage advocacy remains to be seen. But what is interesting is that the original legislative strategy framing the CRA as a minor change to existing law precluded at that time the creation of a new and explicit role for community groups. Instead, groups wanting to participate in CRA enforcement have become adept at using the public comment process generally available for banking regulation. Unlike other policies that establish nonprofits as partners with government, the CRA sets up advocacy groups as "shadow" implementers. When groups use the policy effectively, they risk becoming targets of criticism. In a political climate hostile to the CRA, as the Senate was in 1999, arguments that such advocacy was illegitimate were used to justify weakening the law.

IMPLICATIONS FOR RACIAL JUSTICE

Both the *Fair Housing Act of 1968* and the *Community Reinvestment Act of 1977* represent legislative victories in the effort to reduce housing discrimination. In each case, supporters overcame the structural bias against passage of such laws. They succeeded in channeling benefits to politically weak groups and burdens to politically powerful industries—broadly understood as important players in the private economy. But in each case, passage came at a price. The discursive strategies supporters used as they navigated distinctive issue contexts entailed modest policies with designs that limited in various and continuing ways the prospects for social change.

These designs set the stage for subsequent struggles against discrimination. In the case of fair housing, target-group politics continues as new groups and their advocates become involved. This process may dilute the government's attention to racial discrimination in housing, create competition between advocates for scarce resources, and privilege a focus on individual rights rather than the racially segregated housing patterns that continue to mark our cities. In the case of the CRA, the policy design threatens to destabilize the work of community groups advocating for the poor and for minority neighborhoods. Original efforts to minimize conflict and visibility cast a shadow of illegitimacy on the neighborhood actors, who now attempt to hold banks accountable to communities when regulators do not.

We can understand fair housing politics as an example of consistently degenerative target-group politics that limits government's ability to solve the problems of racial minorities. Community reinvestment supporters initially avoided this type of stereotyping, but opponents later injected it into the policy arena, thanks to elements of the original policy design. Opponents were thereby able to scale back an already modest policy. Whether or not a policy that advances racial justice is framed in racial terms, its benefits remain fragile and open to dilution or contestation.

5

"It Is Not a Question of Being Anti-immigration": Categories of Deservedness in Immigration Policy Making

LINA NEWTON

INTRODUCTION

Immigration policy making is an emotionally charged policy area. While the United States cherishes its identity as a nation of immigrants, cycles of xenophobic and racist reactions to immigrants characterize the nation's history and immigration policies. Generally, outbursts of anti-immigrant sentiment have involved a larger debate over (1) who is worthy of being considered for full incorporation into the nation and (2) who is incapable of assimilating and taking on the characteristics and responsibilities associated with full political and social membership.

Following the amendments that Congress made in 1965 to the *Immigration and Nationality Act of 1952,* it is no longer acceptable for immigration policies to single out groups for exclusion on the basis of race or national origin. Nonetheless, immigration policy continues to distinguish between the "right" and "wrong" kinds of immigrants. Currently, the designations of "right" and "wrong" kinds of immigrants are based on assumptions people share about who contributes to the welfare of the nation and who does not. As a result, today's immigration policies do not need to rely on exclusion of races or people of certain national origin.

Policy evaluation often focuses on the failure of immigration control policies to achieve objective goals. However, I argue that these laws need to be examined for how they continue to define and redefine the nation even when

139

Again pulling apart groups not + unity [handwritten marginalia]

they do not overtly target specific groups for exclusion. We can read official immigration rhetoric for its symbolic designations of groups either as potential citizens, or unassimilable aliens. Immigration policy-making language actually follows a much older American tradition of ascriptive citizenship, which socially and legally categorized some groups as *unqualified* for membership in the nation. In the past, the groups who have occupied these strata have been either native born (women, African Americans, Native Americans) or immigrant (the Chinese, for example), while the groups that have been deemed unassimilable have changed over time.

This tradition of classifying some as incapable of or undesirable for full civic inclusion has occurred through what Rogers Smith (1997) has termed "civic myths." According to Smith, these myths "explain why persons form a people" and specify who belongs to the nation and the dominant values to which members subscribe. Smith's book, *Civic Ideals,* confronts us with a view of citizenship that is nonlinear and that expands and contracts, again over time and in tandem with the changes that the country has encountered in its ethnic composition. Moreover, changing political circumstances force the reevaluation and redefinition of who is eligible for the rights and privileges of full political, social, and economic membership in the nation.

Smith's argument encourages us to view immigration law making as a component of civic myth making. Restrictionist immigration law-making that has typically occurred during times of anti-immigrant backlash involves the creation of a story that highlights the damage of immigration to the nation and to popular values. Similarly, stories that appeal to the nation as an open, immigrant-receiving nation rely on an alternate set of myths and symbols to communicate the ways in which immigrants have contributed to the nation. Both sets of stories enjoy broad resonance in the American context, and political elites manipulate the mythology and symbolism of immigration as they define who constitutes the nation, who makes significant social and economic contributions, and who is better kept out. In short, the policy-making process divides the immigrant population into those who are deserving and those who are undeserving of access to the nation.

Whether elected officials choose to portray immigrants as deserving of membership ultimately corresponds to how officials portray immigrants target groups as they advocate particular policy tools or designs. The relationship between immigrant target group constructions and policy designs follows the pattern that Schneider and Ingram predict in their social constructions of populations theory (1993, 1997). By communicating which immigrants embody values of hard work and self-sufficiency and which immigrants flaunt or undermine these values, official rhetoric and official policy construct immigrant groups positively or negatively in ways that emphasize their contributions to or detractions from American society.

Immigration Policy as a Testing Ground for Social Constructions Theory

Immigration is a key component of American national identity and scholars of American political culture have referred to our immigration history as the cornerstone of the nation's prosperity and the test of the strength of Constitutional and pluralist ideals (Barber 1992; Walzer 1992). At the same time, during periods of economic recession, immigrants have been depicted as stealing jobs from citizens, driving down wages, or as culturally and morally incapable of adopting the "American way" of life.[1]

These social constructions of immigrants, both positive and negative, have become a part of our national discourse on the issue. They also provide important political currency for elected officials, who have the skill and access to avenues of communication through which they can advance these constructions to serve their policy agendas. Politicians are aware that their constituents regularly evaluate their policy stances and, subsequently, expect that the rationales that they provide for their stances must resonate with the values of their peers and constituents (Arnold 1990).

Politicians can depict immigrants as either beneficial for the nation or detrimental to it because this group has, over time, been endowed with a host of positive and negative attributes that persist as social constructions. For example, the category "immigrant" is a legal designation for foreigners with a green card for permanent residence in the United States. Likewise, the category "illegal immigrant" is a legal designation for people who have entered the United States without inspection at a designated port of entry. However, both legal categories are also laden with social meanings which political officials can manipulate to generate support for preferred policy approaches.

Politicians construct immigrant groups in ways that resonate with the fears and hopes of their constituents.[2] Edelman's work on symbolic politics (1964, 1988) speaks to the function of imagery and language in political life and how these reduce politics and policy making to *condensation symbols*. The word "immigrant" serves as a powerful condensation symbol for economic uncertainty, high fertility rates, welfare usage, hard work, and the American dream that all evoke the United States as a nation of immigrants. Schneider and Ingram describe the activity of capitalizing upon images and myths associated with groups as the social construction of target populations (1993, 1997). In their theory of policy design, Schneider and Ingram argue that the type of policy that target groups receive—whether symbolic, punitive, or redistributive—is actually quite predictable, if analysts pay attention to whether target groups enjoy positive characterizations or are burdened with negative connotations. Immigration policy making provides a good test of social constructions theory because a history of both positive and negative social constructions exists for this target population.

Policy making is more than simply linking problems to available solutions. In order to choose among available approaches, lawmakers skillfully link problems and solutions in ways that tap into people's preexisting notions of who is to blame for a social crisis. Issues are not only strategically framed; certain issues often involve groups already defined in the broader society as problematic (Stone 1989). Given the historically ambivalent relationship between immigrants and their host society, U.S. legislators can easily bank on negative constructions that portray immigrants as troublesome, criminal, and deserving vigilant oversight, control, or expulsion.

BACKGROUND: IMMIGRATION REFORM AND CHANGING TACTICS, 1986–1996

Immigration control is about establishing a system of classification for foreigners seeking permanent residence in the United States. Legislators have structured this system of classification based on qualitative aspects, labor needs, and foreign policy considerations. Movements to reform or strengthen immigration controls generally emerge during times when economic downturn triggers anti-immigrant sentiment in a public fearful that immigrants take scarce jobs from Americans. Efforts to reform immigration, then, generally target immigrants for restriction and focus resources on the agencies that regulate their entry into and activities within the United States. These efforts often include new or adjusted mandates for the Immigration and Naturalization Service (INS) and the Border Patrol, which are then complemented with increased budgets. From a strictly descriptive vantage point, the 1996 *Illegal Immigration Reform and Immigrant Responsibility Act* (IIRAIRA), which also contained these stock components, differed little from past efforts at immigration reform.

However, when we look at the design of the 1996 IIRAIRA as an expression of a problem definition which resulted in specific assumptions and expectations about target groups, the IIRAIRA does differ significantly from other reform efforts—particularly its immediate predecessor, the *Immigration Reform and Control Act of 1986* (IRCA). The movement from IRCA to IIRAIRA, which occurred within the span of a decade, shows that something had fundamentally changed in legislators' understanding of what causes problem immigration as well as what course of action would best correct the problem. In order to fully appreciate the role of social constructions in immigration reform in 1996, a discussion of the 1986 IRCA provides a standard by which to gauge the power of target group constructions in immigration policy making.

Regulating Employers, Legalizing Illegals: The 1986 IRCA

The 1986 IRCA was a landmark in U.S. immigration policy. In addition to providing border enforcement measures, the law broke ground with a two-pronged approach to controlling undocumented immigration. First, the law would fine employers who hired ineligible foreign workers and, second, the law included provisions to legalize resident undocumented immigrants who could prove they had lived continuously in the United States and had entered the country before January 1, 1981.

Like other legislation intended to restrict immigration, the 1986 IRCA emerged from a context of anti-immigrant backlash. When the *Immigration and Nationality Act of 1952* and its 1965 amendments lifted many of the bans on Asian and Western hemisphere source countries, the face of immigration changed from European to Asian and Latin American. In tandem with this change in legal immigration, levels of illegal immigration swelled in the 1970s and 1980s, and public concern increasingly focused on stopping illegal crossings at the southern border with Mexico. In 1977 and 1980, *The New York Times* reported findings by the Gallup pollsters showing Americans as being strongly opposed to illegal immigration and favoring government initiatives to stop undocumented migrants, whom they accused of taking American jobs (1980). When the Reagan administration and a newly elected Congress came to office late in 1980, they pledged that they would respond to this public outcry by making immigration reform a priority.

With its passage, the *Immigration Reform and Control Act of 1986* represented a fundamental shift from past immigration restriction efforts in two important ways: (1) for the first time, immigration legislation would punish employers for their role in luring and hiring illegal foreign workers and, (2) the bill created an amnesty program for illegal immigrants who could demonstrate that they had been working and living continuously in the United States for five years. Although the law still targeted the INS and the Border Patrol for additional funding, IRCA signaled an important shift in the reading of the causes of illegal immigration. Until the IRCA, immigration control tools were selected to punish or deter the immigrants themselves for illicit entries. By contrast, the IRCA's sanction tools sought to change the behavior of employers. Of course, sanctions were also intended to serve as a deterrent to would-be undocumented immigrants by making it harder for them to secure employment in the United States. In order to avoid sanctions, employers would have to document their workers' eligibility for employment. The punitive employer sanctions tool, and the subsequent shift of illegal immigrants from direct to indirect targets for punishment, sent a new message about who was to blame for the crisis in illegal immigration.

The legalization provisions of the IRCA are remarkable as well. Also designed to stop illegal immigration, legalization offered those who could prove

continuous presence in the United States a chance to regularize their status, thus
freeing them from a surreptitious existence. The provision was highly controversial,
because many in Congress saw it as unduly benefitting people who had broken the
law and as eventually leading to more illegal immigration. Many feared such a step
would send the message to would-be immigrants that they could expect a chance
for legalization in the future. However, the passage of the IRCA with this component also recognized that some of these "illegals" had accrued social capital and
deserved the opportunity to continue working in the United States. Congressional
supporters of the provision emphasized that these were "hardworking" and "otherwise law-abiding" people with families who deserved to "live the American
dream." Supporters of amnesty argued that as an immigrant-receiving and humane
nation, the United States should extend the legalization opportunity to those who
could demonstrate this embeddedness. About three million illegal immigrants were
able to regularize their status in the United States through the IRCA's amnesty
provisions. Additionally, many of those who were legalized went on to apply for citizenship when they became eligible in the mid-1990s.

Employer sanctions, however, did not fare as well. Lax enforcement of
sanctions severely diminished their deterrent capacity and the INS agents
charged with investigating and administering fines were spread too thin to regulate employers effectively in industries known for illicit hiring. While immigration dropped off initially immediately following the passage of the IRCA,
research showed that the law had little success of significantly curbing illegal
immigration (Fix and Passel 1994). In fact, the extension of border enforcement
efforts with the IRCA is believed to have contributed to the number of resident illegal immigrants by making it more difficult for target-earners and sea-
sonal migrants to return to Mexico at the end of a migratory cycle (see
Durand, Massey, and Parrado 1999 for a summary of research).

Although the 1986 IRCA did not achieve its goal of reducing undocumented migration, it provided an important foil to its successor, the 1996
IIRAIRA. As we will see, the IIRAIRA provisions would invoke different
assumptions about who was to blame for illegal immigration and, therefore, who
should be targeted with punitive tools. Likewise, the 1996 law would redefine
how it was determined that immigrants were investing in society, who was
working, and who, therefore, deserved benefits administered through policy.

The 1996 IIRAIRA and the Limits to Immigrant Contributions

A decade after the failure of either sanctions or amnesty to end illegal immigration, the issue returned to the Congressional agenda. Following the passage
of welfare reform, the *Personal Responsibility and Work Opportunity Reconciliation
Act of 1996,* the emphasis on "personal responsibility" carried over into the
continued quest for immigration control. In 1996, Congress passed a bill
designed to crack down on illegal immigration as well as those immigrants

relying on public assistance. The bill called for stricter enforcement of employer sanctions and document verification provisions of the weak *Immigration Reform and Control Act of 1986.* Additional stipulations for securing the southern border included the extension of deterrence programs already operating along the border in San Diego, California (Operation Gatekeeper) and El Paso, Texas (Operation Hold the Line), which included repairing and reinforcing fences, as well as adding several thousand INS agents per year through fiscal year 2001. The law's expansion of Operation Gatekeeper represented the most comprehensive effort the U.S. government has undertaken to enforce its southern border since the establishment of the U.S. Border Patrol in 1924.[3] In combination with the 1996 welfare reform package, IIRAIRA was also the first time federal law addressed the argument that access to public benefits played a role in encouraging legal and illegal immigration. A summary of the law's chief provisions appears in Table 5.1.

TABLE 5.1
Major Provisions of the 1996 Illegal Immigration Reform and Immigrant Responsibility Act

Enhancement and Enforcement of Immigration Control

More Agents	Increased number of Border Patrol agents by not less than 1,000 per fiscal year beginning in 1997 through 2001. Also provides for an increase of up to 300 support personnel for the same period.
More Barriers	Called for the reinforcement of existing barriers along the U.S. border and construction of second and third fences along the 14 miles stretching eastward from the Pacific Ocean. Authorized $12 million expenditure to carry out construction and waived the Endangered Species Act of 1973 and National Environmental Policy Act of 1969 to "ensure expeditious construction of the barriers and roads."
More Facilities	Calls for increase in INS detention space of 9,000 beds.
More Equipment	Authorized the U.S. Attorney general to use "any federal equipment (including fixed-wing aircraft, helicopters, four-wheel drive vehicles, sedans, night vision goggles, night vision scopes, and sensor units) determined available for transfer by any other agency of the Federal government upon request of the Attorney General."

(continued on next page)

TABLE 5.1 *(continued)*

Enhancement and Enforcement of Immigration Control	
Streamlined Procedures	• Reduction of documents employees can use to demonstrate work eligibility.
	• Facilitates interagency cooperation with the INS by authorizing local agencies to assist in immigration enforcement.
	• At ports of entry allows for removal without hearing (excepted: asylum claims)
	• Removes discrimination barrier stating that employers do not engage in unfair employment practices unless they show *intent* to discriminate.
Limitations on Access to Public Benefits	
New Public Charge Exclusion	Sponsors of legal applicants must provide affidavits of support at 125% of the federal poverty line for 10 years (40 quarters) of employment by admitted legal alien, or until their naturalization.
Ineligibility for Public Benefits	Persons unlawfully in the United States not eligible for Social Security benefits or post-secondary education benefits. Transition of ineligible immigrants out of public housing.

Source: 104th Congress, Sess. II. Statutes at Large, P.L. 104-132.

While the emphasis on border control as a means to control illegal immigration shows the ongoing concern that political leaders have in ensuring the integrity of the U.S.-Mexico border, the portion of the bill addressing the costs of immigration are evidence of the impact of California's popular Proposition 187 passed two years earlier. The 1996 IIRAIRA was replete with the same fundamental logic that appear in Proposition 187—namely, that the way to control legal and illegal immigration is to remove the lure of public benefits.

IIRAIRA extended the logic of Proposition 187 to legal immigration as well, and the supporters of a similar federal policy argued that a restriction of benefits would reduce the flow of legal immigrants. The IIRAIRA would limit Supplemental Security Income (SSI) payments and housing assistance to legal immigrants, and it reasserted the century-old "public charge law" by requiring families sponsoring immigrants to show proof that they could support these relatives at 125 percent of the national poverty level.[4]

Among the more contentious amendments in the IIRAIRA was the Gallegly Amendment, which would have allowed states to deny public education to the children of illegal immigrants. The threat of a presidential veto ultimately forced the removal of the amendment from the final version of the law, but only after appearing twice for consideration in the House of Representatives. Eventually, the *Illegal Immigration Reform and Immigrant Responsibility Act* passed in the House with a vote of 333 to 87 and in the Senate, 97 to 3 during the spring of 1996. The Act was finally included as Division C of the *Omnibus Appropriations Act of 1997,* which passed in the House 370 to 37 and in the Senate, 84 to 15 on September 30, 1996. The breakdown of the votes clearly reflects bipartisan support for the effort.

Social Constructions of Deserving and Undeserving Groups in the IIRAIRA

The function of immigration control policy is to subdivide entering groups and assign them statuses that delineate their relationship to the state. Immigration policy by definition divides a subset of the population—noncitizens—into multiple categories with distinctive rights ascribed to each. One of the primary immigrant status distinctions currently familiar to most Americans is that drawn between legal and illegal immigrants.[5] Members of the first group have the right to live, work, draw benefits and, eventually, to naturalize if they so choose. By contrast, members of the second group have broken the law and maintain an illicit existence as a result of this crime. These distinctions are designed to administer the foreign population living within U.S. territory in a universal and neutral manner.

The IIRAIRA was designed to crack down on a category of people who are criminals by statutory definition. However, the law also penalized *legal* immigrants, thereby lending legislative credence to the idea that all immigrants were damaging the nation. Even though some expert witnesses, leading academics, and agency reports suggested the evidence of a negative impact was inconclusive, at best, the law was grounded in the assumption that *all* immigrants were taking more than their fair share of public resources (U.S. General Accounting Office 1995).

Thus, legal status was not the only set of qualities believed to separate the right kind of immigrants from the wrong kind. As my research on the 1996 IIRAIRA revealed, the distribution of penalties and resources to immigrants rested upon the persistent measurement of immigrants against an ideal that spoke to their potential to become good Americans. The definition of this potential emerged in debates over the reform bill and involved the rhetorical ascription of sets of characteristics and behaviors to immigrants. In turn, these rhetorical ascriptions delineated which immigrants the nation should consider a permanent feature of the social fabric and which immigrants should face expulsion. Congressional characterizations of deserving and undeserving immigrants did not correspond with legal distinctions (and protections) that had existed between undocumented people and permanent resident aliens.

Methods and Data

Schneider and Ingram's policy-making theory is that social constructions exist for politicians to exploit and justify tool selection. With this as a premise, I set out to observe the activity of immigration policy making in order to pinpoint the role that social constructions of immigrant groups play as legislators contemplate various methods to achieve orderly immigration admissions and reduce abuses already in place. In order to do this for policy-making activities that had already occurred, I relied on transcripts of the hearings and debates for the 1996 IIRAIRA (H.R. 2202).

For my research on social constructions in immigration policy making, I conducted a text-based discourse analysis of Congressional hearings and testimony given prior to the passage of each bill. According to Hajer, discourse is defined as a "specific ensemble of ideas, concepts, and categorizations that are produced, reproduced, and transformed in a particular set of practices and through which meaning is given to physical and social realities" (1995, 44). Thus, the analysis of discourse involves (1) looking for ways of communicating ideas that have become ritualized (Hajer refers to these as "storylines") and (2) looking at how specific discourses are routinely practiced by certain groups with specific interests in the problems being discussed.

In order to categorize story lines and explore how ways of communicating about immigration and related problems are shared among legislators, I conducted a specific type of discourse analysis termed narrative policy analysis (Roe 1994). Roe explains the utility of narrative analyses of public policy in this manner:

> Stories commonly used in describing and analyzing policy issues are a force in themselves, and must be considered explicitly in assessing policy options. Further, these stories often resist change or modification even in the presence of contradicting empirical data, because they continue to underwrite and stabilize the assumptions for decision making in the face of high uncertainty, complexity and polarization. (2)

Roe's method requires researchers to look at the policy selection and design process, then begin the analysis by breaking down transcript data into "discrete statements," or the simplest assertions of causal relationships or sets of causal relationships linking problems to their sources. The disaggregation and categorization on the *Congressional Record* for H.R. 2202 produced sixty-seven discrete statements. Once the transcripts were broken down into these recurring discrete statements, I was able to regroup them into the policy "storylines" (Hajer) or "narratives" (Roe) encompassing related discrete statements.

Social constructions are an indispensable part of policy narratives. Essentially, they tell debate participants who are the "good guys" and who are the "bad guys" in the story. Thus, the narratives become a vehicle for the rhetorical reproduction of social constructions. Much of a narrative's credibility depends on tapping into preconceived ideas about who is to blame for the problems or who is deserving of resources or punishments from government action. The official rhetoric employed to garner support for policy designs casts immigrants either as deserving or undeserving of full inclusion in the political community. These constructions allow for restriction to be reconciled with the "nation of immigrants" vision, for they codify criteria for what types of immigrants are good for the nation and what types of immigrants should be kept out.

Official Language as a Source of Social Constructions

A study of social constructions that accounts for elite discourse is elemental to observing how these constructions are employed to achieve certain policy outcomes. As Edelman noted, rhetoric is central to the conduct of political activity:

> The employment of language to sanctify action is exactly what makes politics different from other methods of allocating values. Through language a group can not only achieve an immediate result but also win the acquiescence of those whose lasting support is needed. . . . Talk, on the other hand involves a competitive exchange of symbols, referential and evocative, through which values are shared and assigned and the coexistence attained. (1964, 114)

Generally speaking, the *Congressional Record* is an underutilized but important source of data for analysts wishing to learn about the role of value allocation in policy making. Congress was designed as a deliberative body, a place in which discussion and argumentation among many members would generate the best political solutions. Even with its growth in size and its strict time limits for those occupying the House floor, the institution continues to reflect a commitment to this deliberative tradition.

Congress is the forum in which lawmakers discuss and debate the merits of policy for the public record. Official rhetoric provides an important data source for the study of social constructions, as it represents well the public stance of members of Congress. While few people in the public may choose to watch the debates in their entirety on C-SPAN, footage from debates on especially contentious legislation is often included in newscasts and newspapers print excerpts from the debates. Moreover, what appears in the *Congressional Record* is important to its creators: it is an official historical record of the body's proceedings and members take care to edit their remarks, or have them included when they are unable to attend the actual debate.

DISTINGUISHING GOOD IMMIGRANTS
FROM PROBLEM IMMIGRANTS

Even though the IIRAIRA was designed to stem the fiscal costs of immigration, those speaking in support of the new legislation appeared aware that they

dif between immigrant and illegal immigrants

must tread lightly in their remarks; immigrants carry a positive social construction—and this positive construction emerged in the introduction of the bill to Congress:

> Legal immigrations continue to provide the United States with a steady stream of hard-working, freedom-loving, patriotic new Americans. Legal immigrants bringing special skills to our workplace have been instrumental in placing American firms, especially many in California, on the cutting edge of high technology. (Dreier 1996)

This statement speaks of immigration as a positive force, comprised of legal immigrants with "special skills" valuable to American businesses. This construction of the "hardworking" immigrant, who ascribes to American values of freedom and patriotism, makes the immigrant similar to American citizens and, in fact, the speaker calls them "patriotic new Americans." Others who spoke in favor of immigrants referred to their hard work and contributions to the nation—particularly their labor contributions.

Similar to this positive construction of the immigrant who contributes was the immigrant who emblemizes the nation's past as an immigrant-receiving country. In fact, as the House debated the merits of IIRAIRA, it was not uncommon for a member of Congress to refer to his or her own immigrant background in statements supporting or opposing H.R. 2202:

> Mr. Speaker, my heritage is German, Irish, Polish, and even a little Bohemian, and my children are all of that plus Norwegian, and I appreciate America as a Melting pot. (Ganske 1996)

> Before we begin the actual testimony, let me state the following premise about which there is little disagreement. It is the obligation of the Federal Government to secure the borders of the Nation from illegal entry and unauthorized invasion. . . . It is not a question of being anti-immigration. This country was founded by immigrants. I am the son of one of them. (Horn 1997)

The recurrence of this type of statement is important because legislators portraying themselves as children of immigrants are also appealing to the American dream myth of opportunity and self-betterment. In this version of the American dream, the children of immigrants can grow up to be members of Congress. These types of positive images of immigrants, moreover, were employed whether the individual was speaking on behalf of or against the new immigration bill. In the third statement, the speaker disassociated the efforts of Congress from an anti-immigration stance by reminding the chamber that he himself is the son of an immigrant.

Statements like these demonstrated how the positive construction of immigration both constrained and enabled lawmakers debating the immigration bill. They revealed a self-conscious effort on the part of legislators to reference the contributions of immigrants even as they debated a bill that would be quite punitive toward legal immigrants. What would emerge was a construction of two categories of immigrant: a good immigrant, portrayed with the qualities described in the statement above (hard work, patriotism, self-betterment, the desire to become American) and a qualitatively distinct immigrant who was, in essence, a problem requiring a legislative solution.

CONSTRUCTING THE PROBLEM IMMIGRANT

While members of Congress employed positive immigrant stories when alluding to their own heritage, those members supporting immigrant restrictions would need to override or change this positive characterization to justify the IIRAIRA. To do so, the bill's advocates would need to show how the immigrants that required control were qualitatively distinct from the immigrant ancestors. This change in social constructions would emerge from narratives depicting immigrants as problematic and undesirable.

The "Zero-Sum" Narrative. One of the most common ways in which members of Congress forged a negative immigrant construction was through a narrative that described immigrants as freeloaders reaping the benefits of hardworking citizens who paid taxes. The narrative juxtaposed citizens and immigrants and supported efforts to restrict access to immigrants by arguing that the provision of goods or funds going to immigrants came at the expense of more entitled citizens. One version of this narrative appeared in debates over immigrant schooling. The statements below speak about the children of illegal aliens—some of whom may be either legal or illegal, though the actual status of the children cannot be derived from the statements—who are seen as diverting public school resources from citizen children:

> Whose children do we care about? Why are we here? Who are we representing? We are supposed to care about the people of the United States of America. All of these children are wonderful children who have been brought here by illegal aliens. We care about them. But we have to care about our own kids first. (Rohrabacher 1997)

Children of illegal immigrants were not the only burdens on the public coffers; House members also argued that legal immigrants tapped into strained resources upon settling in the United States:

> [T]he U.S. welfare system is rapidly becoming a retirement home for the elderly of other countries. In 1994, nearly 738,000 noncitizen residents were receiving aid from the Supplemental Security Income program known as SSI. This is a 580–percent increase—up from 127,900 in 1982—in just 12 years.

The overwhelming majority of noncitizen SSI recipients are elderly. Most apply for welfare within five years of arriving in the United States. By way of comparison, the number of U.S.-born applying for SSI benefits has increased just 49 percent in the same period. Without reform, according to the Wall Street Journal, the total cost of SSI and Medicaid benefits for elderly noncitizen immigrants will amount to more than $328 billion over the next ten years. (Solomon 1996)

Both speakers in these statements call for prioritizing citizens over noncitizens. These members, and those speaking in the following excerpts, supported policy tools that would distinguish between potential charges of the state and those people who are more likely to be self-sufficient:

Our immigration system should reward those who bring skills and initiative into this country, but it is not right to penalize our citizens by forcing them to pay benefits to people who have never contributed to the system. (Fowler 1996)

If we don't require sponsors to fulfill their financial obligations, taxpayers will continue to pay $26 billion annually for legal immigration. Sponsors must honor their obligations so legal immigrants may become self-reliant, productive residents of the United States rather than dependents of the welfare state. (Stearns 1996)

The members who offered these two statements were speaking in favor of revising the visa preference structure for legal permanent residents. According to these legislators, the United States could avoid the fiscal drain of immigration by granting visas to those immigrants most likely to have skills, or the capacity, to work and contribute to the system rather than retire and draw upon it. Additionally, many members argued, Congress could stem the fiscal drain of legal immigrants drawing on welfare by holding sponsors financially accountable. In each of these quotations, the speakers drew the distinction between the "right" and "wrong" kind of lawful migrants: good immigrants become "self-reliant, productive residents," with sponsors who "honor their obligations." Undesirable immigrants, by contrast, are those who "never contributed to the system," and become "dependents of the welfare state."

In each instance of this immigrant freeloader narrative, legislators spoke of resource diversion to unworthy immigrants—both legal and illegal. The statements do not account for the fact that some children of undocumented immigrants are citizens, nor do they account for the 1981 *Plyler v. Doe* ruling that allowed undocumented children to have the right to attend public schools. Instead, supporters of restriction portrayed immigrants as undeserving and easily sublimated the more complex legal distinctions that characterize the resident immigrant population. Like citizens, legal immigrants who work have SSI taxes taken from their paychecks. However, statements like the ones above portrayed citizens as more deserving of public resources than immigrants and, again, legal distinctions appeared irrelevant as speakers promoted the image of immigrants as burdensome.

The "zero-sum" narrative emerged from recurring speeches that portrayed immigrants as profiting from programs without contributing to them. As a result, immigrants were constructed as undeserving of access to government programs. According to the logic of this narrative, the resolution to a misallocation of resources plainly lay in prioritizing citizens over foreigners. In order to accomplish this prioritization, immigrants would need to be barred from participating in public programs. Such bans included the Gallegly Amendment, Title V provisions—to ensure that immigrants not become a public charge—and the Chrysler-Berman Amendment, which would restructure admissions and place new caps on legal immigration.

The "Criminal Alien" Narrative. This narrative emerged from recurring statements linking immigrants to criminal activity or statements that described them as inherently criminal. Much of the IIRAIRA had expanded border and interior law enforcement. Illegal immigrants have, by definition, broken the law, and this element of criminality figured into their negative construction. However, this criminality extended beyond their actual status when legislators attributed other criminal qualities and behaviors to this population:

> Mr. Speaker, just to put into perspective the problem we will be considering over the next 2 days let me begin with a few facts.
>
> No.1: Nationwide more than one-quarter of all Federal prisoners are illegal aliens. According to the Immigration and Naturalization Service, in 1980, the total foreign-born population in Federal prisons was one thousand which was less than 4 percent of all inmates. In 1995, the foreign-born population in Federal prisons was 27,938, which constitutes 20 percent of all inmates. The result is an enormous extra expense to be picked up by the Federal taxpayers. (Solomon 1996)

The negative, criminal construction was a specter surrounding the entire debate over the IIRAIRA. The previous statements illustrate the causal relationship that the speakers drew between illegal immigrants and criminal behavior. In this statement, while the speaker does not identify the crimes, the imagery of prisons—one-fourth of the population of which is illegal immigrants—sends a message about the proportions of the illegal immigration crisis. At the same time, it places a significant portion of these people in the federal prison system.

While criminal activity recurred as a theme throughout the debates, House members also accentuated this criminal construction by reminding their colleagues that illegal aliens are a criminal category of people. Members of Congress speaking in support of the IIRAIRA continually reminded participants that illegal immigrants are criminals by definition as the following excerpt illustrates:

Mr. Speaker, the gentleman from Washington [Mr. Tate] and the gentlewoman from California [Mrs. Seastrand] will offer a commonsense amendment to clarify that if someone violates American laws and enters the country illegally, then they will no longer be eligible to later become a legal immigrant. Legal immigration should be reserved for those who respect our laws. (Dreier 1996)

The Tate amendment, which was included in the final draft of the bill, punished illegal immigrants by denying them the chance to reapply for legal entry. The law, in essence, produced a criminal "mark" on those who cross the border illicitly.

In discussions about portions of H.R. 2202, which limited benefits access for illegal immigrants and their children, an additional crime—welfare fraud— was linked to illegal immigrants. The Fourteenth Amendment of the U.S. Constitution grants birthright citizenship to children born to illegal immigrant parents. Because these children are citizens, they are entitled to Aid to Families with Dependent Children (AFDC); however, because agencies cannot issue checks directly to the children, their undocumented parents receive the disbursements. The system leads this criminal category of people to commit more crimes, like welfare fraud:

So you are in a situation that when you say you are going to give illegal aliens public assistance funds for their children, you are de facto either giving them money to support themselves in violation of the welfare law, or you are condoning the fact that they are working in violation of the law. They are not declaring income, which is a violation of their welfare status for their child. So what we have here is a catch-22 in an absurd situation. (Bilbray 1996)

An analogous act that is not a crime in and of itself, but which calls attention to the questionable intent or character of undocumented adults, emerged in legislators' concerns that illegal immigrants come to the United States to give birth to citizens so that they may "bootstrap" their child's benefits:

I think we have all seen situations in which we have heard the traditional description of bootstrapping your way into a benefit. This is booty-strapping. This is a situation in which, by virtue of the act of illegal entry on the part of a parent, the birth of the child gives the right to benefits from the taxpayers' coffers. (Deal 1996)

These two statements reflect a general refusal, during the hearings, by supporters of the bill to recognize the legitimate citizenship of children born to illegal immigrants in U.S. territory. Even though the Fourteenth Amendment grants these children the rights of full U.S. citizenship, their parents are defined not as parents of citizens, but as perpetual offenders transgressing immigration laws and defrauding federal and state governments. A criminal construction is a negative construction and criminal behavior justifies establishing punitive measures. In addition to general restriction of resources, many of the elements of IIRAIRA emphasized policing and punishing undocumented immigrants through jail, detention, and expulsion.

The "Lawless Border" Narrative. This narrative, containing the image of the southern border that emerged from hearings and debates, depicted it as a territory under siege. From 1994–1996, Congressional discussion of the immigration problem was a discussion of law enforcement problems and, more specifically, border enforcement problems. In the IIRAIRA debates, members of Congress regularly referred to the southern border as a place inundated in unlawful activities, like drug smuggling, vandalism, and prostitution. The narrative located the solution to the problem in the enforcement and protection of the political division between the two nations, as the quotation below illustrates:

> I think that all three Congressmen [at this hearing] know what the scenario was back then [before Gatekeeper]. We were overrun, completely and totally. Our apprehension rates were running anywhere from 2,500 to 3,000 on a daily basis. People were camping on the United States side. There was no delineation of the border. There wasn't a fence; there were remnants of fences. People were all over the place. . . . It was completely out of control. (de la Vina 1997, 62)

Edelman has argued that political language is designed to trigger an emotional response from its audience. The "lawless border" narrative achieves this by tapping into an existing view of the U.S.-Mexico border as a place of disorder and depravity. Scholarship concerning the border and U.S.-Mexico relations has argued that longstanding fears and prejudices that Anglo-Americans have toward Mexico have led to conceptualizing the southern border as a division between distinctive moralities, and it is reified by the political division between the two nations (see Rodriguez 1997 or Martinez 1994, chapter 1). On one side of the border, the rule of law pervades, while on the other side, chaos, immorality (drugs, prostitution), and corruption (moral, political) prevail. The border, in this view, does not simply represent a division between wealth and poverty, but instead characterizes the region as a place of degeneracy, backwardness, and criminality. Illegal immigrants embody the penetration of lawlessness into the United States; thus, the crisis of illegal immigration is a crisis of foreign invasion that further rationalizes the military response of IIRAIRA.

The Pathologies of Federalism Narrative. Although this narrative also involves enforcement of immigration laws, it is different in that it portrays how the federal government is inept and its agencies too cumbersome to implement immigration laws. Illegal immigrants are still depicted as criminals that need to be ferreted out, caught, and punished for their crime. The protagonists of the narrative, however, are the state and local law enforcement officers, who try to do their job only to find their efforts sabotaged by federal regulations. The solution to the problem is to close gaps in law enforcement jurisdiction and, in essence, create a dragnet for capturing illegal aliens. This idea is evident in this quotation:

> All we are saying is that the local law enforcement agencies should have an opportunity to work with INS, to be their eyes and ears out in the local communities. These people are on the frontline. These people are the ones who know if someone has violated a deportation order and is in their community under a criminal act by violating that order, and they should, in fact, have the power to detail, arrest, and transport that individual to INS so that they can be deported. (Latham 1997, 62)

Ultimately, this problem was addressed through the measures in IIRAIRA that enabled interagency information sharing among all levels of law enforcement. The narrative not only portrays local and state enforcement agencies as needing the support (not the hindrance) of the federal government, it also reinforces the "criminal alien" narrative by making illegal immigrants the subjects of law enforcement efforts to protect and maintain order in communities across America.

The "Government Off Our Backs" Narrative. This narrative provides an interesting juxtaposition of the narratives portraying immigrants as the bad guys. It is particularly interesting when one considers the efforts of the 1986 IRCA to criminalize and punish those who employ undocumented workers. In this narrative, employers are doing their best to comply with IRCA's verification requisites for hiring, yet they find themselves ensnared in the inefficient federal bureaucracy. Worse yet, employers are reaping punishments for their adherence to the law's paperwork requirements:

> I've talked to people that have literally been fined $50,000 for forgetting to cross the Ts and dot the Is and you didn't fill out square C, that's another $3,000. And for these people, it's a nightmare. (Hunter 1997)

The narrative's resolution rests in making federal laws more user friendly for employers and characterizes employers as responsible individuals doing their best to comply with excessive federal laws. The narrative argues that government should ease the burden on employers and encourage compliance by facilitating it, as the rest of this member's statement shows:

> In reality, we all know that the I-9 process already exists out there that the employers must use with potential employees. But right now we put these employers in a catch box. As my colleagues know, if they ask too many questions of a potential applicant for a job, they question the documents as to whether they are counterfeit, they can be sued by these applicants. But on the

other hand, if they do not ask enough questions and they hire an illegal, then the INS can come in and fine them.

So we are putting these employers in difficult situations, which this process, by use of the 1-800 number on a voluntary basis, will help alleviate. It will be a defense to those employers. (Bryant 1996)

Both of these examples depict the ways in which businesses are faced with onerous compliance requirements, and each speaker supports a system that would be easier for employers to use. In short, the narrative constructs businesses as undeserving of burdensome regulations for their hiring practices.

Narratives, Target-group Constructions, and Policy Tools

The "zero-sum," "criminal alien," and "lawless border" narratives all involved the social construction of immigrants as a problem group. Often, as in the "government off our backs" and "pathologies of federalism" narratives, the negatively constructed immigrant stands in stark contrast to more positively constructed law enforcement and employer target groups. Table 5.2 summarizes the relationship between narrative and the social constructions of the target groups, as portrayed in these narratives. It also compares the type of policy tools, anticipated by Schneider and Ingram's social constructions theory (1993, 1997), for each target group's construction with the policy tools legislators selected to resolve policy problems.

In reviewing social constructions appearing in Congressional discourse, it important to note that the narratives often advanced or juxtaposed multiple social constructions. Much of the discourse in these debates compared citizens with immigrants. While citizens were not themselves a policy target group, citizens figured into the narratives as victims of immigrants. This approach highlights the ways in which immigrants were qualitatively distinct from the citizen population. For example, in the "immigrant freeloader" narrative, the negative social construction of immigrants abusing the system was frequently contrasted with references to "citizens," who legitimately claim public benefits by birthright, and "taxpayers," who were depicted as hard-working and more deserving of the public benefits they had presumably subsidized. Likewise, citizens were either directly or indirectly suffering the social costs of the "criminal" alien whose activities cost citizens/taxpayers.

Each of the five narratives tells a story about target group deservedness. In the "zero-sum" narrative, deserving people pay taxes or were citizens who were assumed to have contributed to social security. According to these narratives, target groups did not deserve protection of rights or access to the social safety net—even the citizen children of undocumented parents were depicted as undeserving because of their parents' criminal status. In both cases, the criminal and freeloader constructions were strengthened through their juxtaposition with more positively constructed groups: citizens/taxpayers and legal immigrants, who work or who are descended from the people who work.

TABLE 5.2

Policy Narratives and the Social Constructions of Target Groups

Policy Narrative	Target Group	Narrative Portrayal	Social Construction	Anticipated Policy Tools*	Policy Tools Supported Through Narrative
The Immigrant Freeloader	Illegal and legal immigrants Children of illegal immigrants	On welfare Not contributing their fair share Absorbing citizens' benefits	Negative	Punitive, coercive	1. Restrict access to SSI, housing 2. Enforcement of Public charge laws 3. Deny schooling, etc.
The Criminal Alien	Illegal immigrants	Lawbreakers	Negative	Punitive, coercive	1. Identification 2. Incarceration 3. Deportation
The Lawless Border	The INS and Border Patrol (direct)	Overwhelmed Under siege	Positive	Resources	• Barrier construction • Expansion of border patrol and pilot programs

(continued on next page)

TABLE 5.2 *(continued)*

Policy Narrative	Target Group	Narrative Portrayal	Social Construction	Anticipated Policy Tools*	Policy Tools Supported Through Narrative
The Pathologies of Federalism	State and local agencies	• On the front lines • Diligent • Frustrated by jurisdictional divisions • Shouldering the burdens of immigration enforcement mandates from Washington	Positive	Voluntary, positive inducements, self-regulation	• Facilitate information-sharing between jurisdictions. • Federal block grants to states to absorb the costs generated by immigrant populations.
Government Off Our Backs	Employers	• Trustworthy • Diligent • Law-abiding	Positive	Voluntary, positive inducements, self-regulation	• Streamlined I-9 • Streamlined H2-A • Verification hotline • Burden of proof shifted to plaintiffs in discrimination cases

*Based on Schneider and Ingram's social construction of target population theory (1993; 1997).

In the "government off our backs" narrative, employers deserve the benefit of the doubt, rather than strict regulations. They deserve to be trusted to
police themselves and comply with hiring laws. When employers do not comply, it is because the regulations are too burdensome. To ensure compliance
from this target group, policy should be streamlined and compliance facilitated.
This argument follows in the case of law enforcement entities in the "pathologies of federalism" narrative. The jurisdictional divisions elemental to federalism were pitched as too inefficient to protect communities from the illegal
immigrant threat. This threat was further bolstered by the two narratives highlighting the criminality and degeneracy of the illegal population: the "criminal
alien" and "lawless border" narratives.

This is not to suggest that either the narratives or the social constructions
went unchallenged. In fact, the section that follows elaborates on counter narratives, or challenges to the narratives just discussed. It explores the extent to
which different, even contrary, social constructions of these target groups found
voices in the H.R. 2202 debates.

Counter Narratives and Alternative Social Constructions
in the H.R. 2202 Debates

As is customary in debates, those who did not agree with the policy solutions
had opportunity to voice their opposition. The interesting question is whether
or not these challenges shared similar themes and social constructions of immigrant target groups. A counter narrative by definition should provide an alternative story—with its own beginning, middle, and resolution—that is equally
plausible and equally parsimonious as the narrative it disputes. Ideally, a strong
counter narrative would also counteract the negative social constructions of
immigrant target groups appearing throughout the H.R. 2202 debates. For
example, a strong counter narrative to the immigrant freeloader narrative
would not only criticize H.R. 2202 as bad policy for immigrants, but would
also do so by portraying immigrants as people who contribute labor and tax
dollars. Likewise, a counter narrative offering an opposing construction might
highlight how legal immigrants who work pay SSI. Additionally, it might even
argue that even illegal immigrants pay into state tax coffers through purchases
subject to state sales tax (like gasoline and other consumer goods). In short, a
strong counter narrative would provide a positive construction to counter the
negative construction of immigrants as freeloaders.

The "cure-worse-than-the-disease" counter narrative—generally speaking,
objections to the policy that took the form of critiques or rebuttals about particular measures—had nothing to unify these elements other than their shared
objection to the policy. As Roe describes, critiques "tell us what to be against
without telling us what to be for" (1994, 54). They offer policy makers little to
act upon, which becomes problematic once the momentum of pulling together

support coalitions to enact some policy solution has gotten under way. However, the debate transcripts did show one counter narrative warning that, if H.R. 2202 (or specific components of it) passed, a variety of foreseeable problems would result; problems perhaps worse than the ones facing the legislators at present. The "cure-worse-than-the-disease" counter narrative is recognizable for its depiction of the dire consequences resulting from the bill's passage.

The Gallegly Amendment debates, for example, gave rise to a consistently grim scenario should the provision pass and states choose to deny illegal immigrant children the right to an education:

> At a time when juvenile violence is on the rise, this amendment would deprive a large group of children in our communities of the only thing that can keep them out of trouble, and that is an education. . . . Children thrown on the streets by this amendment will not simply disappear. They will be left with nothing to do during school hours, tempting them to pursue a host of noneducational activities. One can only imagine the possibilities. (Richardson 1996)

> These children will not leave the United States simply because they are not in school. They will be, as all of our speakers pointed out, on the streets, joining gangs, left at home alone, for there is a price to be paid in terms of community health and community well-being, not to mention the harm to the children themselves. (Ros-Lehitinen 1996)

These statements follow a distinctive narrative pattern: should the bill include the Gallegly Amendment, the children of illegal immigrants would end up on the streets, in gangs, and create a long-term problem for society.

In a similar manner, the "cure-worse-than-the-disease" narrative disputed the bill's section 607 provisions to stop AFDC and Food Stamp disbursements to illegal immigrants collecting payments on behalf of their citizen children:

> This section of the bill makes it virtually impossible for many American children to receive public benefits. It creates a two-tier caste system where U.S.-born children of immigrants are treated differently from the children of U.S. citizens. This ignores the premise of equal protection, a blatant violation of these children's constitutional rights.
>
> This provision affects far more than just the children of undocumented parents. It also affects the U.S.-born children of legal permanent residents. These are American children of parents who work hard and pay taxes, who start businesses and create jobs. Under these provisions, they too would be unable to file for benefits on behalf of their U.S.-citizen children. (Velazquez 1996; Roybal-Allard 1996).[6]

These members argued that H.R. 2202 was bad public policy because section 607 violated the Constitution and was a solution out of proportion to the size of the problem. However, the social construction of immigrant target groups that emerged in this version of the counter narrative is mixed. The legal and undocumented parents of citizen children are differentiated from the children themselves, who are portrayed as innocent and constitutionally protected by the Fourteenth Amendment.

A final variant of the "cure-worse-than-the-disease" counter narrative emerged as the House debated better ways to verify worker eligibility and improve the Social Security card and make it harder to counterfeit. Both policy "cures" would lead to violations of citizen privacy and push the federal government into the role of Big Brother. An example from the debate over extending the 1-800 employer verification hotline follows:

> OK, [the 1-800 pilot program extension] is the famous camel's nose under the tent amendment. This is the one where it starts off real nice. Not to worry, folks. It is OK. Trust us. We will make it a pilot project. Will that make it OK? We will make it a temporary project. We will make it voluntary. We will do it just like we did the Japanese internment program when we said we are going to find out who the Japanese are that need to be rounded up. And how did they do that so quickly? They used the census data. Government trusters, that is where that came from. So congratulations, voluntary, temporary program for employment verification. (Conyers 1996)

In this statement, the sentiment is clear: do not create an employer verification hotline because it will entice the federal government to trample citizens' privacy. The pilot program is a "nose under the tent" that the House should defeat, lest it prod the nation towards police state tactics. The Democratic representative who made this statement tried to arouse fear of government encroachment by likening the effort to the World War II internment of Japanese. In policy terms, the solutions on the table for monitoring employment eligibility are worse than the problem of undocumented labor. Even designating the verification hotline "voluntary" starts Congress down a slippery slope of distasteful federal intrusion into private lives. The consequences are dire and the only way to avoid the slippery slope is for legislators to vote to strike it.[7]

The Role of Counter Narrative in Shaping Target Group Constructions

By definition, a counter narrative should provide an alternative story, with its own resolution, that is equally plausible and equally parsimonious as the narrative it disputes. But counter narratives are also a discursive tool that can either challenge or reinforce dominant social constructions. So, to what extent did the one true counter narrative incorporate or contradict the social constructions that appeared in the five narratives? Table 5.3 revisits the narratives' social constructions of groups and compares them to how the counter narrative characterized the same group.

In the dominant example of the "cure-worse-than-the-disease" counter narrative, representatives who opposed denying education, medical care, and welfare payments to children of illegal immigrants pointed to the crises the nation would face if children were denied the social safety net. While this produced a substantial contest to the fiscal benefits that the bill's proponents emphasized, the counter narrative did not alleviate the negative social construction of these children. In fact, opposition to the Gallegly Amendment portrayed immigrant children uniformly as little criminals, potential gangsters requiring schooling to curb this tendency toward delinquency. In this regard, the children of illegal immigrants did not dodge the "criminal alien" stigma, even though their right to an education is protected by the Supreme Court decision in *Plyler*. Even the discourse that members of Congress levied in defense of children of immigrants constructed them as potential criminals.

Whereas the immigrant freeloader and criminal alien narratives effectively lumped immigrants of varying legal statuses together with a uniformly negative construction, the social constructions of immigrants in the counter narrative for

TABLE 5.3
Narrative vs. Counternarrative Group Constructions

Group	Narrative Portrayal	Counternarrative Portrayal	Social Construction
Legal immigrants	Freeloaders On welfare Don't contribute	None	Negative
Illegal immigrants	Criminals	Criminals	Negative
Children of illegal immigrants	Absorbing public dollars that should go to American citizen children	Innocent Protected by Constitution Potential delinquents	Mixed
Employers	Trustworthy Diligent Law abiding	None	Positive
Federal government★	Inefficient Punishing the wrong people (employers)	Big Brother Insidious	Negative

★Not an IIRAIRA target group, but a group that was contrasted with target groups and the construction of which, therefore, remained elemental to the policy stories used to justify the IIRAIRA's components.

H.R. 2202 did not provide an equally uniform positive construction of immigrants. Instead, those protesting the bill and its amendments characterized immigrants differently according to their status: citizen children deserve protection, children of illegals should be in school, lest they turn to crime. Legal immigrants are hardworking and deserve access to benefits; illegal immigrants continue to work illicitly and some of them have children—some of whom are citizens. Thus, whereas the pro-IIRAIRA rhetoric successfully consolidated narratives with uniform portrayals of immigrants as making illegitimate claims on the state, the opposition to the bill provided a logical counter narrative that failed to provide an equally solid positive construction of immigrants. Instead, the opposition characterized immigrants according to their status, resulting in an immigrant construction that appeared murky and mixed.

CONCLUSION: IMMIGRATION POLICY AND THE CONSTRUCTION OF GROUP DESERVEDNESS

Immigration as a subject of policy debate evokes positive imagery about the origins of the nation and figures strongly in how the nation defines itself. As the opening remarks from members of Congress showed, the immigrant past is a source of both national and individual pride.

When it comes to drafting and defending immigration restriction policy, legislators must carefully delineate who requires restriction and why. They accomplish this by constructing immigrant target groups as problematic and undesirable. Congressional debates provide a window through which to observe the construction of immigrant target groups for policy purposes. In addition to reflecting the prevailing values of politicians and their constituents, these debates produce recognizable, recurrent depictions of groups—depictions that politicians manipulated and juxtaposed to support the final design of the IIRAIRA.

Generally speaking, the debates over immigration reform from 1994–1996 constructed immigration as a problem and constructed immigrants as parasitic, at best, and, at worst, as deviants. Policy narratives that highlighted these and other negative qualities of immigrants also recommended coercive policy tools and provided justification for punitive tools. While their illegal status facilitates the portrayal of undocumented aliens as undeserving of access to the welfare state, legal status *did not* guarantee which immigrants could make claims on their host nation. Rather, the policy debates portrayed all immigration as being out of control and all immigrants as draining resources. The narrative of the immigrant with the laudable work ethic that made America only appeared in legislators' allusions to their own immigrant backgrounds. Most significantly, this alternative narrative and positive immigrant construction—which would have directly challenged the assertions of the "zero-sum" narrative—was not a part of argument against H.R. 2202. Without a countervailing construction that might indicate deservedness, what emerged were two classes of undeserving immigrants—the criminal aliens and the immigrant freeloaders.

Moreover, no classifications other than "citizen" or "immigrant" emerged from the debates. Absent from these discussions were the large backlogs of immigrants seeking the permanence of naturalization or distinctions between refugees and other immigrants. These latter distinctions are particularly elemental to any real discussion of welfare usage among immigrants. Refugee status—granted to Cuban and Vietnamese immigrants, for example—designates a different class of legal immigrants that the federal government has selected for particularized aid that addresses political concerns as well as the involuntary nature of their departure from the home country. Such political considerations have served in the past as a justification for administering additional public (and sometimes emergency) resources to qualifying immigrants. The IIRAIRA debates, by contrast, did not acknowledge the various classifications among immigrants; instead, congressional supporters of IIRAIRA unilaterally depicted immigrants as undeserving. The result was a legislative designation of "immigrant" as a single class of target group for whom complex legal statuses that once determined distribution of benefits were blurred to suit a larger campaign that sought to affirm that social membership could only be achieved through birthright citizenship.

To illustrate, consider the contrasting constructions that emerged for "citizen" and "immigrant" during the debates. Congressional discourse defined citizens (with the key exception of citizen children of illegal immigrants) as entitled to social protections and publicly funded schools and benefits. By contrast, immigrants' claims were portrayed as illegitimate and unwarranted. Often, statements made on the House floor called for the prioritization of citizens/taxpayers over immigrants. The IIRAIRA debates, in this regard, defined citizenship not in terms of a contract of rights and obligations between government and denizen, but rather in terms of assumptions about who pays into the system and who does not. "Taxpayers" were presumed to be citizens and, therefore, to have the right to state resources and protections. Those constructed outside the boundaries of "taxpayers" were consequently divested of any legitimacy.

Policy Messages and the Construction of Membership

Immigration policy is, at its very core, about ascribing a relationship between a noncitizen class of people and the state under whose jurisdiction they nonetheless reside. In 1986, the legalization program extended social membership to those with the least recognition from the state, illegal immigrants. Legalization removed the stigma and reality of criminality for 2.9 million people. It did so despite the reservation that the mass public held toward this group and despite the fact that the controversial nature aroused many political opponents.

With the IIRAIRA, Congress significantly constricted the idea of membership, making it exclusive to citizens. Furthermore, although the language of the bill did not target immigrants by race or nationality, the language of the debates as expressed in the "lawless border" and "criminal alien" narratives, clearly identified Mexican immigrants as the "wrong" kinds of immigrants, due to their deviancy, their intent to scam the system, their illegal status, and their sheer numbers. Even attempts to classify children of these undeserving immigrants as innocent were insufficient to override the emphatically negative construction of their parents. Nor were immigrant children able to escape their indictment as freeloaders.

What my analysis of the IIRAIRA debates shows is the particular vulnerability of immigrants to elite constructions. Because their legal status places significant limitations on their potential to exercise their political voice and because the diversity of the population limits their ability to organize and communicate a shared or unified interest, the motivations, characteristics, and activities of immigrants are open to manipulation by politicians seeking a popular agenda. The myths and symbols of immigration are powerful emotive tools that cut through partisan divisions and easily serve those who would engage in negative politicking. However, the messages that emerge from this type of discourse have effects that reach beyond campaigns and policy making. Policies have the ability to initiate social learning. They teach us who matters, and who does not; who has a rightful stake in the system, and whose claims are best ignored or even officially stripped of their legitimacy. These messages are not only absorbed by target groups (as Joe Soss's research on welfare policy suggests in chapter 11),` but they are also absorbed by the broader society that is the intended audience of this spectacle.

NOTES

1. While this sentiment corresponded with efforts to restrict certain immigrant "stocks," in the mid- to late-nineteenth century, the concern that some immigrants were not adopting American social and political values became the justification for the Progressive Party's push for "Americanization" programs for immigrants (see Hartmann 1948).

2. In a similar vein, others have argued that political elites can capitalize on particular ways of defining or framing issues in order to take advantage of contextual opportunities (Kingdon 1995; Baumgartner and Jones 1993). I agree with these arguments and show how social constructions are elemental to framing issues in ways that are favorable for elected officials to achieve preferred goals.

3. The 1986 *Immigration Reform and Control Act*'s combination of employer sanctions and legalization programs is perhaps the most significant.

4. The 1882 law stated that customs officials had the duty to deny entry to anyone who might become a public charge, such as "convicts," "prostitutes," "lunatics," and "idiots."

5. In this chapter, I refer to legal immigrants as including those immigrants entering via family reunification sponsorship and refugees admitted in conjunction with U.S. foreign policy considerations.

6. Representatives Nydia Velazquez and Lucille Roybal-Allard (D-CA) cosponsored an amendment to strike Section 607. The House ultimately rejected the amendment 267 to 151 (D 58–129; R 211–21).

7. The verification program survived these and similar critiques. Initially, the vote on Chabot-Conyers was delayed and the amendment was modified to strike the provisions of H.R.2202 for increasing the number of INS and Department of Labor inspectors who specialize in employer violations. The House defeated the modified Chabot-Conyers amendment 260 to 159 (79–152; D 79–108) *Congressional Record* 1996.

PART III

Nonprofits, Neighborhood Organizations, and the Social Construction of Deservedness

ANNE L. SCHNEIDER AND HELEN M. INGRAM

The tendency to divide people into categories, where some members are far more deserving than others, is a recurring theme in certain policy arenas—particularly those that involve race, ethnicity, gender, poverty, and other forms of disadvantage. We have seen in previous chapters, however, that policy makers sometimes attempt to overcome disadvantage through the pursuit of policies that emphasize themes of justice or pragmatic problem solving rather than manipulation of images for political gain.

Policy making is not complete when statutes are adopted, and the subsequent processes of policy implementation, in which many of the details of the policy are developed, carry very important implications for the social construction of target populations. Implementation may be carried out exclusively through local government agencies, but in other instances, policy is implemented by nonprofit organizations or neighborhood-based associations.

Besides implementing statutes or agency guidelines, grassroots organizations and nonprofits may engage in the "coproduction" of public policy, in that they provide direct services to selected groups of people or localities. These services may be partially funded by government or entirely free of government restrictions.

The next two chapters examine the capacity of nonprofit and neighborhood organizations to serve disadvantaged populations at the local level. The chapters focus on whether local-level organizations offer a viable alternative to federal welfare policies and the ways in which nonprofit and neighborhood organizations socially construct those they serve.

Chapter 6, "The Construction of Client Identities in a Post-Welfare Social Service Program: The Double Bind of Microenterprise Development," by Nancy Jurik and Julie Cowgill, is a study of the construction of client identities in a microenterprise development program and the ways in which identity affected access to program services.

The underlying assumption of these programs is that the poor actually are hard working and highly motivated, but they have been marginalized and denied sufficient access to the global economy. In contrast with traditional welfare approaches of paternalism reflected in the Aid to Families with Dependent Children (AFDC) program and the Temporary Assistance to Needy Families (TANF) program, microenterprise programs offer loans, training, and access to the mainstream economy. They attempt to empower clients by creating lending circles that will hold one another accountable for repaying the loans. The intent of microenterprise is not to change or resocialize clients, but instead to provide them with opportunities to succeed in a business-like environment.

Drawing on data from a survey of fifty U.S. microenterprise programs and a longitudinal case study, the authors found that although the Microenterprise Development Program (MDP) succeeded in extending some economic opportunities to many women, minority, and low- and middle-income individuals, it did not live up to the ideals that have been claimed for these programs. The pressures of accountability and fund raising resulted in staff screening clients to find those with the greatest potential for success in a business-oriented culture. Over time, the program slipped into one that served the "not quite so poor." Junik and Cowgill examine the dynamics of the client construction processes and how staff came to engage in some of the same types of disempowering social constructions of the poor that are found in traditional welfare program delivery systems. In this sense, MDPs further contribute to the illusion that there are adequate "post-welfare" programs for the poor.

In chapter 7, "Deservedness in Poor Neighborhoods: A Morality Struggle," Michelle Camou examines more than twenty neighborhood-based organizations that provide services in a high-minority, low-income community. But her findings are quite different from those of Jurik and Cowgill, as these organizations did not divide their possible client populations into "right" and "wrong" kinds of clients and "cream" those clients most likely to succeed. Instead, they stayed intently focused on an institutional mission of serving the most disadvantaged people. Similar to Jurik and Cowgill, however, Camou found that the organizations did establish ideas about lifestyles that should be emulated. They also directed their efforts at changing people to better fit the preferred lifestyles.

Camou argues that there is a process of establishing deservedness or entitlement in high-minority, low-income neighborhoods, and that it often involves a morality struggle in which neighborhood organizations attempt to establish lifestyle standards for their communities. Her analysis of several different kinds of organizations in an African-American, low-income community in Baltimore shows that the process is very different from the degenerative policy making sometimes found in legislative arenas. Legislatures focus on providing benefits to advantaged groups and punishment to deviants, whereas the neighborhood organizations she studied provided services to the most needy and most disadvantaged rather than to various middle-class or white populations. Why? The dominant story line, she found through interviews with service providers, is that residents have made poor choices about their lifestyles and need to change. The poor are socially constructed as dependent, needy, and lacking proper values, and this is exactly what the organizations wish to address. Their mission is to resocialize and change people who have deficits so that they can meet the standards of competence and become contributing members of the neighborhood. The dominant story line is one of deficits. This construction dominates, even though Camou argues that the organizations could just as easily have focused on making infrastructure changes that might help people get jobs, or physical redesign that might protect the value of housing and interest in home ownership. There is an odd mixture of condescension and hopefulness, she says, and a belief that residents can—if they receive proper services and try hard enough—reject street values in favor of mainstream ones.

Camou found interesting differences across three different kinds of neighborhood organizations. The more professionally oriented, nonprofit organizations disproportionately allocated resources to behavioral change activities and tended to construct people as deserving but needing help in changing their behavior. Faith-based delivery systems were operated more by persons from outside the immediate neighborhood. The faith-based narrative doubts that the problems can be solved "once and for all," or that people can change. Instead, they were much more inclined to simply provide help to the needy. Resident associations were the only ones that had reconstructed the more typical pattern of advantaged, dependent, contender, and deviant, in that they more clearly identified deviants who needed to be punished and excluded from housing. Camou explains that the social constructions of each organization are consistent with the institutional culture, mission, and resources. The faith-based organizations, for example, do not have the resources or expertise to engage in behavioral change interventions. The professionalized nonprofits, who must allocate scarce resources, justify their actions on the grounds that they should first provide for the most desperately needy groups. Serving the most needy is the rationale of choice, as it is the one most consistent with how they view their mission and their calling. Apparently, they are not held accountable for actually bringing about behavioral change.

These chapters produce several observations. The neighborhood organizations that had the least connection with government funding or outcome accountability measures were the most likely to avoid negative constructions that divided people by race, ethnicity, social class, or gender. A construction of "deviant" and, therefore, not to be included in the distribution of benefits, was rare in the neighborhood programs, where an institutional culture seemed to guide service delivery toward the most needy. This did not mean, however, that there were no social constructions of clients. Instead, clients were constructed as people who had made poor choices and who, with proper treatment,` could be resocialized into mainstream values.

The MDPs, in contrast, were much more tied to federal mandates for their target populations and to outcome measures of success. The result was that the federal mandates required the program to stay within the target population guidelines, but the need to produce positive outcomes resulted in "creaming" and serving only those who best fit the business-oriented entrepreneurial model.

6

The Construction of Client Identities in a Post-welfare Social Service Program: The Double Bind of Microenterprise Development

NANCY JURIK AND JULIE COWGILL

Social service organizations are important sites for constructing client identities and transmitting dominant cultural discourses about deservedness and entitlement (Miller 1989; Trethewey 1997; Holstein and Miller 1996). Historically, social service organizations generally, and welfare organizations in particular, have been charged with distinguishing deserving from undeserving program applicants. Ironically, this process has produced a situation wherein, despite their ostensible role in extending opportunities to the disadvantaged, welfare agencies promote discourses, ideologies, materials, and practices that reinforce images of many poor as undeserving and unentitled (Quadagno and Fobes 1995; Schneider and Ingram 1997).

In recent years, political discourse has been filled with the rhetoric of welfare reform. "Reform" advocates allege that welfare benefits create dependency among recipients and strain state and federal resources (Naples 1997). The increasingly negative imagery and accompanying political rhetoric surrounding welfare recipients have fueled movements to "reform" the welfare system (MacLeod, Montero, and Speer 1999). The *Personal Responsibility and Work Opportunity Reconciliation Act of 1996* (typically referred to as "welfare reform legislation") restricted the availability of welfare subsidies, emphasized work requirements, and otherwise sought to promote "self-sufficiency" in lieu of "welfare dependency" (Bartle 1998, 24). Although proponents claim that such changes will promote independence and empowerment of the poor, the net effect of reform rhetoric and legislation has been to deny that the poor are entitled to long-term economic assistance or "safety net" programs (Naples 1997).

During the decade prior to welfare reform, and in the years since, microenterprise development programs (MDPs) gained increasing popularity in the United States (Howells 2000). Microenterprises typically are defined as very small owner-operated businesses with less than $20,000 in capital investment and five or fewer employees. MDPs extend loans and training opportunities to individuals starting their own very small businesses.

Like economic development and welfare job training programs of the past, MDPs aim to alleviate poverty and extend opportunities to least-advantaged citizens (e.g., women and persons of color). Unlike traditional welfare programs, MDPs want to help poor and low-income persons gain independent means of earning an income (Edgcomb, Klein, and Clark 1996, 1). Rather than seeking to change the personalities of the poor, MDPs promise to invest in them through business loans and training (Servon 1999; Stoesz and Saunders 1999). MDPs offer the hope of a practitioner movement that could reconstruct the image of society's poor from helpless dependents to that of resourceful, motivated entrepreneurs (see Schneider and Ingram 1997, 102).

MDPs also promise to challenge images of entrepreneurship as the strict domain of elite, white men (Servon 1999; Light and Pham 1998). A number of programs target poor and low-income mothers, often women of color, who need to earn an income and care for small children. Many MDPs also target men of color.

This chapter focuses on the construction of client identities in an MDP and on the ways in which those identities frame client access to program services. Our data reveal that MDPs do extend some economic opportunities to many women, minority, low- and middle-income individuals. However, we also find that just as in traditional welfare programs, MDP staff evaluate client worthiness and attempt to resocialize them as well as shape access to further services. Some roots of these client constructions are found in extra-organization demands from funding sources that the programs simultaneously assist disadvantaged clients and avoid loan losses and large operating costs. Staff assessments of successful and unsuccessful clients are also influenced by white, middle-class, male-centered standards of business. Such imagery is problematic for many women, minority, and poverty-level clients.

LITERATURE REVIEW AND RESEARCH QUESTIONS

Conservatives and liberals alike have criticized welfare programs for promoting client dependency and passivity (Moynihan 1965). Progressives point out the oppressive role of welfare programs in the cultural reproduction process.

Research shows that welfare programs not only replicate existing societal divisions of labor and remuneration, but also construct clients as passive recipients of benefits and as victims whose defective personality or culture leaves them vulnerable to joblessness and poverty (Schneider and Ingram 1993; Quadagno and Fobes 1995). Staff definitions of clients as morally unworthy or unwilling to change often lead to denial of benefits regardless of their case eligibility (Sarat 1990). Programs use therapeutic language that isolates clients as individuals and obscures the structural roots of their problems (Quadagno and Fobes 1995; Trethewey 1997; Young 1990).

MDPs purport to avoid welfare paternalism by taking a "business-like" approach to clients (Servon 1999; Stoesz and Saunders 1999, 397). U.S. MDPs were inspired by and, in many cases, directly imported from programs in developing countries (e.g., the Grameen Bank and Accion) (Balkin 1989). There are now more than 300 MDPs operating in the United States (Langer, Orwick, and Kays 1999). They base their lending decisions on the feasibility of clients' business plans; the money is loaned, not granted (Edgcomb, Klein, and Clark 1996). Dispensing money is a business transaction that encourages active client self-help (Light and Pham 1998). Advocates argue that this business-like orientation avoids the traditional welfare focus on resocialization and moral assessment of clients (Light 1998; Stoesz and Saunders 1999, 397).

The popularity of MDPs as a solution for persistent unemployment and poverty complements neoliberal policies of tight money, shrinking government expenditures, and the demise of safety-net programs (Joankin and Enriquez 1999; Jurik and Cowgill 1998; Howells 2000). MDPs exemplify a post-welfare trend described by Quadagno as a societal shift from the welfare state to the "capital investment welfare state" (1999, 3), also referred to as welfare capitalism (Stoesz and Saunders 1999). This shift is visible in efforts to shrink government and restructure public benefits to better reflect the operating principles of the private sector. In this vein, programs aim to promote individual rather than collective responsibility through incentives for personal investing, savings, and accumulation (Quadagno 1999, 3; Stoesz and Saunders 1999). Thus, MDPs appeal to the post-welfare mentality of U.S. liberals and conservatives alike by emphasizing investment and self-help through business ownership.

Microenterprise has been praised as an avenue for mothers to combine paid work and child care. Until recently, masculine models of entrepreneurship dominated research and development efforts. Women entrepreneurs had to meet male-centered visions of motivation, management style, and growth objectives to be treated as legitimate candidates for counseling, training, or loan assistance. Brush (1992) argues that while men tend to see businesses as distinct economic units, women are more likely to view their businesses as an interconnected system of relationships. MDPs promise to direct attention toward women's entrepreneurship. Numerous programs were designed to focus on women clients and help them overcome barriers, such as the lack of access to capital, the lack of business expertise, and the absence of social networks (Servon 1999).

Many MDPs function as nonprofit service providers. Despite sharp contrasts with government welfare programs, MDPs still exhibit key elements of human service organizations. They offer scarce services that are, to some extent, subsidized by governmental and philanthropic funding (Hasenfeld 1992). In contrast to popular images of nonprofit organizations as altruistic, innovative, and devoid of red tape, research reveals that successful social movement and nonprofit organizations often grow dependent on government funding for support and, consequently, become bureaucratized and professionalized over time (DiMaggio and Powell 1983). Program services become less innovative and less client oriented (Smith and Lipsky 1993).

Despite the excitement surrounding MDPs, they do not have access to unlimited resources. Research on human service delivery and organizational resource allocation argues that attempts to resocialize or morally assess client worth are inevitable in any organization where staff must allocate scarce resources to clients (Lipsky 1980; Holstein and Miller 1996). Staff evaluate client attitudes, comportment (language and dress), and work practices (Quadagno and Fobes 1995). Moral judgments of client character often accompany these evaluations.

In a case study of one MDP geared for low-income and welfare women, Ehlers and Main found that program staff encouraged women to start businesses in "small-scale, under-capitalized, barely profitable 'pink-collar' businesses" (1998, 424). Training classes socialized them to accept traditionally male entrepreneurial models (e.g., competitiveness, aggressive marketing, risk taking) that ignored the often unique strategies and practices that women bring to the world of business. Special barriers and problems facing poor women entrepreneurs (e.g., conflicts between business and family responsibilities) were ignored and women were told that they could succeed in business if they had sufficient determination to do so. Clients learned to blame their failure on a lack of determination or "lack of the right entrepreneurial stuff"; the structural forces that produced marginalization went unnoticed (438).

This chapter focuses on the construction of client identities in MDPs—that is, images of deserving and undeserving clients. We focus on client-staff negotiation of entrepreneurial identities. We consider several dimensions of the identity-production process, including the dynamics of staff ideologies, job demands, and staff-client interactions. We also consider the extra-organizational context of staff concerns about and definitions of clients.

We find that to sustain funding, MDP staff had a vested interest in recruiting clients who would be successful in their program. Despite the best of intentions, staff developed guiding definitions of worthy and successful clients (e.g., their orientation, loyalty, and productivity). These definitions were linked to the need to show funding sources demonstrable outcomes of program success. Individuals who did not fit staff definitions of worthiness were viewed negatively and labeled dreamers and entitlement seekers. With varying degrees of salience, these assessments were also class-laden, gendered, and racialized. Program training content and outcome measures tended to rely on business models that ignored the racial, ethnic, and gender disadvantages so often faced by women and minority entrepreneurs (Jurik 1998). In line with the findings of Ehlers and Main (1998), we find that instead of promoting woman-oriented models of entrepreneurship, the program tended to rely on traditional models of business. The more concerned they became about program success, the more staff relied on traditional models.

In the following sections, we discuss our research methodology. Then, we turn to an outline of the extra-organizational pressures that encouraged MDP staff to screen out high risk clients. Next, we describe the process whereby staff attempted to select and mold successful clients. Then, we discuss the negative funding consequences when MDPs are proclaimed to be poverty alleviation programs, but weed out too many poor clients. We conclude with a description of our study's implications for social policy.

METHODS

Our analysis draws on case study and cross-sectional data. The case study follows the planning and first six years of operation of one MDP. The cross-sectional study includes surveys and telephone interviews with key program staff at fifty MDPs across the United States.

The case study was based upon the experiences of Micro-Enterprise, Inc. (a pseudonym, hereafter referred to as ME), an MDP located in a large, western U.S. metropolitan area (population of more than two million).[1] ME was a nonprofit community organization governed by a board of directors that included representatives from large private companies, local human service agencies, city government, a university, and several small business owners. ME began providing training and loans to clients in 1994. Loans were provided through a peer lending methodology, whereby clients formed borrowers' circles of up to eight individuals to make lending decisions, provide peer support, and encourage loan repayment.[2]

During its first six years of operation, approximately 64 percent of ME clients were women; 62 percent were persons of color. Sixteen percent were unemployed when they entered the program, but less than 5 percent received welfare or food stamps at the time of entry. Seventeen percent had incomes at or below the federal poverty line, and another 53 percent met the low-income criteria of the U.S. Department of Housing and Urban Development (HUD) (see Table 6.1). Like the clients of most American MDPs, ME clients were well educated: about 61 percent had at least some college experience (Edgcomb, Klein, and Clark 1996).

TABLE 6.1
1999 Income Guidelines for Federal Housing Assistance

Number in Household	HUD Low-Income Guidelines	HUD Very Low-Income Guidelines	Federal Poverty Guidelines
1	$28,100	$17,550	$8,240
2	$32,150	$20,100	$11,060
3	$36,150	$22,600	$13,880
4	$40,150	$25,100	$16,700

Prior to borrowing, ME clients were required to complete a training course and develop a business plan. The fourteen-week training classes were divided into a four-week course for people who were starting new businesses and a ten-week course for those already in a business and for "graduates" of the four-week session. The training covered basic business skills such as marketing, preparing financial reports, and constructing business plans. Clients met with business counselors for additional technical assistance. ME began with two paid staff and some volunteers, had five paid full-time staff by its third year of operation, and nine paid staff by its sixth year. Business counselors and instructors were paid as hourly consultants. After completing the ten-week course, clients were eligible to join a borrowing circle.

After forming a circle, ME borrowers faced a six- to eight-week certification period in which they were asked to forge business relations, develop peer support, elect officers, write by-laws, and make lending decisions. Loan amounts for first loans were $1,200, up to $3,000 for second loans, and up to $5,000 for third loans. Once lending decisions were made, circles met biweekly to make loan payments, provide peer support and repayment pressure, and receive continuing education. A ME staff member attended the circles to facilitate meetings and repayment. To remain eligible for subsequent loans, members had to make timely payments and attend circle meetings. ME also ran an alumni association and a mentoring network for graduates.

The case study data included observations and interviews with ME staff and clients. Between September 1994 and October 2000, we conducted observations of training sessions and meetings of circles, staff, and board of directors. We conducted approximately forty formal interviews with clients, staff, board members, training instructors, circle facilitators, and bank officers working with the program. Both staff and clients appeared to welcome an opportunity to speak about organizational strengths and weaknesses and to make recommendations for future improvements. We conveyed their suggestions to staff and board members in ways that would promote organizational improvement while safeguarding confidentiality.

Our national MDP data came from a combination of purposive and random sampling techniques. Sources for the sample included the Self-employment Loan Project's directory of U.S. MDPs and the registration list of program participants at the 1996 annual conference of the Association for Enterprise Opportunity, a national association of microenterprise providers and supporters (Severens and Kays 1997). From these sources we developed a list of MDPs grouped by lending methodology (peer, individual methods, or both). We oversampled programs with peer lending components for two reasons: (1) We wanted to compare peer lending programs with those using more traditional, individual lending methodologies and (2) Less than 19 percent of U.S. MDPs at the time of our study used peer lending. We mailed short questionnaires to the 104 programs selected and asked for their participation in telephone interviews. Fifty-nine programs (57 percent) agreed to our requests, but we eliminated nine programs from our sample because they did not offer microloans (loans of $25,000 or less). We conducted phone interviews with key staff (executive directors, program managers, lending officers) at the remaining fifty programs. Peer lending-only programs comprised 20 percent of this final sample, 18 percent of our sample offered *both* peer and individual loans, and 62 percent offered individual loans only.

While the crux of our analysis relies on case study data from the ME program, we draw on findings from our national fifty-program sample as well as findings from other research studies to better address the generalizability of the ME experience to the larger U.S. MDP population.

EXTRA-ORGANIZATIONAL PRESSURES ON MDP PROGRAM AND STAFF

In order to understand staff constructions of MDP clients, it is necessary to examine the extra-organizational demands on these programs. Staff exhibited a strong desire to assist their clients in a sensitive and respectful manner, but they were constantly confronted with the need to balance competing demands of providing quality client services and maintaining program resources. Demands with regard to clients included recruiting new clients, overseeing training, managing circles, handling client complaints, promoting client business successes, and ensuring loan repayment. Organizational demands included running the program office and securing funding for lending and program operations.

Only 8 percent of our sample programs were part of state agencies, and even they had to justify their continued existence and attract additional funding from local community, government, and private sector sources. Staff

fund-raising activities included grant writing and networking with local business leaders, community advocates, and lending sources. MDP staff named
increasing competition for funding as their most serious program problem:

> As we . . . open more and more . . . programs, there's actually becoming less
> and less money . . . to be distributed among more and more programs. . . . [My]
> experience is that you find a lot of non-profits that are sort of competing with
> each other.

Programs had problems obtaining sufficient funds for staff salaries, client training, and the day-to-day management of their operations. Many funding agents,
especially banks that needed to meet federal *Community Reinvestment Act*
requirements for lending to low-income communities, were willing to provide
loan pools for MDPs (Santiago, Holyoke, and Levi 1998). However, funding
sources were less interested in providing operations monies. Thus, most programs sought to keep these costs to a minimum:

> We want to provide services without . . . building a whole new bureaucracy.
> We have total assets of . . . around $400,000, and operating costs of around
> $65,000. . . . I look at most loan programs and they have a loan pool of about
> $100,000 and operating costs of about $400,000. Then, you have to go after
> grant money to pay for your $400,000 staff.

Funding appeals necessitated the development of measures of program
effectiveness: service utilization, loan repayments rates, and increasing clients'
employees, business profits, and household incomes. Chief among the outcome
measures was the rate of loan default and delinquency. Some staff argued that
funding concerns pressured MDPs to sacrifice program quality by promoting
"quick and easy success measures." Although most programs emphasized the
importance of accountability, respondents also argued that concerns with meeting outcome measures often discouraged a focus on less easily measured,
longer-run outcomes:

> And it's coming from a desire to do something good, but we all get caught up
> in numbers. And you get so caught up in that [and] you get very confused as
> to who your target market is . . . who you're going to serve, and how to really
> give them quality education. It should be working with people, and not just
> to fulfill a number. . . . It's basically learning how to balance . . . answering to
> your grants *and* answering to your customers.

The ME program experienced these funding pressures. Its operating funds
came from a variety of sources—city, state, and national grants, private foundations, and corporate or individual donations. The loan fund was provided first
by a community development bank and later by an SBA loan fund. Its use of

the peer lending method was a deviation from traditional lending, but the peer model has been credited with high rates of repayment around the globe (Balkin 1989; Microcredit Summit 1997). Despite the reputation of peer lending, local bankers were leery of it. It was clear to ME staff and board members that continued funding would be dependent upon demonstrating that ME could replicate the Grameen repayment record.

Before agreeing to lend to ME's "high risk" clients, the lending bank insisted that all loans be 100 percent guaranteed since the businesses were "quasi start-ups [with] no historical operations." During the first phase of lending, loans were delayed four to six weeks as the city, state Department of Commerce, and ME solidified an agreement to cover any unpaid loans. One ME board member explained:

> We got the backing from the state on our loan pool. Now we have to keep the support from our funding sources. We have to show that our model works, that people pay the loans back.

Despite guarantees, upon reviewing ME clients' proposed businesses, one bank officer balked at making the first loans. An ME staff member describes his reaction:

> It is the midnight hour, the loans are supposed to go out, and Arthur says they are not going to loan us the money. He thought their business ideas were just crazy. I could not imagine how I was going to tell the clients who have already waited longer for these loans than they think they should have. I called Fred [board member and bank officer at another bank]. . . . He said *his* bank could loan us the money. I called Arthur back and told him [about arrangements to borrow from another bank]. Then he said. "Well, wait, I think we can work things out to loan you the money."

Staff and board members reiterated that it was important to "show a good repayment record to prove to the CDB and other funding sources that ME and its clients were good risks." They realized the importance of organizational impression management in maintaining and attracting funding sources and wanted "to identify several successful clients as quickly as possible, and feature them in the local newspapers and program newsletters" to attract public interest and support. Similarly, a staff member in our national sample said:

> The first [concern] is making sure that you have enough funds. My . . . agency . . . put out approximately $30,000 a year for my salary, my part-time secretary, . . . space rent, telephones. And, you know, they're not going to . . . do that forever.

Therefore, in addition to a primary objective of high-quality service delivery, MDP staff were concerned with organizational impression management.

They viewed strong repayment records as integral to organizational longevity (Gulli 1998). Identifying clients with success potential became an element central to ME board and staff member agendas.

SCREENING

Staff in both our case study and national sample selected clients who were most appropriate for their services and who were most likely to be successful after completing the program. Client screening occurred at different stages across programs: before being admitted, during training, during technical assistance, and before lending (see also Balkin 1993; Servon 1999). While all MDPs screened clients at the admission stage to make sure they met the organization's target population requirements (e.g., income, gender, and geographical restrictions), some reported more in-depth methods to select potential clients. The executive director of a program serving Asian immigrants explained their screening process:

> We screen our potential clients first by income, annual gross income. . . . And, number two, [we look] into their income [to see] where they it get it from.

While some screening processes may work to guarantee that a program serves disadvantaged clients, many programs screened to select the most capable clients (Edgcomb, Klein, and Clark 1996; Jurik and Cowgill 1998). A staff member described her program's rationale for screening:

> [W]ith this more streamlined process, we might be able to reach just as many people, or granted, by *creaming* them a little bit. Because now we're not dealing with the people who say "yeah, I'm *thinking* about a business." . . . We can provide loans to people who *already* exhibit strong entrepreneurial characteristics, and that's a key distinction.

An example of one of the more rigorous screening processes was described by a staff member of a Northeastern program that offers both peer and individual lending:

> We have a very intense screening process to even get *into* the program. [People] have to turn in an application, take a math test, submit a writing sample, do a group activity, [take] an individual interview, and [complete] a personality interview. . . . We usually have 75–80 people apply . . . then we select 30 of them.

We observed client screening in the ME case to be an emergent process that entailed both assessment and socialization of clients in terms of basic eligibility, orientation, loyalty, and productivity. The evaluation of moral worthiness was a component of this process. As ME grew more concerned about loan repayment rates, it increased efforts to screen clients. A board member suggested:

> Now that we have been doing this a few months, we need to identify some methods for selecting clients for circles and loans who are *right* for our program, clients who will be likely to succeed.

This screening pattern coincides with reports that we received from staff in our fifty-program sample. The next section focuses on the process of client screening as it emerged in the ME case and as it paralleled programs in the national sample.

THE SUCCESSFUL ME CLIENT—TRUE ENTREPRENEURS

The ostensible focus of ME was on the quality of a client's business idea. Lending was made without traditional forms of collateral so that to a degree, the lending was character-based. Unlike small local communities in which peer lending models developed (e.g., rural Bangladesh), in large urban communities, little is known of an individual's reputation. ME staff and, later, ME circle members, had limited information upon which to base decisions about distributing training and loan money. Staff developed theories about the client personality-type that would most likely be successful in the program. Moral assumptions about clients were often implicit. From the program's inception through its first four years of operation, we observed that staff and board members became more concerned with recruiting the "right type" of client for the program.

In the following subsections, we demonstrate how staff identified clients as legitimate recipients of ME's resources. Staff viewed successful clients as being on the path toward becoming "true entrepreneurs." These were individuals who exhibited: (1) an *orientation* toward self-improvement, professionalism, and training; (2) *loyalty* to ME; and (3) *productivity* in meeting prescribed program and business outcomes. True entrepreneurs were contrasted with their negative counterparts—"entitlement seekers" and "dreamers." Staff came to define entitlement seekers as those who confused ME with traditional welfare programs, who thought loan money was an entitlement rather than a business transaction. Dreamers had unrealistic expectations for themselves and their business.

Orientation

True entrepreneurs were oriented toward self-improvement, presented themselves in a professional manner, and focused more on training than on borrowing. Staff constructions of true entrepreneurs were informed by American cultural images of professionalism and rationality. A staff member described his preferred clients as being "sincere, committed, hardworking, and disciplined" individuals who had a "rational, practical dream."

One indicator of a successful client orientation was a "professional" demeanor in the client's "presentation of self" (see Goffman 1963). This included personal appearance (clothing, speech, demeanor), social capital (networking ability), and symbolic factors (a typed business plan).

Dominant images of professionalism have been criticized for reflecting white, middle class notions of propriety (Young 1990). Staff promoted traditional notions of professionalism even as they tried to respect clients' social and economic positions. They viewed clients as "unsophisticated," but believed that, with training, hard-working, realistic clients could become good business people. Although staff members mentioned clothing, they did not expect "the clients to be dressed up, just to present themselves as neat and tidy." A staff member said:

> It goes back to attitude and how you think of yourself and your business. If they take this seriously, they dress appropriately. . . . [T]hey don't need a business suit . . . but they should show that they take themselves and their business seriously. They need . . . to make an effort to say this is my business and it's important to me.

Another indicator of a successful orientation was a client's willingness to focus on the training rather than lending aspects of the program. From the outset, loans clearly drew clients to the ME program. However, when members of the earlier classes began to grumble about the length of training and other "obstacles" that delayed borrowing, staff began to emphasize training and networking opportunities over the small loan offerings. Moreover, client interest in training became an indicator of worthiness. As one staff member described it: "Serious clients realize the value of this educational process." Participants who focused primarily on loans, and who spoke about training as a barrier to loans, were suspected of being entitlement seekers. A staff member said:

> We have some that may have had ulterior motives. . . . They're not really there for the spirit of the program like we want it. And the program was new . . . [and] some of these people may have slipped through and [just wanted] the loans, [but they] didn't get into the spirit of the program which is educational.

Another staff member said:

> It is our job to get them to recognize that these are business loans and not something that they are entitled to. People are so used to welfare that they slip into this mentality.

Initially, the ME program aimed to assist the poor, especially women and minorities. The images of making loans to women selling tamales on the streets, and of helping welfare mothers to get off welfare by starting their own businesses, were frequently referenced in planning session discussions of ME's target population. When initial contacts with funders discouraged a predominant focus on welfare and poverty level clients, ME adopted HUD standards as their criteria for low-income clients. HUD low-income guidelines are significantly higher than federal poverty guidelines (see Table 6.1). Despite their acquiescence to pressures for targeting higher income clients, ME planners reiterated a commitment "to preserve at least some part of our resources for lending to these very poor women."

Within the first year of program operations, ME board and staff members became increasingly aware of the negative images of welfare programs and of the greater needs and risks associated with poverty-level clients (see Quadagno 1999). Eighty-eight percent of the first client cohort was comprised of poor or low-income individuals; slightly less than half of this cohort either had numerous late payments or defaulted on their loans. Alarmed staff and board members sought to disassociate ME from a welfare clientele. A board member said, "I think it is clear that our program works best for low-income individuals, and not the very poor. The very poor just do not have the resources to get their businesses off the ground." A staff member said:

> Our program has appeal because it is *not* a welfare program. It is a business program. We do not have the resources to work with welfare clients and the risks are just too great. They think the money is a right, not a loan.

ME officials feared that potential funders would see them as being similar to welfare programs. Drawing on assumptions that resembled conservative versions of a culture-of-poverty perspective (Moynihan 1965), staff and board members increasingly worried about client behaviors and attitudes that they associated with low-income, unskilled, and less educated people. One staff member said:

> We don't have a lot of people on welfare in the program now and I think part of the reason for that is entrepreneurship requires a certain mentality in order to be successful at it. I think a lot of people on welfare get bogged down in their current situation and have troubles looking forward to things, which makes it hard to start a business.

This was also a common theme in our national sample:

> Our primary objective . . . is to help people to produce their own income and not to rely on welfare.
> [W]e're not trying to develop a pattern of dependency; we're trying to facilitate and provide a tool which helps people get on their feet.

Although ME clients faced many structural disadvantages, training classes focused on traditional models of business planning, emphasizing success through hard work and deferred gratification. Guest speakers recounted Horatio Alger-type stories of how their businesses went from rags to riches. Clients were told that if they just worked hard enough, they too could be successful in business (Ehlers and Main 1998). ME training classes devoted little attention to societal barriers such as racial, ethnic, and gender discrimination, work-family conflicts, monopolistic business practices, or government regulatory and tax structures that disadvantage very small businesses (Van Auken 1999).

Despite the traditional course content, ME business trainers and staff were concerned with developing training that was suited to clients. An instructor said that ME clients differed from the established business people she worked with:

> Some ME clients haven't taken any . . . classes since high school or college. We
> assumed a certain level of knowledge on a certain subject, and if we could see
> that we weren't getting through . . . we would back up [and] do something
> more basic.

ME staff wanted to help clients, but also wanted to reinforce the view that business success was the individual client's responsibility, not the program's. In response to client objections about guest speakers who were elite, white, and owners of large businesses, staff invited more minority and smaller business owners to visit classes. However, discussions of structural barriers to client success remained outside the program's purview (Ehlers and Main 1998; Van Auken 1999).

Loyalty

Staff were sensitive to a second dimension of client behavior—whether they were "team players." Specifically, they wanted clients who would obey ME rules and negotiate organizational problems without rancor. For example, in the first cohort of clients, ME faced service delivery dilemmas that included delays in the lending process, instructors inexperienced in working with low-income clients, incomplete training workbooks, and an untrained circle facilitator. These problems created tensions between ME staff and clients.

Staff preferred clients who negotiated hurdles without openly criticizing the program. For example, one participant, Ben, challenged an early ME policy. Instead of complaining, Ben turned a training session into a forum to express his concern and discuss solutions. His diplomacy led to the policy being terminated. Karen, an instructor, said that Ben's feedback was invaluable and helped her improve subsequent classes:

> A lot of the changes we made were due to Ben. Ben came in during the second session and he was all excited. He said, "This is really great, Karen, but there are some things that you could do and you're not." Boom, boom, and I was writing like a madwoman.

In contrast with clients who threatened to take complaints outside the ME organization, Ben's more "constructive approach" was welcome. He became a key source of feedback for the program.

Productivity Outcomes

Staff judged client success by outcomes that would bolster funding efforts. Prior to joining borrowers' circles, clients had to have an approved business plan. Staff examined the plan to see if it was a realistic idea. Clients were expected to be realistic about their planned needs, including start-up capital, profitability, cost projections, and marketing. Staff viewed it as essential that businesses grow out of clients' prior work experiences. For example, a low-income woman who wanted to manufacture environmentally safe laundry disks was dismissed as a "dreamer." Her business plans were "unrealistic" for someone of her income status, work experience (waitressing), and lack of previous business experience. A realistic business was also supposed to be commensurate with the client's financial and time restrictions. It should be compatible with personal demands, such as other paid work and child care demands. Clients whom staff perceived as having unrealistic business plans were described as "dreamers."

Of course, staff desires for "realistic" business ideas were practical and well intentioned. They were also sensitive to the differential resources of clients, generally, and to the child care demands for women clients in particular. Yet, in the long run, this "realistic" concept also reinforced the marginalized status of ME clients. Given the gender, racial, ethnic, and class positions of clients, the encouragement to keep business ideas compatible with resources and past work experiences meant that most client businesses were undercapitalized, labor intensive, and low profit (Servon and Bates 1998). Pressures to be "realistic" also reinforced existing gender stratification patterns in business, because most women clients' prior work experiences were in "pink collar" occupations. ME women clients' enterprises were typically in this category. Business ventures in pink collar industries tend to be even more undercapitalized and low paid than those in stereotypic male ventures (Ehlers and Main 1998).

Staff often recommended changes in client business ideas to make the ventures "more realistic." At times, staff assessments of client business ideas were implicitly racialized or class biased. One short-term instructor criticized a client who wanted to sell photographic art in the southern part of the city. This area was known as a low-income, African-American and Latino/Latina community. The instructor told her that most people would not view the materials from that area as art.

Client responsiveness to staff suggestions was important. For example, one training instructor commented on the clients' business ideas:

> Sometimes I can tell they have unrealistic expectations of what their business is going to be all about. . . . If they refuse to change it early on, or refuse to be even receptive to it [change], they won't make it.

Staff believed that a realistic business plan should produce timely and measurable results. Modest goals and quick successes were important to ME staff.
They believed that it was important for clients, many with low self-esteem, to
experience some success as soon as possible. Also, ongoing efforts to raise funds
were facilitated by client successes. Staff encouraged clients to start their businesses promptly and show small, quick returns. Clients who did not follow this
advice were viewed negatively. One staff member said:

> We don't need a lot of procrastinators . . . the way that we're getting rid of
> those people is we're basically going to start having them prove that they have
> done something in the six months of the first loan for a [new] business. . . . If
> they haven't done anything with their business in six months, I don't think
> we'll be dealing with them any further. We're talking certification, licensing,
> business cards, customer base, income statement.

Because it gave clients a quick sense of success and gave the program some
successful outcomes, this strategy was practical in the short run. Unfortunately,
this strategy further pressured clients to start very small, undercapitalized, labor
intensive businesses in lieu of waiting for better financing opportunities, or
seeking to build cash reserves. It also excluded clients who might not be able
to handle the added financial burdens (e.g., tax liability), or to meet citizenship
requirements for quickly formalizing their businesses.

These quick, small goals complemented ME's concern about losses. During the first year of ME operation, loan amounts were lowered from $1,200 to
$500 for people with start-up businesses. When combined with prompt loan
repayment and good circle attendance, quick, albeit small successes showed staff
that clients were serious about their businesses. Such clients were considered
more favorably for future loans.

Staff avoided the technical terms "microenterprise" and "micro-
entrepreneur," because they believed that such terms demeaned clients. They
emphasized that despite limitations confronting client businesses, there was
considerable continuity between microentrepreneurs and large-scale entrepreneurs. One instructor said:

> An entrepreneur is just somebody who wants to take risks and doesn't nec-
> essarily need to have a steady paycheck all the time, . . . and on a micro-
> scale, we're just talking smaller dollars, but we're talking the same kind of
> risks psychologically.

Despite staff sensitivity to client status, an emphasis on shared characteristics
underestimates the greater relative barriers confronted by ME microentrepreneurs when compared with those faced by entrepreneurs in large businesses and corporations (Van Auken 1999).

Successful Circles

In addition to shaping individuals into professional business owners, MDPs that used a peer lending approach also had to be concerned about developing successful circles. The circle served as the collateral of the peer-lending method, and successful circles were believed to increase the likelihood of loan repayment. One staff member in the national sample said:

> The peer group lending model has been exciting . . . [and] it is a challenge, because when you bring groups of women together . . . it becomes difficult sometimes to get people to want to work together over the long period. . . . [A]n enterprise agent has a very sensitive position in that they can't tell a circle what to do, but they have to find these very creative ways to guide them through group dynamics.

Over time, ME staff also developed notions about successful circles. Staff wanted circle members to support each other, but also to critically assess each other's business plans and repayment prospects prior to lending.

ME staff pressured circles to avoid letting supportive functions overshadow their roles as "rational lending decision makers." Staff devalued circles who based decisions on personal allegiances instead of on analysis of business plans:

> We want to bring out more . . . that this is a business. [At first,] we had wanted them [circles] to have a family atmosphere. We found that's not really what we wanted. [We know] that you let family run over you sometimes, and do things that you would not let a person do in business. We want them to look at it in a business manner always.

Successful circles demonstrated commitment to the program through regular attendance at circle meetings and smooth, organized circle meetings. Dissension among circle clients upset the flow of meetings and consumed extra staff time. Circle members who were unable to mediate potentially volatile situations were especially problematic for staff.

Circles also had to negotiate program hurdles. For example, delays in lending and unclear policies sometimes posed problems for ME clients, especially those in earlier cohorts. Circles that responded to such problems by complaining and challenging staff and program legitimacy were viewed as "troublemakers" and "entitlement seekers." In contrast, true entrepreneurs belonged to circles that supported and worked with ME staff to solve problems. A staff member from our national sample described successful circles as being comprised of individuals who were active in the program and in developing their business, and who had "a good relationship" with the program. Staff hoped that these types of circle characteristics would lead to a successful circle with successful businesses and strong repayment records.

STAFF EFFORTS TO CREATE
SUCCESSFUL CLIENTS AND CIRCLES

Over time, ME staff assumed greater control over virtually every stage of the ME program. This tendency was triggered initially by circle attendance problems, staff-circle conflicts, and the loan delinquencies of the first client cohort. However, even after these problems were stabilized, staff continued to exert control over more program areas, especially client circles. In line with processes identified in the literature on social movements and social organizations, these later changes appeared to coincide with increases in staff size, in grant reporting requirements, and in overall program growth (Smith and Lipsky 1993; DiMaggio and Powell 1983). The changes included increased staff screening of clients joining borrowers' circles, exerting control over circle meetings and lending decisions, and developing additional client socialization activities. A ME staff member said:

> There are people in the [current] borrowing circles now that we wish weren't. We just didn't think they were ready to take that step. . . . Now we are taking a more careful look at the business plans before letting clients join circles. . . . We are also going to require staff approval for loans. The circles will still recommend, but a staff committee will have to give final approval after we consider the soundness of the request.

Staff also sought greater control over the structure of circle meetings. They provided sample by-laws and monitored circle officer elections. A staff member discussed these changes after she implemented parliamentary procedures:

> Used to be . . . there was no structure, . . . and one individual would dominate the . . . meeting. We don't allow that [any] more. Basically, we got a rule: If we're trying to get something passed and somebody wants to talk, you know to sway the vote or something then . . . we will dictate how many minutes we're going to give them to talk.

More rigorous controls included compulsory training to apply for additional loans and denying additional loans to those with excessive circle absences.

Socialization activities included providing business mentors, an alumni association, a client business directory, and "trade fairs" to promote client businesses. Staff also developed mock circle demonstrations to encourage the critical assessment of circle member business plans.

These sorts of programmatic changes were common among the peer-lending programs in our fifty-program sample, especially for those with peer-lending components. Three programs eliminated peer lending altogether because of the "problems and costs" associated with managing circles. Four programs kept peer lending, but modified it in ways that were similar to ME program changes: one program added a tracking mechanism to monitor circle attendance, while three programs increased staff control and supervision of circle activities and decision-making. A staff member in our national sample stated: "Our facilitator has final say on the loans. He hasn't rejected any, but he does evaluate them."

Interestingly, there were three or four programs in our national sample that maintained a high degree of participation among poor and very low-income clients, significant autonomy for circles, and even client participation in program governance. A few programs also incorporated coverage of issues of racism and sexism and other structural concerns into their training and mentoring curriculum. Ten programs (20 percent) developed partnerships with child care providers and twelve programs (14 percent) obtained funding for transportation assistance to aid clients in their business pursuits. For the most part, however, MDP respondents described business-as-usual curricula and increasing efforts to screen, monitor, and control clients as programs matured.

THE CONSEQUENCES OF SCREENING: SERVICE DELIVERY AND FUNDING ISSUES

Policy makers and social scientists suggest that poverty alleviation is, and should be, a primary MDP goal (Edgcomb, Klein, and Clark 1996; Microcredit Summit 1997). MDPs are frequently presented as an alternative to welfare in today's era of welfare reform (Else and Raheim 1992; Howells 2000). Another goal is to assist women, minorities, and other marginalized people (e.g., refugees, the disabled) to start businesses. In our national sample, 12 percent of the programs targeted the poor and 64 percent targeted low-income individuals as their service population. Forty percent targeted women and 46 percent targeted minorities.

In addition to fueling the popular support of MDPs, poverty alleviation goals generated considerable funding for programs. Initiatives from the U.S. Small Business Administration, HUD, Community Development Block Grant Programs, and private support from banks seeking credits under the *Community Reinvestment Act* all required that funded programs target the needs of poor and very low-income groups, especially women and minorities (Howells 2000). Some MDPs were developed as demonstration programs for welfare clients (Else and Raheim 1992), and more recent funding, linked to federal welfare reform legislation, will require that MDPs provide services for welfare-to-work clients (Pate 2000, 1).

Despite the incentives to focus on poor and low-income groups, research indicates that programs serve clients who are better educated on average than the general U.S. low-income population, and while MDPs serve low-income individuals, most fail to serve many clients at or below the poverty level (Servon and Bates 1998; Schreiner 1999; see Table 6.1). Researchers question the appropriateness of MDPs for low-income, poverty-level clients, especially those formerly on welfare. It is difficult, they suggest, for people with limited educational and financial resources to develop businesses that can sustain their households. Microloans may simply increase their indebtedness (Servon and Bates 1998; Ehlers and Main 1998; Howells 2000). In contrast, others argue that MDPs are helpful to such disadvantaged groups, if only to provide an additional source of income (Else and Raheim 1992; Clark and Kays 1999).

Many practitioners in our national sample agreed that MDPs were not appropriate for poor and very low-income clients. They found that such clients were more difficult to assist and required more services. Extra services increased operating expenses significantly, but without them, more disadvantaged clients were doomed to failure (Servon 1999; Gulli 1998; Servon and Bates 1998). In turn, failures reflected poorly on programs and hurt fund-raising efforts:

> A lot of programs ... are trying to be full-scale service providers and it's very costly, very time intensive, and they don't always have a lot to show for it because often times people aren't really starting their businesses and getting them running. ... We have to think about what we do best, ... what we *don't do* best is provide full-fledged counseling, literacy credit counseling, ... helping them explore what business they want to start.
>
> You have to be business-like in your approach ... otherwise you're going to be out there begging for money ... there is a social cost and somebody has to pick up the tab.

Some programs provided training and technical assistance to poor and very low-income clients, but typically did not give them loans. Servon (1999) discovered this pattern in her study of MDPs. The Self-employment Loan Project's survey data suggest that about 30 percent of clients served by MDPs are poverty-level clients (Severens and Kays 1997). Yet, because these figures do not differentiate client demographics for the type of services received, it is likely that they overestimate the percentages of poor clients and welfare clients served by MDPs.

In analyzing ME's service delivery data over its first six years of operation, we found that the program maintained a high level of service to women (over 60 percent), minority populations (over 60 percent of clients), and HUD, low-income-level populations (72 percent). In keeping with staff desires to reduce service to welfare and poverty-level individuals, the percentages of clients in this category decreased over time (from 26 to 16 percent) (Table 6.2). The percentage of clients who had at least some college experience increased over time from 46 to 71 percent for the advanced training class and from 35 to 86 percent for the lending phase.

Staff and board members agreed that clients who had more educational and income resources seemed to do better in the program. While it is possible that improved general economic opportunities for the poor during our study period disproportionately discouraged them from entering the ME program, staff believed that their increased screening efforts had effected these client demographic changes. They also believed that their screening efforts had produced a lower rate of loan default after the first client cohort. Despite these seemingly positive program effects, however, lowered rates of services to poor and very low-income clients also held potentially negative repercussions for future program fund raising.

According to staff estimates, for the first half of the seventh year of program operation the proportion of poverty and low-income clients was 51 percent. At a planning meeting, staff and board members expressed concern. A board member noted:

> When we present these figures to banks, they will question whether they can justify CRA [Community Reinvestment Act] credits.... Fifty percent or more low income clients is easily justified under CRA credit criteria. If the number is less than 50 percent, then it is not as straightforward to justify that we are an organization that serves low income individuals. It raises more questions.

Facing increased competition for local funds, ME has recently begun to apply for welfare-to-work funding and promised to increase its services to welfare clients. This pressure poses a contradiction for ME staff and board members, who feel that the program is not really appropriate for welfare clients. Nationally, MDPs are searching for new ways to tap in to welfare funds (Pate 2000). Thus, MDPs struggle between conforming to popular conceptions of

TABLE 6.2
ME Poverty-Level Clients and HUD Low-Income Clients Over Time

Year of Entry	Meets Poverty Guidelines	Meets HUD Low-Income Guidelines	Total HUD & Poverty Clients	Total Clients All Income Levels
1994	13 (26%)	31 (62%)	44 (88%)	50
1995	32 (24%)	79 (59%)	111 (82%)	135
1996	43 (26%)	93 (55%)	136 (81%)	168
1997	28 (19%)	89 (60%)	117 (79%)	149
1998	49 (18%)	124 (47%)	173 (65%)	266
1999	47 (16%)	160 (55%)	207 (72%)	289
Total All Years	**212 (20%)**	**576 (54%)**	**788 (75%)**	**1057**

them as welfare alternatives and poverty alleviation programs, and funders' demands that they meet certain success criteria (e.g., high loan repayment, client business successes). These competing demands led to screening procedures that increased the numbers of clients with moderate income and educational levels. Staff must then justify declines in services to low-income and poverty-level clients and to funders concerned with these issues (Bhatt, Painter, and Tang 2002).

CONCLUSION

An important agenda for policy studies is documenting the social construction of deservedness and entitlement in social policy. This chapter examines the construction process in one type of post-welfare social service organization. MDPs have been praised for empowering marginalized individuals—low-income, white women, and men and women of color—both economically and socially by providing opportunities for clients to "help themselves." Advocates claim that these programs demonstrate that the poor—especially women and minorities—are more resourceful, hard working, and self-sufficient than traditional welfare programs recognized (Microcredit Summit 1997). In particular, peer-lending MDPs are credited with giving clients extensive control over training and lending processes, while avoiding efforts to resocialize or morally assess them. These self-help and business-like dimensions have fueled MDP popularity and visibility in the post-welfare era. The fact that so many MDPs are independent nonprofit service providers has also furthered hopes of developing a more innovative, less bureaucratic, local, and nongovernment service sector.

Our findings suggest that, although MDPs provide important services to many clients trying to start and operate their own very small businesses, programs fall short of these ideals. MDPs are in an unfortunate double-bind. The demands of fund raising and accountability pressure staff to develop indicators for identifying clients with the greatest success potential. This screening process leads to the exclusion of more disadvantaged clients. However, screening may cause MDPs to exclude too many poor and otherwise disadvantaged clients and thereby lose funds associated with their image as poverty alleviation programs.

In contrast with images of MDPs as alternative and innovative nonprofit service providers, we find that as programs matured, increasing bureaucratization and staff controls eroded client empowerment and local autonomy. Despite the locally controlled and nonprofit aspects of many MDPs, these programs are increasingly dependent on government funding for significant components of their budgets. With government funds come reporting and staffing requirements that increase bureaucratization. Even programs that are not dependent upon government funding must meet the standards of bureaucratization and institutional isomorphism so often required to gain the financial support of foundations and corporate donors (DiMaggio and Powell 1983). Our findings support Smith and Lipsky's (1993) argument that the separation between government and nonprofit service providers is not as clear as popular wisdom claims.

Our findings suggest that to meet funding pressures, MDPs, like welfare programs, develop practices to screen or "cream" more desirable clients (Ehlers and Main 1998; Blumberg 1995). These mechanisms increase program success, but they also propogate negative character assessments of clients who fail.

It is significant that so many MDP clients experienced training and lending opportunities that otherwise might not have been available to them and their very small businesses (Servon 1999; Severens and Kays 1997). However, problems arise when funding for these organizations is justified on the grounds that they are (1) poverty alleviation programs, (2) substitutes for policies that promote large-scale employment opportunities, or (3) alternatives to welfare and other safety net programs. Most evidence suggests that MDPs work best for individuals with higher levels of economic and educational resources than those possessed by most poor and low-income individuals in our society (Servon and Bates 1998). A clear majority of staff in our program sample, as well as the staff in our ME program case study, did not believe that their programs worked well for very low-income, poor, or welfare-to-work clients. Therefore, although MDPs are helpful to some low-income individuals, their continued identification (Else and Raheim 1992; Microcredit Summit 1997) as alternatives to welfare and solutions to declining paid employment opportunities for the poor is highly problematic and contributes to a degenerative policy-making context (Schneider and Ingram 1997, 102–05). In particular, the continued lobbying efforts of MDPs to gain eligibility for welfare-to-work funding seems particularly misleading.

Another problem with many MDPs, particularly with the ME program in this study, is that business training focuses on transmitting individualistic explanations of economic success and implicitly blames clients for economic failures (see also Ehlers and Main 1998). The "business-as-usual" approach never systematically engaged the structural disadvantages faced by economically and socially marginalized ME clients. Accordingly, the program failed to significantly challenge white, masculine, and elite-based definitions of doing business. In the absence of such challenges, and in this era of declining services for the very poor, MDP organizational discourse supports and disseminates a capital-investment welfare ideology to socially and economically marginalized clients and to a general public that only hears about MDP program "successes," "poverty alleviation," and "welfare alternatives." By offering only nominal financial support through small loans, by emphasizing personal growth, and by ignoring myriad structural disadvantages faced by clients, MDPs reinforce economic and cultural marginalization (Howells 2000). Those poor and

very low-income women and minority individuals who fail to "lift" themselves up out of poverty through microenterprise will continue to be viewed
as helpless deviants and are scorned by policy makers.

NOTES

1. Some peer lending programs offered both individual and peer loans. After its first
five years of operation, the ME program added an individual lending component. Individual loans typically were larger than peer loans and were made only to established
businesses. There were too few individual loans at the time of our study to evaluate them
or the lending process associated with them.

2. Although not the focus of the present chapter, it should be noted that some
clients actively resisted and reinterpreted dominant ME organizational constructions of
themselves and of entrepreneurship more generally. We will focus on client resistance in
a future paper.

7

Deservedness in Poor Neighborhoods: A Morality Struggle

Michelle Camou

Introduction

Policy-making responsibility in the United States is a dispersed responsibility. Traditionally, scholars have focused on legislatures and bureaucracies as the prime sites of policy making. But, by devolution, the civic sector and its diversity of organizations have become more important. This is especially the case with urban revitalization policy as *neighborhood* organizations[1]—including nonprofit service providers, advocacy organizations, and resident associations focused within neighborhoods—assume much responsibility for identifying and tackling urban problems. Neighborhood organizations have become the new "street level bureaucrats" (Lipsky 1980), fulfilling a similar policy-making role as government agencies that identify, articulate, and attempt to resolve urban problems. In this role, neighborhood organizations allocate resources for collective purposes and become intimately involved in determining questions of who will be served and why.

I examine the policy-making role of neighborhood organizations and how they socially construct deservedness in a case study of Sandtown-Winchester, a low-income, African-American community in Baltimore, Maryland. In this chapter, I argue that the process of establishing deservedness or entitlement in poor neighborhoods is often a morality struggle in which neighborhood organizations attempt to establish lifestyle standards for specific communities. Because of their leadership role, institutional backing, and control of resources, neighborhood organizations are able to validate certain lifestyles, but they do so in ways that differ from legislative and nonprofit sectors. Nonprofits frequently "cream," and legislatures typically confer benefits on individuals who are more powerful and well-regarded. Neighborhood organizations, however, largely ignore the more positively constructed groups within the neighborhood. Instead, they focus attention on members of target groups whom they believe lack the "correct" norms and values and attempt to resocialize them into an acceptable way of life. The basic strategy for many neighborhood organizations observed in this study was to bring about behavioral and attitudinal change. The notion of deservedness is intermingled with a language of deficits: people who lack the "correct" norms and values are worthiest of neighborhood resources. This approach results in a construction of deservedness where competence, contribution, and power count less than need.

SOCIAL CONSTRUCTIONS IN NEIGHBORHOOD POLICY-MAKING CONTEXTS

Schneider and Ingram's original work focused on the degenerative policy making sometimes found in legislative arenas, as contrasted with policy making in a scientific/managerial dominated arena (Schneider and Ingram 1997). Although they examined various implementation styles and agency strategies employed to deal with the policy designs that emerge from degenerative politics (Ingram and Schneider 1990, 1991), they did not focus on policy making by nonprofits or neighborhood organizations. Thus, this chapter contributes to a theory of social constructions of policy by examining how nonprofits and neighborhood organizations socially construct the client groups they serve.

Taking neighborhoods as arenas for policy making accepts the idea that actors in neighborhoods decide questions for the collective by identifying common problems, developing agendas, collecting and allocating resources, and crafting solutions. It is a myth to think that, in the devolved policy-making context of federalism, neighborhood actors simply carry out policies formulated by cities, counties, states, or federal governments. In reality, many neighborhood organizations operate in the absence of governmental funding of any kind. Even when neighborhood groups rely partly or fully on funding from government sources, their discretion in policy implementation is constrained only by grant guidelines.[2] As a result, neighborhood organizations place their own "stamp" on urban polices, and neighborhood strategies reflect the discourse of community decision-makers in specific neighborhoods.

While neighborhood decision-making can occur within either formal or informal organizations, the focus here is on formal neighborhood organizations, associations, and groups, legally incorporated as nonprofits under Internal Revenue Service designation 501(c)(3) or its equivalent, that operate within specific territorial boundaries. Everything from highly structured, technically oriented organizations to groups of citizens that meet in church basements fall in this range. This definition excludes funding organizations and government agencies that may take special interest in particular neighborhoods but, nonetheless, are based outside of neighborhood boundaries and are not engaged in the day-to-day implementation of neighborhood-centered strategies.

Because of their sustained and ongoing control of resources for public pur-poses, neighborhood organizations are also in the business of determining who is deserving. As this case study points out, neighborhood organizations also rely on making judgments of personal competence and contribution in their deci-sion-making, just as "traditional" policy makers do. Yet, because they operate in the absence of electoral motivations, they face few pressures to systematically reward populations without legitimate needs. Operating under different incen-tive structures and with a fixed population, neighborhood organizations in low-income neighborhoods equate "deserving" and "entitled" with "incompetent" and "deficient"—not "meritorious" or "successful." Ultimately, this leads them to focus on the tough cases.[3]

This significant difference with the legislative arena reflects the different motivations, accountability concerns, and mechanisms of reward in neighbor-hoods. Motivations are not rooted as much in personal gain as they are by insti-tutional cultures that emphasize service to the most needy. Furthermore, key constituencies include funding sources and neighborhood residents—none of whom can, for instance, remove individuals from their policy-making role by voting them out. More important, not all constituent groups feel entitled to benefits from neighborhood organizations, as in the case of foundations that exist to provide rather than consume resources. This dynamic removes much of the impetus for rewarding advantaged targets.

In addition, neighborhood organizations are fundamentally limited in *how* they can reward and punish. In contrast to the power of elected policy-making bodies, neighborhood groups generally cannot tax or give tax breaks, nor do they possess the coercive authority of the state to fine lawbreakers or remove them from the neighborhood. All of these factors militate against defining deservedness in terms of rewarding powerful, well regarded persons since there are fewer incentives and means for doing so. Thus, attending to people without legitimate needs is not a high priority.

Creating Entitlement in Sandtown-Winchester: A Case Study

Sandtown-Winchester is an African-American neighborhood in Baltimore with a population of ten thousand to twelve thousand, a rich tradition of neighborhood activism, and a large number of neighborhood organizations of various types. Bal-timore's loss of its manufacturing base has been hard on Sandtown. In recent years, the neighborhood has become an area marked by concentrated poverty, low edu-cational and employment attainment, high rates of crime, female-headed house-holds, population loss, and housing deterioration (McDougall 1993, 137).

Since 1992, Sandtown-Winchester has also become the site of several high profile public-private partnerships involving the Enterprise Foundation, the

City of Baltimore, and the Empowerment Zone project of the U.S. Department
of Housing and Urban Development (HUD). Directly involving about half of
Sandtown-Winchester's neighborhood organizations, the partnerships aim to
produce "neighborhood transformation,"[4] primarily around housing, health,
crime, and employment. These partnerships have received national acclaim as
comprehensive approaches to community revitalization focused on changing
behavioral and changing some structural sources of neighborhood decline.

Research has tended either to focus on the major players in these partnerships—especially the Centers for Disease Control (CDC) (Goetz 1997; Liou
and Stroh 1998; Von Hoffman 2001, 11–22) or a handful of other programs
(McDougall 1993)—and/or has failed to differentiate between funding and
administrative organizations (e.g., The Enterprise Foundation, Baltimore
Empowerment, Community Building in Partnership) and the frontline organi-
zations/programs charged with implementation. However, Lipsky (1980) cau-
tions that this may be a significant oversight, since the process of implementation can transform policies, as frontline decision-makers import their own
views and establish allocation guidelines. This opens the possibility that programs, as practiced, do not always internalize the visions of external partners. It
also means that existing knowledge about urban revitalization in Sandtown-
Winchester may be slanted toward external players' interpretations.

This chapter focuses only on frontline organizations physically based in
Sandtown-Winchester that do not conduct activities beyond neighborhood
boundaries.[5] Using the *Sandtown-Winchester Community Directory,*[6] I identified
twenty-eight separate neighborhood programs/organizations active in Sandtown-Winchester in 1998. Half of the groups engage in implementing partnership activities and the other half are independent. I was able to interview individuals from twenty-five programs or organizations, virtually the entire
population, in July and August 1998. Primarily, I used qualitative interviews in
the style of Rubin and Rubin (1995) to investigate neighborhood revitalization.

In Sandtown-Winchester, organizations vary according to the institutional
setting in which they operate. Institutional setting varies along two dimensions:
secular or religious orientation and professional or voluntary leadership. Secular or religious orientation refers to whether or not organizations are affiliated
with a church; professional or voluntary leadership refers to whether the organization's *management* (those presiding over day-to-day activities) are volunteers
or paid.[7] While it is certainly possible to classify organizations using other criteria—such as issue area, funding sources, or radical versus conventional worldviews—I contend that classification along the secular/religious and profes-
sional/voluntary dimensions makes the most sense for this and many other
low-income neighborhoods. Since radical organizations tend to be rare, funding sources do not determine the content of strategies, and issues are varied,
these dimensions provide the best foundation for examining the constraints and
norms faced by organizations at a more generalized level.

Institutional setting describes organizational capacities to construct and carry out goals. On the one hand, it circumscribes the resource base (time, money, and expertise) that organizations bring to their approaches to problems. Yet, it also delineates peer communities in which neighborhood organizations participate. Through interaction, they develop common outlooks and standards of propriety that, over time, constrain visions of legitimate activity. Both of these elements—resources and organizational community—help set the parameters in which organizations operate and make decisions.

In terms of this typology, the professional/voluntary distinction communicates much about resources as well as organizational worldview. Professional organizations tend to be richer in terms of time, money, and (usually) expertise, so they can entertain time- and labor-intensive strategies not even imaginable by volunteers. Professionalized neighborhood organizations are also likely to share normative perspectives because of joint participation in meetings, informal networks, trade publications, training seminars, and the like. The secular/religious dimension also speaks to this question of worldview, since religious organizations in Sandtown-Winchester also tend to participate in their own informal networks and joint projects. Table 7.1 shows the frequency distribution of the four institutional types in Sandtown-Winchester disaggregated by issue area for the twenty-five programs/organizations in the sample.

TABLE 7.1
Frequency Distribution of Institutional Types by Issue Area

	Secular	Religious
Professional	**12 Total**	**4 Total**
	3 Health	1 Job Readiness
	3 Job Readiness	1 Education
	2 Housing/Home ownership	1 Health
	1 Children/Youth	1 Home ownership
	1 Basic Needs Provision	
	1 Crime and Safety	
	1 Economic Development	
Voluntary	**5 Total**	**4 Total**
	3 Homeowner Associations	4 Basic Needs Provision
	2 Resident Associations	

Note: Four of these organizations are separate programs of one neighborhood organization. The true number of organizations is twenty-one.

The Morality Tale

Partnerships of internal and external actors reflect the belief that "neighborhood transformation" requires comprehensive, multifaceted approaches directed at people and systems inside and outside of the neighborhood. In practice, however, they entail a division of labor that, on the whole, assigns behavioral change activities (job training, youth development) to neighborhood organizations and structural components (business investment, middle-class home ownership) to external partners.[8] The primary and secondary stories about neighborhood decline and revitalization reflect this division of labor so that, overwhelmingly and across the types of organizations in Sandtown-Winchester, the dominant story of the neighborhood's problems emphasizes internal causes.

In the aggregate, Sandtown-Winchester's morality tale accepts the premise that residents do not possess skills and mind-set needed for success. Across the interviews, neighborhood decision-makers use a language of deficits, suggesting that many residents are deficient in some way. As one organizational representative explains:

> Unfortunately, since most of the programs are deficit-oriented, many of the participants have some type of deficit. We focus on people who do not have employment, high school diplomas. They don't have jobs. They are looking for more adequate and affordable housing and, I think, one of the things most common is that these people are looking for ways to *improve themselves*. So irregardless of what their challenges may be, they are willing to work at removing the barriers if they can be connected to the right services.

Clearly, this focus on deficits is a valid assessment; many people in Sandtown-Winchester are lacking certain things. But, other interviews connect these deficits to attitudinal failings rooted in the pervasive "street culture" in Sandtown-Winchester. One organizational director explains:

> No matter what's going on in the house, there's a whole culture out there, and there's a rite of passage that is preferred now for young people. Where once upon a time, you'd think about young people—I don't know about when you were growing up—but rites of passage was your first date, and your prom, and your graduation, and maybe your driver's licence. You know, you have these stages. But now, rites of passage is you are able to carry a piece and, you know, sometimes it's even being able to kill somebody. It's a rite of passage. You kinda made it through the rules of the streets, I mean, in terms of belonging. I mean, for some kids, that's—it might be crazy—but there's a sense of support and belonging in the street that they may not be getting in the household.

While this surely describes some Sandtown-Winchester residents, many organizations generalize this as the dominant neighborhood culture.

With attention focused on people farthest from the mainstream, many neighborhood organizations focus on resocializing residents lacking the "correct" skills and values that neighborhood decision-makers associate with success. Consistent with the culture-of-poverty thesis, the dominant story is an odd mix of condescension and hopefulness that Sandtown-Winchester residents can reject street values in favor of mainstream ones, including employment, nonviolence, family cohesion, delayed gratification, and respect for property. The story culminates in resocialization and, through resocialization, Sandtown-Winchester residents can be brought into the mainstream, eventually transforming the neighborhood in the aggregate.

Basic Elements of the Story—An Elaboration

The language of deficits—or the inability of target group members to take control of their lives without interventions—recalls Schneider and Ingram's dependent construction and is the primary theme in the stories told by Sandtown-Winchester's neighborhood organizations. Of the twenty-five organizations, sixteen conceive of their particular target population as lacking *something,* whether it be tangible items (3), practical life skills (8), access and opportunities (3), or freedom from drug addiction (2). Eleven of these concepts relate to individual—not systems—failings.

Many organizations make moral statements about their target populations. A job readiness/youth development director describes:

> Typically, the individuals we bring into the program are individuals who have a lot of idle time and have mixed their priorities up. Their priorities have been mixed up with hanging with peers or socializing with those who aren't trying to succeed in life. They're generally those who have low self-esteem about themselves and their talents and such and such. And they are also individuals who have a problem with controlling, I don't want to say emotions. With controlling their attitudes, you know, attitudes to adjust to authority, authoritarian figures. And basically, they're just folks who are screaming out, reaching for help. But at the same time, they're still following the in-crowd. And sometimes, it's difficult to pull them from that particular lifestyle.

The moral dimension to this story intends to link flaws in attitudes and skills with neighborhood problems. Six out of the sixteen professional (church and secular) organizations and three out of the four resident associations discuss this moral dimension. Five professional organizations resist moral typecasting by emphasizing material deficits or lack of opportunity as the main problems faced by their target populations. The remaining organizations offer dual or multiple characterizations that combine moral and material explanations of deficits.

The moralistic interpretations are not absolute, and all neighborhood organizations share the basic view that values can be rechanneled and people reshaped through organizational activities. The same director explains this potential:

> Because, like, when we bring in participants that have a high school diploma, sometimes those individuals are basically, they just need a little extra push or an extra opportunity to success. They're basically on the right track. . . . Many of our men who come in the program have been exposed to the drug culture. And that drug culture, I describe those individuals as those who want to succeed who have a tremendous amount of talent because they're involved in that particular field of activity that brings with it many necessary skills for it to run. But at the same time, they have a problem with the instant gratification. They, like, they want it overnight. And it's difficult for them to visualize past a year, past five years.

Here, even the toughest people have redeeming qualities that can serve as the basis for their personal transformations.

This prevailing tale, focused on moral deficits, leads to two basic strategies aimed at dependents that are focused on behavioral and attitudinal change. I characterize these as *direct* or *indirect* strategies.

The most common strategy, used by twelve of the sixteen professional organizations, is the *direct, change-the-person* strategy. In large measure, the propensity of the professional organizations to use this strategy is shaped institutionally, since professional organizations possess the unique organizational capacity to adopt such a proactive, time-intensive approach. But, institutional capacity does not *determine* the content of ideas about problems, and the heavy use of this strategy also reflects professional organizations' common interpretation of Sandtown-Winchester as beleaguered by street culture.

Direct behavioral change strategies aim to alter members of the target populations whose behaviors or attitudes, or both, are deemed counterproductive. Sometimes this relates to personal habits, as the director of a job readiness program explains:

> We want to make sure . . . they have successfully completed the application because they're going to use that as a model when they go out looking for a job. They'll need to fill out an application, and they'll have a model in front of them with all the pertinent information. Goes over that and then, if necessary, if the job requires it, we'll develop a resume for them from the application and conversation. . . . We send people out on interviews, we provide (bus) tokens if necessary, job interviewing skills, sit down with them and make sure they're ready, make sure they're dressed right.

Here, interpersonal skills and dressing habits are the objects of instruction.

Other times, neighborhood organizations want to change worldviews. The director of a woman's health program explains:

> There are so many things that we have to offer. It's just getting the women to buy into it. And a lot of what we're up against is just the feeling of hopelessness. A lot of our clients just don't see themselves making it. You know, their

mothers didn't make it, and they don't see that happening. And everything
around them is saying you're not going to make it and the odds are, they feel
the odds are against them. But if they took advantage of the program, you
know—I've had clients who came here as mothers who are heavy into drug
use that have two children, nobody to watch their kids, and now they're in
college. So there it is, you just have to get them to believe.

Many of these organizations express great faith in their ability to change
targets. The director of a youth program explains:

> We have to help them because you're always going to get people that are going
> to stay in that same mindset. And only by showing them are you going to be
> able to change their mind. [Interviewee begins to role play.] "You ain't going
> to be able to do nothing with those youth." I hear it every day. "Oh, you crazy.
> Oh, you work down here with those? Oh, how do you do it?" "You know,
> come down and watch them." And then they come and "Oh, I didn't know
> they don't act like that [bad] all the time." You know, looking in this window
> right now, you know, a lot of assumptions could be made. But, until you come
> in and see and actually let the community—you know, that's why the com-
> munity paper is so powerful because it shows the community what we're
> doing. And, if they pick up that paper—and maybe even look at the pictures if
> they can't even read—they'll say, "Hey, somebody doing some stuff down in
> that little building on (Name) Street. You know, they're doing some stuff."

This last statement illustrates that professional organizations seek to combine
direct and indirect behavioral change strategies, since their obvious hope is that
nonparticipating target members will also change by ripple effect. This is the
essence of the *indirect, behavioral change* strategy. Indirect behavioral change is the
primary approach to dependents for Sandtown-Winchester's resident associations; one hundred percent of the active associations use this strategy with
dependents. As one explains:

> We're hoping to accomplish, for one thing, to get more people involved. . . .
> And we thought if they saw us coming out, coming out together, doing var-
> ious activities, doing various clean-up activities, planting flowers and things of
> that nature, they would also want to get involved.

This is a strategy of leading by example or, perhaps less charitably, using peer
pressure to change how target populations live in public spaces. However,
unlike the direct strategies aimed at changing behaviors, the resident associations using this strategy can only hope that target populations are paying attention to the standards they are setting for public space. Here, institutional capacity again affects the approaches available to neighborhood organizations.
    Taken as a whole, neighborhood organizations in Sandtown-Winchester
have developed a tale of dependence that identifies "street values" as interfering

with the quality of the neighborhood. Many believe that they can transform the neighborhood by transforming individuals and ridding them of these values. Street values run the gamut from anti-authoritarianism and instant gratification to ideas that educational and employment opportunities are off-limits, that private property is not sacred, and that violence indicates manhood. However, the story also expresses a deep faith in the ripple effect and that all Sandtown-Winchester residents have the capacity to change. As a health worker explains:

> Because I think it has a ripple effect. Totally. T. [Name of a resident who has some fame in the neighborhood as someone who turned her life around through programs.] People see T. She goes up to a person she's known. I mean, they know all these people. The way they talk to each other is just hysterical. "Well, you gotta get yourself off of drugs." And he looks at her. He knows she's been on the street. And, she really was there. I mean, she was really down. And, so, he'll see that she's not only off of drugs but that she's employed. We've just seen that effect; we've seen it. . . . And I think that when you see people succeed in a place like this [meaning the organization]—because this is a very visible place—and 'cause I don't think this community ever expects anything on a large scale. . . . So, you—I think that every little bit. If you're going to do a transformation, you've got to start with number one and just hope it goes around.

This notion of dependency in Sandtown-Winchester is a positive one, positing that people have inherent capabilities to recognize ideal behaviors and then to act on that recognition. Organizations do not view dependents as inept or fully incapable. Rather, they see them as able to reproduce successful models of behavior. As a job readiness/youth development director explains:

> I travel throughout this community. It's only a seventy-two square-block community—so. But, I travel through the community a lot. And I see, one by one, those that this community feels are a loss and there's no saving them who come and approach me, whether it be walking past the corner or they see you walk into a store. And they'll whisper in my ear, you know not literally whispering, but they don't want anybody to hear. "What's going on? Can I get some training down there? Is there any GED [General Educational Development] classes down there? What can I do with myself?" They yelling up to me and then I walk out the door and then they're back on the street, the majority of individuals who aren't doing anything! So, the majority that aren't doing anything, one by one, they'll come out. That particular population is the one that I would love to grab. Because the persons that are selling drugs in the community—in just any community I believe, but in this community specifically—I just really wish that I could just go and recruit them and bring them in. [The program has limited enrollment.] Because it's all it would take for someone to approach them and tell them that we have ABCD and, if you're interested in ABCD, I want to see you here at XYZ. And that is generally the

way I have seen a lot of students turn their lives around, when they're approached in that manner. Because they understand they only have—there's only two ways that they're going to end up in that situation, either in jail or dead. And when you look them in the eye and say, "You know, you're headed for jail or, you know, you're headed for death, right, and I have ABC for you," they know that ABC is something they have to do. The ABC is something inside their spirit, whatever you want to call it, nags at them and lets them know, "I have to check this out."

In this construction, Sandtown-Winchester dependents have the personal wherewithal to recognize that they need to change their lives. Behavioral change is the key to revitalizing Sandtown-Winchester.

SECONDARY STORIES

The dominant theme, focused on dependency and ensuing resocialization, occurs in sixteen of twenty-five stories proposed by Sandtown-Winchester neighborhood organizations; seventy-five percent of the professional organizations and eighty percent of the resident associations offer this tale. Yet, the neighborhood also offers secondary stories about the sources of the neighborhood's problems that do not point to resocialization as the logical strategy for neighborhood transformation. Oftentimes, however, the same organizations articulate multiple story lines so that these secondary stories do not so much compete as coexist with behavioral change arguments.

Story 1: Help, Not Change

This story asserts that Sandtown-Winchester residents need help, not change. The basic approach to target populations is to offer assistance with "no strings attached." The *no strings attached* strategy simply posits that people need to be helped with their basic needs; it is used by eight of the twenty-four organizations in the sample with programmatic activities. These words from a food pantry director illustrate this strategy:

> Right now, we more or less do things to help them, you know, in emergency cases, really. One time we tried to establish something where we'd try to give them training on how to prepare the food, but they didn't really seem interested in it. Most of them just want to come in, get the food, and go on somewhere. That's mainly what we do now, give them the food, you know, as needed.

The use of this strategy is most common in church-based, voluntary organizations; one hundred percent of these organizations employ the strategy. This is in contrast to resident associations, none of which uses the strategy, and professional organizations, of which only twenty-five percent use the strategy. The propensity of churches to use this strategy is conditioned by institutional factors and their unique take on their target populations.

In terms of social construction, the most distinctive element of this story is the refrain from moral commentary on the characters or culture (or both) of the target group. Like the secular and professional organizations, church groups similarly adopt a terminology of deficits, with three of the four mentioning lack of self-sufficiency as the main deficit of their target groups. But, unlike the moralistic tales of the other organizational types, churches avoid taking their interpretations of problems beyond that. As an example, one soup kitchen director justifies his program's aid to able-bodied, working-age men by stating, "Not everyone can be independent." The unwillingness to draw moral implications extends beyond even this level when a food pantry volunteer discusses her clientele:

> I think most of them are drug users. A few of them, we have some older men who come in. But most of our customers, our clients, are the young males who really—I don't know. Sometimes it's very discouraging because you don't know whether they really need the food or whether they just gonna take it down to the street corner (to sell it). Because we feel like if they say they need it, let them have it.

Despite skepticism, this volunteer decides to take at face value the target group's claims on neighborhood resources.

As mentioned, the "help, not change" story is almost unique to church-based, voluntary organizations like soup kitchens and food pantries. Ironically, it is the *churches*—traditionally in the business of passing judgment and providing salvation—that produce the least stigmatizing tales in Sandtown-Winchester. Ultimately, much of the explanation for this, again, stems from institutional constraints on the development of social constructions that would require more involved interventions into the lives of target groups. Institutionally, churches are limited in the range of options they can consider. As voluntary organizations managed and staffed part-time by retirees, they do not realistically have the capacity or the training for sustained contact with target groups that is required by the behavioral change strategies. Institutional parameters seem to limit the ideological positions that organizations develop. The resulting norm is that churches avoid making moral assessments about constituents' lifestyles.

Story 2: Deviancy

Given the high crime rate and prevalence of the drug economy, I initially expected that stories of deviancy would figure prominently in Sandtown-Winchester's understanding of its problems. Yet, tales of deviancy are exceptionally rare, as well as the corresponding punishment activities that have increasing currency in the official policy arena.[9] In fact, resident associations are the only organizational types that use this construction in their explanations of neighborhood decline. But, importantly, this is not the only story they tell. Simultaneously, resident associations articulate the behavioral change tale, sometimes applying deviant and dependent labels to the same groups of people. This merely reflects that problems—and people—are multidimensional, and a single story is not adequate for capturing the complexity of the situation. Interestingly, the simultaneous use of multiple constructions for a target population is unique to resident associations.

In Sandtown-Winchester, the deviant tale is the inverse of the dependent tale. It identifies highly disruptive members of the community that must be removed if the neighborhood is to improve. In all of the interviews, I asked respondents to identify disruptive groups of people in the neighborhood that they would not want participating in their organizations. Many people had difficulty understanding the question and ultimately could not identify such groups. Homeowner organizations were the exception. As the president of a homeowner's group describes:

> The thieves, the drug addicts, and the murderers. Yes sir, those people, whoever they may be. And, so, I don't know who they are or where they come from, but they're here. And they're wreaking havoc on the neighborhood.

Following from this understanding of the neighborhood and some of its residents, resident associations adopt the *punishment strategy* that Schneider and Ingram associate with the deviant construction. It is important to point out that resident associations do not possess the coercive authority or the protection from risk that is at the disposal of the formal policy community, so their use of this strategy is of great significance. The implementation of the strategy involves appealing to law enforcement authorities to remove "undesirables" from the neighborhood. As the president of a block association says:

> We have done some nuisance and abatement cases. We had several drug houses that were being used for stashing drugs, selling out of the houses, selling drugs. And the Community Law Center told us how to do the nuisance and abatement cases, where we take the landlord to court as well as we would keep observation logs. We had Western District (police) to help us keep a record of any drug bust that would be made. If the drug bust didn't take place directly in the house, if the person lived in the house was caught in another area selling drugs, we could still use that information for nuisance and abatement cases.

This story, and the ensuing strategy, recall the morality struggle that dominates the dependent tale and strategies—but with a twist. The deviancy tale does not accept the saveability of everyone in the neighborhood, and this is a significant departure from the dominant discourse about people and problems in Sandtown-Winchester.

It is important to reemphasize that these two story lines represent different interpretations of the very same population. From the social construction perspective, there is no particular reason why the other organizational types fail to develop this interpretation about certain subcultures in Sandtown-Winchester. Again, I think we must look to institutional factors to understand this pattern.

First, as with church-based groups, resident associations are part-time propositions, directed by people without any particular expertise in "social work" and notoriously burdened by trying to find people willing to volunteer. Furthermore, they have the most precarious access to funding of any organizational type, often operating on budgets of five thousand dollars per year or less. Clearly, these institutional features limit their choices to relatively hands-off approaches. While it is true that they share in the hopes of changing people's attitudes and behaviors, they reserve their leading-by-example activities for lower stakes problems like neighborhood beautification and property maintenance. The tougher problems, like drug dealing, warrant tougher approaches; but, institutionally, they cannot begin to consider the "savior" strategies available to their professionalized peers. They have no choice but to work within their limits.

Furthermore, the social setting compounds the desirability of punishment as an option. Drug dealing and murder affect members of resident associations in ways not experienced by professional organizations. One resident association president reported to me how activists have received death threats from neighbors targeted by nuisance and abatement proceedings. Unlike professionals, activists in these resident associations are not shielded by security guards, professional credentials, and the ability to remove themselves from the physical locale at 5 p.m.[10] Institutionally, neighborhood associations are more vulnerable.

Institutional factors also make it more likely that professional organizations, whether religious or secular, will gravitate toward perceiving themselves as teachers and moral authorities, not as "punishers." First, as funded organizations with trained staffs, they have the capacity to devote considerable and ongoing resources to trying to change the attitudes and behaviors of target group members. Second, professional organizations operate in a culture that legitimizes certain approaches and ideas about urban decline. Today, the behavioral change and "personal responsibility" approaches to reducing poverty have currency both inside and outside of Sandtown-Winchester, and it is consolidated in the peer communities of these professionals who interact and receive training inside and outside their communities.[11] As Fisher suggests, the third sector has become more "conservative" today than in the 1960s, for instance, when the goals of neighborhood organizations were more likely to be oppositional and transformative (Fisher 1996, 43). The institutional structure, the division of labor imposed by external partners and other foundations, and the professional community's views about ineffective strategies has led to a broad tendency to focus on individual behaviors.

Story 3: Structures

The individualistic interpretation is not monolithic, and some of Sandtown-Winchester's neighborhood organizations recognize external and structural causes of neighborhood decline. However, this view is expressed and integrated into programmatic approaches by a minority of organizations.

Of thirty-four goal statements by which organizations can express more than one goal, twenty-six are focused on the individual. Specifically, these goals are to: meet the basic needs of people (6); facilitate upward mobility for individuals (4); increase individuals' involvement in the community (4); give people constructive activities (2); change people's skills and attitudes (2); help with any problem (2); improve people's health (1); get people to follow covenants (1); improve people's knowledge for better personal decision making (1), make families stable (1); set an example for others (1); and connect people to the church (1). Only five organizations express their goals in terms of the structure of the neighborhood: to eradicate unemployment, eliminate vacant housing, and maximize existing (health) service networks (2); to maintain property values (2); to make the area liveable (2); and to relax covenants.

The activities that accompany some of these structural goals include improving housing stock and home ownership rates, creating linkages to health care providers throughout the city, operating a school, and developing a transportation network to suburban jobs. These activities recognize external targets, as well as the idea that reversing neighborhood decline is not in the complete control of actors in the neighborhood. Nonetheless, this view remains a minority view, and two of the three organizations espousing it simultaneously articulate the *cultural values* storyline as well. Despite the influence of partners such as the Enterprise Foundation that promote external linkages to Sandtown-Winchester, many neighborhood organizations remain insular. Neighborhood organizations are, by definition, inwardly focused (Fainstein 1987, 389) and their scope of action is inherently limited. The inward focus is the more pragmatic and realistic approach; it is much easier to attempt to affect a spatially bounded population of ten thousand to twelve thousand than a global one.[12]

Story 4: The Advantaged

Finally, stories of advantaged target populations do circulate in Sandtown-Winchester, though neighborhood organizations tend not to connect relatively privileged residents to their tales of neighborhood revitalization. Mostly, neighborhood organizations reserve positive constructions for their volunteers. As one resident association explains, "The typical person [who volunteers] is a person that sees a need for something to be done and steps up to the plate to do it—because it's a voluntary thing for most of the people who come on board and so it comes from the heart." Generally, the advantaged construction of volunteers is independent of social class considerations, but some organizations stress the middle-class character of the advantaged. For instance, the president of a resident association is very aware of the professional affiliations of board members, describing "most of the people that are in my organization, the younger ones, are up and coming. Some of them, I mean we've got three executives, one lawyer, one guy who works for the State's Attorney in Baltimore County. He's a deputy."

Interestingly, neighborhood organizations integrate advantaged targets, especially the black middle class, in only superficial ways, despite the fact that the "suburbanization" of the black middle class is well publicized in Baltimore and repopulation is a goal for partnerships. Strategies directed at advantaged groups are symbolic at best, related to self-esteem building and low-level material rewards (such as block picnics and events for children). One organization leader describes these benefits, "We provide them with the vehicle to actually make a difference, and they feel good because they come on as a partner." Resource allocation is minimal.

While it is not a majority sentiment, some residents/workers criticize transformation activities for not paying more attention to the advantaged, upwardly mobile residents. One resident/staff person in a transformation-related organization says:

> Programs are set up based on the fact that this is a 99.9% African-American community, not even engaging the fact that there are subcultures here, that there are different moral and spiritual backgrounds here. Everyone is just put into one category of being black and so, when you have job training programs, they're set up for people who have little education, no GEDs, no high school diplomas. I have yet to see a program set up in Sandtown-Winchester dealing with the work force that says if you need job training to move into the work force or if you want to advance in your career. See? It's set up for one segment of the population: AFDC. We're moving you from welfare to work, you know. Well, what about those residents who are working in the community, who are making minimum wage or just a little better who want to go beyond that in terms of education, in terms of career? It's nothing there. Most of the community advocates [a job title of many of the frontline jobs created in the "transformation" process] who work in this community are going to be advocates. Why? Because nothing is set up to move them to the next level. So even if [an organization with a large staff] folds today or tomorrow, most of their advocates have been there for years, but do not have the training nor the education to move to another level. They would need [to find] another advocacy position.

Given the emphasis on dependence, Sandtown-Winchester's neighborhood organizations have an underdeveloped sense of how advantaged targets fit into their strategies, other than as organizational volunteers, despite various possibilities to promote career advancement, business incubation, continuing education (as opposed to GEDs), and the like. That this idea of serving the relatively accomplished residents does not enter neighborhood discourse, I posit, is quite telling and suggests strong sanctions against focusing on advantaged populations in Sandtown-Winchester.

Implications for the Social Construction of Deservedness

While not hegemonic, Sandtown-Winchester's frontline organizations have placed conduct, lifestyle, and street culture at the center of neighborhood discourse about revitalization. This problem definition favors resocialization and behavioral change as the best approaches to neighborhood transformation. This approach has interesting implications for the social construction of entitlement and deservedness that are quite different from other contexts.

First, neighborhood organizations in Sandtown-Winchester link deservedness to the needs of the most disadvantaged—those who are dependent, as they have defined it for their setting. In contrast to the legislative and nonprofit arenas, neighborhood organizations do not oversubscribe benefits to advantaged target groups and they tend not to "cream." Instead, benefits to the advantaged tend to be symbolic, and this is not just a matter of resource constraints. Rather, evidence from Sandtown-Winchester suggests that neighborhood organizations do not expect to provide for the advantaged or offer incentives for staff to subscribe benefits to people not perceived as needy. It seems that attention to the needs of advantaged residents has to come from external groups, and this attention is focused more on work-related issues than housing and health issues.

An interesting question raised by the Sandtown-Winchester case is why there are so many incentives to focus on the disadvantaged while so many other programs resort to "creaming" (see Jurik and Cowgill, chapter 6). Funding pressures can explain some of this, especially for professional organizations. As Table 7.2 shows, professional organizations are most likely to receive private monies, foundation grants, and city contracts.

Especially in the era following the "Contract with America," foundations and city agencies have been more interested in welfare-to-work and service delivery as a replacement for the public service provision. Foundation and city influence has shifted the institutional mission and culture of neighborhood organizations to focus on dependents rather than advantaged groups, especially in areas with heavy welfare dependency like Sandtown-Winchester. Despite public-private partnerships that claim comprehensive approaches, the evidence

presented here suggests that external partners delegate behavioral and individualized components disproportionately to neighborhood organizations. In the
context of this low-income neighborhood, these components are more about
combating street values than expanding the opportunities of the working poor
who have already internalized mainstream values.

However, funding pressures alone cannot explain the neighborhood's general oversight of advantaged targets—especially considering that not all organizations receive grants and other organizations receive grants in amounts of one
thousand dollars or less, which suggests other factors at play.

Among the other factors, these organizations operate in an environment
where problems (such as drug addiction, deteriorating buildings, and poverty)
are highly visible. For example, in my field work, I sat in on a summer program
for children who were asked to write and read aloud an essay on how to make
Sandtown-Winchester a better place to live. One essay implored residents not to
urinate in the streets; for this girl, neighborhood transformation means having a
neighborhood that does not smell like urine. That this was the most pressing
issue that came to mind for her indicates the extent of deprivation[13] in this
neighborhood. In Sandtown-Winchester, neighborhood decline and abject
poverty are sensory experiences that command attention, whereas stifled upward
mobility is not. In a neighborhood with so much visible deprivation, it is hardly
surprising that neighborhood organizations gravitate toward the toughest problems, even though it may be disempowering to advantaged target groups.

Also, neighborhood organizations face resource constraints in an environment marked by relentless demand. Allocation decisions are made in a face-to-
face setting where staff must provide reasons for their decisions on the spot.
Since many of the people involved in the organizations (as frontline and direc-
torial staff) are Sandtown-Winchester residents, there is added pressure because
they could encounter people they have denied. Basing decisions on the most
desperate cases is the preferred rationale and the one most consistent with the
institutional culture and mission. It also helps reduce the likelihood of the
neediest residents challenging the legitimacy of neighborhood organizations. A
clear focus on the most disadvantaged helps establish parameters and legitimacy
for making allocation decisions.

TABLE 7.2
Organizations with Grants as a Source of Funding

Professional Organizations Receiving Grants	93.75%
Church-based, Voluntary Organizations Receiving Grants	50
Resident Associations Receiving Grants	60
Organizations (All Types) with No Grants	24

COMMUNITY SANCTIONS AGAINST "CREAMING"

Unique features of Sandtown-Winchester as a *place* may also reinforce the neighborhood's emphasis on needs and norms against "creaming." An important characteristic of Sandtown-Winchester is that, even in the professionalized organizations, more than half of the directors are themselves long-time residents, often born and raised in the neighborhood, with many others having only recently moved out. Interviews reveal a communitarian ideal and collective memory of the neighborhood as a more cohesive and tightly knit place where interpersonal relationships between neighbors were dominated by feelings of "fellowship." As the president of a resident association explains:

> And back to the unity thing, there is none. When I grew up on these streets as a little girl, everybody knew my mother and, if I was out of place, before I got home my mother probably knew about it. So, it's things like that. They babysat for everybody; there was no one particular. Everybody looked out for everybody. But, if you go to these people today—especially the younger mothers or whatever—and say something about their children, you have to virtually fight the parent. So, you know, that's where the unity part comes in again. There's none of that, no fellowship. I always knew, always felt comfortable, that I could go to a neighbor's house and knock on their door if I needed something. Or if my mother wasn't home, I knew that I was okay because my neighbors were home, you know, so it wasn't no problem. But my house is so locked up now. I mean, it's a shame because you're a prisoner inside your own house. So, they (other residents) make things hard where it don't have to be hard.

Given this collective memory, neighborhood organizations' focus on issues of morality and cultural standards is consistent with a communitarian ideology, where individual expression is secondary to the good of the whole. In Sandtown-Winchester, people active in neighborhood organizations have defined the good of the whole in relatively mainstream terms. I do not think that organizations promoting this concept of the neighborhood's problems intend to stigmatize. Rather, it signals a "tough love" approach that would assume a different connotation if pursued by outsiders.

As previously noted, church-based, voluntary organizations do not share this cultural interpretation of Sandtown-Winchester. Some of the reasons have to do with institutional capacities and church norms surrounding charity. However, evidence also suggests that this is because church organizations do not share this collective memory.

Of all of the institutional types, volunteers/staff in the church organizations are least likely to live in the neighborhood. Here, their connection to the neighborhood is really to the church that, oftentimes, was a church they joined as small children in Sandtown-Winchester. However, my interviews reveal that many church-based programs in Sandtown-Winchester are from "commuter"

churches, with pastors and congregations traveling to the city from the suburbs for church services and activities. Many of the volunteers in my sample
report had moved away long ago. Additionally, churches are the least integrated
into the transformation project of all the organizational types. As a representative of one of the neighborhood organizations heavily involved in the transformation explains:

> We're really working to pull the clergy in. As I said, Sandtown-Winchester is
> seventy-two square blocks with fifty-two churches here. That's almost a
> church for every block. And they have an umbrella organization named
> (Name), and we're really working hard to bring them on board and get them
> to support some of the initiatives. . . . That's one group we're really working
> hard on. We've met with them over the last few months but, again, they're
> kind of slow to the draw because they're still formalizing themselves.

Distance from both the collective memory and the dominant discourse seems
to alter the kinds of claims that churches are willing to make about the neighborhood and its population, reinforcing the institutional checks against moralistic interpretations.

CONCLUSION

The evidence from Sandtown-Winchester suggests that neighborhood organizations in low-income communities may play a unique role in the process of
urban revitalization. In Sandtown-Winchester, their role in public-private partnerships (as well as their institutional structures) predispose neighborhood organizations to posit individualized, behavioral reasons for urban decline and the
majority of organizations focuses on individuals. Yet, this does not result in activities aimed at supporting neighborhood residents already deemed successful or
"creaming" for residents most likely to produce measurable success. Instead,
Sandtown-Winchester's neighborhood organizations dealing with individuals
focus on the "tough cases"—welfare dependents, drug dealers, high school
dropouts—aiming to correct what they see as moral and material deficiencies.

Unlike degenerative policy making, Sandtown-Winchester's attention to
morality does not often lead these organizations to frame residents involved
with the street culture as deviant or to propose punishment strategies. Rather,
with few exceptions, neighborhood organizations accept the redeemability of
everyone. In fact, "ripple effects" are important components of neighborhood
approaches. Emphasizing the power of residents to respond to examples of positive change, neighborhood organizations believe that individual transformations—even in small numbers—lead to neighborhood transformation.

This points out the importance of place in neighborhood-based social
construction of policy. On the one hand, neighborhoods are, by definition,

small territories. This smallness, combined with (perhaps eroding) face-to-face interaction in Sandtown-Winchester, may have direct bearing on why the neighborhood emphasizes people with legitimate needs. Individual successes are detectable in this neighborhood in ways that they are not detected in larger territorial units, such as cities. With a concentrated population, relative cohesiveness, and a contingent of lifelong residents, results are felt and perceived in Sandtown-Winchester so that, for instance, getting one homeless addict off drugs and into stable housing and employment packs more punch than helping one hundred certified nursing assistants climb the career ladder to become licensed practical nurses. The impact of such a success would be lost in other policy arenas, including other nonprofits dealing with more dispersed target populations; thus, nonterritorial nonprofits must find more concrete methods of documenting impacts. Neighborhood organizations can afford to focus on the marginal.

Additionally, the communitarian outlook in Sandtown-Winchester frames this process and further crystallizes attention on the neighborhood's neediest. Because the personal histories of many neighborhood decision makers are rooted in Sandtown-Winchester, the organizational leadership has a collective memory of community values and cultural standards from the neighborhood's prime. In this setting, residents most out of line with notions of community standards are even more noticeable to neighborhood organizations. A policy approach that rewards residents who already meet the accepted morality does not achieve much, since the goal is cultural regeneration. The Sandtown-Winchester case suggests that, when the attachment to place coincides with the right institutional supports—such as professional staffs and residential voluntary associations—resocialization becomes the favored strategy. Ultimately, this limits policy designs centered on "creaming," rewards the successful, and punishes the deviant.

NOTES

The author wishes to thank Susan Clarke, Rodney Hero, Jeffrey Kopstein, Anne Schneider, and Helen Ingram for comments on earlier versions of this chapter.

1. This term should not be confused with the term *neighborhood association,* which commonly refers to voluntary associations of renters and/or homeowners.

2. It is important to keep in mind that grant guidelines rarely dictate the *content* of proposals and strategies, while they do specify rules (such as prohibitions against discrimination).

3. This approach contrasts with nonterritorial nonprofits dealing with citywide or regional populations. The larger population pool may enable them to be more selective with clients/participants.

4. The Enterprise Foundation coined this term to describe the targeted activities they fund to achieve comprehensive change. Elaboration of Enterprise Foundation and Baltimore Empowerment Corporation activities are beyond the scope of this paper.

5. Since the focus of this study is the role of organizations based in the neighborhood, I do not analyze the full range of partnership activities or the social constructions offered by external partners. As this chapter points out, these may not be equivalent.

6. This is compiled, published, and distributed by one of the major community centers in the neighborhood, so it is separate from the regular telephone directory.

7. Structurally, and by law, all nonprofit organizations and associations have volunteers, but my point is that organizations with professional staffs are qualitatively different from those relying exclusively on volunteers, especially in terms of institutional capacity.

8. To illustrate this division, the City of Baltimore initiated several home ownership projects in the neighborhood, primarily aimed at middle-class professionals (see McDougall 1993, 137), while private housing groups tend to target low-income people from within the neighborhood. Additionally, economic development activities are similarly divided. The Baltimore Empowerment Corporation handles business relocation and contacts with outside businesses, while the neighborhood "village center"—until 2000—dealt with neighborhood residents looking for jobs and other services. This village center has since been discontinued by the Baltimore Empowerment Corporation for failure to make progress.

9. As evidenced by the growth in "three-strikes-you're-out" approaches to crime fighting.

10. Importantly, more than half of the directors of the professional organizations also live in the neighborhood and have proximity to these populations and activities. Yet, because their activities are associated with the workplace, they are more invisible when they go home at night, since they are no longer congregated spatially and potential threateners are less likely to know where they live. Resident associations are spatially close to their targets.

11. One organization reported attending a conference as far away as Denver.

12. Effecting demographic and economic changes in Sandtown-Winchester has been exceedingly difficult. In 2000, the Baltimore Empowerment Corporation closed down the neighborhood's "village center," the community-based arm of Empowerment Zone projects in the physical neighborhood, for failure to realize program goals. Interestingly, this village center was one of the few professional organizations in Sandtown-Winchester that executed on behavioral and structural views of neighborhood decline, including housing, microenterprise loans, and creating transit to suburban labor markets.

13. In Sandtown-Winchester, there are sizeable homeless/transient/drug-addicted populations without regular access to bathrooms.

PART IV

Constructions by Moral Entrepreneurs and Policy Analysts

HELEN M. INGRAM AND ANNE L. SCHNEIDER

Social constructions of deservedness are undergirded and rationalized by well-accepted narratives, or story lines, in which various groups are portrayed as playing more or less positive roles in contributing to the national well-being. While constructions are highly emotional and symbolic, for policies to have "traction" in policy settings, they must be well worked out through causal narratives that link the groups being portrayed to policy problems and their solutions. Story lines take on a life of their own and are a force in themselves, as Lina Newton's analysis of the construction of Mexican-Americans in immigration policy (chapter 5) makes clear. This part of the book addresses the critical role that moral entrepreneurs and policy analysts play in the process of constructing and reconstructing the social construction of particular ethnic groups as being included or excluded from the "underclass" or the "dangerous class." In the three chapters that follow, the necessary conditions for translating negative public sentiment into policy choices are examined and suggestions made for what it might take to undo the damage.

While any number of groups in American society are held in low regard by the public, sometimes for long periods of time, only some of these deviant groups become the target of policy sanctions. This part begins with a chapter by Sean Nicholson-Crotty and Kenneth Meier, who argue that the presence of issue activists, or "moral entrepreneurs," who hold institutionalized power bases and who can lend legitimacy to the emergent narrative, is critical to emergence of policy. Such actors are able to typify the behavior of certain target groups so that they can be identified as the root of a social problem. Thus, muckrakers were able to construct a narrative that linked Chinese opium smokers with urban moral decline at the turn of the twentieth century. Closer to our own time, the portrayal by prominent academics of inner city Black males as pursuing a jobless way of life and supporting drug habits through crime has clearly been linked to draconian crime policies. Of course, entrepreneurs cannot construct such narratives out of whole cloth. There must be preexisting receptive biases, images, and predilections on the part of some of the public to paint certain groups as evil. There also must be rising concern for problems for which a scapegoat can relatively easily be blamed. The rise of crime and joblessness in urban areas did coincide in the 1980s, but it took a moral entrepreneur to forge the link with moral decline among urban black males.

Because experts have reputations for reason and objectivity, their narratives are particularly potent. According to Progressive logic, which continues to greatly influence policy making and the study of public policy, democracy is best served when unbiased experts exert a countervailing power to the influence of politicians, lobbyists, and special interests. Experts are reputed to be evenhanded and disinterested. Policy experts are supposed to bring "truth the power" (Wildavsky 1979). The ambitions of the founders of policy analysis, like Harold Laswell and Yzekial Dror, were to bring the best possible policy information to the service of policy making (Schneider and Ingram 1997, 30). Even policy analysts of a critical persuasion—who recognize that truth is, at least in part, a social construct—subscribe to the notion that policy analysts can supply important perspectives and critiques that otherwise would be absent in policy making (Fischer 1990; Schneider and Ingram 1997). The chapters by Dionne Bensonsmith and Sanford Schram teach the lesson that without intending to do so, well-meaning policy analysts can contribute to damaging social constructions and the perpetuation of unfair policies.

Dionne Bensonsmith, in her chapter "Jezebels, Matriarchs, and Welfare Queens: The 'Moynihan Report' of 1965 and the Social Construction of African American Women in Welfare Policy," focuses upon the emergence of a convincing, discursive story line at a critical moment. In the life cycle of policy issues, prevailing public policies reach critical junctures or turning points at which it is possible to reframe issues and redesign policy elements. While a variety of forces may come together to create this juncture or policy window, it is often essential to have well-conceived causal logic. Bensonsmith argues that the Moynihan Report provided just such a convincing logic because, while it seemed to utilize important research findings, it also drew upon existing racial, sexual, and class stereotypes that portrayed African-American women as wonton breeders ("Jezebels" and "Sapphires"). The reinforcement and legitimation that the Moynihan Report provided to these longstanding stereotypes served to submerge a more sympathetic and deserving image of welfare recipients as deserted mothers struggling to support their children. The report, Bensonsmith argues, supplied the causal link or rationale between race, receiving welfare, and pathological behavior that has continued to dominate discourse over welfare to the present. By focusing on the African-American family and the economic/social parity of its men and women—or perhaps the superiority of women over men—the report shifted the focus from the systemic, societal causes of racial discrimination and poverty to indidivudal and family pathologies as causes. Bensonsmith observes that the legacy of the Moynihan Report was to justify and rationalize subdividing the poor into two categories: the deserving, "working poor," who were mainly white; and the undeserving, who were closely bound to race and gender. Maintaining the existing gendered and racialized power structure is clearly a fundamental, if unintended, premise of this policy analysis. The black matriarch, who exhibits too much independence, is the cause of poverty, male abandonment, crime, and illegitimacy.

Bensonsmith's argument appears to be directly at odds with Sanford Schram's position in chapter 10, "Putting a Black Face on Welfare: The Good and the Bad." Bensonsmith supports the deracialization of welfare discourse as the antidote to damaging social constructions. In contrast, Sanford Schram deconstructs the statement commonly made by expert policy analysts who advocate for the poor that "everyone who knows anything about welfare knows that most recipients are white." Such claims, Schram argues, are not only factually untrue and ultimately unjustifiable, but are also quite damaging to the interests of the poor. Only by acknowledging the disproportionate numbers of persons of color on welfare, Schram asserts, can the bias and racial inequality of the larger society and economy be exposed.

However, a fundamental issue of agreement between the two authors far outweighs their apparent disagreements. Both argue that the roots of social and economic differences among the races need to be traced to fundamental structural inequities in opportunities afforded by the economy, government, and society. Until these fundamental imbalances in power, privilege, and access are addressed, race and class problems will persist in America. Implicitly, both Bensonsmith and Schram agree that policy analysis can and should try to refocus debate upon such fundamental structural differences. This book serves as one contribution to that large project.

8

From Perception to Public Policy: Translating Social Constructions into Policy Designs

Sean Nicholson-Crotty and Kenneth J. Meier

Introduction

Numerous scholars, including many of the contributors to this volume, have provided evidence that social constructions often influence the policy design choices of elite decision makers. In this chapter, we undertake a more explicit examination of how the perceptions of groups sometimes become translated into public policy. Through a review of literature from sociology and political science, we develop a set of necessary conditions that typically exist before that process can take place. We examine the utility of those conditions through a historical case study analysis of U.S. policies passed in 1909 and in 1984. Our central argument is that the causal link between social constructions and policy designs is not inevitable and that numerous intervening factors mediate the connection between the two. The case studies illustrate that the characteristics of the target group, the activities of "moral entrepreneurs," and the availability of policy champions or "political entrepreneurs" all help to determine when target group construction is successfully transformed into specifically designed policies.

The editors of this volume, along with several of the contributors, rightfully note that "entrepreneurship" is a powerful force in determining social constructions and consequent policy designs. They suggest that political actors can often build political capital by exploiting widely shared negative perceptions of certain groups (see especially chapters 3 and 5). The coalitions necessary to pass policy legislation can often be built, according to these authors, through "degenerative politics," whereby negatively perceived outgroups are identified as being responsible for social problems. These shared negative stereotypes thus become a binding force between actors who might otherwise have very diverse interests. The negative constructions of certain groups created during this process of scapegoating often become persistent and entrenched, as targeted coercive policies exacerbate existing problems among these groups, who are, in turn, blamed for their inability or unwillingness to adhere to social and political standards (see Schram, chapter 10; Ingram and Schneider 1991).

In order to build upon these works and their insights regarding the role of political entrepreneurs in the social construction/policy relationship, we investigate further how negative perceptions of certain groups are translated into public policies. Rather than beginning with the assumption that the identification of a blamable group necessarily overcomes the many political "transaction costs" in the policy development process, we hope to identify the conditions where that is indeed the case. Numerous political scientists have attempted to describe the policy process parsimoniously. Each has recognized that a fortuitous set of circumstances must intersect in order for a public issue to become a public law (Kingdon 1995; Anderson 2000). To even secure a spot on the public agenda, issues are typically redefined numerous times in a variety of institutional venues (Cobb and Elder 1980; Baumgartner and Jones 1993). Like all other types of legislation, public policies designed to target socially constructed groups must compete with myriad other public issues for scarce legislative attention. Most such policies will fail to survive the process and will be abandoned or forgotten before they can become law.

In this chapter, we argue that the social construction of a particular group, even when aggressively exploited by a political entrepreneur, does not guarantee that a legislative body will pass legislation specifically designed to target that group. That variability suggests that we examine more explicitly the process of translating the perceptions of groups into public policy. Through a review of literature from sociology and political science, this chapter develops a set of necessary conditions that we believe typically exist before that process can take place. We then illustrate the utility of the conditional framework through a historical case study analysis of U.S. policies passed in 1909 and in 1984. Our central argument is that the causal link between social constructions and policy designs is not inevitable, but that numerous intervening factors mediate the connections between the two. The characteristics of the target group and the availability of issue entrepreneurs, as well as the political and cultural environments, all help to determine when perceptions become policy.

A THEORY OF THE JOURNEY FROM PERCEPTION TO POLICY

Developing theoretical expectations about the journey from social construction to policy design is important in order to address several unanswered questions. For example, why do the constructions of certain groups suddenly intensify to the point where behaviors become identified as public problems worthy of political attention? Similarly, why does the perception of a particular group sometimes penetrate the popular agenda but does not become a political issue? Finally, why do many proposed policies designed for a specific target group fail to become law? Throughout modern history, there has always an array of groups constructed as "advantaged," "contenders," "dependents," or "deviants." At any given time, however, a majority of subgroups in each category essentially has been ignored by the policy process. Homosexuals, for example, typically have been perceived by society as deviants, but their activities were not the subject of public policy until a rash of "sexual psychopath" ordinances was passed in the 1930s, 1940s, and 1950s (Sutherland 1950a, b).

Drawing from various bodies of scholarship, this chapter develops a theoretical set of conditions to answer the questions posed above. It suggests how negative perceptions of a particular group are sometimes transformed into the more comprehensive and compelling notion of a social construction, demonstrates how these constructions make certain groups the targets of political action, and identifies the factors that influence the success or failure of these initiatives. The conditions outlined below are intended to clarify the policy process only as it relates to those groups constructed as "deviants." The applicability of this framework to groups in the other categories is probably inappropriate. The political power of groups perceived as "advantaged" and "contenders" and the positive perception of those categorized as "dependents" fundamentally changes the dynamics of the policy process. The journey from perception to policy design is likely different for initiatives targeting these groups.

The first condition that must be met regards the characteristics of the target group. If a specifically targeted policy is to succeed, the target group must be readily identifiable to both the mass public and to political elites and must hold a marginal position in society. This condition may seem redundant in light of our focus on deviants; but even among negatively perceived groups, some are more marginal than others. Groups that are subject to "value-laden" stereotypes, those that lend themselves to clear cut assumptions about right or wrong, are more likely to provide decision makers with policy rationales (Donovan 2001). Mucciaroni (1995) argues that value-based stereotypes can be the most important factor in determining the allocation of state resources. Furthermore, sociologists suggest that stereotyping is a subtle and *dynamic* process, producing a hierarchical ordering even among groups generally perceived positively or negatively.

When a clearly identified group is widely associated with an intensely negative stereotype, political decision makers are more likely to consider that group as a potential target for sanctions. Edelman (1977) argues that "the archetypal device for influencing political opinion is the evocation of beliefs about the problems, intention, or moral condition of people whose very existence is problematic." If the portion of the population with political power considers a group to be marginal, then the "political opinion" of rational elected officials will likely become biased against that group. This process can occur quite rapidly if a sufficient portion of the public becomes convinced that the marginal group is immune to normal means of social control, such as family, neighborhood, and occupational structure (Janowitz 1978; Simon 1993). When a group is thus perceived as "out of control" or incorrigible, it becomes politically advantageous to design coercive policies to enforce the boundaries of societal norms (Cavender 1982).

Before these general perceptions of a marginal group can be translated into public policy, however, broad-based social anxieties must be focused on the actions of that group. The second condition, therefore, requires the availability of a moral entrepreneur who is willing to draw attention to the actions of a marginalized group and convince others that those actions constitute a fundamental threat to society (Ben-Yehuda 1990; Hills 1980). The notion of a moral entrepreneur assumes that deviance and criminality are subjectively defined (Schur 1980; Morris 1994; Becker 1963). These may at times be universal definitions but, more often, an individual or group within society aggressively seeks to define some behaviors as deviant. "Moral entrepreneurs," according to Goode and Ben-Yehuda, "are crusaders who believe that some members of society are involved in damaging behavior and are not being sufficiently punished for it" (1994, 80).

Moral entrepreneurship is an activity rooted in the differential power of groups within society. The definition of deviance or criminality typically represents the values of a powerful group juxtaposed against those of a group with fewer political, social, or economic resources (Gusfield 1955; Becker 1963). Conrad and Schneider argue that "constructions of deviance are inevitably closely linked to the dominant social control institutions in a society" (1980, 17). Becker (1967) similarly notes that societies have "hierarchies of credibility" based upon assumptions about social standing and moral character. Some groups, via their position in society, are perceived as more credible than others when defining appropriate behavioral norms. The efforts of moral entrepreneurs reflect and represent the views of these groups and gain legitimacy because of their power (Goode and Ben-Yehuda 1994).

Thus, the power of moral entrepreneurs is drawn in part from the power of the groups whose values they espouse. These individuals are also successful in their attempts to isolate and stigmatize certain groups, however, because of their own position within society. Moral entrepreneurs often draw upon an institutionalized power base, such as church or government, when identifying deviant behavior. If not members of the clergy or government officials, these individuals may rely on educational credentials to lend legitimacy to their proclamations. Whatever the source, entrepreneurs must be able to claim a high level of expertise regarding the moral issue at hand. Alternatively, the general public must believe that entrepreneurs can correctly identify both the dominant value system and groups that deviate from it.

Even with an institutionalized base of power or expertise, entrepreneurs are more likely to define deviance successfully when they can identify an entire group with a particular behavior and create fear that the behavior represents a danger not only to that group but also to the rest of society. *Typifying* is a powerful rhetorical tool, often used to help define public problems (Best 1995; Lowney and Best 1995). In the process of typification, the moral entrepreneur not only identifies behavior X (e.g., crime) as a problem, but labels it as a certain type of problem (e.g., moral) associated with a certain group of people (e.g., young black males). When a problem can be readily identified with an entire group, the perceived threat to the social order becomes greater than if the behavior was isolated in a few individuals. The group/behavior linkage creates the perception of a "dangerous class," which lives *en masse* outside acceptable social boundaries (Morris 1994; D. Gordon 1994; Beckett 1997). Because such groups are demonized as threats to the very social fabric of society, they are blamed for a number of larger social problems that often have little connection to the original behavior for which they were singled out (Stedman-Jones 1971; Reinarman and Levine 1995).[1]

Through typification and the creation of a dangerous class, moral entrepreneurs can place the activities of a particular group on the public's agenda; but increased salience and public concern does not guarantee a political response. The third and final condition that must be met in the journey from perception to policy is the presence of a political entrepreneur, or policy champion, with sufficient incentive to shepherd an initiative through the policy process. Moral entrepreneurs may be, and often are, political actors. When we distinguish between moral and political entrepreneurs, therefore, we are drawing a distinction between the roles they play in the process and not arguing that they are necessarily different people. Moral entrepreneurs use typifying and stereotyping behaviors to generate anxiety about a particular group and place the actions of that group on the public agenda. Political entrepreneurs/policy champions rely on different tools and motivations to translate those concerns into public policy.

A large body of literature investigates the role of entrepreneurs in law making (see Doig and Hargrove 1987; Riker 1986; Kingdon 1995). In recent work on this topic, Schneider and Teske (1992) outline a set of conditions that help to determine when political entrepreneurs emerge, and their argument assumes that the costs of entrepreneurship are high. Potential players must, therefore, anticipate sufficient reward or profit. The first way to increase potential profit is to decrease initial cost, or in other words, reduce the barriers to entry. By identifying a politically weak or socially marginal group as a threat to society, moral entrepreneurs have already greatly reduced the political cost of proposing legislation targeting that group, thereby increasing the likelihood of finding a policy champion. Meier (1994) even suggests that political actors will rush to become associated with such policies long after public concern has diminished.

Decreased barriers to entry are not always sufficient, however, to justify the costs of political entrepreneurship or guarantee that an entrepreneur will be able to advance an innovation successfully. Otherwise, all public concerns would inevitably result in specifically designed public policy. In reality, argue Schneider and Teske (1992), entrepreneurs must generate and distribute selective incentives in order to secure a winning electoral coalition and overcome the collective action problem of the legislative process. To increase the eventual probability of success—which undoubtably influences the initial decision to become involved with a proposal—entrepreneurs must be able to guarantee profits for other political actors, as well as for themselves. To do so, the political payoff of a proposed policy must be larger than, and often conceptually distinct from, the one attained by simply sanctioning a marginal group. We acknowledge that there is often significant electoral benefit in pandering to public fears or addressing high-salience issues (Becker 1963; Meier 1994). Because public attention to issues is often fleeting (Downs 1972; Hilgartner and Bosk 1988), however, a potentially broader payoff increases the probability that a political entrepreneur will champion legislation.

We have outlined three necessary conditions for perceptions about a group to translate into specifically designed policy targeting that group. Only together are they sufficient to influence policy outputs and, even then, they are intended to describe the process only as it applies to those groups classified as "deviants." Briefly revisited, the conditions include first the presence of a readily identifiable and socially marginal group with a value-laden stereotype. Second, a moral entrepreneur must focus public attention and fear on the actions of that group. Finally, there must be sufficient political profit to entice a policy champion to place the issue on the political agenda and work to secure passage of a targeted policy.

Two Illustrative Case Studies

The following section examines two cases that illustrate the presence of conditions outlined above in the journey from perception to public policy. The initial case examines the federal government's first anti-narcotics law banning the smoking of opium in 1909. The second case looks at the *Comprehensive Crime Control Act of 1984* (*Congressional Record* 1984a), perhaps the federal government's most sweeping statement on criminal justice policy. We look at policies adopted in different historical periods in order to probe the external validity of the conditions outlined previously and to reassure the reader that the process we describe is not contextually or temporally specific. We believe that the variability of these cases, on a host of indicators, suggests that those conditions hold in a variety of circumstances and contexts.

The "Yellow Peril" and Opium Regulation. In 1909, President Theodore Roosevelt signed into law the nation's first anti-narcotics legislation. The law banned the

importation of smoking opium but continued to allow other opiates to enter
the country unabated. At the time of the law's passage, Chinese immigrants in
the major cities of California were the primary users of smoked opium, while
the use of Laudanum, an equally popular opium derivative, was restricted primarily to white middle-class Americans (Morgan 1981; Courtwright 2001).
Numerous scholars have suggested that the ban was specifically designed to
sanction the Chinese rather than address any real concern over opium addiction (Brecher 1972; Zimiring and Hawkins 1992). The evidence supports this
conclusion, but the theory outlined above suggests that a number of conditions
facilitated the translation of bias into targeted public policy.

The Chinese were the consummate marginalized group during the
decades surrounding the turn of the twentieth century. Originally encouraged
to emigrate in the 1840s and 1850s to provide much-needed labor on the
nation's growing rail network, the Chinese were initially celebrated for their
industriousness, temperance, and penchant for hard and dangerous work (Yung
1999). When the economic depression of the 1870s slowed production, however, Chinese immigrants quickly became surplus labor and were viewed as a
threat to white employment (Wu 1972). This was particularly true after recent
immigrants became the predominate workforce in several industries, such as
cigar making, laundry services, and woolen mills (Cather 1936). The historical
evolution of Chinese immigrant constructions from positive to negative in the
last half of the nineteenth century is particularly interesting in light of the
opposite shift experienced by Japanese Americans at the end of the twentieth
century (see chapter 3). The fluidity of anti-Asian sentiment in the United
States, even in the absence of a narcotics connection, reinforces the notion that
negative perceptions can be manipulated into social constructions, which in
turn provide the foundation for targeted policies.

Public animosity toward the Chinese found expression in the popular press,
as well as in state and local government actions. The vehemence and frequency
of anti-Chinese rhetoric placed that group at the bottom of an already highly
stratified society. So low was the group in public esteem, that a California Attorney General was willing to go on record saying, "I believe the Chinese have no
souls to save, and if they have, that they are not worth the saving" (quoted in Wu
1972). Similar comments appeared regularly in major newspapers and other outlets of popular culture; the Chinese were portrayed as "dangerous," "criminal,"
and "inferior from a mental and moral point of view" (Schriek 1936). "It is
remarkable," noted one San Francisco editor, "that nature and custom should
combine to produce so much individual ugliness" (quoted in Nash and Weiss
1970, 110). Fear and hatred of the Chinese also penetrated deeply into widely
read national publications. An 1878 article entitled "The Yellow Peril," in the
North Atlantic Review, asked readers: "Is not the Mongol a Thistle in our fields?
Shall we pluck it up as does the wise husbandman, or shall we . . . leave the battle to the chances of natural selection?" (quoted in Wu 1972, 135).

Moral entrepreneurs played an important role in translating a general animosity toward the Chinese into a widespread fear that the Chinese represented a pressing threat to American society. Activists were particularly successful in identifying Chinese as a "dangerous class" when they focused on the immigrant population's connections to the importation and use of smoked opium. Prior to 1875, opium smoking was confined almost exclusively to immigrants in western cities and mining camps. The first recorded use of a pipe by a Caucasian was not until 1871 (Courtwright 2001; Booth 1996; Kane 1881). When addiction to opium smoking posed a threat only to Chinese laborers and prostitutes and was restricted geographically to "Chinatowns" throughout the West, the practice aroused little concern among reformers. After 1875, however, a new class of white addicts began to emerge (Courtwright 2001). Though accounts of the day suggest that the majority of white users were prostitutes, gamblers, criminals, and other marginalized members of society, reformers nonetheless became increasingly vocal about the threat of opium smoking (see Kane 1881; Williams 1883; Dobie 1936). Specifically, moral entrepreneurs warned Americans that opium smoking, and the Chinese who introduced it to this country, posed a significant threat to respectable white women and the cultural institutions that they represented (e.g., motherhood, feminine modesty) (Dobie 1936; Courtwright 2001).

Warnings about an assault on feminine virtue by Chinese immigrants were a particularly effective rhetorical tool at the turn of the twentieth century. Women's historians have argued that concern over changing social mores and female sexuality in the late Victorian era had reached a critical level. They contend that, by the turn of the century, accounts in the popular press had convinced many Americans that modern society was filled with seducers waiting to prey upon young women who were too weak-willed to resist (Odem 1995; Freedman 1996; Kerber, Kessler-Harris, and Sklar 1995). The desire to safeguard American society by curtailing promiscuity and social rebellion among adolescent girls led to several questionable policy responses, including vigorous antivice campaigns in urban centers and state laws permitting the sterilization of wayward girls (Odem 1995). Moral entrepreneurs who wished to publicize the threat posed by Chinese immigrants simply drew public attention to yet another threat to feminine virtue: the opium den.

Although many contemporary writers and reformers helped to make a "dangerous class" of the Chinese, one of the most widely read was Jacob Riis. In 1890, early in the muckraking period, Riis published *How the Other Half Lives: Studies among the Tenements of New York*. Though the tone of the book was generally sympathetic toward the plight of the inner city poor, the author held no such sympathies for Chinese immigrants. Riis began his chapter on Chinatown with a somber admonition to readers who might hold naive views about the condition of the Chinese soul. "Ages of senseless idolatry," warned the author, "have left him without the essential qualities for appreciating the gentle teachings of a faith whose motive and unselfish spirit are beyond his grasp. . . . [H]e adopts Christianity, when he adopts it at all, with ulterior motives"(1970 [1890], 63). Riis' primary concern about Chinatown, however, was not the lack of Godliness, but rather the prevalence of opium and the effects that opium smoking had on white users:

> The chinaman smokes opium as Caucasians smoke tobacco, and apparently with little worse effect upon himself. But woe unto the white victim upon which this pitiless drug gets its grip. . . . From the teeming tenements come the white slaves of its dens . . . hapless victims of a passion which, once acquired, demands sacrifice of every instinct of decency. (65)

Despite his obvious desire to publicize the dangers of Chinese opium for all whites, Riis was particularly concerned with its deleterious effects on white girls. The addictive power of the drug, argued the author, meant houses in Chinatown were full of:

> girls, hardly yet grown to womanhood, worshiping nothing save the pipe that has enslaved them body and soul. Easily tempted from their homes, they rarely or never return. Mott Street gives up its victims only to the city's Charity hospital or Potter's Field. (66)

Nor was Riis convinced that these girls entered the trap of addiction of their own free will. Rather, he insisted that the "cruel cunning" of Chinese men lured underage girls into dens of vice, where they bound them with addiction to opium. To emphasize the point, the author reported "the arrest of a chinaman for 'inveigling little girls into his laundry,' one of the hundreds of outposts of Chinatown that are scattered all over the city, as the outer threads of a spider's web that holds its prey fast" (67). The most insidious thing about the Chinese and their opium, insisted Riis, was that hapless female victims became too ensnared to even feel remorse about the abandoning their appropriate role:

> On the depth of their fall no one is more aware than the girls themselves and no one is more unconcerned. The calmness with which they discussed it is disheartening. There was no shade of regret in their voices, nothing but indifference and surrender. (66)

The appeals of Jacob Riis and other moral entrepreneurs were successful in heightening public awareness of opium smoking, as well as mobilizing bias against the group with whom the practice was most readily associated. Historians of the muckraking period insist that *How the Other Half Lives* and Riis' second book, *Children of the Poor,* "stirred hundreds if not thousands of sympathetic readers who joined his attack with energy, with influence—and with funds" (Harrison and Stein 1973, 4). These historians also suggest that Riis was widely recognized as an expert in the subcultures of the American urban environment. His legitimacy came largely from his association with the *New York Times,* to whom he was a regular contributor both as a journalist and as a photographer. As a reformer, Riis' activities also drew the attention of prominent national officials. Among them was President Teddy Roosevelt, who termed Riis "the most useful citizen of New York" (quoted in Alland 1972, 67). Recognition by the President and other prominent figures further enhanced the legitimacy of the author's claims that the Chinese and their opium were denigrating the other upstanding, though impoverished, residents of New York's tenements.

The increasing prevalence of media accounts concerning the dangers of opium use and the Chinese also indicates that the work of moral entrepreneurs was successful in placing the issue on the public agenda. In 1889, the *New York Times* published no articles about opium smoking, opium dens, or Chinese use of opium. By 1909, the year that smoked opium was banned, the number of articles had risen to fifteen (*New York Times Index,* 1889–1909). The growth of media concern was more evident in popular magazines, where the number of opium-related articles increased by almost 200 percent from 1890 to 1909 (*Readers Guide to Periodic Literature,* 1890–1909).

The success of moral entrepreneurs in creating a Chinese "dangerous class" placed the problem on the public agenda, but the activities of political entrepreneurs were ultimately responsible for translating public concerns into public policy. Anti-opium legislation found a champion in Elisha Root, President Roosevelt's Secretary of State (Musto 1999). The final version of the bill that became law represented not only the lower political costs of targeting smoked opium and the Chinese, but also the broader political payoff to be gleaned through quick passage of the nation's first anti-narcotics legislation.

In 1907, the State Department, under Secretary Root, asked Congress for twenty thousand dollars to fund a three-person commission to study the prevalence and dangers of opium use (Booth 1996). The Secretary chose prominent men for the commission seats, including Dr. Hamilton Wright, whose work on early drug prohibition earned him the title "the father of American narcotics laws" (Taylor 1969). Largely at Wright's behest, the commission launched a series of fact-finding missions and prepared a number of reports for both Root and a congressional audience (see, for an example, Wright 1910). The statistics in these reports were similar to those offered by moral entrepreneurs in the popular media. Musto insists that "they were usually interpreted to maximize the danger of addiction, dramatize a supposed crisis in opiate consumption, and mobilize fear of minorities" (1999, 33). Acting on Wright's surveys and reports, the commission proposed several fairly comprehensive bans on the importation and domestic use of opiates.

Secretary Root realized, however, that total prohibition was likely to arouse opposition among physicians, pharmacists, manufacturers, and a number of other powerful groups (Musto 1999). Although increasingly concerned about opium addiction, American doctors were still lauding the palliative effects of opiates when properly administered by a medical professional (Courtwright 2001; Beard 1881). Recognizing the political power of the medical community, Root decided that legislation prohibiting only the importation of opium for smoking purposes was most likely to win quick congressional approval. The growing national concern over the Chinese, and the deleterious effects of their habits on white Americans, meant that the political cost of such a proposal was almost nil. In 1908, Root proposed to Congress legislation that closely resembled the 1905 ban on importation of opiates into the Philippines. He modified the language of the previous bill, however, to allow the importation of opiates not intended for smoking purposes (Musto 1999).

In addition to the obvious electoral benefit of passing anti-narcotics legislation that targeted only a feared and marginalized group, Root could offer a much larger political payoff to members of Congress when he proposed the ban on smoked opium. The State Department Commission on Opium Use was actually convened to help the United States prepare for an international conference on the opium trade. Though the conference, scheduled for early 1909 in Shanghai, China, was conceived by President Roosevelt, the United States faced the real possibility of being the only attending nation without a national law limiting the use, importation, or sale of opium (Taylor 1969; Booth 1996). In order to have any legitimacy when calling on other nations to crack down on opiate production and importation, the President and Congress alike felt that the United States must have some type of anti-narcotics law on the books by the opening day of the conference (Musto 1999; see also Zabriskie 1948). A law targeting only a practice widely associated with the Chinese was most likely to meet such a strenuous deadline and, indeed, the ban on the importation of smoking opium was passed into law on February 9, 1909, twenty-one days before the opening meeting in Shanghai.

Crime as Social Threat and the Comprehensive Crime Control Act of 1984

In 1984, Congress passed what was arguably the most far-reaching federal criminal justice legislation in history. The *Comprehensive Crime Control Act* (CCCA) contained twenty-five provisions toughening sanctions for federal offenders and extending the national government's involvement in state and local law enforcement efforts. In brief, the bill eliminated the presumption that defendants were entitled to pretrial release, eliminated discretionary parole release, extended judges' authority to supervise ex-felons after sentence completion, expanded the government's ability to seize the assets of certain offenders, increased fines for most drug offenses by as much as 400 percent, federalized a number of crimes committed with a firearm, and created the Office of Justice Programs to oversee a greatly expanded number of criminal justice grant initiatives (P.L. 98473). Critics have argued that the *CCCA* simply pandered to public fears about crime rather than addressing any real crisis of lawlessness and that it disproportionately targeted minorities and the underclass (Beckett 1997; Tonry 1995; Scheingold 1991; Simon 1993). Though all of these accusations may be true, the interesting question is: Why did it take until 1984 to pass legislation designed to garner electoral favor by targeting negatively constructed and politically powerless groups of minority lawbreakers? Legislators had, after all, been trying to pass similarly punitive provisions for more than eleven years (*Congressional Record* 1984a).

Part of the answer is that, by the mid-1980s, criminals occupied a more marginal place relative to the remainder of society, than they had in previous decades. This assertion may seem strange to those who see criminality as uniformly negative, but we believe that it is accurate for a variety of reasons. Crime and criminal activity are themselves socially constructed concepts that vary over time and across groups (Becker 1963; Ben-Yehuda 1990). That conceptual flexibility allows survey respondents to identify petty thieves, but not white-collar offenders, as "criminals" (Schrager and Short 1980). Similarly, it is the reason why labor unrest can be perceived as lawlessness in one historical period and legitimate employee action in another (e.g., gold miners in 1890s Colorado versus United Auto Workers in post-war Detroit). Apart from changing definitions of criminality, however, criminals had become more marginalized by 1984 for two additional reasons. First, assumptions about the causes of crime underwent a profound transformation during the 1970s and early 1980s, placing greater emphasis on individual rather than societal culpability. Second, scholars argue that, during that same period, fear of crime and criminals became a vehicle for racial animosities that could no longer be expressed openly in political discourse (Browning and Cao 1992).

The debate concerning the causes of criminality was between advocates of structural and culturalist explanations. Culturalists argue that the ethos of certain groups provides a breeding ground for social pathologies—such as crime, drug use, and delinquency—among group members (Moynihan 1968). Structuralists, on the other hand, insist that historical inequities, economic privation, and pervasive societal bias better explain why some groups cannot break the cycle of poverty and crime (Morris 1994; Clark 1970). Throughout much of the post-war era, the second perspective was dominant, at least among political elites. In keeping with the structural view, President Lyndon B. Johnson's national crime commission confidently declared that "warring on poverty is warring on crime. A civil rights law is a law against crime. Money for schools is money against crime" (President's Commission on Law Enforcement and the Administration of Justice 1967).

By the early 1980s, however, the popularity of structural explanations was waning; the culturalist perspective had gained prominence (Beckett 1997). As Bensonsmith notes in this volume, it was the very public positions of impor-

tant culturalists, such as Patrick Moynihan, that hastened the erosion of legitimacy for structuralist explanations. In his first major address on crime, President Ronald Reagan criticized the "social thinkers of the 1950s and 1960s
who discussed crime only in the context of disadvantaged childhoods and
poverty stricken neighborhoods" (quoted in Gross 1983, 87–88). In response
to criticisms that his famous book, *Thinking About Crime,* did little to address
"root causes" of crime, James Q. Wilson replied that "a free society can do so
little about attacking these 'causes' that concern for their elimination becomes
little more than an excuse for doing nothing" (1983, 6). He went on to insist
that "if kindness, better housing, improved diets, or lessened child abuse can
reduce crime then I favor them. I only ask that . . . their employment for crime
reduction purposes not be at the expense of society's desire to see justice done
to those who have violated its moral imperatives" (7). In 1984, President Reagan best summarized the changing assumptions about crime and society's relationship to criminals. "We are told," he remarked, "that the answer to this
problem is to reduce poverty. This isn't the answer . . . government's function
is to protect society from the criminal, not the other way around" (quoted in
Beckett 1997, 48).

In addition to changing assumptions about the causes of crime, criminals
became a more marginalized group by the early 1980s because criminal activity had become associated primarily with minority groups (Tonry 1993).
Numerous scholars argue that anti-crime rhetoric became a thinly disguised
substitute for explicit racism among political conservatives (Beckett 1997;
Browning and Cao 1992). According to Michael Tonry (1993), in law-and-
order politics, "the text may be crime but the subtext is race." There are two
explanations for the adoption of this strategy by political elites and its influence
on mass opinions about crime. The first centers on the search for electoral
advantage following the realignment of the South during the civil rights movement, while the second addresses anxieties among many Americans about the
speed and scope of race reform during that period.

The civil rights movement, and the subsequent increase in black electoral
power, alienated many southern Democrats from their party and provided an
opportunity for Republicans to gain an advantage in that region. Rieder argues
that "millions of voters, pried loose from their habitual loyalty to the Democratic party, were now a volatile force . . . without the channeling restraint of
party attachment" (1989, 243). As early as 1961, Barry Goldwater and other
conservatives recognized that this block of predominately poor, white, southern voters—along with blue collar and rural Midwesterners—could be courted
on the issue of race (Rieder 1989). The Republicans mobilized this "New
Majority" by wedding their traditional platform to a new conservative stance
on social issues. They appealed to anxieties about race in these constituencies
by focusing on the rapid social transformation and the need to reassert control
over the dangerous elements in society (Crawford 1980). Racially charged code

words within these appeals "referred indirectly to racial themes but did not directly challenge popular democratic or egalitarian ideals" (Omi 1987).

According to scholars of the race issue, the willingness to accept indirect attacks on racial equality in criminal justice rhetoric and policy stemmed from widespread popular anxiety about the speed and extent of racial reform (Schuman, Steed, and Bobo 1988). In the 1970s, studies found that 42 percent of those who disapproved of racial reform efforts identified crime as the country's number one problem, compared with only 13 percent of respondents who strongly supported racial reform (Beckett 1997). The link between these attitudes may not indicate explicit racism but rather the perception among whites, especially poor whites, that blacks now enjoyed a favored status among government, employers, and others in positions of power (D. Gordon 1994). Whatever the reasons for its tacit acceptance, the subtle infusion of race and racism into law-and-order rhetoric greatly contributed to the negative social construction of criminals. As Gordon notes, "For many whites, the criminal justice system is all that stands between them and a world dominated by black criminals and the violence and sloth they are presumed to represent" (151).

Gordon's statement draws attention to the importance of moral entrepreneurs in convincing Americans that crime and criminals represented a real threat. The accounts provided by these individuals helped to define street crime as a serious public problem and were instrumental in placing it on the public agenda. In many ways, the portrayal of crime in the media also served to heighten awareness and anxiety over criminality during the 1960s, 1970s, and 1980s. In perhaps the most comprehensive study of crime coverage and its impact on public opinion, Graber (1980) concludes that news coverage distorted the frequency and severity of crime, while serving as the primary source of information on the subject for almost 95 percent of Americans. Numerous other scholars also argued that the news media played an important role in constructing the crime issue for modern Americans (Surette 1998; MacGillis 1983; Barak 1994). Despite the importance of the media, however, it is difficult to demonstrate that biased coverage was intended to convince readers or viewers that criminals were a public problem because they posed a fundamental threat to the larger society. For that reason, we will limit our discussion here to individuals who did make such claims explicitly and, therefore, better fit our description of moral entrepreneurs.

The reformers who insisted that crime and criminality were pressing societal threats did not simply burst onto the national scene unannounced in the early 1980s. More than a decade before Ronald Reagan became president, moral entrepreneurs were explicitly connecting crime to the downfall of society. In the opening line of their book *The Lawbreakers,* Medford Evans and Margaret Moore told readers that "crime, like pain, has some unpleasant but necessary uses. It is a warning signal which tells us that the organism is diseased or wounded" (1968, 13). They went on to argue that, in the case of the United States, the disease might well be fatal:

> Every community operates in terms of a consensus about the way that its
> members are supposed to act. If and when this social framework ceases to exist,
> the community will, in the real meaning of the word, also cease to exist. (14)

Evans and Moore were careful to explain that crime was not simply an inevitable byproduct of a large, industrialized nation and that blame for the problem was not uniformly distributed among different groups within society. Instead, they argued, crime and the resultant threat to the social order was the product of groups who embraced the "new morality." Responsibility, claimed the authors, lay with the "topless dancers, profane preachers, go-go girls, and pill pushers" who exemplified the decline in traditional values evident in 1960s America (34). The adherents to the new morality did not, Evans and Moore admitted, commit every crime but they were responsible for nurturing an ethos that created the larger problem:

> Certain connections between the "new morality" and crime are apparent . . .
> continuing assault on the presuppositions of civilization itself, which is the
> essential program of the "new morality," is in a larger sense the very definition
> of crime. (45)

Moral entrepreneurship in the 1970s and 1980s found its most eloquent expression in James Q. Wilson and his widely read *Thinking About Crime* (1975; 1983; 1985). Wilson's commentary on the social threat of criminality was a good deal more staid than warnings issued by other reformers.[2] His influence on policy makers and the mass public was probably greater, however, than any other single individual due to the popularity of *Thinking About Crime* and his position on President Reagan's advisory commission on crime, law enforcement, and drug abuse (MacGillis 1983). Though his analysis was more subtle than those attributing crime to go-go girls and sexual deviants, Wilson was nonetheless clear about his belief that "predatory crime does not only victimize individuals, it impedes and, in extreme cases, prevents the formation and maintenance of community" (1985, 26). The author also warned that when social controls were weakened, or when they disappeared altogether in a society, criminality could quickly become a threat:

> Such an area is vulnerable to criminal invasion. Though it is not inevitable it
> is more likely that here, rather than in places where people . . . can regulate
> behavior by informal controls, drugs will change hands, prostitutes will solicit,
> cars will be stripped, . . . muggings will occur. (79)

While Wilson aggressively publicized his belief that crime represented a pressing societal threat (see Wilson 1973; 1983), his most compelling argument concerned how to regulate those groups responsible for criminal behavior. Social controls that had limited crime in the past were quickly losing their efficacy due to an "ideology of personal liberation and radical individualism" (Wilson 1985, 247). Wilson did not directly criticize these developments but, rather, suggested that increased individual liberty necessitated a larger and more coercive role for the state in regulating criminal behavior:

> Societies that are not free need not rely as much as we on the police appara-
> tus to control crime for, if they manage their "unfreedom" skillfully, they can
> use schools, political parties, and mutual spying to control behavior. (248)

Wilson acknowledged that the absence of tyranny necessitating more coercive criminal justice policy was a difficult logic to digest, but he was quick to warn readers that the modern liberal ethos left little choice:

> We have made our society and we must live with it. We must labor as patiently
> as we can to make a liberal society work and to make the best and sanest use
> of our laws to control behavior without feeling embraced that by invoking
> "The Law," we are denying our liberal creed. Far from it; we are reaffirming
> it. (1985, 249)

In making these arguments Wilson not only connected crime and social decay, he also suggested that punitive criminal justice policy was the only way to make a liberal society "work."

The writings of Wilson and other moral entrepreneurs had a substantial impact on national concern about criminals and criminal activity. After remaining stable at 0 to 2 percent between 1950 and 1968, the percent of Americans who identified crime as the most important problem facing the nation fluctuated between 5 percent and 29 percent during the period from 1968 to 1983 (Gallup 1950–1983). During the same fifteen-year period, the number of annual Congressional hearings on crime and crime-related issues increased from fourteen to seventy-four (Baumgartner and Jones 1993). Although determining the number of hearings spurred by growing public concern versus those launched for other reasons is impossible, the trend nonetheless indicates the rising salience of the issue.

The success of moral entrepreneurs in framing crime and criminals as a pressing social threat increased the probability that a policy entrepreneur could successfully place the issue on the political agenda. The *Comprehensive Crime Control Act* actually owed its eventual passage largely to the efforts of two champions, President Reagan and Representative Dan Lungren (R-California). Both men, in different ways, helped to ensure that a public concern was successfully translated into a political problem and that there was sufficient profit to overcome the collective action problem of the legislative process.

President Reagan deserves a good deal of the credit for initially placing the bill on the agenda and providing early and vigorous support for the issue. Though crime control had always been high on the President's domestic agenda, he officially announced a sweeping revision of criminal justice policy as one of his top priorities during the 1983 State of the Union address. "It is high time," declared Reagan, "that we make our cities safe again. . . . This administration hereby declares an all-out war on big time organized crime and the drug racketeers who are poisoning our young people" (Reagan 1983). On March 16, 1983, Reagan sent to Congress an anti-crime package that contained most of the major provisions included in the final version of the CCCA. A bill closely resembling Reagan's initial proposal, including sentencing reform and revision of the pretrial detention codes, passed the Senate by a 91–1 vote on February 2, 1984 (*Congressional Quarterly Almanac* 1984; *Congressional Record* 1984c, S 1762). Following passage, Reagan continued to elicit support for the bill in Washington and around the country. At the first televised press conference following the Senate vote, Reagan declared that the legislation was "long overdue" and criticized the House of Representatives for "dragging its feet" on the issue (quoted in *Congressional Quarterly Almanac* 1984). In an address to the Annual Convention of the National Sheriffs Association in June 1984, the President urged support for the legislation and reminded participants that:

> Choosing a career in crime is not the result of an unhappy childhood or a misunderstood adolescence; it is the result of a conscious willful choice made by some who consider themselves above the law, who seek to exploit the hard work of their . . . fellow citizens. (Reagan 1984, 886)

Despite Reagan's support for crime control legislation, however, the House of Representatives was slow to act. Several elements of the Senate package had been passed as individual pieces of legislation, but two of the most important provisions, regarding sentencing and bail, continued to languish in the House Judiciary Committee (*Congressional Record* 1984a). At this point, Representative Lungren became a prominent figure in the history of the legislation. By chance, C-Span began broadcasting House proceedings around the same time as floor debate began on provisions of the anti-crime package. In an attempt to take the message of the Republican minority directly to the public, thereby bypassing resistant House leadership, Lungren began using the one-minute floor statements to which all members were entitled to popularize now familiar slogans such as "truth-in-sentencing." "We had to learn to tame that creature of C-Span," admitted Lungren. "We very consciously decided how we would pitch our arguments on the floor differently" (quoted in Gest 2001). In addition to pitching important provisions of the crime package on the floor, Lungren also attempted to build support by recruiting crime victims to testify at committee hearings (Gest 2001).

Lungren supported an omnibus crime bill that would encompass the majority of conservative provisions within a single piece of legislation. His ardent support reflected more than simply a desire to address the crime issue or "carry water" for the president. First, Lungren knew that anything short of a comprehensive crime package was likely to be vetoed by the President. Reagan had, in fact, rejected crime legislation in 1983 because it failed to contain most of the fundamental reforms that he envisioned (*Congressional Quarterly Almanac* 1982, 419–20). More importantly, however, Lungren enthusiastically pushed the *CCCA* because it represented a rare opportunity to force conservative legislation past the Democratic opposition.

Lungren joined the House in 1979, just as the Conservative Coalition of Republicans and southern Democrats was beginning to regain some power in the Congress. Members of the coalition, tired of seeing their agenda ignored, were determined to attain more visibility for conservative core goals (*Congressional Quarterly Almanac* 1980, 34-C). The Republican leadership looked favorably on the junior representative from California, who had a bit of notoriety as the son of President Richard M. Nixon's physician, and assigned him to the Judiciary subcommittee responsible for rewriting the criminal code (Gest 2001). Coalition members were particularly interested in penetrating the Judiciary Committee, which had "preserved its standing as the graveyard of conservative initiatives" (*Congressional Quarterly Almanac* 1982, 371). Over the next four years, Lungren worked in committee and on the floor to publicize a comprehensive conservative anti-crime package (Gest 2001).

In fall 1984, the opportunity to pass a conservative crime bill became a reality. Congress had not enacted all thirteen of the appropriations bills necessary to keep the government running and was forced to pass a continuing resolution maintaining current spending levels (H.J. 648). Recognizing that the Democratic leadership had presented an opportunity by allowing some provisions of substantive legislation to be attached as riders, Lungren moved to attach crime legislation to the Fiscal 1985 continuing appropriations resolution (*Congressional Record* 1984a). The House bill (HR 5963) was identical to the crime package passed by the Senate and the motion to attach it to the appropriations resolution passed 243–166 (*Congressional Record* 1984b). Before the modified funding bill returned to the floor for a vote, Lungren gave an impassioned speech in favor of passage. He insisted that it was "time to put up or shut up" on the crime issue and reminded members that they would be defending their votes on the campaign trail within a month (*Congressional Record* 1984b, H10094). The continuing resolution, with the crime bill attached, passed easily and a similar piece of legislation was signed into law on October 12.

CONCLUSION

Recognizing the important contribution of social construction theory to the study of policy design, this chapter investigated the process that lay between perception and policy. Relying heavily on literature from sociology and political science, we argue that the transition from the social constructions of deviant groups to targeted policy is characterized by three conditions. First, a readily identifiable and socially marginal group is widely associated with a value-laden stereotype. This condition assumes that even among those groups perceived as *deviants,* certain groups are more feared and more marginalized than others. Second, in order to turn public concern about a group into an impetus for action, a moral entrepreneur is needed to focus public attention on the actions of that group. Finally, in order to convert a public problem into a political one, there must be sufficient political profit to entice a policy champion to place the issue on the political agenda and to work to secure passage of targeted legislation.

The case studies we presented invite a set of interrelated conclusions about the complexity of the policy process and the importance of entrepreneurs and the constructions they create within that process. The anti-opium laws of the early twentieth century and the *Comprehensive Crime Control Act* passed during the Reagan era both demonstrate that it is a circuitous journey from perception to public policy. As we argued at the outset, the negative stereotypes assigned to Chinese immigrants and to lawbreakers, respectively, did not guarantee that the state would produce policies targeted at each. Instead, there was a multistep process in which the actions of each group became a matter of concern for the general public and then for political actors. Once the issues of opium and criminality had been forced onto the political agenda, they were then only able to produce public policy once the substantial transaction costs of the legislative process had been overcome.

As the case studies demonstrate, however, it would be a mistake to assume that such a progression through the process is organic and unassisted. In the case of anti-narcotics and anti-crime policies, notable individuals played key roles in creating and magnifying social constructions that facilitate the journey from negative perception to policy. Drawing their legitimacy from social institutions such as media, religion, government, or the educational system, these moral and political entrepreneurs helped to focus latent social anxieties on the activities of certain groups and then parlayed those heightened concerns into targeted, and often politically profitable, public policy. Some of the chapters in this work have drawn attention to the sometimes unintended consequences of political analysis and commentary (see especially chapter 9). While we acknowledge that coercive policies can sometimes result from the best of intentions, we also think it is important to remember that negative social constructions and the policy designs that they produce may often be the result of the conscious effort of individuals with something to gain.

If that is indeed the case, then it is also important to note the dangerous and destructive nature of such degenerative politics. While negative social constructions, like the ones that gave rise to the *Comprehensive Crime Control Act,* are undoubtably an efficient way to build political capital, they are also a long-lasting burden to the group in question and perhaps the society as a whole. More than five million people have come under some sort of correctional supervision since the passage of the CCCA. If we define them all as members of a dangerous class, as the proponents of that legislation did, then we have, by definition, a huge group of Americans who are incapable of living within the moral confines of our society. That supposition presents us with two immense problems—one individual and one structural. First, for the individuals who are classified as members of the dangerous class, any chance of reintegrating into society is lost. Being classified as such almost guarantees that they will, in fact, be forced to live outside of the mainstream. In a broader sense, a large group within the population who are formally disenfranchised or informally ostracized and thus inefficacious, presents a real challenge for a democratic system such as ours. As previous experience (circa 1965) has demonstrated, segregated systems of citizenship often disintegrate in a violent and rending fashion. Taken together, the individual and social consequences of degenerative politics seem far too great to justify the short-term political payoff.

NOTES

1. Radical criminologists argue that the designation of a "dangerous class" is, in fact, fundamental to the origination and maintenance of the legal order in our society (Chambliss 1964; Chambliss and Seidman 1971).

2. Wilson has done some work on predicting criminality using body type and other questionable techniques, which is uncomfortably reminiscent of eugenics research that characterized nineteenth century criminology (see Wilson and Hernstein 1985). We have chosen not to review this work, however, because it did not enjoy the widespread popularity and influence of *Thinking About Crime*.

9

Jezebels, Matriarchs, and Welfare Queens: The Moynihan Report of 1965 and the Social Construction of African-American Women in Welfare Policy

DIONNE BENSONSMITH

INTRODUCTION

K nowing that race, gender, and sexuality have been, and continue to be, constructed through welfare debates and policy is essential for understanding how the American welfare state developed. Studying how race, gender, and sexuality are talked about helps place these into a larger context. When we use symbolic language, which has helped produce such cultural icons as the welfare queen, we not only construct the "other"—the operative "they" to our "we"—but we construct ourselves as well.

This article discusses specific constructions of African-American women that have emerged during the past thirty years as we have expanded and retrenched the American welfare state. First, I examine the constructions that initially worked to exclude black women from welfare programs and then, once they were finally included, served as the basis for welfare state retrenchment. I argue that, during the 1960s, the welfare state became explicitly defined around stereotypes of African-American women. Specifically, this chapter examines how social constructions and stereotypes of African-American women mediated the debate over welfare. More importantly, it asks: What can these constructions teach us about race and gender?

At the core of this chapter is a critique of the social construction of race, sex roles, and the African-American family in the 1965 report, *The Negro Family: The Case for National Action* (hereafter the Moynihan Report). Moynihan's central thesis was that the "breakdown of the Negro family" was the primary cause of African-American poverty and disenfranchisement. Studying the report, as well as critiques that both support and refute it, we can illustrate the ways in which social constructions inform and structure policy discourse.

In addition to reviewing the Moynihan Report, this chapter examines the consequence of stereotypes generated within the report for discourses on race, gender, and class. This analysis does not assign causality; nor does it argue that the Moynihan Report was the sole cause or the only source of negative constructions of African-American women and families. In fact, the report itself drew from the works of prominent African-American scholars of the time. In addition to citing these scholars, the Moynihan Report drew upon existing racial, sexual, and class stereotypes. However, the report highlighted particular beliefs—like the idea that African-American women are uncontrollable breeders who cause dysfunction within their families (the Jezebel or Sapphire stereotype)—and submerged others, like the long-standing stereotype of the "innocent" and ignoble deserted woman who receives needed public assistance to keep her family (mainly children) intact. This chapter also places the Moynihan Report, and the African-American women's constructions it contained, within historical context. Rather than emphasize Moynihan's structural impact on welfare policy and institutions, it uses a historical lens to observe the discursive influences the report had on social welfare policy and poverty debates.

Many changes in welfare and social policy debates, specifically those concerning who should receive what types of aid, occurred during the 1960s. The expansion of African Americans' civil, political, and social rights was also debated in this period. In this way, the Moynihan Report is about more than just race. Some of the more pernicious constructions produced by the report were sexist and most were influential in constructing who were the deserving versus the undeserving poor. The report's gendered and racial analysis of African-American family structure reflects the historical time period in which it was written and significantly influenced how debates about poverty and the family developed.

Origins of the Moynihan Report

President Lyndon B. Johnson laid the groundwork for the War on Poverty programs in his 1965 Howard University commencement speech *(To Fulfill These Rights: Remarks of The President at Howard University, June 4)* (Rainwater and Yancey 1967, 1; Quadagno 1999, 10–13). The speech highlighted African Americans' social and economic plight throughout the entire country (Rainwater and Yancey 1967, 125). In this address, Johnson applauded recent efforts to expand their civil rights, but cautioned that the statutory remedies contained in the *Civil Rights Act* and the *Voting Rights Act* were not enough (125–32).

In an attempt to illustrate the "widening gulf" between blacks and whites, Johnson cited a litany of facts, stating, "since 1947 the number of white families living in poverty [had] decreased 27 percent, while the number of poor non-white families decreased by only 3 percent." Johnson also noted that in 1940, the nonwhite infant mortality was only 40 percent greater than whites, but just twenty-two years later that percentage had increased to 90 percent (Rainwater and Yancey 1967, 127). Acknowledging that the causes of poverty are complex and differentiated among individuals, Johnson nonetheless cited the breakdown of African-American families as the primary cause of black poverty:

> Perhaps the most important—its influence radiating to every part of life—is the breakdown of the Negro family structure . . . the family is the cornerstone of our society. More than any other force it shapes the attitudes, the hopes, the ambitions, and the values of the child. When the family collapses it is the children that are unusually damaged. When it happens on a massive scale the community itself is crippled. So unless we work to strengthen the family, to create conditions under which most parents will stay together—all the rest: schools and playgrounds, public assistance and private concern, will never be enough to cut completely the circle of despair and deprivation. (1965, 130)

To strengthen the family and curb the "circle of despair and deprivation," Johnson called for income assistance programs, more jobs for African-American men, and home subsidy allowances so that African-American families could move to better neighborhoods. Finally, Johnson announced a White House conference, at which he would convene "scholars, and experts, and outstanding Negro leaders—men of both races—and officials of government at every level," dedicated to explicating and understanding the causes and cures for African-American poverty (Rainwater and Yancey 1967, 131).

Johnson's speech served as a preview of what would be discussed at a White House conference focusing on poverty and race in America. Written in conjunction with then-Assistant Secretary of Labor Daniel P. Moynihan, the speech outlined the main ideas contained in his report. The speech itself caused little or no controversy. Once unveiled, however, the Moynihan Report sparked one of the most contentious and enduring national debates, changing the way poverty, race, and welfare were talked about for the next thirty years.

The report served several overlapping purposes—political, academic, and theoretical—for Moynihan. As Assistant Secretary of Labor, Moynihan sought to use the report to tackle long-standing poverty and disenfranchisement problems experienced by African Americans and poor Americans in general. However, Moynihan's interest in social welfare, race and ethnicity, and public policy topics started long before he joined the Johnson Administration. As a political scientist, Moynihan had studied the causes of poverty and disenfranchisement among the poor (Rainwater and Yancey 1967, 17–18). Moynihan was part of what was characterized as a "new breed of public servants, the social scientist-politicos, who combine their background both social science training and experience and full-time involvement in political activity" (18). Moynihan also sought to use the report as a way to transform the government's role in the social policy process, and his office in particular, moving into the area of *defining* problems as well as offering solutions to them.

The report was Moynihan's attempt to explain why the assimilation pattern that had worked for white immigrants in the early 1900s failed to move African Americans into the mainstream. His report unquestionably assumed the assimilation theories of Gunnar Myrdal and E. Franklin Frazier and quoted from them at length.[1] The idea was that a "pathological aspect of black culture which only full assimilation could cure" existed (Rainwater and Yancey 1967, 17). Assimilation and culture of poverty theories, coupled with his readings and study of the works of black intellectuals, such as Frazier, led Moynihan to conclude that the primary effect of African-American poverty and disenfranchisement was the disintegration of the African-American family (1965, 17, Introduction). His remedy would be "a national effort . . . directed to a new kind of national goal: the establishment of a stable Negro family structure" (17, Introduction). In this way, Moynihan acted not only as a "moral and political entrepreneur," but as the "policy champion" for his particular definition and solution for African Americans' disenfranchisement (1965, Introduction).

However, as many articles in this volume demonstrate, in defining and "solving" the problem, Moynihan (the policy entrepreneur) created several new issues. The report's one enduring legacy was the racialization of the culture of poverty. Moynihan combines social pathologies—such as drug abuse, broken families, and criminal behavior associated with the underclass—with 1960s stereotypes and misperceptions of African Americans. He asserts that slavery destroyed patterns of two-parent family formation for African Americans. In addition, high unemployment caused by racism undermined the primary family role of African-American males—namely their ability to provide for their families. Moynihan writes: "[A]t the heart of the deterioration of the fabric of Negro society is the deterioration of the Negro family" (Nicholson-Crotty and Meier, this volume; O'Connor 2001; Rainwater and Yancey 1967).[2] However, it is the relationship between black men and women, and the economic independence of the latter, which receives sustained attention in the report. The remainder of this chapter focuses on the characterizations of African-American women as welfare-reliant, emasculating matriarchs. Additionally, it addresses the report's influence on race, gender, and social policy scholarship and discourse.

Constructing African-American Women:
Matriarchy, Independent Women,
and the "Tangle of Pathologies"

The Aid to Dependent Children (ADC) program (1935–1937) was transformed into the Aid to Families with Dependent Children (AFDC) program
in 1967 and then into the Transitional Aid to Needy Families (TANF) program
in 1996. During this period, discourse on U.S. poverty became increasingly
racialized and feminized, while the welfare policy discourse feminized race and
racialized gender. The two concepts—race and gender—intersected and were
personified in African-American women's images and constructions. The
Moynihan Report, and the debate that followed its publication, marked a key
moment in this transformation. It was published at the height of the national
debate over expanding civil, political, and social rights for African Americans.
Since then, many of the stereotypes constructed and reconstructed in the report
have become an integral part of the U.S. national lexicon on race and gender.

Although Moynihan wrote the *Negro Family: The Case for National Action*
with the stated intent of supporting programs designed to advance rights for
African Americans, an unintended consequence was the construction of three
pernicious stereotypes. These stereotypes, however, would plague African
Americans, poverty discourse, and welfare policy in the years that followed. The
emasculating black matriarch, the overly fertile and lazy welfare mother (later
transformed into the iconographic welfare queen) and the shiftless black male
are stereotypes that, upon closer inspection, originated during slavery.

It should be noted that the welfare queen construction did not become a
dominant archetype until former president Ronald Regan coined the term in the
early 1980s. The Moynihan Report, though, did contain many of the behavioral,
economic, and social antecedents to this stereotype. More accurately, the report
characterized black, female welfare recipients as "welfare ladies" (Patricia Hill
Collins [1990] used this term in *Black Feminist Thought*). The causal link that
Moynihan established between race, receiving welfare, and pathological behavior,
however, gave rise to the welfare queen construction. This construction contributes
to the discourse used by conservatives to attack welfare and welfare recipients.

The Moynihan Report constructed and supported its thesis with respect
to sex and gender roles in the family and matriarchy—black women and single motherhood to which the matriarchy thesis is related—in several ways. As
he developed his thesis around these variables, Moynihan constructed an argument calling for the "policy of the United States [to] bring the Negro American full and equal sharing in the responsibilities and rewards of citizenship."
Through this discussion, however, the report focused debates over race, gender,
and social policy. That is, it focused on the dysfunction of female-headed
households and not the social, political, and economic structures responsible for
African-American poverty and disenfranchisement.

Sex and Gender Roles and Their Influence on Family Structure

> There is no one Negro problem. There is no one solution. Nonetheless, at
> the center of the tangle of pathology is the weakness of the family struc-
> ture. Once or twice removed, it will be found to be the principal source of
> most of the aberrant, inadequate, or antisocial behavior that did not estab-
> lish, but now serves to perpetuate, the cycle of poverty and deprivation.
> (Moynihan 1965, 5)

Moynihan begins the report by highlighting the perceived disintegration
of the black family, stating, "[T]he family is the basic social unit of American
life; it is the basic socializing unit. By and large, adult conduct in society is
learned as a child." He then attempts to explain African-American disenfranchisement by focusing on black behavior:

> The fundamental problem, in which this is most clearly the case, is that of
> family structure. The evidence—not final, but powerfully persuasive—is that
> the Negro family in the urban ghettos is crumbling. . . . [A]t the heart of the
> deterioration of the fabric of Negro society is the deterioration of the Negro
> family. It is the fundamental source of weakness of the Negro community at
> the present time. (5)

In his discussion of sex and gender roles and their effect on family structure, Moynihan advances two stereotypes. First, he juxtaposes African-American family "types" with those of whites. Citing the perceived dysfunction in the
black family, he implies that when it pertains to gender and sex roles in the
family, the behavior of African Americans is responsible for their poverty and
discrimination. Moynihan does this by setting up binaries between the black
and white poor, between urban and rural, between maleness and femaleness,
and between the "natural" and the "unnatural." In constructing his analysis
around binary thinking, the Moynihan Report replicates the "us versus them"
dichotomy criticized by scholars of race and gender theory. It also consigns
blacks, more specifically black families headed by women, to a lower class status. He states:

> But there is one truly great discontinuity in family structure in the United
> States at the present time: that between the white world in general and that
> of the Negro American. . . . The white family has achieved a high degree of
> stability and is maintaining that stability. (1965, 5)

In bold lettering in the original report, he goes on, "[b]y contrast, **the family
structure of lower class Negroes is highly unstable, and in many urban
centers is approaching complete breakdown**" (5). Thus, Moynihan
defined what he believed to be the first characteristic of the black lower class,
an urban geographical setting.

Juxtaposing white and black children, Moynihan again extends the benefit of the doubt to lower-class whites stating, "[W]hite children without fathers
at least perceive all about them the pattern of men working. Negro children
without fathers *flounder* and *fail*" (35) [emphasis added]. If we take this statement on face value, the presence of fathers in the home is the most important
factor in determining poverty and social dysfunction in families. The presence
of a dominant male in the home is only followed by race in the variables that
determine economic and social dysfunction within the black community.

Matriarchy: Black Women, Female Heads of Household, and Single Mother Families

The second cause of African-American disenfranchisement and poverty,
according to Moynihan, is female-headed, so-called "broken homes." Moynihan cites a litany of statistics pointing to the rise in separation and divorce rates
among "nonwhite" families (Moynihan 1965, 8). He writes, "[N]early a quarter of Negro women living in cities who have ever married are divorced, separated, or are living apart from their husbands . . . 26 percent of Negro women
ever married are either divorced, separated, or have their husbands absent" (8).
He continues:

> In essence, the Negro community has been forced into a matriarchal struc-
> ture which, because it is so out of line with the rest of American society, seri-
> ously retards the progress of the group as a whole, and imposes a crushing bur-
> den on the Negro male and, in consequence, on a great many Negro women
> as well. There is presumably, no special reason why a society in which males
> are dominant in family relationships is to be preferred to a matriarchal
> arrangement. However, it is clearly a disadvantage for a minority group to be
> operating on one principle, while the great majority of the population, and
> the one with the most advantages to begin with, is operating on another. (29)

This statement demonstrates it is not merely the father's absence from the
home that causes dysfunction. According to Moynihan, it is merely the state of
having the home headed by a woman—those with fathers in residence and
those with fathers outside of the home—that contributes to dysfunction and
poverty within the black community. For Moynihan, the "problem" of female
heads of households is so severe that it warrants its own separate section within
the report. Moynihan begins his analysis of the "real" cause of problems within
the black community with a section headed: "almost one-fourth of Negro families are headed by females" (1965, 9).

Neither Moynihan nor the current discourse on the deviancy/pathol-
ogy of "broken homes" comments on the status of single-parent families
headed by men. The reader either assumes that these families do not occur
or that they are somehow free of the dysfunction and pathology associated

with families headed by women. That the dysfunction happens when women are family heads, regardless of whether or not there is a male present, represents the double standard applied to male and female gender and to sex roles within the family. Historically, welfare and social policy considered women to be the "harbingers of democracy," the group responsible for socializing little girls and boys into their "proper" gender roles (Mink 1990). Men, then, were to provide the proper financial security. That way, the wife can perform her intended gender role of taking care of the home, raising the children, and serving her husband.

According to Moynihan, the primary dysfunction in African-American families is that the majority of them fail to fit this pattern. He writes: "[A] fundamental fact of Negro American family life is the often reversed roles of husband and wife" (1965, 31). This inversion of gender roles negatively affects African Americans' ability to assimilate into mainstream American society. Moynihan notes several of these effects within the report. With respect to slavery's role and how Jim Crow affected changes in gender roles in the black family, he states:

> [U]nquestionably these events worked against the emergence of a strong father figure. The very essence of the male animal, from the bantam rooster to the four-star general, is to strut. (16)

Pointing out the ways in which female heads of household produce "bad" children, Moynihan observes: "[R]esearchers who have focused upon the 'good' boy in a high delinquency neighborhood noted that they typically come from exceptionally stable, intact families." He continues:

> Recent psychological research demonstrates the personality effects of being reared in a disorganized home without a father. One study showed that children from fatherless homes seek immediate gratification of their desires far more than children with fathers present. Others revealed that children who hunger for immediate gratification are more prone to delinquency, along with less social behavior. (1965, 39)

More important for Moynihan, however, is that African-American men are *feminized* because of their inability to take their rightful place at the head of the family. To illustrate this point, he cites sociologist Edward Bakke's study of the effects of unemployment on families. Bakke writes that the effects of unemployment on family structure can be observed in four stages, "the first two stages end with the exhaustion of credit and the entry of the wife into the labor force. The father is no longer the provider and the elder children become resentful" (1965, 19). It is the third stage that is "most critical" for Moynihan, for in this stage there "commences a new day-to-day existence." Again quoting Bakke, Moynihan observes:

At this point two women are in charge: Consider the fact that relief investigators or caseworkers are normally women and deal with the housewife. Already suffering a loss in prestige and authority in the family because of his failure to be the chief breadwinner, the male head of the family feels deeply, this obvious transfer of planning for the family's well being to two women, one of them an outsider. His role reduced to that of errand boy to and from the relief office. (19)

To counteract the disastrous effects of female-headed households, which include "reduced intelligence, illegitimacy, crime and delinquency," Moynihan advocates traditionally masculinizing activities such as military service (1965, 39). In addition to providing a place where black men can excel, due to its imposed "meritocracy," Moynihan advocates military service for black men because "it is an utterly masculine world" (42). He goes on:

Given the stains of the disorganized and matrifocal family life in which so many Negro youth come of age, the Armed Forces are a dramatic and desperately needed change: a world *away from women,* a world run by *strong men* of unquestioned authority; where discipline, if harsh, is nonetheless orderly and predictable, and where rewards, if limited, are granted on the basis of performance. (43)

Moynihan's belief that dependency feminizes men has deep historical roots and is consistent with early constructions of gender roles that provided the impetus for welfare programs from the late 1800s to the present. In her analysis of the early welfare state, Gwendolyn Mink notes the ways in which welfare proposals and arguments for state-administered social policy often revolved around the perceived relationship between men and women, the masculine and the feminine, and the provider and the dependent. Though Mink is analyzing welfare policy in the late 1800s and 1920s, her observations regarding the construction of the masculine and feminine in welfare policy are relevant with respect to the Moynihan Report as well. She writes:

By assigning feminine traits to ethnic men, old-stock Americans not only neutered allegedly servile and dependent men but marked them as a peril to republican liberty as well. For while woman's dependency was the mainspring of woman's virtue, men's dependency was the sign of men's inadequacy. The flip side of dependent womanhood was virtuous motherhood; the flip side of dependent manhood was the germ of tyranny. (1990, 96)

This lack of familial instruction as to the proper sex roles, caused by female dominance in the family and the feminization of black men, is the primary cause of political, economic, and social alienation within the African-American community. Thus, it is the cause for "a national effort . . . that will give a unity of purpose to the many activities of the Federal government in this area, directed to a new kind of national goal: *the establishment of a stable Negro family structure*" (Moynihan 1965, Introduction).

The Controversy: Criticisms and Defenses of the Moynihan Thesis

Most of the praise and criticism that resulted from the report's publication focused on Moynihan's depiction of the African-American family and his analysis of the causes and consequences of African-American poverty. Very few reviewers took issue with Moynihan's construction of African-American women as emasculating matriarchs or with his ascribed remedies to the "problem" of gender inversion within the African-American family. Early critiques did note, however, the potentially negative effects the report could have on debating the causes of and remedies for disenfranchisement within the African-American community. Christopher Jencks summarized the critiques of the report in his review for the *New York Review of Books* stating:

> Moynihan's analysis is the conservative tradition that guided the drafting of the poverty program. . . . The guiding assumption is that social pathology is caused less by basic defects in the social system than by defects in particular individuals and groups which prevent their adjusting to the system. The prescription is therefore to change the deviance, not the system. (Jencks 1965, quoted in Rainwater and Yancey 1967, 217)

However, few scholars, journalists, or politicians took issue with Moynihan's depiction of gender and sex roles in the family, nor his portrayal of African-American women and the deviancy of households which they headed. While the report drew protest from various leaders ranging from George Gilders—founder of the National Welfare Rights Organization—to African-American scholars like Robert Staples, most of the critiques focused on Moynihan's analysis of the African-American family. More specifically, they called into question his depiction of African-American men. The matriarch construction was hotly contested, but it took place mainly in relation to how this thesis reflected on African-American men. Prominent black social scientists—like Joyce Ladner, Andrew Billingsley, Robert Staples, and Angela Davis—refuted Moynihan's depiction of the African-American family as "pathological" (Giddings 1984). Ladner and Billingsley stressed the benefits of a nontraditional family structure, questioning the validity of using as a norm white, middle-class families, many of which were in crises due to rebellious and disaffected youth (Ladner 1973, 326; Billingsley 1968).

As Paula Giddings notes in her essay *Strong Women and Strutting Men,* "though many took issue with Moynihan's view of the problem, however, few criticized his suggestion for resolving it—which was even more malevolent" (1984, 328). Specifically, Giddings refers to Moynihan's contention that black men have been unsuccessful in education and in the job marketplace while black women have experienced a relatively high degree of success in both areas.

In their study of the aftereffects of the report on the policy-making community, Rainwater and Yancey write that, "Moynihan felt that jobs had primacy and that the government should not rest until every able-bodied Negro man was working even if this meant that some women's jobs had to be redesigned to enable men to fulfill them" (quoted in Giddings 1984, 328). This points again to one of the most sexist elements of the report. For Moynihan, single mother heads of households are clearly not the heart of the "Negro problem." Rather, it is the perceived economic and social supremacy of black women over black men or their parity with black men in both single-parent *and* two-parent households.

An Ironic Legacy? The Discursive Impact of the Moynihan Report on Race, Gender, and Poverty Debates

The main thrust of the report is aptly summarized in its title: *The Negro Family: The Case for National Action.* The report's political and institutional legacies helped provide justification for shifting government intervention from the public (institutional structures that cause poverty and disenfranchisement) to the personal (namely the family and the individual). The link Moynihan made between the disintegration of the African-American family and welfare dependency foreshadowed one of its most troubling legacies. The report connected out-of-wedlock childbearing with the breakdown of the African-American family. This conclusion heavily influenced welfare policy discourse and is central to the conservative attack on welfare policy that would take place in the 1980s and 1990s.

The report posits that African Americans have been consigned to a "structure" or "culture of poverty" that has, in turn, created a "tangle of pathologies." These pathologies are both the cause and the consequence of African-American poverty and disenfranchisement. One of the main points of my analysis has been to illustrate how the Moynihan Report racializes the tangle of pathologies in such a way that they begin to become synonymous with racial groups and move beyond behaviors attributed to class. The report's linkage of different types of pathological behavior—such as crime, out-of-wedlock childbearing, and welfare dependency—provided the impetus for the conservative attack on welfare policy that emerged in the following decades.

A look at research on the causes of poverty and its impact on behavior points to the impact the Moynihan Report has had on poverty research and scholarship (O'Connor 2001; Reed 1999). The Moynihan thesis is most evident in the work of scholars like William Julius Wilson. In *The New York Times'* retrospective on the life of Moynihan, Wilson is quoted as praising Moynihan's work, stating, "Moynihan's study of the relationship between poverty and family structure provided the framework for scientific investigation that has—especially since the mid-1980s, when the research on the black poor was revived—influenced research ideas and the development of research topics across social science disciplines" (*The New York Times* 2000, 9). In fact, Moynihan's thesis played an integral role in creating a "new" construction and analytic category of poor people, the underclass.

In his book *Stirrings in the Jug,* Adolph Reed, Jr. provides an intellectual history of the underclass concept. He traced its development in the works of scholars like Richard Nathan, Isabel Sawhill, David Ellwood, and William Julius Wilson. Reed critiques the constructions of the underclass by these authors who, in keeping with the Moynihan constructions, characterize them as urban dwellers or the "ghetto-poor," single-mother households, rampant unemployment, out-of-wedlock childbearing, and welfare dependency (Reed 1999, 184). Summarizing the analytical framework used in most depictions of the "underclass," Reed's analysis serves to underscore the similarities between more recent underclass constructions and those contained within the Moynihan Report. Of these depictions, he states:

> They also share certain features, despite the considerably different political and programmatic agendas to which they are connected. All zero in on inner-city blacks and Hispanics; all focus on behavior, values, and "culture"; and all in fact converge on an overlapping list of behavioral indicators. Yet they do not tell us very much about a distinct, discernible population. (184)

In her 1992 article, *Black Ladies, Welfare Queens, and State Minstrels: An Ideological War by Narrative Means,* Wahneema Lubiano focuses on the gendered legacy of the report, tracing the effects of the Moynihan thesis on subsequent debates involving African-American women. Lubiano uses the Anita Hill testimony—during the Senate Confirmation Hearings for Clarence Thomas's nomination to the Supreme Court—as the focal point for her analysis. She demonstrates how the matriarch construction posited in the report is used against African-American women apart from welfare and social policy debates.

She posits that the negative reaction to Hill was in part due to the fact that she was placed into one of the negative stereotypes of African-American women. Hill, as the "black lady," was juxtaposed with Thomas's sister (Emma Mae Martin), the "welfare queen," another long-standing negative stereotype of black women. Important for this analysis, however, is the way in which Lubiano draws parallels between these two stereotypes of black women and their construction in the Moynihan Report. Noting the report's contributions to both narrative tropes, Lubiano writes:

The lesson implied by the Moynihan Report . . . in many ways the Urtext for the simplistic "culture of poverty" discussions as they are represented in the media, is that the welfare-dependent single mother is finally the synecdoche, the shortest possible shorthand, for the pathology of poor, urban, black culture. . . . [T]he welfare mother is the root of greater black pathology. But the flip side of the pathological welfare queen, as Moynihan's own language tells us, is the other kind of black woman—the black lady, the one whose disproportionate overachievement stands for black cultural strangeness and who ensures the underachievement of "the black male" (1992, 338).

Unlike most critics of public policy and the Moynihan Report, Lubiano illustrates the complex interplay between race, class, and gender contained within the report. She also contributes to the body of knowledge regarding the ways in which social constructions influence the outcomes of the political and policy process—in this case, the confirmation of Clarence Thomas for the Supreme Court. More importantly, Lubiano demonstrates the ways in which dominant stereotypes of African-American women (the welfare queen and the black lady) are bolstered by "official" government documents like the Moynihan Report and can work against black women.

According to Lubiano, when a black woman makes a public claim, like Hill did, we immediately attempt to "categorize" and place her, to *construct* her experience, so to speak, and place it within the existing paradigm or narrative regarding black women and their societal role. Two of the most identifiable and most pernicious stereotypes of black women, largely due to the Moynihan Report, are the welfare queen and the black lady. As Lubiano demonstrates, both stereotypes were invoked in the Thomas-Hill fiasco. Of the complex interplay between historical stereotypes of African-American women and the role they play in public discourse, she concludes:

> Across history, and certainly at this moment, one of the most reliable all-purpose scapegoats has been the black woman. In this moment both the "welfare queen" and the "black lady" are pathologies created by an erring state: welfare queens are poor and pathologically dependent because of state-welfare handouts, and black ladies are pathologically independent because state-influenced or assisted affirmative-action programs keep such ladies from what they might otherwise become: the spousal appendages of successful black patriarchs. (1992, 339)

SOCIAL CONSTRUCTION AND THE WELFARE STATE

Since its creation, AFDC (formerly ADC, now TANF)[3] was a controversial policy. It was drafted as part of the *Social Security Act of 1935*. Critics of "widow's pensions" charged that such government benefits would break up the traditional family; that is, it would allow a woman to leave her husband "just because she's unhappy with him." Thus, men would be relieved of their primary responsibility: providing for their families (Gordon 1995; Mettler 1998). On the other hand, welfare advocates worried that undeserving and unsuitable women—those who willingly left their husbands, or those who mothered children out-of-wedlock—

would receive aid earmarked for the "good" widowed mother (Gordon 1995; Mettler 1998, 38–43).

AFDC's detractors attended to these concerns by making the benefit structures and cash assistance as meager as possible. Welfare advocates (primarily female social workers), however, kept a tight rein on recipients, ensuring that only those who were "pure of heart" and with "saintly virtue" received aid (Mettler 1998, 38). These two factors worked together to sanction African-American women and children from the program. In addition, prohibiting African-American women from receiving ADC and Social Security benefits helped give rise to and reinforce constructions of black women as mammies and matriarchs. They were seen as domestic workers and caretakers of white families; that is, economically and socially independent women, neglectful of their own families.

Until the 1960s, the nucleus of AFDC policy was the idea that, in the absence of the man (the father/husband), the state would take on the primary job of supporting the family. This would enable women to continue to stay at home and raise the children. However, in the wake of the Civil Rights Movement and the War on Poverty came a new construction of welfare and its recipients. Although statistically untrue (see Schram, chapter 10), welfare became viewed largely as a black program. In national discourse the dominant, promiscuous, and lazy black woman replaced the innocent white widow as the primary stereotype of the average welfare recipient.

As briefly noted in this chapter, these constructions occurred through both institutional and extra-institutional channels. The constructions were the results of a complicated interplay between government reformers (like Moynihan), politicians (Russell Long), leaders of various social movements (NWRO) and a political climate in which African Americans, women, and the poor were demanding greater economic, social, and political inclusion) in American institutions.

All of these groups offered different and contested interpretations and constructions of welfare and its recipients. More important, these groups articulated different visions of citizenship: what constituted a citizen, a citizen's responsibility to the state, and the state's responsibility to the citizen. These factors play an important role in how we construct and implement our social policies. As Schneider and Ingram note, policy designs are a result of an interplay between ideology, political institutions, and the general public (1997, 5). They explain, "[P]olicy designs reflect the social constructions of knowledge, target populations, power relationships, and institutions in the context from which they emerge, and these are conveyed to citizens through the messages, interpretations, and experiences that people have with public policy" (5).

Implications of the Discourse on Race and Social Policy

The social construction of African-American women in welfare policy helps us understand developments, especially recent ones, in the welfare state. They also can help us understand developments and ideas regarding race. Social constructions in the welfare state act as much more than a rhetorical device used by politicians, scholars, and reformers. Social constructions act as an organizing device through which we decide "who gets what, when and how" (Laswell 1936). Hence, those who have the power to construct the debate, as well as define the parameters for discussion, have a decided advantage with respect to controlling the outcomes.

In the 1960s, the state, activists, and reformers explicitly constructed welfare recipients in terms of their racial and behavioral characteristics. These constructions are symbolic with respect to what has value and what types of behavior we want to encourage. They also are instructive as to who is valued and whose voice counts in the policy-making process. As Schneider and Ingram observe, social policy conveys meaning to the larger public.

Documents like the Moynihan Report explicated the characteristics that make up the under class and the lower class and constructed them in *racial* terms. This process helped define which characteristics and behaviors were associated with African Americans (social pathologies, welfare dependency, illegitimacy, matriarchy, and crime) and which ones were associated with whites (middle-class values, work, patriarchy, and education). Here, race is not simply phenotype, but is constructed around and constitutes characteristics that are definable by values, actions, and behaviors.

From the 1960s to the present, race debates and discussions over welfare have tended to reflect the construction of "American values" as framed by the Moynihan Report. More importantly, however, they influenced the 1960s discourse on welfare when they also articulated and constructed white identity and behaviors.

Scholars as diverse as Ruth Frankenberg and Rogers Smith have observed the ways in which African Americans, even after adopting the desired characteristics that constitute American citizens, still failed to assimilate into the mainstream of American life. In this way, African-American constructions and stereotypes that emerged during debates over welfare go further to help explain, inform, and instruct white identity. Social constructions, like the welfare queen, instruct Americans in general—white Americans in particular—on the behaviors and characteristics that comprise the "good" citizen (Wellman 1997).

Many people point to various appropriations and misappropriations of categories and constructions (depending on where you sit) contained within the Moynihan Report as one of the most ironic aspects of Moynihan's legacy. While it may not be fair to characterize the Moynihan Report as an intentional act of racism, the negative constructions of race, gender, and the African-American family were born out of racial ignorance and arrogance. Conversely, linking race, pathological social behaviors, and poverty provided the foundation for creating a second category of poor people. With construction of the "new underclass," poor people were separated into two distinct categories—one deserving and white (the working class), the other undeserving and racialized (the underclass).

The welfare state also constructs and offers lessons regarding gender and race roles. Welfare policy teaches white women the desired heterosexual behaviors by juxtaposing them with and constructing the black welfare queen. The welfare queen is sexually and socially independent from men and the opposite of what we believe embodies good women (virtuous traits like abstinence, marriage, homemaking, and dependence on men). Moynihan's matriarch operates as an example to white women of what too much independence brings (poverty, male abandonment, crime, and illegitimacy).[4]

However, the debate over the relationship between race, poverty, and the underclass illustrates one more inequality that currently exists between blacks and whites. That inequality concerns the power and control over how you are constructed, by whom and, most importantly, how much influence those perceptions and stereotypes have in your day-to-day existence. In the poverty debate, like many others, whiteness confers upon its members the power to construct and shape the world according to their imagination. Then they can structure the experience of others to fit that reality. White people are the only individuals in the United States who can construct an existence where they never have to encounter anyone different. This is *not* a privilege afforded strictly by class and income. Bill Cosby or Oprah Winfrey, for example, could never organize their existence so that they have no day-to-day contact with whites. In any number of small towns and suburban enclaves, however, Joe and Jane Doe live without ever coming into contact with people who are "different" from themselves. This is one of the most important privileges of being white: living in, as opposed to reacting to, a world of your creation.

NOTES

1. The Moynihan Report's expressed purpose was to make a case for more government programs that would *actively* pursue the goal of equal opportunity and outcome for African Americans. In his introduction to the report, Moynihan quotes Myrdal's famous warning: "America is free to choose whether the Negro shall remain her liability or become her opportunity." He then describes the ways in which African Americans' progress has been hampered by slavery and segregation/racism. While acknowledging the middle-class African Americans' progress, as well as leaders such as Martin Luther King, Moynihan's real concern is for the vast majority. He sees African Americans—due to structural impediments—stuck in a continued cycle of poverty and deprivation (1965, 1–4). For Moynihan, the Federal government has a special role in assisting African-American progress. Referencing court decisions, legislation like the *Civil Rights Act,* the *Voting Rights Act,* and the first programs of The Great Society, Moynihan argues that, "the principal challenge of the next phase of the Negro revolu-

tion is to make certain that equality of results will now follow. If we do not, there will be no social peace in the United States for generations" (3).

2. The political strategy behind Moynihan's activities: his behind-the-scenes lobbying in the Johnson Administration, his role in the White House conferences on poverty and race, and his influence on welfare policy are detailed in Rainwater and Yancey (1967) For a more recent analysis of this phenomenon and its effects on social welfare policy, see O'Connor (2001).

3. When ADC (Aid to Dependent Children) was introduced in the *Social Security Act of 1935,* the program mainly covered just children of single parents—specifically, children whose fathers had deserted or divorced their mothers. In the 1960s, as part of the 1962 and 1967 Social Security Amendments, ADC was broadened to include both single household heads—Aid to Families with Dependent Children (AFDC) and unemployed parents in two-parent homes (AFDC-Unemployed Parent). These programs, AFDC and AFDC-UP, remained in existence until 1994, when Congress passed the *Personal Responsibility and Work Opportunity Reconciliation Act* (PRWORA). As part of the PRWORA, AFDC was dismantled and replaced with a state-administered, block grant system called Transitional Aid to Needy Families (TANF) (Department of Health and Human Services 1995).

4. Patricia Hill Collins notes that there is no coincidence that the matriarch construction emerged and gained prominence at the same time that the women's movement began to tackle issues of economic and social equality through proposals like the Equal Rights Amendment (1990, 79).

10

Putting a Black Face on Welfare: The Good and the Bad

SANFORD F. SCHRAM

"Everyone who knows anything about welfare knows that most recipients are white." This is a common statement made in conversation among people concerned about racist representations of welfare in the mass media. It often goes unchallenged. In fact, in recent years it seems to have taken on the status of an unquestioned truth among those who know better than to accept popular myths and stereotypes about welfare. This statement has been used repeatedly in attempts to undermine the prevalent notion that welfare is largely a "black program" that is needed because low-income African Americans are trapped in a "black underclass," mired in a "culture of poverty," bereft of "personal responsibility," and unable to break out of an intergenerational cycle of "welfare dependency."

Yet, at least since welfare reform was enacted in 1996, this statement is not only factually questionable, it is also politically problematic. In this chapter I argue that failure to acknowledge the changing racial composition of the welfare population will only compound the problems that social policies pose for people of color, African Americans in particular. I argue that such reticence will only serve to "whitewash" the racial disparities in the U.S. economy that in recent years have increased the extent to which low-income persons of color rely on public assistance. I contend that this will likely become a growing problem, given that welfare discourse in recent years is increasingly encoded with implicit racial connotations (Schram 2000). In other words, contrary to the conventional understandings about the best way to depict welfare, it is important to recognize the good and the bad in highlighting the color issue in welfare.

Analysis suggests that putting a "black face" on welfare is not as clear-cut an issue as it is often depicted.[1] There are pitfalls either way. Emphasizing the disproportionate numbers of persons of color on public assistance can reinforce attempts to denigrate welfare as a "black program" for those "other" people who are irresponsibly not conforming to the standards of white, middle-class society. Yet, accepting depictions of welfare that do not account for race leaves unchallenged the racial disparities that are reinforced by welfare policy. White or black, the face of welfare that we project poses political risks.

In what follows, I note the importance of recent scholarship on how racial representations of welfare undermine support for public assistance; but I also suggest that such scholarship all too often fails to appreciate the political complexities of race and welfare. In particular, such scholarship does not sufficiently examine the artificiality of racial categories, the political uses of deploying different constructions of race, and the ways in which "race talk" about welfare, or the lack thereof, can become self-defeating. These problems spill over into questions of advocacy. I conclude that studying racial representations of welfare involves layers of political consideration and poses a variety of strategic problems for political activism. I recommend that we focus not so much on the *frequency* of racialized depictions of welfare in the mass media, but on how the broader society, the culture, and the prevailing modes of perception that prime people to use particularly tendentious racial categorizations and then rely on them to interpret issues of race and welfare (see Mendelberg 1997). My recommended response is to not avoid the construction of race categories in discussions of welfare, but to deploy such constructions in politically sensitive ways. Putting a black face on welfare risks reinforcing racial stereotypes. Only by acknowledging the disproportionate numbers of persons of color relying on welfare can we challenge racial inequality in the economy.

In undertaking this line of inquiry, I suggest that understanding the racial dimensions of welfare can help promote racial justice. To get racial justice, we need to be willing to ask hard questions and break with conventional wisdom. Given that welfare discourse has become implicitly encoded with racial connotations, there is a need to "call out" those insinuations. Since welfare reform has disproportionately affected persons of color, the need to highlight the racial dimensions of welfare has intensified. Taking race into account may be more necessary now than before.

THE MOYNIHAN PROBLEM

Breaking with conventional wisdom has its own political pitfalls. The risk here is what I call "the Moynihan Problem"; that is, studying welfare use along racial lines may be associated with the most controversial work on the subject—Daniel P. Moynihan's *The Negro Family: The Case for National Action* (1965). This short (seventy-eight page), U.S. Department of Labor internal report emphasized the theme, well accepted at the time, of pathology among economically marginalized African Americans. It was leaked to the press by Moynihan in the aftermath of the Watts riots in 1965 (Lemann 1991, 171–72). It ended up being seen not as an effort to highlight racial unfairness in the broader society, even though that might have been part of its author's intention (O'Connor 2001, 203–10). Instead, the "Moynihan Report," as it was quickly dubbed, was criticized for serving to essentialize race differences, reinforce racist attitudes, and generally promote the idea that low-income African-American families were mired in their own "culture of poverty," thereby making them personally responsible for their plight. This was a widely accepted interpretation of the report by civil rights advocates and others concerned about poverty among African Americans. The Moynihan Report quickly fell into disrepute. In particular, it was criticized for unfairly stressing racial background as the key factor in producing poverty among African-American families to the neglect of the political and economic roots of that poverty. Although Moynihan was rarely explicitly labeled a racist, his work was seen as being part of a broader perspective that encouraged "blaming the victim" for poverty (Ryan 1971).

Regardless of the intentions behind the report, its effects indicate that it deserved such an interpretation. It was rather quickly appropriated by conservatives as justifying cutbacks in welfare on the grounds that public assistance was a major contributing factor to promoting "welfare dependency" and a lack of "personal responsibility" among low-income African-American families (O'Connor 2001). This was a campaign theme of the political right for three decades, finally ending welfare as an entitlement in 1996. In spite of Moynihan's own pained resistance to that act of disentitlement, the seeds for the *Personal Responsibility and Work Opportunity Reconciliation Act of 1996* (PRWORA) were sown in the Moynihan Report (Katz 2001).

The report's conclusions created a bad impression on the basis of bad research. The statistical claim most often cited in the report was the weakening of the ostensible link between African-American male unemployment rates and welfare caseloads. The Moynihan Report seized on this shift to suggest that, while changes in the number of families on welfare tracked changes in the black male unemployment rate, the welfare participation rate for African Americans in the early 1960s was starting to become "unglued" and welfare caseloads continued to increase even as the black male unemployment rate declined. Growth in the welfare rolls was interpreted as becoming an autonomous problem disconnected from the status of the economy and indicating that the black family was becoming wrapped in a "tangle of pathology" (see Katz 1989). To underscore its importance as a finding of social science, Moynihan would in time proudly call this phenomenon the Moynihan Scissors (Moynihan 1985). Nonetheless, this analysis has been consistently criticized for inappropriately tying the unemployment rate of black males with the welfare caseload for all races; subsequent research has shown the correlation to be unsubstantiated (O'Connor 2001, 205–06).

William Julius Wilson has most prominently highlighted the problems with this statistical claim (see Wilson and Neckerman 1984). Yet, Wilson himself was to go on to trumpet Moynihan as a prophet who was unfairly castigated for pointing out the growing problems of social breakdown among what Wilson called the "black underclass" (Wilson 1987). Wilson laments in particular that the firestorm of criticism over the Moynihan Report may have induced self-censorship among social scientists who feared being labeled racist for raising issues of family formation among African Americans. Adolph Reed and others have effectively questioned whether this self-censorship ever really happened (Reed 1999, 93; Schram 1995, 31). Instead, a better explanation for self-censorship might be that in the wake of the controversy over the Moynihan Report, researchers who, like Moynihan, had emphasized the "culture of poverty" argument were now more sensitive about avoiding the racist canard that low-income African-American families were the source of their own poverty. Researchers instead sought to find new ways to understand how poverty could create conditions that some times made it difficult to adhere to conventional moral standards of personal responsibility. Rather than speculate that an underclass had come to indulge in a culture of poverty, they found more meaningful ways to understand the causes of what was previously called "pathology." The Moynihan controversy, therefore, was not, as Wilson suggested, a cautionary tale about the premature dismissal of good research that prophetically predicted the demise of the traditional, nuclear family among low-income African Americans. Instead, the Moynihan controversy was more about the risk that emphasizing race as a factor in receiving welfare might be correctly interpreted as a sign of blaming the victim.

Still, the controversy surrounding *The Negro Family* does, indeed, provide a cautionary reminder of the dilemmas associated with raising issues of race and welfare. Its thesis of cultural pathology touched off a firestorm, and it was roundly criticized for imputing to African Americans a lack of commitment to what policy makers today call "family values." There are good reasons, then, for wanting to be sensitive about introducing race into the analysis of welfare. There is the chance that your research can be associated with the Moynihan Report and its blame-the-victim outlook. Yet, there are problems in the other direction as well. While Reed is correct to dismiss Wilson's unsubstantiated claims about self-censorship, there are legitimate reasons to fear that analysis of the disproportionate use of public assistance by African Americans will be left in the dust. It could be a casualty of another kind of self-censorship, grounded in a concern not to reinforce racist stereotypes about who uses welfare and why. Yet, there are also pitfalls to not putting a black face on welfare, as I demonstrate in the following section.

Myths about Myths

In 1996, the *Personal Responsibility and Work Opportunity Reconciliation Act* was enacted into law, ending welfare as an entitlement. As part of the battle to prevent this from happening, numerous efforts were made to inform the public about the real facts concerning welfare. Most of this work was quite valuable in pointing out misunderstandings circulating among the public about welfare. Yet, analyses that were sound in other respects often mischaracterized the racial composition of the welfare population. One example is *Welfare Myths: Fact or Fiction? Exploring the Truth about Welfare,* published in 1996 by the Welfare Law Center. Even this scrupulously researched and clearly written publication parsed its statistics on race and welfare in a problematic way. *Welfare Myths* stated:

MYTH: Almost all of the families receiving AFDC are Black or Hispanic.

FACT: Many more White families than Black families or Hispanic Families are helped by the AFDC program.

In the Internet version, to the left of "MYTH" is a button to push for "More Info." That additional information turns out to be statistics that cover the "facts," such as "the percentage of Black families and of Hispanic families that receive cash assistance is larger than the proportion of White families who do, as is the proportion of Black and Hispanic families that are in poverty." Yet, the main point emphasized is that even though poverty forces African Americans and Latinos to rely on welfare more frequently than whites, whites make up a majority of welfare recipients. The factual basis for this claim is reported as follows:

A study of families receiving AFDC between January 1990 and June 1992 found that less than 3 in 10 women receiving AFDC for the first time were Black and 1.6 in 10 were Hispanic. Looking at all families receiving aid during a given period of time, White families still outnumber Black families, although the percentage of Black families in the total caseload is higher than the percentage among first-time recipients. White families make up 38.3 percent of the caseload, Black families 36.6 percent. Hispanic families account for 17.8 percent of all families receiving aid while Asians and Native Americans amount to a total of 4.2 percent.

There are numerous problems with this "myth versus fact" presentation. First, the study from which the supporting calculations are drawn is cited nowhere in the publication. Second, the primary statistic used by the report is about the percentage of first-time users of welfare; this measure neglects to count people who are reapplying for benefits after having not received them. These "recyclers" are left out of this statistic and are not counted at all. This measure also does not count people who are still receiving assistance they initiated before the start of the time period studied. In short, the statistical claim presented, that most recipients are white, is constructed in a highly selective fashion.

There are many ways to measure the racial composition of the welfare population. While none is perfect, several are an improvement over looking only at first-time users. One common approach is to examine the racial composition of the rolls in a representative month (say January or June, or better, the average monthly breakdown for twelve months in that year). This approach is reported in Figure 10.1.

The data in Figure 10.1 are the more commonly reported data from the federal government and indicate that for the decade before welfare reform, roughly equal proportions of recipients at any one time were white or African American, with Latinos at a lower but increasing rate during the 1985–1999 period. These data are by no means consistent with the popular claim, often made in political discussions that most welfare recipients are white, indicating as they do that whites and blacks received welfare in approximately equal numbers for most of the years since 1985, while the number of Hispanic recipients was somewhat lower. Data indicate that since the mid-1990s, the number of recipients for all three groups has declined, fastest for whites and slowest for Hispanics, so that blacks were the largest group by the end of the 1990s. It should be emphasized that a major part of the explanation for the disparity between these data and those reported in *Welfare Myths* is that the federal government data include the people on the welfare rolls at any one point in time, regardless of whether they are using assistance for the first time.

The federal government, however, excludes from its data people who have gone off the rolls but had received welfare during that year. Therefore, we might want to try still another method, which estimates the racial composition of all family heads that received any assistance during a calendar year, regardless of

FIGURE 10.1
The Distribution of Welfare Recipients by Race, 1985–1999

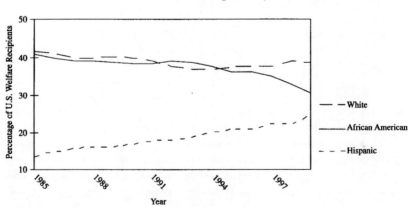

Source: Department of Health and Human Services, 1995–1998.

whether it was their first time or not. Table 10.1 presents data from the Panel Study of Income Dynamics (PSID) on the racial breakdown of welfare recipients. The PSID is a national longitudinal study with a sample population in any one year exceeding 2,000 families.[2] The data are weighted to ensure representativeness by race.[3]

The data in Table 10.1 are from the annual PSID waves for selected years 1970–1993.[4] The data presented are the percentages of all the PSID married women or independent female heads of households with children who indicated receiving any amounts of public assistance at any time during the preceding calendar year. In these figures, blacks outnumbered whites in 1970. Whites slightly outnumbered blacks in 1975 and 1980. Blacks outnumbered whites in each year after 1980. For 1991, 57 percent of all the mothers who indicated receiving any public assistance were black, 42 percent were white, and 1 percent were other races. In 1992, 53 percent were black, 43 percent were white, and 4 percent were other races. In 1993, 50 percent of recipient families were black, while 46 percent were white and 4 percent were other. These calculations sort by race identification alone so that Latinos, for instance, are sorted into either Black or White categories and the Other category refers to Native Americans, Asians, and other racial groups designated neither white nor black. The calculations are based on all the married women and independent heads of households who had children and had received any welfare benefits in the preceding calendar year. Therefore, this is an inclusive sample that maximizes the chances of counting even a middle-class, suburban woman who received only a partial welfare benefit for one month while, say, making the transition from being in a marriage to being divorced. This calculation, therefore, does not systematically exclude whites. Still, the percentages indicate that *in each year examined from 1985 on, more black women than white women received assistance.*

TABLE 10.1
Welfare Receipt by Race, 1980–1993
Percent of Married Mothers and Independent Female Heads of Households
Who Received Welfare During the Calendar Year

Race	1970	1975	1980	1985	1990	1991	1992	1993
Black	46	44	46	50	54	57	53	50
White	45	50	50	49	45	42	43	46
Other	9	6	4	1	1	1	4	4
Total	100	100	100	100	100	100	100	100
N	281	361	350	304	301	302	314	292

Source: University of Michigan, Panel Study of Income Dynamics (PSID), annual waves.

These larger PSID numbers for blacks were for essentially the same time period covered by *Welfare Myths* data. During that time period, the average number of whites and blacks receiving welfare at any one point in time (e.g., in any one month) was essentially the same, according to government statistics (Administration on Children and Families 2000). Yet, according to the PSID data, the total number of blacks who had received assistance during the calendar year exceeded the number of whites.

These data, therefore, are different from both the *Welfare Myths* data and those reported by the federal government. Part of the explanation is that the government and the *Welfare Myths* data report Latinos separate from race. Another difference that is important for the contrast with both *Welfare Myths* and the federal government data is that the PSID data account for recycling back onto welfare, while still counting each family only once, regardless of how many times they received welfare. Looking only at first-time users ignores the fact that, compared with whites, African Americans who have left public assistance are more likely to return later, largely due to lower marriage rates (Edin and Harris 1999). Therefore, presenting a racial breakdown of the first-time users, as *Welfare Myths* does, cuts out more African-American families than white families. In the case of the federal data, what is not counted are all the people who are not currently receiving assistance, including recyclers who are disproportionately nonwhite.

Another difference with the *Welfare Myths* data is that by concentrating only on people who initiate the receipt of welfare, those data miss people who began using welfare before the time period covered. This leaves out longer-term users who are already welfare recipients. According to available research, these people are more likely to be nonwhite (Blank 1997, 154; Duncan, Harris, and Boisjoly 2000). This is critical, especially since long-term use has for years been the main source of concern about welfare in the mass public. Therefore, looking only at first-time receipt or only at who is on welfare at any one point in time takes the focus off the more controversial, long-term welfare population, which happens to be comprised even more disproportionately of nonwhites.

The PSID data, however, do not fully solve these problems. These data produce a small sample, making their generalizability suspect. In addition, the inclusion of anyone who receives welfare for even the shortest period of time and in the smallest amounts fails to address the claim that longer-term users are the more significant population. An even better estimate would weight the population by how long each family received welfare and how much they received. When this measure is done, the racial composition of the welfare population would in all likelihood be even more heavily skewed toward persons of color because, as mentioned, various studies have indicated that nonwhites are likely to receive welfare for longer spells (Blank 1997, 154).

Therefore, I would suggest that the data on the racial breakdown of persons receiving welfare is subject to much debate. One thing is clear: in the run up to welfare reform it was questionable to claim, as many did, that most welfare recipients were white. This claim operated as its own unquestioned myth among those seeking to repudiate the equally suspect notion that welfare was a "black program" for those "other" people who were not conforming to white, middle-class work values and family values.

There was, however, at least a good rationale for the myth-busting about race even if it was factually suspect. Martin Gilens (1999) has effectively demonstrated that beginning in the 1960s, the mass media—both print and electronic—began to overrepresent African Americans in negative stories about poverty and, to a lesser extent, about welfare. Gilens also notes that beginning at that time, the mass public began to regard welfare as a "black program" that coddled low-income black families and rewarded them for not adhering to middle-class work values and family values. Gilens goes on to demonstrate persuasively that both the mass public and journalists were likely to grossly overestimate the proportion of welfare recipients who were black. There came a need to challenge the highly racialized image of welfare recipients that was, and continues to be, ascendant in the culture and among the people in positions to influence opinion.[5]

Gilens's work is important in highlighting mass media's role in providing a racially distorted image of the welfare population. He is effective in suggesting that this role encouraged the denigration of welfare as a program for "other" people who were different and not adhering to white, middle-class work values and family values. Yet, there is a need to consider how the problem transcends the mass media and its racialized depictions of welfare (Neubeck and Cazenave 2001). We need to *recognize* that the problem transcends such racialized depictions. For instance, what do we do when these depictions become accurate because the welfare population has, in fact, become disproportionately nonwhite? We need to ask: Why is the mass public reluctant to see black welfare recipients as deserving? In other words, we need to examine why some segments of the white population are predisposed to looking negatively upon blacks receiving welfare and are, therefore, already primed to respond negatively to media depictions of them (see Mendelberg 1997).

As the "most recipients are white" mantra of popular discourse, cited at the outset, becomes an increasingly popular myth-busting claim among antipoverty advocates, less attention is given to how welfare recipients are "different" in racial composition and other ways—especially in terms of how society treats them. As a result, less attention is given to examining how this relatively distinctive group came to require assistance. The lure of "almost all recipients are white" is the prospect of unracializing welfare, of "whitening" it. If that can be accomplished, an opportunity is created for greater equity in the treatment of welfare recipients. Further, if advocates can make the case that the welfare population's racial composition is no different from that of the society overall, there is a stronger empirical base for insisting on more equitable treatment of recipients. This conclusion is necessary because they do not need to be treated as some alien "other" group to be singled out for distinctive treatment under a punitive welfare system. The goal of equitable treatment is laudable and well-established among advocates for a more progressive welfare state. But trampling over basic demographics and creating a distorted image of the racial composition of the welfare population is a strategy that is doomed to fail. It will founder on the shoals of factual disputation, which will not help realize the larger goal of equity.

In addition, while we might want to downplay race as socially constructed, it has real consequences as a way of organizing social life (Loury 2002). Ignoring the racial composition of the welfare population, on the grounds that race should not matter, unfortunately overlooks the fact that it does matter. Therefore, we need to recognize how it counts and deal with the consequences. As much as we want to sweep the fictions of race into the dustbin, they continue to haunt social life. A disproportionately black welfare population is a subject that needs to be addressed for no other reason than to resist racist interpretations of welfare. When the welfare population increasingly becomes disproportionately nonwhite to the point that the myth-busters' myth about a white welfare population can no longer be sustained, where are we then?

One answer is: the present. That is exactly where we are right now. Today, we confront the prospect of arguing for equity on grounds other than the distorted image that the demographic profile of welfare recipients mirrors the general population. It has not mirrored the general population for a long time and it increasingly does not. Although during much of the 1980s it might have been true that whites and blacks were about equal in the government's monthly tabulations of welfare recipients, it is no longer the case. As Michael Brown (2003) has emphasized, with welfare reform in 1996, the welfare rolls declined dramatically through 2000, with whites leaving welfare faster than other groups, making the welfare population even more disproportionately nonwhite and creating an even greater prospect that welfare will be marginalized as a "black" program for "other" people (also see Neubeck and Cazenave 2001).

Unfortunately, the main source for tracking this change has been the aforementioned federal government's statistics on the characteristics of the welfare population (Administration on Children and Families 2000). These data combine race and ethnicity to report not only on "whites" and "blacks," but also on "Hispanics," which is not a racial designation. Nonetheless, these data supply the evidence that, since welfare reform was enacted in the mid-1990s, there has been a rapid increase in the proportion of welfare recipients who are nonwhite—even if one makes the conservative assumption that about half of Hispanics on welfare are nonwhite (Grieco and Cassidy 2001). In 1985, for the average month, 40.8 percent of adult welfare recipients were white, while 41.6 percent were black and 13.6 percent were Hispanic. In 1999, the percentage of whites had fallen sharply to 30.5, while the percentage of blacks had only dropped to 38.3 and the percentage of Hispanics had risen to 24.5 (Lower-

Basch 2000). (See Table 10.2.) Under the heading "AFDC/TANF Trends in the 1990s" and the subheading, "Racial/Ethnic Composition of Families," the Administration on Children and Families (2000) noted these figures:

> The racial composition of welfare families has changed substantially over the past ten years. In 1990, it was 38 percent whites, 40 percent blacks and 17 percent Hispanics. In 1999, however, it was 31 percent whites, 38 percent blacks and 25 percent Hispanics. In addition, the small percentage of the welfare population which is Asian has grown slowly but steadily over the period from just under 3 percent to about 3 and one-half percent. Viewed over the decade there has been a shift from white to Hispanic families which is consistent with broader population trends. This shift has been accelerated since 1996 and is particularly pronounced in California, New York and Texas. Thus, in 1999, 70 percent of all Hispanic welfare families were in three large States (California, New York and Texas), as compared to 65 percent in 1996. In California, the proportion of Hispanic welfare families increased to 46 percent in 1999 from 38 percent in 1996. In addition, black families which had been a declining proportion of the caseload have trended up slightly since 1996. The upshot of these changes is that the proportion of welfare families that were minorities has increased from three-fifths to just over two-thirds over the decade, primarily driven by the growth in Hispanic families.

Given the racial diversity of the Latino population, we can conclude that part of its growth in the proportion of recipients further adds to the increase in the nonwhite proportion of the welfare population. Since welfare reform in 1996, blacks have increasingly been established as the largest group and nonwhites as the overwhelming majority of recipient families at any one point in time. (See Table 10.2.)

These figures, however, point to a dimension of the issue that is discussed even less often. Comparing these figures with raw population numbers, we can suggest that the probability that African Americans rely on welfare is much greater than it is for whites. We can estimate that, on average, in any single month in 1999, approximately one in one hundred whites and eight in one hundred blacks were receiving welfare. While the probability of receiving welfare is low for both racial categories, persons designated as black had an eight-fold higher probability of using welfare than those designated as white.

What are we to do now, under these circumstances, with a welfare population as racialized as this one? The welfare population remains diverse, but it is increasingly composed of nonwhites—more so than the overall U.S. population. Arguments for equity based on a distorted image that the welfare population is largely white, or that it is like the overall population, were always questionable; now they are irrelevant.[6] How are we to build the case for equitable treatment of welfare recipients now? For a long time, equity arguments should have been made on a basis different from the misleading grounds that most

TABLE 10.2
Percent Distribution of TANF Families by Race,
October 1998–September 1999

	Total Families	White	Black	Hispanic	Native American	Asian	Other	Unknown
U.S. Total	2,648,462	30.5	38.3	24.5	1.5	3.6	0.6	1

Source: U.S. Department of Health and Human Services, Administration on Children and Families, Office of Family Assistance, National Emergency TANF Datafile as of April 4, 2000. Available from http://www.acf.dhhs.gov/programs/opre/characteristics/fy99/tab06_99.htm.

(Last Updated August 27, 2000). Figures are for the average month.

welfare recipients were white; for a long time, they needed to be made not by neglecting race, but by explaining how African Americans in particular, and other racial minorities as well, were more likely to be living in poverty and in need of public assistance at higher rates. Equity arguments need to be urgently made now to take race into account, to acknowledge that African Americans and Latinos need to rely on public assistance more frequently and that there are good reasons why they should be seen, if only in this regard, as "different." They face different circumstances, often experience greater need, and more often require the assistance of welfare. The situation is critical, since research indicates that blacks constitute a large majority of the recipient families that are predicted to be affected by the new time limits under welfare reform. It is estimated that blacks constitute more than two-thirds of the families who will reach the newly imposed sixty-month federal limit for receiving welfare (Duncan, Harris, and Boisjoly 2000). Taking race into account is now, perhaps more than at any other time in the history of the welfare program, an unavoidable necessity.

As long as advocates cling to the myth of a white welfare population, we will neglect the problems of racism, the issue of racial barriers, and the extent to which race-related differences need to be addressed (Loury 2002). Such neglect is dangerous and it can ignore the systemic sources of poverty for low-income families of color. Yet, this failure is not just a conservative deficiency, but part of a pattern of political inadequacy among liberals unwilling to discuss what they see as potentially troubling facts about welfare recipients.

While this gentility is understandable, it is also harmful. The unwillingness to address more forthrightly the racial composition of the welfare population springs in part from a fear that conservatives will use such information to reinforce their arguments that welfare recipients are "different." This reticence extends to discussing the "differences" associated with all single mothers on welfare, black or white, thereby often leaving the field open to conservatives to decide how differences are interpreted.

There are many parallels for this sort of reticence. For instance, for years liberals were reluctant to examine seriously what was alleged to be "welfare fraud" when recipients were not reporting all of their other, small sources of income. Traditonally, the topic was dominated by conservative viewpoints that led to states developing obsessive practices to track down and punish violators who failed to report all of their income, even if the underreporting was minimal. "Welfare fraud" had become another way to harass economically distressed welfare recipients and depict them as undeserving. Finally, after decades of cracking down on these alleged welfare abuses, studies—such as the one by Edin and Lein (1997)—offered an alternative perspective, showing that low benefits left recipients no choice but to supplement their welfare checks with unreported income. Unfortunately, by the time these results were published, the campaign to combat fraud and withhold aid from "cheaters" had held welfare benefits down for more than two decades. Benefits had, on average, declined in real value by more than 40 percent since the early 1970s (Moffitt 1992). The long-term failure to discuss the reality of "welfare fraud" was, therefore, at best unhelpful. This avoidance, in turn, enabled states to tighten access and reduce benefits, in effect punishing people in most cases for just trying to survive by combining inadequate welfare benefits with small amounts of unreported income.

Reluctance to discuss particular issues about welfare and poverty can have negative effects. But the whole point of getting involved and discussing potentially difficult issues about welfare and poverty is to prevent those issues from being framed in tendentious ways. Talking about the disproportionate numbers of nonwhites receiving welfare does not have to involve buying into the Moynihan "tangle of pathology" perspective that ends up blaming the victim. Yet, if only the Moynihans of the world get involved in highlighting the racial composition of the welfare population, that is just what might happen. Others need to engage these issues not just to check the facts but, more importantly, to check how the facts are being framed and how assumptions of "otherness" are informing the interpretation of those facts.

VISUALIZING RACE

Racialized depictions of welfare recipients are not just a problem of numbers. They are perhaps an even greater problem when we turn to issues of visual culture. There has been a great and longstanding concern that visual depictions of African Americans on welfare only serve to reinforce the stereotype that welfare is strictly a "black" program. Such images inevitably risk reinscribing the notion that only blacks use welfare because there is something in their personal characteristics, behavior, and culture that leads them to rely on assistance. These images reinforce the worst racist stereotypes about why African Americans use welfare.

A cultural dynamic underlies racialized images. The denigration of "black" supports the privileging of "white." The socially constructed designation of "black" is continually manufactured and given life largely to sustain the privileges associated with the equally suspect category of "white." If "black" had not existed, therefore, in the quest to validate "white" identity and culture, something else would have had to have been created. Hortense Spillers has stated: "Let's face it. I am a marked woman, but not everybody knows my name . . . 'Sapphire' . . . or 'Black Woman at the Podium': I describe a locus of confounded identities, a meeting ground of investments and privations in the national treasury of rhetorical wealth. My country needs me, and if I were not here, I would have been invented" (as quoted in Lubiano 1992, 323). In a more abstract register, Slavoj Zrzek has seconded this assessment and pointed it toward how the "black welfare queen" has been constructed out of need for an "other" to legitimate the middle-class white man of virtue who practices personal responsibility and has no need for assistance from the government. Zrzek adds:

> [E]ach universal ideological notion is always hegemonized by some particular content which colours its very universality and accounts for its efficiency. In the rejection of the social welfare system by the New Right in the U.S., for example, the universal notion of the welfare system as inefficient is sustained by the pseudo-concrete representation of the notorious African-American single mother, as if, in the last resort, social welfare is a programme for black single mothers—the particular case of the "single black mother" is silently conceived as "typical" of social welfare and of what is wrong with it. . . . Another name for this short-circuit between the Universal and the Particular is, of course, "suture": the operation of hegemony "sutures" the empty Universal to a particular content. (1997, 28–29)

Zrzek emphasizes that the abstract categories need to be filled with content from the existentially experienced world of social relations. The idea of a welfare queen is one of black, single mothers who rely on public assistance, making the abstract idea seem more credible and consistent with real life. Yet, most women on welfare are not as the stereotype depicts; that is, they are not lazy, unmotivated, irresponsible, promiscuous, and so on. They are often actually "heroes of their own lives," exercising initiative and independence by putting themselves on welfare in order to make the best of a bad situation and provide for their children (Gordon 1988). Furthermore, most white middle-class "men of virtue" rely on the government for various tax advantages, subsidies, and other forms of assistance. Nonetheless, the contrast between the black welfare queen and the white middle-class man of virtue resonates very strongly in popular culture, scholarly critiques notwithstanding.

The images of women on welfare help reinforce this biased distinction and reinscribe notions of black inferiority and white supremacy. The history of racist depictions of African Americans in the United States—creating a rich reservoir of racist iconography that reinforces stereotypes and exploits black images to access white privilege—is a recurrent pattern in our culture. We need reach no farther than the well-established, if now repudiated, practice of white entertainers performing in "blackface." Begun in the 1840s in minstrel shows, it was popularized first among Irish and, eventually, among Jewish entertainers (Figure 10.2). Michael Paul Rogin has written:

> Blackface is a form of cross-dressing, in which one puts on the insignias of sex, class or race that stands in binary opposition to one's own. . . . Assimilation is achieved via the mask of the most segregated; the blackface that offers Jews mobility keeps blacks fixed in place. Rabinowitz turns into Robin, but the fundamental binary opposition nevertheless remains. That segregation, imposed on blacks, silences their voices and sings their names. (1996, 30, 112)

Blackface facilitated assimilation for white immigrants, demonstrating that they must be white because they had to paint their faces in order to make them look black. The Jew becomes white by way of demonstrating he was not black until painted. The cultural dynamic of invoking blackness in order to privilege whiteness is enacted all over again.

Creating whiteness via denigrating blackness is an immense topic that has only begun in recent years to undergo serious study by white scholars (Roediger 1991; Frankenberg 1993; Ignatiev 1995). African-American intellectuals, however, have been commenting on this issue for some time, highlighting that "becoming white" was the goal of many immigrants. This made the American dream something that was not accessible to African Americans in ways that it was to other groups. James Baldwin (1984) once emphasized:

> No one was white before he/she came to America. . . . It took generations and a vast amount of coercion before this became a white country. . . . There is an Irish community. . . . There is a German community. . . . There is a Jewish community. . . . There are English communities. . . . There are French communities. . . . Jews came here from countries where they were not white, and they came here in part because they were not white. . . . Everyone who got here paid the price of the ticket, the price was to become "white." (90–92)

The use of blackness to legitimate whiteness has prevailed in recent years (Figure 10.3). In a controversial photo, Christie Todd Whitman, former governor of New Jersey, was caught on film frisking an innocent black man, for what exact purpose remains unknown. One possible explanation is the imbrication of race and gender: a female Republican governor felt the need to prove she was as tough as some of her white, male conservative party members when it

FIGURE 10.2
Using Blackface to Reinscribe Otherness and Legitimate the Self

Al Jolson Publicity Photo. *Source:* U.S. Department of Health and Human Services, 1995–1998.

FIGURE 10.3
Another Form of Blackface?

Christie Todd Whitman, then Governor of New Jersey, Frisks a Black Man. Associated Press photo. Reprinted by permission.

came to cracking down on crime. In the photo, Whitman is dressed in white, frisking a black male, underscoring her claim of access to white male privilege. As a woman, she was adopting the traditional role in American society of the white male overlord. She was perhaps, too, thoughtlessly and inexcusably exploiting a black man in order to prove she was tough enough to be like a white man herself. She erased her gender on the back of a black man.

With this visual display, her wish to be not just Governor Whitman but also Governor *White*man was fulfilled.[7] In the process, she unwittingly ratified the practice of racial profiling by the New Jersey State Police. The systematic stopping and harassing of African-American motorists on the New Jersey Turnpike was to continue even after the state settled out of court in a controversial case. In that instance, the state all but admitted responsibility for the shooting of two young black males and a young Latino male. Sufficient evidence had been produced, including the Whitman photo, about the state's willingness to allow racial profiling to continue (*The New York Times* 2001). The racist practices of the state police were not to be repudiated until Whitman left to head the federal agency dedicated to making our environment clean. The racial connotations from white clothes to clean environment make the Whitman photo all the more troubling.

Therefore, racialized images have a long history of reinforcing white privilege in the broader society and not just with respect to welfare. This history makes some thoughtful people understandably reluctant to put a black face on welfare. The photograph in Figure 10.4 appears on the cover of Martin Gilens's book on the mass media's racialization of welfare. His editors probably depicted an African-American woman on the cover in part because his main thesis is that beginning in the 1960s, the overrepresentation of African Americans in stories and accompanying pictures about welfare led to increased opposition to welfare programs.

Yet Gilens's cover suggests something else is at work as well. The hand shown is multi-shaded, suggesting ambiguity and highlighting how viewers are forced to make their own judgment about who is taking welfare and why. In this sense, the photograph is what W. J. T. Mitchell (1994) calls a "metapicture"—a representation that refers not so much to some visualized object but more importantly to the process of visualization. This metapicture highlights how all representations require viewing subjects to make the viewed object coherent, and that these judgments are, to varying degrees, grounded in the prevailing culture.[8] White viewers often harbor negative conceptions of persons of color on welfare, even before reading slanted news stories. As it turns out, the racially ambiguous hand proved to be too troublesome an image and was removed from the cover of the book's paperback version (Tryneski 2001).

Racialized images of women on welfare are often interpreted in ways that reinforce prevailing cultural biases against persons of color, against women, and against public assistance (Schram 2000). Such images are crucial to reinforcing

FIGURE 10.4
The Act of Visualizing Race

The cover of *Why Americans Hate Welfare,* by Martin Gilens. *Source:* Reprinted by permission.

white privilege in society. Yet, my major point is that these pictures alone do not achieve this effect; they require an act of supplementation. Paul de Man (1986) once defined reading as supplying what is missing to a text. Texts are inert until they are read; reading breathes life into them, making them interpretable. The net result is that each reading supplies its own text, making the idea of one objective reading of any text unattainable and the definitive meaning of any text something that is infinitely deferred and ultimately undecidable.

Additionally, we are, in turn, shaped by texts in ways that are less than predictable. The same is true with images. Pictures are nothing until they are seen. What we see is an act of visualization, as multivalent and polyoptic as texts are undecidable. Every picture produces as many visualizations as the number of people who see it. Maybe more. This is Mitchell's point about what the metapicture tells us. It teaches us about visualization in the abstract in general; and part of that act of visualization is its unavoidably subjective character, inevitably destined to produce multiple readings that loop back to influence their viewers in multiple ways.

A larger point here is that visualization is a dynamic process; it is not one in which pictures impose their imagery on passive viewers. Viewers must be enlisted into the viewing process in order for visualization to occur. Pictures of black women on welfare do not necessarily in and of themselves mean anything in particular. They need to be visualized; they need viewers to interpret them before they can become meaningful representations. Additionally, when viewers draw on the rich cultural traditions of reconstructing white privilege on the backs of black people, then pictures of African-American women on welfare take on added significance, conveying black inferiority in the name of consolidating white supremacy (see Mendelberg 1997).

Therefore, we need to go beyond Gilens's analysis. It is not enough to emphasize that the mass media exaggerate the extent to which the welfare population includes African Americans. We also need to explain how our culture primes people to read news reports and see images in a certain way. Of one such image that appeared in the press in the wake of welfare reform, I have written (Schram 2000):

> The woman depicted . . . had in 1997 been sanctioned to the point where she was being removed from the welfare rolls. Reduced to cooking family meals on an outdoor grill, she sits outside and stares blankly away from the camera while her teenage son looks on. She seems to be an enigma, refusing to work and claiming undetectable maladies, though not even trying to defend herself against a welfare bureaucracy that rejects her story. Her inscrutability creates doubts in our minds, allowing us to decide that she is incorrigible in her insistence on taking welfare. Her passivity becomes a form of active defiance. Her blank face is a blank slate on which welfare discourse can write its stigmatizing story of the welfare queen. Her body language is therefore not of her own making but a discourse that reads her a certain way. Simply being there, in poverty, on the welfare rolls, in the backyard, cooking on the grill, she is open to being read by welfare policy discourse. Without knowing anything about her life, her personal experiences, or her hopes and fears, welfare policy discourse appropriates her body and judges her passivity as a willfully chosen dependency. (54–55)

Therefore, for me, it is important to emphasize how preexisting prejudices operating in society prime people to read, in particular ways, racialized images of welfare recipients. I also want to highlight how cultural prejudices not only reinforce negative views of persons of color receiving welfare, but also necessitate the greater frequency with which persons of color are forced to rely on public assistance. It is necessary to put a black face on welfare *and* to make more visible how those biases are operating and to what effect.

Such pictures, appropriately framed and placed, may have several redeeming features. They can highlight in politically constructive ways how race and welfare are often connected. They can also, if done in a sufficiently self-reflective fashion, remind us that the act of viewing demonizes welfare recipients at least as much as the picture themselves. If such photos—even when they show women of color in uncritical ways—are frequently read as telling the same old tendentious tale of black insufficiency, then we need to ask how and why these photos are read in such a demonized way. The answer, one suspects, will be found more in our hearts and in our heads than on the page or in the photo. And until we are willing to interrogate the rich cultural reservoir that funds such prejudice, manufacturing and demonizing black welfare queens will surely continue.

PUTTING A FACE ON ADVOCACY

Questions of representation spill over into questions of advocacy. A common dilemma among advocacy and welfare rights groups is who should represent welfare recipients in public forums. One response is to choose white single mothers who have been divorced, who have only one or two children, and who are in transition from welfare to work (Brenner 2000). The goal is often to suggest that welfare recipients are no different from the average middle-class family. All families should be supportive of welfare, because it is really a program for all of us and all our families may need to rely on it at some time in our lives. This, of course, is not true. Most families will never need welfare, even during divorce. Many women do go on welfare for short periods of time during divorce; however, they do not comprise a majority of divorcing families—let alone all families—nor do divorced families make up a sizable proportion of welfare recipients (Duncan and Hoffman 1995; Hoffman and Duncan 1991).

Yet, there are more serious problems than factual misrepresentations. Putting a white face on welfare and then pretending that recipients are just like middle-class families risks encouraging policy makers to reform welfare on the basis of that assumption. Then we face the prospect that welfare policies will be even less attuned to the real circumstances and struggles that families needing welfare actually confront. If we represent welfare mothers as people who are "job ready," who are only going to need to rely on welfare for a short period of time while they transition to paid employment, then we are more likely to get public policies that are insensitive to the fact that some mothers will need to rely on welfare for extended periods of time. Our policies may, then, disregard the fact that many individuals are not able or ready to secure employment that can pay them enough while they maintain full responsibility for their children on their own. This is exactly the kind of welfare reform we have been getting—reform that seems oblivious to the realities that confront most welfare mothers, of any color. Presenting the welfare population as being just like the middle-class population leads to public policies that assume that welfare mothers can begin acting middle class tomorrow, when in fact many mothers on welfare confront dire circumstances that make that assumption ludicrous.

The more effective responses lie in recognizing the diversity of welfare recipients so that white or black, divorced or unmarried, "job ready" or not "job ready" will do. Only when we begin representing welfare families in all their diversity, in all their colors—highlighting how many of them are confronted by numerous social and economic obstacles—will we begin to understand their plight. Only then can we begin to convince others to join us in trying to remove those barriers. In particular, we need to highlight that large numbers of welfare mothers are in very difficult circumstances that are often the result of having been marginalized by class, race, and gender discrimination. They are not ready to act middle class because the structure of society has ensured that their inequitable access to education, their lack of opportunities to form traditional families, their lack of economic opportunities, and their overall poverty were not of their own making but, rather, a result of being left out of mainstream society. Only when welfare recipients in all their diversity get to articulate, in their own voices, that they have been marginalized will we begin to see how putting a full face on welfare is a better alternative than whitewashing the welfare population with strategic misrepresentations.

Conclusion

The United States has a bifurcated welfare state (Nelson 1990). In this construction, citizens qualify for the more generous social insurance programs on the basis of their participation in the labor market, requiring others to settle for the inadequate benefits of public assistance programs. The privileged, under this system, can qualify for retirement benefits, survivor benefits, disability insurance, and unemployment compensation; while those who have not worked enough in the right jobs, or who were not married to someone who worked enough in the right jobs, must rely on welfare.

There is also something to be said for the notion that this bifurcated welfare state is based on invidious distinctions, socially constructed to achieve the political effect of privileging some families as more deserving than others. The deservedness of top-tier families is not the result of politically neutral, fair, economic processes. Instead, the distinctions between deserving and undeserving are politically suspect, reinforcing longstanding class, race, and gender biases about which types of people and families are more appropriate for our social order. The traditional two-parent family with a "breadwinner" and a "homemaker" is privileged, especially families where the breadwinner works in an appropriate job long enough to qualify for benefits. This privileged status was more often accessible to white middle- and upper-class families. It is no surprise, then, that the welfare state's bottom rungs are disproportionately populated with low-income, nonwhite, single-parent families. A mother is left, therefore, to do the double duty of being a breadwinner and a homemaker for her children in ways that make her less likely to qualify for top-tier benefits.

Writing about the conservative push for welfare reform in the early 1980s, Frances Fox Piven and Richard Cloward (1982) wrote:

> [W]hen the several major policy initiatives of the Reagan administration are laid side by side, something of a coherent theory can be detected. . . . [T]he coherent theory is about human nature, and it serves the class interests of the Reagan administration and its business allies. It is the archaic idea the people in different social classes have different human natures and thus different basic motivations. The affluent are one sort of creature and working people are another. It follows that these different sorts of creatures require different systems of incentives and disincentives. The affluent exert themselves in response to rewards—to the incentive of increased profitability yielded by lower taxes. Working people respond only to punishment—to the economic insecurity that will result from reductions in the income support programs. (38–39)

There are, therefore, institutional roots behind the concern for reinforcing the idea that welfare recipients are these "other" people (Rank 1994). By highlighting that welfare recipients are different in any relevant way, including their racial composition, we risk being appropriated to the service of the right-wing agenda that constructs welfare recipients as these "other people." This easily slides into more ambitious attempts to highlight the "otherness" of welfare recipients as deviants who fail to conform to white, middle-class work values and family values. Focusing on the differences between welfare recipients and others can reinforce attempts to blame welfare mothers for their own poverty, allegedly attributable to their failure to try to be like the rest of us.

Yet, there is also the risk that if we fail to indicate how welfare recipients are different and why, those differences will not be taken into account when fashioning welfare reforms. Then social policy becomes even more obtuse than it normally is, imposing an intensive set of assumptions on recipients and expecting them to live up to them immediately. Welfare reform then becomes focused on enforcing work values and family values on welfare recipients, even when they are not always ready immediately to take a job and work their way off welfare and out of poverty. Obtuse welfare reform that fails to account for differences can end up insisting that welfare recipients be "job ready," make "rapid attachment" to the labor market, take paid employment, and so on, without noting that recipients might, for instance, face race and gender biases and barriers in the workforce and on the job. In fact, that is what we have today: obtuse welfare reform that, in its ostensible neutrality, masks the extent to which it reinforces racial inequities. Such a racially encoded welfare policy fails to account for difference, fails to understand how the welfare population is disproportionately comprised of people of color, and fails to try to do anything worthwhile to address the racial dimensions of our social and economic structure that make race the salient reality of welfare today.

We need to learn to be able to walk and chew gum at the same time. We need to learn to see the differences among welfare recipients, including the racial differences, but not be so blinded as to assume immediately that traits specific to these different individuals account for their being on welfare. We need to challenge how we see and how we think. Otherwise, we will remain blind and ignorant.

In other words, it takes more than numbers and images to create racism. It takes more than statistics and pictures of black women on welfare to reinforce that they are undeserving. The racist premises that inform such interpretations must already be available before these pictures can do their work. Yet, given that those prejudices are there, racial representations of welfare need to be sensitive to the fact that they will possibly tap those reserves and reactivate such tendentious interpretations of why some people need to use public assistance more than others.

There is a need to acknowledge that race does figure into the receipt of welfare. The difficulty is in introducing such topics in a culture that is predisposed to talk about such issues in the worst possible ways, which serves to further reinscribe the prejudices and racial barriers that create the racial injustice in the first place. Yet, until we find ways to talk about race and welfare, the predicament will continue. Persons of color—African Americans and, in particular, Latinos—will continue to be overrepresented in the welfare population. Our willingness to openly discuss the racism and racial barriers that put them there, however, will remain off the public agenda. The dilemma is that if we take race into account, we risk reinscribing racial prejudice; however, if we do not, we risk not calling such prejudice into account for the crimes of poverty that it has inflicted on some groups more than others.

Under welfare reform, as the welfare population becomes increasingly nonwhite, the dilemma intensifies and the situation becomes even more urgent. To achieve equity for welfare recipients, we need to begin highlighting their differences and their often inequitable situations. We cannot afford *not* to talk about race. In particular, we cannot afford not to talk about the assumptions about race that infiltrate discussions of welfare. Just as it takes more than numbers and images to create racism, it takes more than numbers and images to undo it. Examining these assumptions, more so than waging wars of images and numbers, becomes critical to advocacy for racial justice in welfare, in particular, and in social relations more generally. As Paul Gilroy (2000) has suggested, in order to be "against race," we need to account for it and take responsibility for it in the most explicit terms possible.

NOTES

1. Linda Williams (2001) uses Leslie Fiedler's distinction to suggest that, historically, race relations in the United States have unavoidably been expressed in melodramatic terms of either "Tom" or "Anti-Tom" (as in "Uncle Tom"). Williams suggests that the entirety of race relations is always at risk of being discussed in melodramatic terms that do real injustice to its subject matter. She suggests that Americans, to a great degree, cannot talk about race but melodramatically. Americans are continually talking about race in melodramatic ways if for no other reason than that race itself is a melodramatic construction of questionable politics. Therefore, the choice to take race into account or not, in either case, is equally fraught with political pitfalls that must be negotiated.

2. "The PSID is a longitudinal survey of a representative sample of U.S. individuals and the families in which they reside. It has been ongoing since 1968. The data were collected annually through 1997, and biennially starting in 1999. The data files contain the full span of information collected over the course of the study. PSID data can be used for cross-sectional, longitudinal, and intergenerational analysis and for studying both individuals and families. The PSID sample, originating in 1968, consisted of two independent samples: a cross-sectional national sample and a national sample of low-income families. The cross-sectional sample was drawn by the Survey Research Center (SRC). Commonly called the SRC sample, this was an equal probability sample of households from the 48 contiguous states and was designated to yield about 3,000 completed interviews. The second sample came from the Survey of Economic Opportunity (SEO), conducted by the Bureau of the Census for the Office of Economic Opportunity. In the mid-1960s, the PSID selected about 2,000 low-income families with heads under the age of sixty from SEO respondents. The sample, known as the SEO sample, was confined to Standard Metropolitan Statistical Areas (SMSAs) in the North and non-SMSAs in the Southern region. The PSID core sample combines the SRC and SEO samples. From 1968 to 1996, the PSID interviewed and reinterviewed individuals from families in the core sample every year, whether or not they were living in the same dwelling or with the same people. Adults have been followed as they have grown older, and children have been observed as they advance through childhood and into adulthood, forming family units of their own" (available from http://www.isr.umich.edu/src/psid/overview.html).

3. The PSID's representativeness is subject to some debate since some families, over time, leave the study and the PSID did not include new immigrants arriving after its start in 1968. Yet, John Fitzgerald, Peter Gottschalk, and Robert Moffitt (1998) have concluded: "[W]e find no strong evidence that attrition has seriously distorted the representativeness of the PSID . . . and considerable evidence that its cross-sectional representativeness has remained roughly intact."

4. The calculations in Table 10.1 were graciously provided by Thomas Vartanian.

5. Using the PSID, Boisjoly, Harris, and Duncan (1998) find that the percentage of all children receiving welfare in any one calendar year who are black gradually moved upward from 1973 to 1990 from the low 40 percent range to 52 percent, suggesting that the proportion of the welfare population who are black was lower when the press began to overrepresent welfare as a "black program" in the 1960s and 1970s.

6. For an alternative perspective, see Clawson and Trice (2000). They provide evidence that the mass media continued to overrepresent blacks in news stories about poverty and welfare in the 1993–1998 period when welfare reform was being debated and assessed. Yet, while this is certainly correct for poverty, it is less so for welfare, if we compare their calculations to the various data presented in this chapter.

7. Steven Levine provided the point that Christie Whitman suffered from "e" envy. Lacking an "e" in her last name prevented her from being a "Whiteman."

8. Michel Foucault (1973) has emphasized that pictures only become coherent by virtue of a "cycle of representation" whereby a circuitry connects a picture to interpretations by the viewing subject that are needed to visualize the viewed object. Foucault stresses that the cycle of representation necessarily combines the image of a picture with the text of interpretations to make the viewed object better conceived as a text/image, or what Foucault calls a "calligram."

PART V

Social Constructions, Identity, Citizenship, and Participation

HELEN M. INGRAM AND ANNE L. SCHNEIDER

In this book we argue that citizenship should be expanded to include a positive social construction of all citizens. Such a positive social construction is essential to identity, to allegiance to the state, to a sense of efficacy related to participation, to social mobilization, and to political participation of all sorts. People who suffer a negative construction cannot join with one another in political action and tend not to enjoy any of the benefits of citizenship except perhaps those that are legally required and enforced by court action.

The history of American democracy is one of continued expansion of the meaning of citizenship. Early in the evolution of American democracy, the focus was upon extending the franchise and acquisition of related rights, such as freedom of speech, the right to assembly, and protection from unwarranted government exercise of coercion. Bit by bit over time, the impediments to the exercise of the right to vote were swept aside for most people. It is no longer necessary to be a property owner, male, white, and more than twenty-one years of age in order to vote. There are clear limits to the openness of the franchise, however, as previous chapters in this volume have demonstrated. In chapter 1, Kay Schriner illustrates the extent to which the mentally and emotionally disabled as well as those convicted of a wide range of crimes are excluded from the franchise. Further, government has singled out some citizens and imposed particular burdens upon their exercise of speech, assembly, and the right to be free from coercion. America has a continuing history of exclusionary and discriminatory policies toward immigrants with certain ethnic and racial backgrounds. Stephanie DiAlto (chapter 3) chronicles the local, state, and federal governments' formal and informal policies and practices that diminished the civil and political rights of Japanese Americans throughout the first half of the twentieth century. Mexican American and other ethnic minorities have been similarly targeted by policies that diminish their rights, including the passage in some states of English-only laws.

At least since the era of the Great Society in the 1960s, economic rights have joined civil and political rights as fundamentals of citizenship. The argument made by T. H. Marshall (1964) is that economic security is essential to the exercise of citizenship. A citizen suffering from poverty—including inadequate food, housing, and health care—cannot freely exercise political rights. Governmental guarantees of a basic standard of living, or the availability of a safety net, arguably must accompany civil and political rights for full citizenship to exist. That such rights are far from secure is illustrated in a number of the foregoing chapters, including those dealing with poverty and housing (see chapters 4, 6, and 7). Impediments to access to the welfare system by legal Mexican-American immigrants are examples of how economic rights are still constricted for some (see chapter 5). The increased economic risk under which these immigrants labor undoubtedly affects their progress toward naturalization.

A lesson of this book, and especially the capstone chapter that follows by Joe Soss, "Making Clients and Citizens: Welfare Policy as a Source of Status, Belief, and Action," is that citizenship needs to be extended to include deserving and enabling social construction. Thus far, government have been quite discriminatory in their allocation of positive social constructions. As Laura Jensen points out in the first chapter, the federal government used designations of deservedness and entitlement to bind some, but by no means all, citizens to the state. Revolutionary War Veterans, she argues, were an especially crucial clientele for the new and weak central government, and therefore were singled out for the receipt of pension benefits. By officially recognizing some as deserving and entitled, governmental policy, by implication, labeled others as less deserving and entitled. In more modern examples, targeting aid to middle-class African Americans, in the case of housing (see chapter 4) and to professionally oriented microentrepreneurs, in the case of small business loans (see chapter 6) not only deprived certain persons of government aid, but also stigmatized them as undeserving and unentitled.

Government has gone far beyond the passive construction of some citizens as undeserving and unentitled by omission, however. As other chapters of the book illustrate, some policies have actively stigmatized certain classes of citizens (see particularly chapters 2, 3, 5, and 9). In the case of Mexican immigrants, elected legislative leaders built political capital by associating themselves with and amplifying negative social constructions (see chapter 5). While perhaps well meaning, the influential Moynihan Report's social construction of the African-American family as pathological (see chapter 9) amplified and perpetuated constructions of African-American women as castrating vixens with loose morals. Negative social constructions affect the social standing of people, but more importantly for our examination, they diminish their propensity to take up positive roles of citizenship.

Policies that promote democracy can construct rationales or narratives for punishing certain persons that do not necessarily involve assigning a negative group identity or stigma. Bad acts should be identified and addressed, but the perpetrators do not need to be permanently stigmatized as "evil." Allocation of scarce benefits should take justice and fairness into account and take care not to elevate some into a modern aristocracy. The emphasis in policy narratives should be upon the connections between the actions required of target populations and the desired results for the society. Policies should be cognizant of constructing citizenship as a positive experience for all, not just for some.

In the final chapter, Joe Soss traces welfare policy feedback to its effects upon recipients' identity, social mobilization, participation, political power, and citizenship. Soss builds upon his previous work (Soss 2000) comparing two very different programs—Social Security Disability Insurance and Aid to Families with Dependent Children that have vastly different impacts on recipients. Welfare policy in the United States has always had a superior tier of programs associated with and designed for the more deserving groups, such as the disabled and the elderly, who have proven work histories. The inferior tier of programs service relatively disadvantaged groups, such as poor women and people of color. Drawing upon data from in-depth interviews of clients of these different programs, he examines how the differences in policy design impacts the patterns of political thought and action among clients. He traces how experiences with these very differently administered welfare agencies result in quite distinct inferences by recipients about what a citizen is likely to experience from government in general. Further, welfare recipients gain clear notions of their identity as efficacious or helpless in their relations with government and how and whether their participation as citizens matters. Soss argues that policy designs convey cues regarding status and stigma that have a considerable impact on clients' beliefs about whether or not their fellow recipients are morally deserving and whether clients share political interests. These cues have an important impact upon identity and the propensity of clients to take collective action. This chapter explicitly connects social constructions of deservedness and entitlement to positive identities and participation and negative identities of unworthiness with alienation, resignation, and failure to participate politically. There is clear evidence to suggest that future advances toward a more democratic society in America depend importantly upon policy designs that fairly and equitably construct citizens as deserving and entitled.

11

Making Clients and Citizens: Welfare Policy as a Source of Status, Belief, and Action

Joe Soss

Over the past two decades, the question of how to cultivate "good citizenship" has come to play a remarkable role in American welfare politics. Debates that once centered on how much aid should go to low-income families now focus on how the terms of assistance can be used to promote work, sexual restraint, and other behaviors deemed to be social responsibilities. The intellectual force behind this shift has been the *new paternalism,* a movement that promotes directive and supervisory uses of public policies to enforce civic obligations and to provide a moral teaching to the poor (Mead 1997a; Besharov and Gardiner 1996). In federal and state governments, paternalist ideas have captured the legislative imagination and helped to underwrite a major realignment of social policies (Weaver 2000). To a striking degree, welfare provision in the United States has become detached from the goal of income support and entwined with aspirations to make better clients and citizens (Schram 2000).

The paternalist turn in welfare has coincided with a much broader surge of interest in the potential for public policies to strengthen or harm democracy (Schneider and Ingram 1997; deLeon 1997). Scholars have recently begun to pay more attention to the diversity of ways that policies create "feedback" in political systems (Pierson 1993). Policy designs, for example, create arenas for making political demands and for constructing the subject positions that citizens occupy in their interactions with government (Cruikshank 1999; Mettler 1998). These policy designs distribute incentives and resources in ways that shape the calculus of strategic political action (Lowi 1964; Skocpol 1992). Policies consolidate particular ways of thinking about social problems and social groups (Stone 1997). They convey symbolic cues that can arouse or pacify constituencies, invite rebellion, or legitimate existing governmental and distributive arrangements (Edelman 1971).

Because policy feedback takes on such a multiplicity of forms, it is no simple matter to determine *how* a policy design will affect the political process or *which* policy designs are most likely to "empower, enlighten, and engage citizens" (Ingram and Smith 1993, 1; Pierson 1993). In the welfare domain, for example, paternalists focus on the potential for program rules to have "tutelary effects, either supporting or undermining good habits and attitudes" (Fullinwider 1988, 261). Starting from the premise that poor people have become too irresponsible "to merit the esteem of others [or make] a community of equal citizens imaginable," they suggest that democracy will be best served by program designs that teach civility, self-restraint, and compliance with social expectations (Mead 1997b, 229).

Paternalist policies may or may not instill the virtues they are designed to teach; empirical researchers have only begun to provide relevant evidence (Wilson et al. 1999). For those who hope to bolster democracy, however, it is important to avoid an overly narrow approach to asking how welfare policy might affect the practice of citizenship. A policy that successfully enforces civic expectations may, nevertheless, fail democracy in a variety of other ways. To gauge its overall effects, we must think more broadly about how policy designs affect status, belief, and action in the citizenry.

This chapter offers a non-paternalist account of how policy design constructs citizenship for clients of the U.S. welfare system. Welfare paternalism is built on a distinctive set of political priorities: it values social order over social justice and civic compliance over political engagement (Mead 1998). Such values must play a role in any stable polity; but in this chapter, I begin from the premise that democracies require more than just compliant and orderly subjects. Flourishing democracies need citizens who are efficacious and engaged, aware of public issues, and conscious of collective interests—citizens who enjoy a modicum of dignity and security, who are not afraid to assert themselves, and who expect responsive action from government (Barber 1984; Pateman 1970). Such characteristics emerge out of many experiences gathered over a lifetime. But like civic compliance, they can be supported or undermined by public policies. These characteristics depend, to a significant degree, on the ways policy designs position individuals in relation to the state and to one another, and equally on the ways that policy experiences shape individuals' beliefs about themselves, their groups, and their government.

In this essay, I use citizens' encounters with welfare policy as a basis for assessing and elaborating on Schneider and Ingram's theory of target populations (1997). Three points suggested by the authors guide my approach. First, to gauge the political consequences of policy design, one must pay attention to what individuals learn through their "direct, personal experiences with public policy" (141). Second, lawmakers frequently design policies that convey distinct messages to different target populations (104). Accordingly, some important political effects can only be illuminated by a comparative analysis of groups that encounter different policy designs. Third, people "act on their interpretations [of policy designs], which may be quite different than designers' intentions" (1). Individuals do not passively absorb the teachings of policy makers. They actively interpret their experiences as a way to make sense of their place in the world. As a result, the messages conveyed by a particular policy cannot be known from a distant appraisal of its design. The meanings of policy design and implementation must be pursued empirically, by going to the interpreters themselves.

To do so, this chapter draws on fifty in-depth interviews I conducted in 1994–1995 with clients in two social welfare programs. The first group of clients participated in Social Security Disability Insurance (SSDI), a social insurance program commonly associated with "deserving" beneficiaries. The second group participated in a public assistance program generally associated with the "undeserving" poor, Aid to Families with Dependent Children (AFDC), which was replaced in 1996 by Temporary Assistance for Needy Families (TANF).[1] As described in the following section, clients in the AFDC and SSDI programs encounter very different policy designs. This chapter's purpose is to show how experiences with these designs provide distinctive source materials for clients' political beliefs and action orientations. Specifically, it focuses on three areas: (1) perceptions of client status and related beliefs about whether it is wise or fruitful to be assertive in this role, (2) perceptions of how government works and related beliefs about the effectiveness of political action aimed at government, and (3) perceptions of one's fellow recipients and related beliefs about whether it is justified or desirable to engage in collective political demand making.

DUAL WELFARE PROVISION AS A DEGENERATIVE POLICY SYSTEM

> Degenerative policy-making systems are characterized by an unequal distribution of political power, social constructions that separate the "deserving" from the "undeserving," and an institutional culture that legitimates strategic, manipulative, and deceptive patterns of communication and uses of political power. . . . In degenerative policy-making systems, the construction of persons or groups often revolves around divisive concepts . . . [that] serve as guides for the allocation of respect, privilege, and status. (Schneider and Ingram 1997, 102, 107)

In a degenerative policy system, group-based political inequalities and divisive policy designs reinforce each other in ways that threaten democracy (Schneider and Ingram 1997). Social groups are targeted for different types of policy designs depending on their political power (weak or strong) and social construction (positive or negative). These policy designs, in turn, produce feedback effects in the political system. They shape the experiences that individuals have with government and the types of cues individuals use to make sense of the political world. They provide individuals with different kinds of information about how government works, how it is likely to respond to them, and how it values their particular social group. In a degenerative system, "each type of target group receives a rather distinctive set of messages that influences its orientation toward government and its political participation" (Schneider and Ingram 1997, 104).

All else equal, a group with a positive public image will tend not to be viewed as needing coercion or punishment, and a group with political resources will find it easier to protect itself from policy burdens. As a result, policies aimed at politically advantaged groups tend to distribute more generous benefits and emphasize incentives and opportunities. According to Schneider and Ingram, the messages conveyed by such policies enhance the political standing of their targets and encourage them to participate in the political process. Group members learn to expect, and to feel they deserve, government responsiveness. The positive messages embedded in these policies also encourage group members to identify with one another, recognize their mutual interests, and perceive their particular wants as commensurate with the common good.

Politically disadvantaged groups, by contrast, will be less able to win tangible benefits or protect themselves from burdens. Accordingly, they tend to be the targets of policies that are less generous and more directive. In many cases, policies for disadvantaged groups will isolate or stigmatize their targets, setting them apart from the majority as an object of pity or scorn. Policy designs in such cases tend to treat group hardships as personal problems and emphasize the need for individual cooperation or reform. At a minimum, Schneider and Ingram suggest, designs for politically weak groups will portray "the game of politics [as] a bureaucratic game in which [group members] wait in line and eventually get what others want them to have." For groups construed more negatively, as deviants, "the dominant messages are that they are 'bad' people whose behavior constitutes a problem for others" (1997, 144). The theory of target populations predicts that groups dealt with in this manner will eventually learn to retreat from government and view one another with suspicion.

The U.S. welfare system provides an ideal case for investigating this general model of policy feedback. The system's two-tier structure sorts individuals into income-support programs that differ sharply in their designs and cultural connotations (L. Gordon 1994). The superior tier of social insurance programs serves target groups who are typically viewed as "deserving" and who tend to be moderately well organized in American politics. At the heart of this tier lie the Old Age, Survivor, and Disability Insurance (OASDI) programs, often referred to as "Social Security." Although these are redistributive policies that pay benefits to particular categories of individuals, such as elderly or disabled people, they are often described as "universal" programs and understood as contributory insurance plans. Social insurance programs are federally administered; their benefits are pegged to prior wage earnings and indexed to price inflation; and, according to many observers, they produce positive constructions of their targets as "rights-bearing beneficiaries and purchasing consumers of services" (Fraser 1987, 113).

The lower tier of the income support system consists of means-tested public assistance programs that disproportionately serve disadvantaged groups such as people of color, women, and people who have lived in poverty (U.S. House 1998). These programs are frequently associated with the "undeserving" poor and tend to be far less popular than social insurance programs (Gilens 1999). They are generally administered at the state or local level of government and they offer benefits too meager to lift recipients out of poverty (Edin and Lein 1997). In contrast to social insurance clients, who enjoy a depersonalized financial relationship with a federal agency, public assistance recipients enter a personal casework relationship and confront a thicket of rules and services aimed at their social and economic behaviors (Mettler 1998; Schram 1995).

Because of these and other design differences, Schneider and Ingram (1997) identify the U.S. welfare system as a particularly clear case of a degenerative policy system:

> The welfare policy case nicely illustrates one of the central lessons of our work for improving policy design for democracy. The delineation of targets in Social Security . . . was the better design for democracy. It empowered [its recipients] and added to their political power and positive social construction. In contrast, AFDC, targeted to match economic and later racial and social classes, disempowered its intended targets. (Schneider and Ingram 1995, 445)

In what follows, I assess and expand on this claim through a "bottom-up" analysis of welfare policy and its political consequences. Drawing on interviews conducted for my book, *Unwanted Claims* (Soss 2000), I explore the ways that clients respond to the policy designs they encounter in SSDI and AFDC. As I describe below, evidence from the welfare caseload generally supports predictions drawn from the theory of target populations. The approach taken in this chapter, however, focuses less on hypothesis testing than on presenting a process-oriented account of *how* welfare policies influence individuals' political orientations. In particular, I am interested in how clients draw political lessons from their welfare experiences and how they use these lessons as guides for behavior. I begin by describing how AFDC and SSDI recipients differ in their program experiences and, as a consequence, acquire divergent beliefs about how welfare agencies work and clients should behave. Next, I explain how resources and political lessons conveyed by welfare policies affect the broader ways in which individuals think and act as participants in relation to government. Finally, I show how "deserving" and "undeserving" images of client groups shape how clients think about their fellow recipients and assess the desirability of collective action.

The Citizen as Client:
Position and Voice at the Welfare Agency

The growth of modern welfare systems over the past century created new arenas for political action and instruments for governance. Today, welfare institutions are major channels for demands on government and important tools for protecting and controlling marginal groups (Piven and Cloward 1993). Welfare claims allow individuals to articulate immediate needs to government and seek targeted policy responses in the form of selective benefits. For applicants, the institutional conditions that regulate these claims can be as important as any rule governing access to a court or a voting booth. Some claimants get turned away, retreat out of fear or pride, or find they are unable to negotiate agency procedures. Those who succeed win material relief. But they also become *clients*—occupants of a relatively weak role in an unusually direct and continuous relationship with government. Welfare clients are highly dependent on the financial and information resources controlled by agency officials, who also hold authority to interpret rules, demand information, and decide eligibility. Thus, the client role offers unique opportunities to gain assistance from government, but it is also a vulnerable position that entails real threats to privacy, dignity, and material security. For large numbers of Americans, treatment and responsiveness in the welfare system are not administrative sidebars to democratic governance. They are, in their own right, critical measures of what citizenship means in practice.

The categorical architecture of the U.S. welfare system ensures that people who seek benefits from AFDC and SSDI have dissimilar experiences with government. The SSDI program is designed to provide a detached relationship of financial support for people of all income levels whom the government certifies as unable to perform "substantial gainful work" (Mashaw 1997). In contrast, the AFDC program offers temporary aid to low-income adults (mostly single women) who have dependent children and who are assumed to be capable of paid work. As I describe in a later section, this sharp contrast of target groups— the idea that AFDC and SSDI serve distinct "types of people"—is partly a creation of the welfare system itself. But it is a fiction with considerable power. It pervades every aspect of policy design in the AFDC and SSDI programs, defining the terms of participation for applicants and clients.

On its face, the SSDI application process might seem to be more difficult than its AFDC counterpart. The SSDI program offers what amounts to a long-term exemption from the labor market (Stone 1984). Accordingly, its standards of eligibility are relatively stringent. Applicants must document a history of payroll contributions and supply clinical proof that they have a disability severe enough to physically prevent them from working.[2] The AFDC program, which offers less generous benefits and only a partial reprieve from the labor market, has more modest eligibility standards—mainly verification of dependent children and financial need. Formal eligibility requirements, however, are only means by which policy designs shape the application process. A closer look at the rules and procedures reveals that SSDI, the program designed for the more "deserving" target group, does far more than AFDC to accommodate and encourage applicants. Indeed, people who seek AFDC benefits encounter a sequence of unpleasant procedures that lead many applicants to conclude that they are not valued and their claims are unwanted.

The SSDI application process offers claimants a number of advantageous design features. To help applicants overcome transportation difficulties, the Social Security Administration (SSA) accepts applications via a toll-free phone line and supportive documents sent through the mail. Applicants can set up a phone appointment for a time they find convenient or, if they prefer, have a face-to-face meeting with a federal administrator. Aside from documenting their work histories and medical conditions, claimants are asked to provide little additional information. Their domestic arrangements are left private and they do not have to establish any sort of virtuous personal behavior as a precondition for benefits. SSDI application forms provide spaces for individuals to describe their problems in their own words, and SSA workers ask for personal accounts of how and why individuals are experiencing impairment-related problems.

The result of these and other design features is that SSDI applicants tend to leave their first encounter with the SSA feeling that the agency is professional and accommodating. Some express their distaste for bureaucracy or criticize the time required to process completed applications. But in the main, SSDI applicants come away feeling that their claims are welcome and that the SSA can be counted on for reasonable service. Francis, one of my interviewees, recalled, "I was really surprised when I called up. It wasn't much of a hassle. I called up and the wheels got moving, and it happened. . . . I was surprised at how easy it was applying to [SSDI]. It wasn't a whole lot of hassle."

The SSDI application experience offers a telling contrast when held up next to the procedures designed for poor women with children. Like disabilities, young children and poverty can make it difficult for would-be applicants to get to a local welfare office. AFDC applicants may lack access to a car or even to public transportation. The AFDC design, however, requires applicants to appear in person: no electronic or postal alternatives are allowed. Often with one or more children in tow, applicants go to the welfare agency, where they find a waiting room with a layout similar to what Charles Goodsell (1984) has termed the "dog-kennel design" because of its authoritative and maze-like configuration.[3] There are rows of hard plastic chairs bolted to a tile floor and, despite the ubiquity of children, no play areas or places to warm up baby bottles. Agency personnel sit behind protective glass barriers; a sheriff watches from one end of the room; and lines drawn on the floor show applicants where to stand when the loudspeaker directs them to go to a door marked A, B, C, or D. Waits in these rooms vary in length, but it is common for applicants to sit for several hours before seeing an intake worker. One client I interviewed reported sitting at the agency for three days before receiving attention.

Upon leaving the waiting room, applicants proceed to a series of interviews with overburdened agency workers. These workers ask a wide variety of domestic questions but have little time to explain why specific questions are relevant or to solicit applicants' own accounts of their circumstances. Who lives in your home? Do you have a boyfriend? Where does he live? Where do your children go to school? Have you paid your rent? Do you prepare your own food? The questions stretch on, each demanding a brief factual response and offering no space for explanation. Not surprisingly, AFDC applicants tend to come away feeling pigeon-holed and silenced. Worse yet, some questions leave applicants feeling exposed and humiliated. Unlike their SSDI counterparts, who are free to pursue or forego child support services offered by the state, AFDC applicants cannot receive benefits unless they first cooperate with child support enforcement. To do so, AFDC applicants must answer paternity questions that require them to divulge portions of their sexual history to a stranger they have just met. Kisha complained, "They ask questions that are unbelievable. They want to know about your sex life and your sex partners and different places you had sex. It's terrible. When I went in there, I wanted to walk out at first because of those questions. But I needed the money, so I had to take it."

As Kisha's comments suggest, difficult aspects of the application encounter lead some AFDC claimants to give up or leave in disgust (Bennett 1995). Others press on, but with a new appreciation for their inability to resist procedures they find objectionable. Under the TANF program that replaced AFDC in 1996, such design features have proliferated. Many states have implemented formal diversion policies that require claimants to seek help elsewhere before turning to public assistance. Many also now require claimants to submit to fingerprinting and drug-testing procedures and to sign "Individual Responsibility Plans" as part of the application process (Schram 2000, 73–84). Such procedures seem likely to enhance applicants' perceptions that they are suspected of illicit behavior and of not really wanting to be self-sufficient. At a minimum, they add to the procession of unpleasant requirements that clients see as blows to their pride and evidence of their low status. Alissa spoke for many when she described herself as being herded and prodded through a degrading AFDC application process:

It's a big system. "Stand in this line." You feel like cattle or something being prodded. That's how I felt. You go all the way through this line to do this, and then this line to do that. It's like a cattle prod. It's like you're in a big mill. I felt like a number, or like I was in a prison system. . . . It feels like you're in a cattle prod. They're the cowboys, and you're a cow. I feel like a cowboy would have more respect for the animals because he knows that the cattle are his livelihood. But these people are like, "I'm helping you. This is something I'm doing for you. So just be quiet and follow your line."

The feelings of subordination AFDC clients develop in their application encounters carry forward as a signal difference between clients' experiences in AFDC and SSDI. By design, citizens who enter these two programs are positioned very differently in relation to government. SSDI clients have a distant financial relationship with the federal government that involves little interpersonal contact. The SSA regularly sends clients information through the mail but, in most cases, SSDI clients find that they are the ones who initiate more substantive communications with the agency. The SSA does not assign clients to personal caseworkers or subject them to mandatory case reviews. Clients are not obliged to attend job training or life skill classes, nor do they have to fulfill work or community service requirements. When clients need assistance or want to question an agency decision, they usually call the SSA and speak to the first available worker. Most clients report that SSA workers are helpful and professional in these interactions. Darryl expressed the generally positive sentiment of his fellow clients when he told me, "If I ever need anything, I know that's their job. They'll be there. I believe they will."

Through such experiences, most SSDI clients develop a basic sense that they can be effective initiators and that the SSA can be a responsive institution. Clients rarely describe being demeaned in their dealings with the agency. Some clients, such as Donna, compare their agency experiences to everyday consumer transactions "like returning something to Target." Because SSDI clients do not have a personal caseworker, they tend to develop relatively mild views of agency workers as competent, occasionally friendly, but largely disinterested and unremarkable bureaucrats. To clients, SSA employees appear to be interchangeable cogs in the machine—implementers who apply rules they do not make and cannot change. When asked to talk about the SSA, SSDI clients rarely focus on workers *per se*. Instead, they emphasize the size and complexity of the institution and its elaborate system of binding rules.

A heightened awareness of rules leads many clients to view the SSA as complicated and confusing. Starr echoed a common lament when she complained, "I don't know how it works. And I personally would like to know how things work." This kind of uncertainty, of course, can impede client engagement. But on balance, the salience of rules tends to bolster efficacy among SSDI clients by making them feel protected against arbitrary authority and more confident that they can gain responses to legitimate requests. As Donna put it,

"They have to follow the rules and so do I." Most SSDI clients do not think
they can get whatever they want, but they do believe they have the standing
needed to question or challenge agency decisions. Sarah captured this view
when she observed, "Well, if there is any power, I guess they have more than I
do. But I haven't come into a situation where I've seen it. . . . I always feel like
I have some say so in the process." Most SSDI clients find it hard to imagine
how raising a grievance might open them up to retribution. Bridget commented, "I would feel comfortable bringing anything up with them. Why not?
What could the problem be?"

Welfare relationships in the AFDC program proceed according to a different logic. Clients are placed in a personalized casework relationship that medi-
ates their interactions with the welfare agency. Meetings with caseworkers are
organized by a regular schedule of case reviews in which clients must prove
their continued eligibility for benefits. Although they are guided by agency
rules and are accountable to supervisors, AFDC caseworkers tend to hold considerable discretionary power over clients (Handler 1992). They control information about available services; they can assign individuals to or exempt them
from program elements; and ultimately, they have authority to cut off the benefits that clients depend on. Not surprisingly, clients become extremely focused
on whether their worker is personally kind or mean, and they are anxious not
to provoke or irritate their worker. Nona Mae explained:

> Your life is in their hands. Your kid's life is in that worker's hands. If that
> worker don't like you, if you don't smile at that worker, she'll make your
> check late, or whatever. She can do anything she wants to. She can send you
> your check or she can't. If your information is not all there, and she thinks
> you're supposed to have it all there, then she can not send you a check. But if
> it's a good worker, she understands that you might have lost something or you
> can't find your Social Security card. She'll give you a couple weeks to get it.
> They're all in power. You feel like nothing when you go down there. . . . We
> all fear our caseworkers. Caseworkers are feared because they have control
> over our financial abilities.

The AFDC policy design also departs from the SSDI design by addressing
a broader array of client behaviors and by doing so in a directive manner. American poverty policy is marked by a long history of attempts to "improve the
poor" by reforming their values and behavior (Katz 1995).[4] For most of the
twentieth century, programs for poor women placed a particularly heavy
emphasis on behavioral virtue (Abramovitz 1988). Legal challenges in the
1960s pushed many forms of "morals testing" into abeyance for a time. But
starting in the 1980s, AFDC policy began to place renewed emphasis on personal behavior. During the 1990s, the period during which I conducted my
interviews, new program elements proliferated under the AFDC waiver system
(Fording 2003). State lawmakers targeted AFDC clients for stiffer job-search

and work requirements, as well as a host of new measures aimed at reproduction and family life. After 1996, under the TANF system, such terms of participation became a priority of federal law. Individual Responsibility Plans now expose clients to sanctions if they or their children fail to live up to "family-life obligations," such as school attendance, immunization, cooperation with child support enforcement, health visits, drug testing, parenting courses, and family planning courses that often emphasize abstinence.[5]

For clients, these sorts of obligations translate into a steady stream of programmatic "hoops," any one of which might place their income assistance at risk. AFDC clients routinely receive summonses to appear at the agency or directives to attend classes—blunt instructions backed up by the threat of benefit termination for noncompliance. In these interactions, clients rarely get to act as initiators or see the welfare agency act as a responsive or representative bureaucracy. Case reviews typically involve long waits followed by a brief meeting with a weary caseworker who has little time for personal stories but great authority to request information and determine the disposition of an individual's case.

Over time, these and other experiences lead AFDC clients to develop a characteristic set of beliefs about their own status and the agency's power in relation to them. First, a substantial majority of AFDC recipients report feeling humiliated and vulnerable in their encounters with the welfare agency. Second, they come to see the agency as a pervasive threat in their lives, as a potent force the limits of which are unclear. Third, they perceive their welfare relationship as a one-way transaction in which the agency issues directives and the client is limited to two choices: compliance or exiting the program. Fourth, their view of agency decision-making emphasizes the personal discretion of individual workers rather than the rules of the institution. Fifth, they come to understand the agency's capacities for action as an autonomous power over them, rather than as the power to act on their behalf.

Clients' accounts underscore two points about this belief system: it arises from direct, personal experiences with policy design, and it has a chilling effect on client assertiveness. Discussing the client role in meetings with caseworkers, Nancy explained:

> I think it's that you learn not to [say anything]. Because you learn that if you upset this woman or make her angry (or this man, but it's mostly women that work there) that if you upset this person in any way, you're going to pay for it. And so, you don't do that. You learn to be quiet, and just take whatever is dished out.

Only one out of twenty-five SSDI clients in my sample (4 percent) reported she would not question or challenge the SSA if she had a major problem. By contrast, 68 percent of AFDC clients said they would be unwilling to raise a grievance under almost any condition.[6] AFDC clients come to believe that silence at the agency is a rational course of action because they infer from their experiences that speaking out will be ineffective and potentially risky. Alicia expressed both these themes as she explained why she did not raise questions or grievances at the agency. Her comments illustrate the sense of futility that leads many AFDC clients to give up on speaking out, as well as the sense of vulnerability that arises from believing that a caseworker controls one's means of survival:

> **Futility:** You just have to wait and see what they do to you. That's how I feel. Sometimes I do want to say something. But I just leave it at that. Because I feel like I'll get treated the way I've been getting treated anyway. So it wouldn't matter if I said something or not. Whatever they want to do, they're going to do regardless, whether I say something or not. They've got the power, so you have to listen to what they say.

> **Vulnerability:** I figure if I say something back, they know a way of getting me cut off of AFDC. And then I wouldn't have anything for me and my kids, just because I said something. That's their power, right there. That's the power. That's why nobody complains.

In sum, policy designs construct *contexts of transaction* and *subject positions* for citizens who enter the welfare system. In so doing, they do not strictly "determine" the outcomes of administrative interactions. Rather, they establish baseline terms of power and voice for interactions between clients and officials that, ultimately, unfold through an open-ended, political process. Client actions within these political processes are guided by beliefs that are based, at least in part, on subjective experiences of institutional functioning accumulated over the course of program participation. Through program experiences, SSDI clients come to see themselves as secure subjects with full standing to assert themselves. They feel safe enough to contest agency decisions and believe they can actually influence decision-making processes. Because their program experiences highlight the binding force of agency rules, SSDI clients expect to be effective if they persevere in advancing legitimate claims. By contrast, AFDC clients come to believe that they occupy a suspect position, that they are dependent on caseworker benevolence, and that they are vulnerable to retribution. They come to see agency decision-making as an autonomous process, unconstrained by rules, and unresponsive to client demands. As a result, a two-thirds majority of AFDC clients report that they are reluctant to raise questions or assert themselves on issues that are critical to their own well being.

Policy design is not the only factor that affects client assertiveness in SSDI and AFDC. Individual characteristics almost certainly make a difference, as do cultural contexts, social networks, and the peculiarities of specific administrative relationships. Individual contacts with political groups and alternative policy designs offer two sources of countervailing beliefs that should be of special interest to target group theorists. A small number of AFDC clients in my sample were involved with welfare advocacy groups that directly encouraged a more rightful and vocal client stance. Not surprisingly, these clients were especially likely to be among the minority who expressed a greater willingness to speak out. A second group of clients in this minority bears even closer attention because it highlights an important fact about the effects of policy design: any single individual is likely to be affected by multiple policy designs that overlap, intersect, and possibly contradict one another.

Client Self-Advocacy Through Head Start Programs

Of the twenty-five AFDC clients interviewed for this study, eight had children who were enrolled in Head Start programs. The policy design of Head Start requires parents to participate in policy councils that help run local centers by making day-to-day program decisions (Head Start Bureau 1992, §1304.5-1–§1304.5-5, Appendix B). Of the eight women with experience on these councils, five were among the minority group of clients willing to voice grievances in AFDC. Their accounts suggest that Head Start programs can provide a critical venue for poor parents to come together for collective decision-making. They also suggest the potential for policy designs to have spillover effects— that is, to teach countervailing lessons about engagement that influence client orientations in other policy domains. Kisha explained, "Head Start gives you an opportunity, by volunteering, to get the feel of doing different things." Karla emphasized how the Head Start design differed from AFDC and encouraged her commitment to speaking up:

> AFDC makes you want to shy away and hold back. Head Start, they work with you. You can see the progress you're making. Me myself, I've made a lot of improvement in the last two or three years. I went into the citywide policy meetings as a shy, quiet person. And now I've begun to open up a lot more. I talk a lot. I participate in everything they have available.

It is also instructive to consider the responses of the three clients who were active in Head Start, yet remained reluctant to assert themselves in AFDC. These clients underscore that lessons learned in one policy context do not automatically shape behavior in a different institutional setting. The lessons of AFDC participation do not become hardened traits in the essential nature of the individual. Rather, their influence depends in part on clients' assessments of particular relational contexts. The contrast between AFDC and Head Start described by these clients demonstrates the constructive power of policy design. If clients' action orientations flowed from inate individual traits, one would expect clients to hold a single orientation toward involvement across different program contexts (AFDC and Head Start). Cheryl, Lisa, and Nancy all shared their fellow clients' doubts about speaking up in AFDC but felt very different sentiments in the context of Head Start. The excerpts that follow offer a powerful illustration of how a more participatory policy design can foster engagement for individuals who are quiescent in the context of a more directive design:

Cheryl: It would be great if I could have a say in AFDC like I can in Head Start.... I get to go to the meetings. And I know the laws of Head Start. And here [at Head Start] it's different. You have to have parents' say so. You have to have a majority of parents present to vote for certain things and certain people. AFDC is not like that at all. I've never seen or heard about it being that I could have a say so. So, why even think about it? But here, I know it. I know I can have input. So, why not get involved? Now, if there was some place in AFDC where I could go say how I feel and what welfare mothers need, then I'm sure I would have done it by now. But that's not the way it is.

Lisa: Being involved with Head Start now, they give me a lot of options. It's helpful for giving you some insight into AFDC and your caseworker. Like they have a lot of parent involvement, and right now I'm on the policy council. And on the policy council they have components set up on health care, social work, disability plans, and all that.... You get to be more involved with Head Start. They don't tell you that you have to do it. They just give you the opportunity to get involved. So, I feel like I'm wanted, like I'm needed to do something. A lot of people are depending on me to do this, and that's great.... With Head Start, they'll say, "Just bring them [your kids] to the meeting, and let them play off to the side." And then I can still get my business taken care of, even with my kids. That's how you know they want you there. And then afterward, you feel like you accomplished something.

Nancy: I have watched parents blossom in Head Start. Parents who never said a word. They never talked because they had just been beaten down. They don't feel like they have anything to contribute. I've watched them get some empowerment from Head Start, and in two years become leaders of this whole city-wide group of people. Two years ago, they wouldn't even open their mouths at meetings.... [The people at Head Start] give you an opportunity to help. They not only give you the opportunity to help with little stuff in the classroom, they give you the opportunity to go to a meeting where you are making decisions. You are actually involved in the hiring. No one can get hired for this program unless they're interviewed by a group of parents. And that in itself is like, "Wow, really? I can do that?" It gives you control over the education your child is getting, the kind of food your child is getting to eat, the kind of curriculum in the classroom, the people that are actually working with your child. That sense of empowerment starts there. But if you get involved in the program, it just keeps growing more and more. Now, not everyone is going to take advantage of it. And I understand that. But if people want to, they can do it.

Head Start parents' councils provide citizens with evidence that participation can be effective and fulfilling. Such experiences do not always spill over to affect clients' orientations in AFDC. But even when they do not, they still underscore the potential for policy design to shape thought and action among clients of social programs. The policy design of the SSDI program is a fundamentally liberal creation. It emphasizes privacy, limited state power, and rule-based decision-making. It does not seek to build community or stimulate participation, as one might find in a more ambitious "maximum feasible participation" program (Marston 1993). But it does cultivate basic conditions needed for political voice: a sense of security and entitled standing, a conviction that officials must respond to clients in ways that accord with the rules. Caseworkers in AFDC, of course, do not operate in a lawless arena of discretion. From clients' perspectives, however, the rules that guide caseworkers remain obscure. The policy design of AFDC strongly encourages clients to focus on worker discretion. Rules appear to be traps laid for clients or tools that agency workers can use for good or ill. Decision making seems to be an autonomous and directive process carried about by agency officials. In a majority of cases, speaking up seems like a sucker's bet: a foolish waste of time and a good way to land yourself in trouble.

THE CLIENT AS CITIZEN:
GOVERNMENT AND PARTICIPATION

A central contention of the theory of target populations is that policy designs have political effects that extend beyond their immediate institutional arena. A growing body of research, for example, now suggests that the structure of the welfare state has powerful effects on when, where, and how social groups become politically organized (Mettler 1998; Skocpol 1992). At the individual level, however, far less is known about the political consequences of welfare programs. In what ways, if any, do welfare policy designs actually affect the potential for individuals to function as citizens actively engaged in the process of self-government? In all likelihood, there can be no simple answer to this question. Policy designs affect individuals' lives in many ways. As one looks beyond the immediate context of the agency, the effects becomes harder to trace, more complex and contradictory. In this section, I focus on just two processes that can be expected to produce political feedback at the individual level. The first has to do with resource distribution. The second concerns the potential for welfare relationships to function as vehicles for adult political education.

Perhaps the most salient design feature of the AFDC and SSDI programs is that both distribute cash benefits. Money is an important political resource for any group (Verba, Schlozman, and Brady 1995, 288–303), but it takes on special significance for people who live at or near poverty levels. Low-income people labor under a number of distinct disadvantages in the political process, some of which operate at the individual level (Piven and Cloward 1997, 271–86). The daily struggle to make ends meet leaves individuals with little time or energy to follow public debates, participate in political organizations, or hold elected representatives accountable. In an affluent society, poverty also threatens the equal respect and dignity needed for citizenship. Those who cannot "live the life of a civilized being according to the standards prevailing in the society" risk marginalization and shame (Marshall 1964, 72). Equally important, poverty cultivates dependency and vulnerability in everyday life. The threat of deprivation becomes a kind of coercive force, stripping individuals of the ability to walk away from or stand up to the people who control resources they need (Ehrenreich 2001). By providing a bulwark against these sorts of conditions, welfare policy actively enhances the possibilities for meaningful democratic citizenship among the poor.

Because AFDC has a means test set well below the poverty line, clients usually experience considerable hardship before applying for benefits. Many recipients report a lack of food, an inability to pay bills, and unstable housing situations or homelessness. The SSDI program does not have a means test, but its clients are also likely to experience material hardship prior to claiming benefits. Low-income people are more likely than other groups to work dangerous jobs and to lack adequate health care, nutrition, and housing. As a result, the diseases and injuries that give rise to SSDI claims are disproportionately likely to strike the poor (DiNitto 1995). In addition, health problems can be a cause of poverty in their own right. Disabilities lead to lost wages and increased health care costs, a potent combination that can quickly eat up savings for middle-class families and strain informal support systems.

Although friends, family members, and lovers are often willing to help out, it is never easy to predict whether this support will come with "strings attached." With the threat of destitution looming in the background, individuals can suddenly find that they are trapped in a relationship that is manipulative or threatening. Friends and family members are sometimes the culprits, but for women in AFDC, the most common coercive relationships involve male lovers or husbands. Some clients describe the subtle losses of autonomy that arise when a woman is financially dependent on a male breadwinner; others recount more overt encounters with coercion in cases of domestic violence (Raphael 2000). Abuse by a man was mentioned (even if only in passing) by almost half the women I interviewed in AFDC, a disturbing percentage that closely matches figures from national survey research (Tolman and Raphael 2000).

Gender-based violence, of course, is not just a private experience of pain and terror; it is "a problem of democracy . . . [that] affects the community as a public body" (Sapiro 1993, 432, 445). Domestic abuse creates a profound form of social isolation and undermines the autonomy needed for full citizenship. An interviewee named hope, for example, was beaten or raped on almost a daily basis by a husband who guarded her entry and exit from the house. She recalled that "if he found the kids with toys, he would beat me. I lost all of my teeth because of the toys. All of my teeth are dead. If the house wasn't spotless, which it almost always was, I'd get beat." In response to my question about how she was able to escape her husband, she replied, "It was the AFDC that allowed me to do that. Otherwise, I would have been stuck in an abusive situation." While Hope's situation may seem extreme, it is hardly unique. Debber, for example, explained why she applied to AFDC, recounting that when her husband "threatened to take my life, me and the kids, I said, 'You are not my husband no more.' And I took the kids and left."

Like their counterparts in AFDC, SSDI clients also emphasize that claiming welfare benefits allowed them to escape threats to autonomy. For some, SSDI provides a way to stave off institutionalization. Bridget recalled, "If I hadn't applied, I would have had to go to a nursing home when my savings ran out. SSDI allowed me to maintain my independent living situation. . . . I didn't want to be stuck in some nursing home depending on other people for everything." Darryl's story is even more striking. On the day that I met Darryl, the schizophrenia that had once ruled his life had been subdued by medication; he was maintaining his own apartment and holding down a part-time job. After describing how SSDI helped him get medical care and financial security, he recounted his earlier experiences of poverty and marginality:

> I'd be walking the streets because I was homeless. And I would get hungry, and I didn't have cigarettes. So, I'd steal a pack of cigarettes, and then go in a restaurant and order a meal. And I'd eat the meal, and then tell the manager, "I don't have any money. I can't pay for this meal." And then they'd lock me up in jail. So, without SSD[I], I would just go back and forth between the street and jail—staying on the street until I got hungry enough to not care about maybe going to jail.

By offering a means of escape from these sorts of conditions, welfare benefits enhance the possibilities for individuals to participate in their communities. In this respect, programs in both tiers of the U.S. welfare system support a more inclusive civic and political order. By design, however, SSDI and AFDC do not offer equal protections. The SSDI program is designed to distribute higher benefits and to prevent their erosion over time. Payments are indexed to inflation, which means their nominal value rises automatically to keep up with price changes. Public officials do not have to vote for or justify a benefit increase for the target group. In AFDC, the opposite is the case. Benefits have always been set low (partly to promote work and the formation of two-parent families), and there is no safeguard against inflation. When public officials do nothing, the real value of AFDC benefits declines. This design feature ensures that benefits can only hold their value if state lawmakers vote to increase transfers to a stigmatized target group. Not surprisingly, such acts of political bravery are rare. The real-dollar value of AFDC benefits has declined by about one half over the past twenty-five years (Albelda and Tilly 1997).

As a result, AFDC claimants gain access to fewer resources than their counterparts in SSDI and other social insurance programs. While SSDI benefits have considerable "antipoverty effectiveness," AFDC clients do not receive enough to lift them out of poverty or even to cover all their basic necessities (Danziger and Weinberg 1994). To make ends meet, they must continue to depend on aid from family, friends, and local organizations (Edin and Lein 1997). They remain more vulnerable to social coercion and less able to provide themselves and their children with the basic material items that "respectable" people have. They gain less relief from the daily struggle against poverty that diverts their attention from broader civic affairs. AFDC clients are forced to live within a very small margin of error: a routine mishap, the wrong decision about what to buy when, an altruistic cousin moves out of town—almost anything can disrupt the fragile stability and order of their lives.

Thus, two points should be kept in mind when thinking about the individual-level effects of benefit distribution. First, SSDI and AFDC benefits help individuals fend off life conditions that might otherwise prevent even minimal participation in civic and political affairs. Whatever degradation clients may encounter in welfare programs must be measured against the conditions they would face without financial assistance. In the absence of welfare benefits, many clients would be far from "self-sufficient." Certainly, most would find it difficult to become actively engaged in the political process. Second, in the area of benefit distribution, some welfare policies do more than others to bolster the security and status of their clients. By design, the "undeserving" targets of AFDC policy are kept quite poor. The more "deserving" beneficiaries of the SSDI program are given far greater relief from the politically enervating effects of poverty.

Financial benefits make up only one dimension of welfare policy. Other design elements shape the lessons that clients learn as they participate in the welfare system. Because welfare institutions are sites of political action, they are also sites of adult political learning (Sigel 1989; Sapiro 1994). In the preceding section, I described how experiences with policy design provide individuals with a basis for developing political beliefs that shape the ways they carry out the client role. Such lessons would be politically significant even if their influence were limited to the welfare arena. But, in fact, the lessons of welfare have a more general impact. Experiences in welfare programs provide individuals with cognitive resources that they use to make sense of government as a whole and to evaluate the effectiveness of political participation in general.

As a group, people who receive means-tested welfare benefits have very low rates of conventional political participation. Part of what makes this pattern noteworthy is that it contrasts with participation rates among social insurance clients, who are "at least as active as the public as a whole" (Verba, Schlozman, and Brady 1995, 210). The disparity across target groups arises from many factors. In addition to being held back by poverty, AFDC clients tend to come from segments of the population where a variety of important political resources and skills are less abundant (411). They are more likely to be affected by institutional barriers to participation (Piven and Cloward 2000) and less likely to be targeted by mobilization efforts of the elite (Rosenstone and Hansen 1993).

Even after controlling for a variety of background characteristics, however, AFDC clients remain significantly less likely than SSDI recipients to make themselves heard by government; they are also less politically active than others in the population that shares their demographic profile (Soss 2000, 161). These patterns suggest at least two conclusions. First, low participation rates among AFDC clients may be traced, at least in part, to some factor associated with welfare itself. Second, whatever the welfare-related factor might be, it is not simply the receipt of cash benefits: SSDI clients receive more generous benefits but are far more politically active. The missing link here—ignored in most conventional research on political action—is adult political learning in welfare programs. AFDC clients are less active than SSDI clients and less active than people who share their demographics—partly because the political disadvantages they already carry are reinforced by the lessons they learn as they participate in AFDC.

Perhaps it should not seem surprising that policy designs in AFDC and SSDI shape clients' beliefs about the effectiveness of making their voices heard at the welfare agency. But why would these beliefs, developed in the context of a specific welfare program, spill over to affect individuals' more general perceptions of government and of political participation? The answer lies in welfare recipients' tendency to view government as "one big system." Lessons learned in SSDI and AFDC are, in many respects, specific to a particular relationship. But for clients who view government as "one big system," experiences at the welfare agency come to be understood as an instructive and representative example of their broader relationship with government as a whole.

Lessons learned about specific welfare bureaucracies get applied to other government institutions because, in the eyes of clients, government exists as a single entity. In interviews, clients from both AFDC and SSDI regularly identified welfare agencies as institutions of government. They rarely sorted these institutions into neat "administrative" and "political" categories. For example, when I asked Dizzy about the SSDI application process, he said, "Well, it's political. Isn't anything with the government political? Everything with the government is political." In addition to sharing this unified view of government, clients in both programs also tended to suggest that their expectations of government were based partly on their experiences in welfare programs. As an illustration, consider the following statements made by AFDC clients:[7]

Mary: In politics, welfare, SSI, it's all the same.

Hope: I haven't been to most of the government. But I'll bet they just treat you the way the welfare office does. That's my fear. They'll treat you the same way.

Vanessa: When they start talking about voting, I turn the TV. I do. It's no guarantee. This person can make all these promises. But that don't mean they're going to do it. The rest of the government mostly works like the AFDC office. I mean, I don't deal with the government when I can.

Nancy: I don't know if people in the government would be responsive to me. If it's anything like trying to deal with the AFDC system, I don't see how. And to me, AFDC, the Department of Social Services, Department of Child Protection, Juvenile Court, those are all the same system. They're just different departments in the same system. And I have not had luck with any of those systems. . . . I would expect the same sorts of treatment in Congress or wherever. . . . That's why I say the government is all just one and the same program with different departments.

Because the clients I interviewed tended to view government as "one big system," their images of the welfare agency became, in effect, general images of government. To make sense of how government works, they thought about the branch of government they knew most intimately: the welfare system. As a result, the lessons they learned about speaking up at the agency carried over into beliefs about the efficacy of other forms of political demand making.

In our interviews, I asked clients to tell me about politics and government—who and what could influence policy decisions, why political outcomes turn out the way they do, and whether government does what citizens want. Perhaps the most striking result was that AFDC clients were significantly more likely than SSDI clients to view government as an autonomous actor that is neither constrained nor directed by citizens' actions (64 percent vs. 20 percent in SSDI). The widespread belief that "whatever they [AFDC workers] want to do, they're going to do regardless, whether I say something or not" (Alissa) was echoed in near-perfect pitch in clients' descriptions of government policy making: "There's nothing I can do because the government is going to do what they want to do regardless of what us people say" (Debber). Unlike SSDI clients, most AFDC recipients saw government decision-making as a directive rather than responsive process. In explaining why they held this view, they frequently talked about their experiences in the AFDC program.

By contrast, SSDI clients were significantly more likely to view the government as open and democratic (76 percent vs. 32 percent in AFDC). Like the SSA, government, as a whole, appeared to be responsive to persistent efforts to obtain action, and this responsiveness was guaranteed by a system of laws. Bridget, for example, believed that, "In politics, the squeaky wheels get what they want." Phil concurred that citizens can "initiate change" if they "use the process," and explained that "it comes down to the old thing of one person, one vote." By a three-fourths majority, SSDI clients believed that citizens could bring about change, as Starr put it, "within the letter of the law. . . . I know it's a very grueling process. But yes, I think locally we are heard." Approximately 40 percent of SSDI recipients thought that government, like the SSA, had grown too big and too complicated (compared with 8 percent in AFDC). But this concern did not alter their more fundamental expectation that, even if government was slow to act, it would eventually respond to citizens who voted, organized, and lobbied public officials.

In addition to soliciting clients' general images of the political system, I also asked them several direct questions related to political efficacy. Consistent with patterns of client assertiveness, AFDC clients were less likely than their counterparts in SSDI to believe in the efficacy of political action in general. For example, they were less likely to believe that their individual actions could affect government decisions (36 percent vs. 60 percent in SSDI) and that a collective movement of people in the program could influence government actions (56 percent vs. 76 percent in SSDI). The most dramatic differences occurred when I asked individuals whether government officials listen to people like them. While 60 percent of SSDI clients believed that they do, only 8 percent of the AFDC clients agreed.

In sum, the interview results support the idea that the quality of an individual's program experience affects her or his general view of government and level of political efficacy. Further support for this conclusion can be drawn from analyses of other data sets. Based on an analysis of survey responses in the 1992 National Election Study, I found that AFDC participation is associated with significantly lower levels of external political efficacy—even after controlling for differences in a variety of background characteristics. By contrast, the responses given by SSDI clients are indistinguishable from those given by the rest of the population.[8] Corroborating and extending these findings, Jennifer Lawless and Richard Fox (2001) report parallel results from a case study of variation *within* the AFDC population. Lawless and Fox found that agency treatment had a significant influence on AFDC clients' evaluations of their welfare experiences. Only 4 percent of AFDC clients thought the welfare system worked "very well," and low evaluations of the agency significantly depressed levels of efficacy and patterns of participation. Based on their community sample, they estimate that positive experiences with AFDC workers would raise the client's probability of political participation by approximately 20 percent.

All of this evidence suggests a chain of political influence that moves from: (1) welfare policy design to (2) the quality of welfare participation experiences to (3) beliefs about the nature of welfare relationships to (4) clients' willingness to voice grievances in welfare programs. Finally, through (5) clients' tendencies to identify welfare agencies with government as a whole, the chain ends with (6) differences in political efficacy and (7) differences in rates of political action.

In a society in which policy making is often relegated to the status of a distant spectacle and in which the poor occupy a marginal place in the political process, welfare policy designs can serve as a potent source of political knowledge. The heart of the matter is that welfare programs provide many clients with their most direct connection to a government institution. For these citizens, the welfare agency serves as a proximate and reliable source of information about how government works. Client experiences provide a handy indicator of whether demands on government can be effective.

The Client as Group Member: Social Identity and Collective Action

Thus far, I have focused primarily on how welfare policy affects the individual's relationship to government. Policy design, however, is equally important for the ways it constructs and positions clients *as a group* in the polity. By targeting groups for different kinds of treatment, policies convey messages to the public about the particular combination of problems, traits, and values shared by group members (Schneider and Ingram 1997). Such messages not only shape how group members are perceived by lawmakers, they can also influence how group members see their own standing in the polity, how they perceive one another, and how they think about the possibilities for collective political action.

The AFDC and SSDI programs construct their target populations in several politically important ways. First, clients in these two programs do not receive benefits as citizens *per se*. Rather, they qualify for aid by proving they have specific characteristics that set them apart from normal citizens. Their program participation is a signifier of difference (based on wealth or health), as opposed to an equal citizen's rightful claim on the common share. Second, both programs personalize their claimants' life conditions. They pay benefits to deviating *types of people* rather than offering compensation based on problems arising from social structure. The basis of benefit payment is not predicated on the fact that some groups are systematically more likely to suffer discrimination, to develop injuries and health problems, or to be disadvantaged by the lack of workplace accommodations for children or impairments (or all). Rather, benefits are paid to individuals who simply happen to lack income or to have a work-impeding disability. In this manner, the welfare state atomizes individual claims, highlighting personal troubles of milieu while severing them from their sociopolitical roots.

Third, divergent eligibility criteria and separate administration create an appearance that AFDC and SSDI serve distinct, or even opposite, types of people. The first group is able-bodied but poor; the second has needs that arise not from poverty, but from being unable to work. This distinction seems to flow directly from objective group differences, but its clarity is largely a creation of the welfare system. In reality, many SSDI clients would be poor were it not for the benefits they receive (Mashaw 1997), and a considerable number could work if they had access to accommodating jobs (Burkhauser, Glenn, and Wittenberg 1997). Likewise, on the allegedly "able-bodied" side of the dividing line, about 35 percent of AFDC clients meet the diagnostic criteria for at least one mental disorder and about 19 percent report significant physical health problems (Danziger, Kalil, and Anderson 2000). Moreover, 50 to 70 percent of AFDC clients report prior domestic abuse, an experience that significantly increases the odds that a woman will have undiagnosed psychiatric disorders (Tolman and Raphael 2000).

My point is that AFDC and SSDI clients actually come from overlapping populations that experience a diversity of vulnerabilities and needs. Eligibility rules cut a line through this population, and the resulting bifurcation highlights similarities within (and contrasts between) target groups. To be sure, there are important differences between the clienteles served by SSDI and AFDC. But these differences do not reflect "natural" social groupings. They arise because categorical eligibility requirements cleave the citizenry into parts, organizing target groups around a handful of allegedly distinctive traits.[9] A major function of this classification process, according to social control theorists, is to isolate individuals who are viewed as violating social expectations. By separating this group and subjecting it to degrading treatment, welfare policy sends a message about the importance of work, family formation, and other social norms (Schram 1995). As Piven and Cloward explain, "To demean and punish those who do not work is to exalt by contrast even the meanest labor at the meanest wages" (1993, 369). In this view, degradation in the AFDC program is not an incidental feature of welfare provision; it is a crucial form of dramaturgy that functions to shore up work compliance and the family wage system.

Levels of Client Stigmatization

Whatever their origin, the messages conveyed by classification in the welfare system are not lost on clients. AFDC and SSDI clients both identify the feeling of entering a new social status as a salient aspect of applying for benefits. Emerald, a SSDI recipient, explained, "it's like you're in the high, medium, and low reading groups in elementary school. The fish, frogs, and whatever. The kids know what reading group they're in." Most AFDC and SSDI clients share this sensation of being classified, but while some get to be fish, others learn that they are frogs. The roles occupied by AFDC and SSDI clients are anything but equal.

SSDI recipients frequently feel stigmatized for their disabilities, but they are far less likely than AFDC clients to feel stigmatized for welfare participation. Slightly less than half (44 percent) reported that they did not feel any stigma at all for participating in the SSDI program. Bridget commented, "I don't think people view me differently if they know I'm on [SSDI] because they already know I'm very disabled." Marie concurred, "There's a stigma in society toward disability, but not for the program." On the other side, slightly more than half of SSDI clients report feeling some level of stigma—primarily because they think that others suspect them of faking their eligibility in order to "scam the system." This pattern suggests that the degradation of welfare "handouts" in the United States is not restricted to means-tested programs. It spills over to color the meaning of program usage, even for target groups that have a relatively positive construction.

All the AFDC clients in this sample believed that welfare receipt made them targets of social stigma.[10] It is important to note that recipients did not carry the burden of stigma "always and everywhere" in their lives. Many did not feel stigmatized in their relationships with close friends and family. Beyond this circle of significant others, however, they perceived anti-welfare stereotypes and prejudice to be widespread in their communities, in the nation as a whole, and among public officials. Stigma consciousness is not only more common in AFDC than in SSDI, it also has greater depth. AFDC clients tend to believe that, regardless of whether or not they satisfy formal eligibility criteria, their welfare receipt makes them objects of public scorn. The traits that clients cite most frequently as elements of the welfare stereotype include: laziness and a failure to embrace the work ethic, sexual and reproductive irresponsibility, neglectful or abusive parenting, drug and alcohol addiction, television addiction, exploitation of welfare policies, susceptibility to manipulation by men, ignorance and stupidity, overeating and obesity, a lack of cleanliness, and criminal or violent behavior.

In addition to the greater depth of stigma consciousness in AFDC, it is also a relatively salient feature of daily life.[11] Part of the reason for this salience is the relatively high level of attention that media and public officials devote to negative aspects of the AFDC program (Gilens 1999). In addition, as described earlier in this chapter, there are the relatively frequent interactions between client and caseworker demanded by the AFDC policy design—a facet of the program that has expanded further under TANF. Finally, by providing separate nutritional aid in the form of Food Stamps, rather than including this aid in the cash value of AFDC benefits, the AFDC policy design virtually guarantees that clients will have an occasional brush with public humiliation.[12] The following comments offer representative examples of stigma consciousness in AFDC:

Celina: People hear you're on AFDC, and they say "ugh." . . . I mean, you hear about yourself on TV. They're stereotyping you all the time. And I'm tired of it. I'm angry.

Lynn: Our own children are taught to disrespect us because of our source of income. . . . I think the whole bad essence of welfare can really be summed

up in one word, and that's stigma. And it's stigma from the minute you walk
in the door at the welfare building, to when you go and buy your food with
Food Stamps at the grocery, to when you turn on your television and . . . it's
even in the commercials now! Every politician that's running for office is running like welfare is the only frickin' issue on the planet.

Nona Mae: You'll be ashamed to spend your food stamps because you know
they're free. You'll be ashamed to go cash your welfare check. It's all shame. It
makes me feel ashamed. . . . I want to be normal. I want to *feel* normal. I don't
feel normal now. . . . People out there with jobs—with normal lives like I want
to have to be like them—those people think we're dumb, that we're not pos-
itive-minded people, we're addicts, we're not good parents. I think they think
everything less of us. . . . I can feel it. It's in the atmosphere. You know when
somebody doesn't like the fact that you're getting everything free. You're getting a free ride. You're a user. You're not a provider.

A considerable body of research has documented that AFDC recipients
tend to feel stigmatized (Briar 1966; Goodban 1985; Rank 1994; Seccombe
1999). Little is known, however, about what *political* effects flow from stigma
consciousness. One effect worth noting is that welfare stigma intensifies AFDC
clients' pessimism about government responsiveness (described in the preceding section). When SSDI clients talk about whether public officials "listen to
people like them," they rarely suggest that their client status matters. Their statements focus on whether elected officials, in general, fail to listen or are out of
touch. By contrast, AFDC clients tend to believe that their client status would
undermine their legitimacy—their equal standing to speak—in the eyes of
public officials. Regardless of how responsive government might be to other
citizens, AFDC clients tend to feel that, as degraded "welfare mothers," they
could not receive an equal hearing. Alissa explained:

I feel like they [public officials] would listen even less because I'm in this
group of people that they're trying to . . . that they have these stereotypes
against. They [public officials] say, "she's lazy, she's black, she's sitting there, she's
received AFDC for all these years. Why can't she work, what's wrong with
her?" . . . I'm looked at totally differently because of the fact that I am a recipient. Everyone in that category is a lazy person who doesn't know what she's
talking about. [imitating a public official] "So, shut up, I'm trying to hear this
man here who went to Harvard. He knows what he's talking about. I'm going
to listen to him." That's how I feel it is, based on what's been said.

Outside of government, welfare stigma has considerable consequences for
the ways in which clients perceive one another and think about the possibility of collective action. Welfare stigma poses a considerable threat to an individual's self-image (Goffman 1963). Surrounded by degraded images of her
group, the AFDC client must find ways to sustain the belief that she is a

"good" and "normal" person. Perhaps the best known of these defenses, in the welfare context, is what Briar (1966) terms "estrangement"—the tendency for AFDC clients to distance themselves from one another and from the "welfare" label more generally.[13]

Again, it is helpful to consider the less-stigmatized group of SSDI clients as a point of comparison. When asked to describe people in the SSDI program, most SSDI clients either cited positive shared traits (32 percent) or asserted that the group is heterogeneous (64 percent). Very few SSDI clients (4 percent) divided their fellow recipients into "good" and "bad" categories or tried to distance themselves from the group as a whole. This pattern reflects the "deserving" construction of SSDI clients as a target group *and* the contrast of this group with the "undeserving" poor in AFDC. In a sense, the degradation of poor clients in AFDC functions to facilitate cohesion among SSDI clients. Donna offered a typical example of how this reference group bolsters the unity and status of SSDI clients:

> I think the common element is that they [SSDI clients] all, or at least 99 percent of them, have legitimate reasons for being in Social Security. Otherwise, they wouldn't have gotten in the program. I mean, if they didn't want to work, they would have just chosen welfare. Then they would be in the same category with other people who don't want to work. But if you have applied to the disability program, you have a legitimate reason in common with other people in the program. You have some affliction that requires you to do this.

As a more stigmatized target population, AFDC recipients were far less likely than SSDI clients to emphasize positive traits shared by their group (8 percent). Those who expressed a positive view tended to do so by emphasizing the group's heterogeneity (44 percent). This strategy allows clients to grant the existence of some "bad apples," while denying that all group members share a set of common attributes. Equally important, it allows clients to assert that AFDC recipients are no different from "normal" groups that include a diversity of people.

The most striking pattern in AFDC clients' responses is that, relative to SSDI clients, they were significantly more likely to contrast an "undeserving" client majority with a smaller and more virtuous group that includes themselves (48 percent). Unlike clients who see bad actors as one group among many, these clients perceive and sort their fellow recipients according to a binary moral hierarchy: those who "live down" to the welfare stereotype and those who do not. By dividing clients in this manner, AFDC recipients suggest that negative stereotypes are properly applied to the majority but not to themselves. In addition, by showing disdain for welfare recipients, clients affirm that they hold "normal American" values; they position themselves on the same side of the cultural fence as those who stand in judgment. Finally, by identifying a group of immoral counterparts, clients construct a reference group that makes them look good by comparison. The following are representative examples:

Celina: There are pretty much two types [of recipients]. . . . There are the ones trying to get off it, and then the ones with like five kids. . . . I view myself and my friends as separate from those who have five kids, are on dope, and . . . yeh, I view myself separate. I think we're the ones that are trying to get off it, and they're not.

Nona Mae: People do just want to use the system. They don't want to provide. Most people, but not me. See, there's a difference. . . . I know [there are] people that are out there wanting to just sit on welfare and do nothing about their career. They make a career out of having babies and getting welfare checks. . . . There are two kinds of people on AFDC. The first kind is the kind that don't care, and want to stay on. And there's another kind who want to get off. So, those are two different kinds of people on AFDC.

The tendency for AFDC clients to distance themselves from their stigmatized target group can also be seen in two additional patterns in the interviews. To assess whether individuals identified with their client group, I coded whether they used inclusive pronouns such as "we," exclusive pronouns such as "they," or some combination of the two when asked to describe people in their program.[14] SSDI clients were more than twice as likely to signify their own membership by using "we" and "us" when speaking of program participants (36 percent vs. 16 percent in AFDC). AFDC clients were more than twice as likely to locate themselves outside the group by using "they" and "them" (40 percent vs. 16 percent in SSDI). In addition, I asked clients whether they thought their reasons for program usage were typical or not typical of most clients in their program. SSDI clients were three times more likely to classify themselves as typical participants (48 percent vs. 16 percent in AFDC). AFDC clients were many times more likely to say they were not typical at all (28 percent vs. 4 percent in SSDI).

The upshot of all this is that AFDC clients, unlike SSDI clients, are deeply estranged from one another. To protect their sense of self-worth, many AFDC clients identify themselves as something other than a "real" welfare recipient. In the private world of their own thoughts, they classify themselves as misplaced and temporary interlopers who differ fundamentally from those who constitute the true and appropriate members of their social category. All told, less than one fifth classified themselves as typical AFDC clients or as part of an "us" defined by program participation. How does this pattern of group perception affect the ways that clients think about collective action? I believe it erects three kinds of barriers to political mobilization.

Barriers to Political Mobilization for AFDC Clients

First, individuals who view themselves as basically unlike a socially degraded group of others will be relatively unlikely to perceive shared political interests (Turner 1987). In my sample, only 36 percent of AFDC recipients believed they shared political interests with others in their program, significantly fewer than the 80 percent in SSDI. In clients' statements, one can see how beliefs that may protect self-esteem in everyday life function to obscure group-based political interests. For example, when I asked Cheryl whether she might share any political interests with other AFDC clients, she responded: "No. I don't think I would—besides having kids and getting a welfare check. Do we raise our kids the same way? Do we think the same way? No, we don't." When I asked Mary about starting a political group based on clients' common interests, she responded: "You're not going to find a lot of people out there that want what I want, so there ain't no sense in me starting something." Tina said she would rather not join an activist group with other clients "because I would rather be around the same people [as me] that have the same thoughts and feelings and concerns instead of the people that don't really give a shit, because they'll just bring me down."

Second, stigma and estrangement also make individuals less likely to perceive that their group has suffered a collective injustice that merits a political response. When individuals identify closely with a group, they have a stake in attributing negative group outcomes to uncontrollable, external factors (Conover 1988, 63). By contrast, when individuals believe they are atypical group members, they are relatively free to explain their own circumstances in one way and group circumstances in another. The result is that while many AFDC clients cast themselves as victims of factors beyond their control, they nevertheless argue that personal choices explain why the majority of AFDC clients suffer similar hardships. Such clients may speak with outrage about how employers, government policies, or men have thwarted their own good-faith efforts, but then reverse course to explain that other clients have troubles primarily because of laziness and irresponsibility. The possibility of collective injustice is obscured for these clients by a suspicion that most recipients are personally to blame for their own low status:

> **Tina:** They really are lazy, and they're just sitting there getting that money year after year. Yeh, they cruise through their money and learn to work around their rent and learn how to have other people help them. All that money goes toward drugs and alcohol.

> **Nona Mae:** The group that's trying to get off . . . that's just this big [closes thumb and first finger to make a small circle]. And the group that doesn't want to get off, that wants to stay living free forever, that group's that big [holds arms out wide]. . . . They're overpowering us because they don't care about themselves. They just want to get their money, drink what they drink, smoke what they smoke, and do what they do.

Third, and finally, stigma and estrangement also function to undermine the belief that clients, as a group, could work together to achieve political change.

Negative stereotypes provide AFDC recipients with low expectations for how their fellow clients are likely to behave (Oakes 1996). In effect, they create an expectation that other clients cannot be counted on to pitch in and work together for collective goals. AFDC recipients tend to suspect that their fellow clients will be self-serving and lazy rather than trustworthy collaborators. Vanessa captured the crux of the matter when she said, "the people just sitting up here wanting a free ride, they don't care." Lashell, who tended to equate AFDC recipients with black people throughout our interview, explained her expectations as follows:

> They would make me do all the work. . . . "Well, it's her idea—she the one that brought it up. So let her do all the work." And then after I got some people to listen to me, then they would jump in. And that wouldn't do me any good. Because I would need these people to be with me from the beginning to the end. . . . A lot of people in AFDC don't care. They complain because black people do. But they're not really willing to do anything about it. They just want to sit back and complain . . . so it would be hard.

As these examples illustrate, the beliefs that a majority of AFDC clients hold about their group would provide poor soil for political mobilization. Classifying their fellow recipients as different and morally suspect, most AFDC clients see a group of people who are rightly blamed for their own status, who hold foreign values and interests, and who would not serve as reliable or effective collaborators in action. There is, however, a minority group of AFDC clients who emphasize common group interests and express support for the idea of program-based activism. A brief consideration of these contrasting cases helps to clarify that negative social constructions do not *automatically* produce estrangement and demobilization. Their effects depend on how individuals interpret policy messages and the extent to which individuals draw on alternative cultural resources to redefine their group's identity.

Like other AFDC recipients, clients in this minority group felt stigmatized for their program participation and were keenly aware of negative welfare stereotypes. But despite feeling stigmatized, they saw themselves as being typical of many or most AFDC recipients—a group they were comfortable describing as "us." It is not that these AFDC clients were willing to accept degraded images of the "welfare queen" as accurate descriptions of themselves. On the contrary, they rejected such images, but did so in a way that did not distance them from the group as a whole. These clients revalued the group in terms that implied a relatively positive social and moral status—a response to status threat that social identity theorists refer to as *social creativity* (Tajfel 1981).

By far, the most powerful basis for such revaluation among AFDC clients is the motherhood role. For a subset of clients, questions about "AFDC recipients" do not refer primarily to individuals who lack paid work or who rely on government aid; such questions refer to mothers who are trying to raise children under poverty conditions. In the eyes of these clients, mothers occupy a positive social role; they have common needs and share common values; they do important work; they deserve support and respect for their efforts. By equating AFDC recipients with mothers, these clients neutralize group stigma as a motive for estrangement and turn it into a foundation for feelings of injustice. As a point of contrast with the majority in AFDC, consider the themes of identification, attributions of competence, and implicit appeals to care and justice in the following comments by Lynn and Nancy:

> **Lynn:** My brother [and I would] get into these welfare discussions. And I'm not supposed to take it personally, but it's about *me*. When you talk about welfare mothers, I happen to be a welfare mother, so you're talking about me. . . . We [AFDC clients] are all mothers who love our kids enough, and want to raise our children bad enough, to go up against whatever is out there . . . poverty, oppressive neighborhoods, a family that's not supportive. . . . We may not always succeed, but most of us always try to do what's in the best interest of our children. . . . I do the exact same things my [middle-class] mother did . . . only with less money than my mom did. But I am public enemy number one. . . . Mothering is important work. It's important to the children. It's important to the community. And my kids need me a hell of a lot more than McDonald's does.

> **Nancy:** I think the basic common bonds [for AFDC clients] would be a desire to be able to take care of the family. It's that simple—just to be able to take care of the children comfortably. And by comfortable, I don't mean middle class. I mean there's a roof over your head, none of your utilities are going to be cut off, everybody has clothes and food to eat, and if there's an emergency tomorrow . . . I can take care of it. That, to me, is comfortable. And I think that's all any of us want.

Taken as a whole, this evidence suggests some important insights into how negative social constructions may shape the social psychology of collective action in low-status groups. High levels of stigma consciousness tend to undermine group identification, perceptions of shared interest, expectations of effective agency, and feelings of collective injustice. The pivot point for these effects, however, lies in the ways that individuals define themselves in relation to the group. Relative to SSDI clients, AFDC recipients are more likely to use negative stereotypes as their primary point of reference when thinking about people in their program. This framing encourages individuals to classify themselves as atypical and to sort their fellow clients into dichotomous moral categories (the majority who "live down" to the stereotype and the minority who do not). As a result, AFDC clients tend to hold beliefs about group status and joint action that differ sharply from beliefs expressed by SSDI clients. By contrast, the minority of AFDC clients who respond to stigma with social creativity, reinterpreting the group in terms of the motherhood role, appear to neutralize

many of these effects. Among this subset of clients, a negative social coni..
tion appears compatible with group identification as well as a variety of beliefs
that might support collective action.

THE THEORY OF TARGET POPULATIONS:
TOWARD A DIALOGUE WITH POLITICAL PSYCHOLOGY

Because welfare policies are aimed at the most vulnerable segments of society,
they have considerable potential to deepen the democratic character of American politics. Welfare policies offer a way to ensure that the weakest among us
remain able to participate as full and equal community members. They can be
used to protect our access to civil and political rights, ensure our abilities to dis-
charge civic duties, and preserve our dignity against threats such as poverty and
infirmity (Marshall 1964). By drawing citizens together under common institutions, welfare policies have the potential to express "liberal themes of rights
and equal respect; communitarian norms of solidarity and shared responsibility;
and republican ideals of participation in public life" (Fraser and Gordon 1993,
45–46). Welfare policies offer a way to build citizens' capacities for self-gover-
nance and enable them to take the sorts of risks needed for personal and societal advancement (Giddens 1998). By bringing together similarly situated individuals, welfare policies might be designed to enhance associational life and
promote civic as well as political engagement (Goldberg 2001).

The analysis presented in this chapter suggests that such democratic possibilities are, in the main, squandered by the U.S. welfare system. Categorical welfare provision offers a classic example of what Schneider and Ingram (1997)
term a "degenerative policy system." Clients are separated from the broader citizenry and divided according to a moral hierarchy of deservedness. Those
deemed least deserving are given less than adequate aid and placed in welfare
relationships designed to emphasize agency directives and client compliance.
Policy designs in the AFDC and SSDI programs leave different kinds of
imprints on the ways that citizens think about themselves, their client group,
and their government. Unlike their SSDI counterparts, AFDC clients learn to
hold their tongues at the agency and develop a sense that government, as a
whole, is unlikely to be responsive. In addition, the AFDC policy design stig-
matizes and atomizes its targets, diminishing the potential for group solidarity
or collective political action. On balance, policy designs in the U.S. welfare system do much to reinforce (and only a little to diminish) the kinds of political
inequalities that can threaten an inclusive and vibrant democracy.

As a whole, the interview evidence presented in this chapter supports the
theory of target populations advanced by Schneider and Ingram (1997) in *Policy Design for Democracy*. Policy designs in the welfare system are active forces that
shape patterns of status, belief, and action in the citizenry. They convey different

messages to different groups, and these messages do, indeed, serve as important sources of social identity and political behavior. At the same time, however, individual-level research in the welfare context raises some important questions for the target-populations project. The theory of target populations is primarily a macro-level theory addressing policy discourses and social groups. I have taken steps in this chapter toward a micro-level analysis of the social-psychological processes implied by theory. A true dialogue with political psychology, however, remains an unrealized and, to my mind, crucial goal for research on target groups. Toward this end, I conclude this essay by suggesting seven issues that pose challenges for target-group theory and identify avenues for communication with political psychology.

Issue 1. Schneider and Ingram assert that "direct, personal experiences with public policy" constitute a significant influence on citizens' general political orientations (1997, 141). My analysis of client experiences in AFDC and SSDI supports this claim, and similar educative effects have been found for personal encounters with the G.I. Bill (Mettler 2002a) and with law enforcement (Lawless and Fox 2001). By contrast, conventional wisdom in political psychology holds that personal circumstances have very little effect on broader political beliefs. Researchers, often responding to the claim that political preferences are driven by economic self-interest, have tended to find that personal experiences and events have meager effects on general political orientations and policy preferences (Schlozman and Verba 1979; Sears and Funk 1990). The tension between these two sets of findings could be resolved by creating a narrow exception: in contrast to most personal experiences, *direct encounters with government* have the capacity to influence *orientations toward government* as well as closely related aspects of the political system. At present, this statement seems empirically defensible. It also comports with psychological theories holding that attitudes will be more powerful when they have been developed through direct experience with an "attitude object" (see Eagly and Chaiken 1993, 193–202). Nevertheless, I think there are good reasons to resist this tidy, descriptive fix. The target-populations thesis and the emerging contrast of findings in the literature both point, I suspect, to more complex theoretical and empirical questions about how the personal becomes, or fails to become, political. Research addressing such questions should play a central role in the dialogue between target-group theory and political psychology.

Issue 2. The evidence presented in this chapter makes it clear that the lessons delivered by public policy depend not just on design but also on interpretation. Like viewers of television, consumers of policy cues are "active audiences" who participate in the construction of meaning (Fiske 1987, 62–83). Clients in a single public program will frequently draw different lessons from their encounters with the same design elements. Their interpretations cannot be intuited with confidence by a scholar evaluating policy design alone, nor can they be derived from a static description of the "general culture" or "belief system" that prevails in a target group. Rather, the "targets" in target-group theory must be treated as active agents in the social and political process that constructs meaning. To do so, target-group scholars need to make it a priority to construct empirical accounts of "how symbols operate in practice, why meanings generate action, and why actions produce meanings, when they do" (Wedeen 2002, 720). Some insight into these processes may be gleaned from carefully crafted survey and experimental designs. But ultimately, a satisfactory understanding will require some commitment to interpretive field research aimed at illuminating the collaborative "practices of meaning-making through which social actors attempt to make their worlds coherent" (720).

Issue 3. Even when the diverse members of a target group interpret a policy design in a relatively uniform manner, the political effects of this message will inevitably be mediated by additional aspects of each individual's belief system. Lessons learned in AFDC and SSDI spilled over to influence clients' broader beliefs about political participation *because clients tended to see government as one big system.* Without this bridge, the scope of political effect would have been quite different. Likewise, consider the minority of AFDC clients who felt stigmatized by images of their target group, but nevertheless identified with other welfare recipients as mothers struggling to raise their children in poverty. This *social creativity* response did not arise from an alternative interpretation of the policy message; it arose from a different social-psychological *response* to the policy message. These examples underscore the need to study how citizens integrate policy cues into a broader web of political attitudes and how preexisting beliefs may provide grounds for resistance to, or extensions of, lessons learned through policy encounters. Here again, the agency of "targets" looms large for the study of target populations.

Issue 4. From a political learning perspective, claims advanced by target-group theorists raise important questions about *timing* in the life course. Most research suggests that individuals are more open to political learning at some ages than at others (Sears 1990). Early research on political socialization placed a heavy emphasis on childhood. More recently, political psychologists have pointed to a greater potential for adult learning (Sapiro 1994), but have also suggested that political experiences may have their greatest impact among young people between the ages of fourteen and twenty-five (Niemi and Hepburn 1995). This "impressionable years hypothesis"—indeed, any claim that learning varies across the life course—holds implications for the target-populations project. Within target groups, it predicts that policy messages will affect some individuals more deeply than others. Across target groups, it suggests that some policy messages may be especially potent because of the age groups they target. The AFDC/TANF program, for example, targets a relatively large number of individuals during their "impressionable years."[15] The same may be said of the G.I. Bill and its educative effects (Mettler 2002a). Should we expect equivalent effects in a program such as Old Age Insurance? Students of policy-based learning face a significant challenge as we move from general claims about the messages encountered by target groups to specific understandings of how individual characteristics, such as age, condition the processing and impact of policy cues.

Issue 5. An additional challenge concerns the interplay and integration of diverse policy cues. Individuals are members of many groups, each group may be targeted by a variety of policy designs, and each design may convey its own distinctive set of political cues. The result is that any single individual is likely to encounter multiple policy messages, some of which contradict one another. Clients who participate simultaneously in AFDC/TANF and Head Start, for example, receive a different set of messages than do clients who participate in AFDC alone. As described earlier, such combinations can have major effects on the eventual shape of clients' political beliefs. Research on target populations will need to pay close attention to how policies actually intersect in the lives of citizens and interact as sources of political cognition. Likewise, much more needs to be known about the ways that individuals respond to contradictory policy lessons—how these lessons coexist in a state of ambivalence or get reconciled to produce summary judgments.

Issue 6. An extension of this challenge concerns the role of *sequence* in policy-based learning. Students of political development have learned to pay close attention to the role that sequence plays in shaping historical outcomes: path dependencies and conditional effects require close attention to the order in which events occur (Pierson 2000b). This lesson of political history is equally important for understanding political biography. As Sapiro (1994) has argued, a single experience can have very different effects on an individual's political orientations, depending on how it fits into the succession of events in a person's life. For target group theory, this insight suggests a need to ask not only about concurrent policy experiences, but also consecutive policy experiences. Evaluations of policy encounters depend significantly on the standards that clients bring with them from past experience (Soss 2000, 117–18). In my research, for example, AFDC and SSDI clients responded quite differently to encounters with Supplemental Security Income (SSI). The messages conveyed by SSI depended partly on its relative inferiority or superiority to experiences in AFDC and SSDI (Soss 2000, 150–51). Over a lifetime, individuals encounter policy designs that vary widely in intensity and in the messages they convey. We need to know much more about how earlier policy experiences condition the meaning and effects of later policy experiences.

Issue 7. Finally, in addition to questions about how targeted individuals learn from policy encounters, there are more general questions about how target groups are construed by lawmakers and the public. The theory of target populations sorts group constructions along two dimensions: political power and perceived desert. For politically weak groups, the latter dimension is anchored by deviants at the undeserving end and by dependents at the other. Schneider and Ingram (1997) have suggested that "welfare moms" occupy a kind of middle ground between these poles and place this group close to the midpoint between dependents and deviants. The placement is an effective compromise, reflecting the ease with which Americans tend to classify welfare dependence as a kind of deviance in its own right (Fraser and Gordon 1994). By implying an "average" of positive and negative responses, however, the neutral position in this spatial model may obscure more than it reveals about how Americans perceive and respond to welfare recipients. Public opinion research routinely emphasizes that most citizens are ambivalent toward questions of poverty, welfare, and distributive justice: we hold a diversity of poorly reconciled values, thoughts, and feelings about target groups and their treatment (Hochschild 1995). Rather than being "averaged" in a single, middling response, opposing sentiments tend to coexist, providing a variety of considerations that may be appealed to by media stories, public officials, and political activists (Edelman 1971). Target-group theorists have always highlighted this potential for multiple meanings and framing effects (see, for example, the introduction to this volume and chapter 5 by Lina Newton on health care policy for immigrants). But, at the same time, it remains far from clear how the coexistence of opposing sentiments—as opposed to a single, coherent response to a group—should be expected to guide policy design. A political psychology that emphasizes ambivalence almost surely complicates the relationship between social constructions and policy designs suggested by target-group theory. Specifying the relevant political and psychological processes should be a central task for our research agenda.

Over the past decade, the theory of target populations has stimulated a vibrant research program. As the chapters in this volume demonstrate, the theory has proven to be particularly well suited for historical and case-oriented research with explanatory goals. In the present chapter, I have sought to complement these studies by investigating some key claims of target-group theory at the individual level. My analysis suggests a considerable amount of empirical support for the interpretive processes and outcomes that Schneider and Ingram have outlined in their earlier work. At the same time, however, the issues I have raised in this concluding section underscore that the preceding analysis offers only a first step.

Individual-level empirical research is essential for scholars and citizens who hope to learn how public policy can be used to enhance democracy. It offers a relatively demanding way to develop and test propositions about which types of policy designs promote which types of civic orientations. Equally important, it provides fertile ground for efforts to interpret *how* and *why* particular policy designs affect political thought and action. The new paternalist arguments that now prevail in U.S. welfare politics have rarely been subjected to such scrutiny. New paternalists assert that a general syndrome of incompetent behaviors and dysfunctional values undermines citizenship for the welfare poor. Directive and supervisory welfare policies, they claim, offer an effective therapeutic corrective. These arguments have achieved great political influence, but so far we have little evidence that paternalist reforms under the TANF program are actually improving the quality of citizenship for low-income people.

The theory of target populations offers an alternative account of how public policies affect the practice and meaning of citizenship. Existing studies, including the present chapter, appear to support its key propositions. Indeed, they suggest the potential for a long and fruitful dialogue between target-group theory and political psychology. By pursuing this dialogue, scholars may yet contribute to public policies that support a stronger and more inclusive democracy.

NOTES

1. Relative to the SSDI sample, the AFDC clients interviewed for this study have greater racial and ethnic diversity, less gender diversity, a lower average level of education, and a lower average age. Although the individuals included in this study should not be treated as a random probability sample of program participants, these cross-sample demographic differences accurately reflect the broader program populations from which interviewees were drawn. The two samples overlap on each demographic dimension enough to permit some analytic control over group differences. In addition, extensive informal interviews with clients encountered at a shelter for the homeless (primarily AFDC) and a support group for people with disabilities (primarily SSDI) served as a validity check on unrepresentative statements made by clients in the formal interview sample. For details on the sample, as well as methods of data collection and analysis, see Soss 2000 (17–25).

2. Jerry Mashaw (1997, 18–19) notes that the test of disability employed in the SSDI program is the strictest of any disability program in the United States, public or private, and is stricter than the test used in most other Western countries. Tight eligibility requirements have a dual effect: they limit the number of people released from work expectations and they bolster the "deserving" image of people who succeed in becoming SSDI clients.

3. The description in this paragraph refers to the urban welfare office where I conducted most of my field observations. AFDC offices vary considerably in their designs, and waiting areas are likely to be less formal and directive in rural areas. Comparing across similar locales, however, I found that waiting areas provided for SSDI applicants were markedly superior to those provided for AFDC applicants (see Soss 2000, 94–100).

4. The roots of this tradition can be found in the earliest Poor Laws and local responses to paupers (Handler and Hasenfeld 1991). In the early 1800s, with the rise of "indoor relief," the poorhouse became a conspicuous public tool for enforcing work and teaching religious values. Later, in the 19th century, scientific charity movements used "child saving" and "friendly visits" to the home as strategies for reforming the poor.

5. The family life obligations under these plans vary from state to state and have grown far too numerous to describe here. For an informative review, see Jody Levin-Epstein (1998), http://www.clasp.org/pubs/TANF/irastatebystate.html.

6. For tests of statistical significance regarding these percentages and others reported in this chapter, see Soss 2000 and Soss n.d. In light of the purposive sample used in this study, all statistical tests should be taken as measures of internal validity rather than tests of population parameters in the broader universe of program participants. Such tests assume that relevant observations in the sample are generated by an underlying stochastic process; they describe the likelihood of observing specific cross-group differences within the sample if the underlying generative processes were, in fact, identical across groups.

7. The statements listed here bear a striking resemblance to those reported by others who have conducted research with welfare recipients. Austin Sarat, for example, finds that recipients tend to equate legal aid lawyers and welfare caseworkers because they are "both part of government." "Legal services . . . was not only inseparable from but was identical with welfare" (1990, 352). Richard Fox and Jennifer Lawless (2001) report corroborating evidence, including the following quotation from an AFDC client: "I know all there is to know about government from the welfare workers. Bureaucracy makes it almost impossible to get benefits smoothly and to get fair treatment. Bureaucracy will also make it impossible for poor people to be heard everywhere else in the political system."

8. Although space limitations do not allow for a full discussion of results, two additional findings from this analysis of efficacy and political participation are worth noting here. First, just as Head Start participation mitigated AFDC clients' reticence in their welfare program, it also bolstered a subset of AFDC clients' beliefs in the efficacy of political participation. Second, although AFDC clients tend to have lower levels of external political efficacy, they do not appear to have lower levels of internal political efficacy. The problem is not that AFDC clients lose faith in their own ability to engage government; it is that they lose faith in government's responsiveness. For a full discussion of these results, see Soss 2000.

9. To further illustrate this point, consider the case of a working-class woman married to a man who serves as the family's sole breadwinner. If the man "disappears" by abandoning the woman and her children, she will likely be channeled into the AFDC/TANF program, with its meager benefits and harsh terms of participation. Alternatively, if the man "disappears" by dying, she and her children will likely be channeled into the Survivor's Insurance (SI) program, a policy designed very much like the SSDI program described in this chapter.

10. Clients in this study were more likely than those interviewed in past studies to report feeling stigmatized. Goodban (1985), for example, reports that roughly two-thirds of her informants experienced recurrent feelings of shame. I suspect that this difference

reflects the time period of my interviews, 1994–1995. This was a period of diminished welfare rights activism and growing animosity toward welfare programs and recipients. It included the Republican *Contract with America* and a national mid-term election in which candidates engaged in anti-welfare campaigning, proposed plans to abolish AFDC, and even discussed enhanced usage of orphanages for the children of poor single mothers.

11. Because of space constraints, my discussion here leaves aside more complex issues arising from the social-group basis of welfare stigma. Suffice to say that while SSDI recipients tend to feel stigmatized primarily as individuals who might be suspected of fraud, the stigma associated with AFDC derives much of its power from basic fault lines of social identity associated with class, gender, and race. For many clients, the stigma of AFDC receipt is tied to images of being "low class," being a "bad woman," and/or being an example of "what's wrong with black people." For discussion, see Soss, n.d.

12. As Robin Rogers-Dillon explains, "Food Stamps are highly visible stigma symbols, they instantly, and very publicly, reveal the user's economic position and status as a welfare recipient. Even respondents who stated that receiving welfare was nothing to be ashamed of bristled over having their status as public assistance recipients revealed in the course of their daily activities and without their consent" (1995, 48).

13. Scholars have produced a considerable literature on the social and psychological tactics individuals use to protect themselves from status threat (Goffman 1963; Turner 1987). For discussions of stigma management in the welfare context that go beyond the brief description presented here, see Soss (n.d.), Seccombe (1999), and Rank (1994).

14. The simple "we/they" distinction is a central axis of self-definition and has been shown to have powerful effects on group-based cognition (Perdue et al. 1990). This distinction is also identified by Briar (1966, 375) as a key operational component of estrangement.

15. In 1998, for example, 46 percent of adult TANF clients were below the age of thirty and 25 percent of recipient children were over the age of twelve. See U.S. Department of Health and Human Services (1998), "Characteristics and Financial Circumstances of TANF Recipients," available from http://www.acf.dhhs.gov/programs/opre/characteristics/fy99/analysis.htm#list.

References

Abramovitz, Mimi. 1988. *Regulating the Lives of Women: Social Welfare Policy from Colonial Times to the Present.* Boston, MA: South End Press.

Abravanel, Martin D., and Mary K. Cunningham. 2002. How Much Do We Know? Public Awareness of the Nation's Fair Housing Laws [online]. Prepared for the U.S. Department of Housing and Urban Development, Office of Policy Development and Research. (Washington, DC: The Urban Institute [dated April 2002; cited 18 March 2003]). Available from www.huduser.org.

Adams, Charles Francis, ed. 1874–1877. *Memoirs of John Quincy Adams,* 12 vols. Philadelphia: J.B. Lippincott & Co.

Administration on Children and Families. 2000. *Characteristics and Financial Circumstances of TANF Recipients, Fiscal Year 1999* [online]. (Washington, DC: U.S. Department of Health and Human Services, Office of Family Assistance, Office of Planning, Research and Evaluation [updated 27 June 2002; cited 18 March 2003]). Available from http://www.acf.dhhs.gov/programs/opre/characteristics/fy99/analysis.htm.

Albelda, Randy, and Chris Tilly. 1997. *Glass Ceilings and Bottomless Pits: Women's Work, Women's Poverty.* Boston, MA: South End Press.

Alland, Alexander. 1972. *The Human Imperative.* New York: Columbia University Press

Almaguer, Tomas. 1994. *Racial Fault Lines: The Historical Origins of White Supremacy in California.* Berkeley: University of California Press.

Ancheta, Angelo N. 1998. *Race, Rights, and the Asian American Experience.* New Brunswick, NJ: Rutgers University Press.

Anderson, James. 2000. *Public Policy Making,* 4th ed. New York: Houghton Mifflin.

Annals of the Congress of the United States, 1817–1818. 15th Cong., 1st sess. (2 December). Washington, DC, 1817–1818.

Annals of the Congress of the United States, 1819–1820. 16th Cong., 1st sess. (2 December). Washington, DC, 1819–1820.

Annals of the Congress of the United States, 1822–1823. 17th Cong., 1st sess. (2 December). Washington, DC, 1822–1823.

Appleby, Joyce. 1984. *Capitalism and a New Social Order: The Republican Vision of the 1790s.* New York: New York University Press.

Arnold, R. Douglas. 1990. *The Logic of Congressional Action.* New Haven, CT: Yale University Press.

Bailey, Raymond C. 1979. *Popular Influence upon Public Policy: Petitioning in Eighteenth-century Virginia.* Westport, CT: Greenwood Press.

Baldwin, James. 1984. On Being "White," and Other Lies. *Essence,* April, 90–92.

Balkin, Steve. 1989. *Self-employment for Low-income People.* New York: Praeger Press.

———. 1993. A Grameen Bank Replication: The Full Circle Fund of the Women's Self-employment Project in Chicago. Pp. 235–66 in *The Grameen Bank: Poverty Relief in Bangladesh,* edited by Abu N. M. Wahid. Boulder, CO: Westview Press.

Barak, Greg, ed. 1994. *Media, Process, and the Social Construction of Crime.* New York: Garland Publishing.

Barber, Benjamin. 1984. *Strong Democracy: Participatory Politics for a New Age.* Berkeley: University of California Press.

———. 1992. *An Aristocracy of Everyone: The Politics of Education and the Future of America.* New York: Oxford University Press.

Barnartt, Sharon, and Richard Scotch. 2001. *Disability Protests: Contentious Politics 1970–1999.* Washington, DC: Gallaudet University Press.

Bartle, Elizabeth E. 1998. Exposing and Reframing Welfare Dependency. *Journal of Sociology and Social Welfare* 25:23–41.

Baumgartner, Frank R., and Bryan D. Jones. 1993. *Agendas and Instability in American Politics.* Chicago, IL: University of Chicago Press.

Beard, George M. 1881. *American Nervousness: Its Causes and Consequences.* New York: G.P. Putnam's Sons.

Becker, Howard S. 1963. *Outsiders: Studies in the Sociology of Deviance.* London: Collier-Macmillan Ltd.

———. 1967. Whose Side Are We On? *Social Problems* 14:239–47.

Beckett, Katherine. 1997. *Making Crime Pay: Law and Order in Contemporary American Politics.* New York: Oxford University Press.

Bennett, Susan D. 1995. "No Relief but upon the Terms of Coming into the House"—Controlled Spaces, Invisible Disentitlements, and Homelessness in an Urban Shelter System. *The Yale Law Journal* 104 (8):2157–2212.

Bensel, Richard Franklin. 1990. *Yankee Leviathan: The Origins of Central State Authority in America, 1859–1877.* Cambridge, UK; New York: Cambridge University Press.

Ben-Yehuda, Nachman. 1990. *The Politics of Morality and Deviance.* Albany: State University of New York Press.

Bernstein, Mary. 1997. Celebration and Suppression: The Strategic Uses of Identity by the Lesbian and Gay Movement. *American Journal of Sociology* 103:531–65.

Besharov, Douglas, and Karen Gardiner. 1996. Paternalism and Welfare Reform. *The Public Interest* 122:70–84.

Best, Joel, ed. 1995. *Images of Issues: Typifying Contemporary Social Problems*. New York: Aldine De Gruyter.

Bhatt, Nitin, Gary Painter, and Shui-Yan Tang. 2002. The Challenges of Outreach and Sustainability for U.S. Microcredit Programs. Pp. 191–222 in *Replicating Microfinance in the United States*, edited by James H. Carr and Zhong Yi Tong. Washington, DC: Woodrow Wilson Center Press.

Bilbray, Brian. 1996. *Congressional Record. Providing for Consideration of H.R. 2202*, Immigration in the National Interest Act of 1995. 104th Cong., 2nd sess., 19 March, vol. 142, pt. H 2361. Washington, DC: Government Printing Office.

Billingsley, Andrew. 1968. *Black Families in White America*. New York: John Wiley & Sons, Inc.

Blank, Rebecca M. 1997. *It Takes a Nation: A New Agenda for Fighting Poverty*. Princeton, NJ: Princeton University Press.

Blankenship, Jane, and Jong Geun Kang. 1991. The 1984 Presidential and Vice Presidential Debates: The Printed Press and Construction by Metaphor. *Presidential Studies Quarterly* 21:307–19.

Blumberg, Rae. 1995. Gender, Microenterprise, Performance and Power: Case Studies from the Dominican Republic, Ecuador, Guatemala, and Swaziland. Pp. 194–226 in *Women in the Latin American Development Process*, edited by Christine E. Bose and Edna Acosta-Belén. Philadelphia, PA: Temple University Press.

Boisjoly, Johanne, Kathleen Mullan Harris, and Greg J. Duncan. 1998. Trends, Events, and Duration of Initial Welfare Spells. *Social Service Review* 72 (December):466–92.

Booth, Martin. 1996. *Opium: A History*. New York: St. Martin's Press.

Bourdieu, Pierre. 1981. Men and Machines. Pp. 304–18 in *Advances in Social Theory and Methodology*, edited by Karin Knorrr-Cetina and Aaron Cicourel. Boston, MA: Routledge and Kegan Paul.

Brecher, Edward. 1972. *Licit and Illicit Drugs*. Boston, MA: Little, Brown, and Co.

Brenner, Johanna. 2000. Organizing Around Welfare Reform: Activist Notes. Paper presented at the Work, Welfare and Politics Conference, 28–29 February, University of Oregon, Eugene, OR.

Briar, Scott. 1966. Welfare from Below: Recipients' Views of the Public Welfare System. *California Law Review* 54 (May):370–85.

Brookey, Robert Alan. 2001. Bio-rhetoric, Background Beliefs and the Biology of Homosexuality. *Argumentation and Advocacy* 37:171–83.

Brown, Michael K. 2003. Ghettos, Fiscal Federalism, and Welfare Reform. Pp. 47–73 in *Race and the Politics of Welfare Reform*, edited by Sanford F. Schram, Joe Soss, and Richard Fording. Ann Arbor: University of Michigan Press.

Brown, Rupert. 2000. Social Identity Theory: Past Achievements, Current Problems, and Future Challenges. *European Journal of Social Psychology* 30:745–78.

Browning, Sandra L., and Ligun Cao. 1992. The Impact of Race on Criminal Justice Ideology. *Justice Quarterly* 9:685–99.

Brush, Candida G. 1992. Research on Women Business Owners: Past Trends, a New Perspective and Future Directions. *Entrepreneurship Theory and Practice* 92:5–30.

Bryant, Ed. 1996. *Congressional Record. Immigration in the* National Interest Act of 1995. 104th Cong., 2nd sess., 20 March, vol. 142, pt. H 2475. Washington, DC: Government Printing Office.

Buel, Richard, Jr. 1980. *Dear Liberty: Connecticut's Mobilization for the Revolutionary War.* Middletown, CT: Wesleyan University Press.

Burkhauser, Richard V., Andrew J. Glenn, and David C. Wittenberg. 1997. The Disabled Worker Tax Credit. Pp. 47–65 in *Disability: Challenges for Social Insurance, Health Care Financing, and Labor Market Policy,* edited by Virginia P. Reno, Jerry L. Mashaw, and Bill Gradison. Washington, DC: National Academy of Social Insurance.

Burnett, Edmund C., ed. 1921. *Letters of Members of the Continental Congress,* vol. III. (July 5, 1776 to December 31, 1777). Washington, DC: Carnegie Institution of Washington.

———. 1941. *The Continental Congress.* New York: Macmillan Company.

Carlson, Eric T., Jeffrey L. Wollock, and Patricia S. Noel, eds. 1981. *Benjamin Rush's Lectures on the Mind.* Philadelphia, PA: American Philosophical Society.

Cather, Helen V. 1936. *A History of San Francisco's Chinatown.* San Francisco: R and E Research Associates.

Cavender, Gary. 1982. *Parole, a Critical Analysis.* Port Washington, NY: Kennikat Press.

Chambers, John Whiteclay II. 1987. *To Raise an Army: The Draft Comes to Modern America.* New York: Free Press.

Chambliss, William J. 1964. A Sociological Analysis of the Law of Vagrancy. *Social Problems* 12:67–77.

Chambliss, William J., and Robert Seidman. 1971. *Law, Order, and Power.* Reading, MA: Addison-Wesley.

Chiasson, Lloyd. 1991. Japanese-American Relocation During World War II: A Study of California Editorial Reactions. *Journalism Quarterly* 68 (1/2):263–68.

Christiano, Marilyn R. 1995. The *Community Reinvestment Act:* The Role of Community Groups in the Formulation and Implementation of a Public Policy. Ph.D. diss., University of Maryland-College Park. Abstract in *Dissertation Abstracts International* 56–08A:3287.

Chute, Marchette. 1969. *The First Liberty: A History of the Right to Vote in America, 1619–1850.* New York: Dutton.

Cincotta, Gale. 1977. *Community Credit Needs: Hearings before the Committee on Banking, Housing, and Urban Affairs.* 95th Cong., 1st sess. (23–25 March), S. 406. Washington, DC: Government Printing Office.

Clark, Ramsey. 1970. *Crime in America: Observations on its Nature, Causes, Prevention, and Control.* New York: Simon and Schuster.

Clark, Peggy, and Amy Kays. 1999. *Microenterprise and the Poor.* Washington, DC: Aspen Institute.

Clawson, Rosalee, and Rakuya Trice. 2000. Poverty As We Know It (Media Portrayals of the Poor). *Public Opinion Quarterly* 64 (1):35–64.

Cobb, Roger W., and Charles D. Elder. 1980. *Participation in American Politics: The Dynamics of Agenda Building.* Baltimore, MD: Johns Hopkins University Press.

Collins, Patricia Hill. 1990. *Black Feminist Thought: Knowledge, Consciousness, and the Politics of Empowerment.* Boston, MA: Unwin Hyman.

Congressional Quarterly Almanac. 1975. 94th Congress, 1st sess., vol. IV. Washington, DC: Congressional Quarterly Inc.

Congressional Quarterly Almanac. 1980. 96th Congress, 2nd sess., vol. V. Washington, DC: Congressional Quarterly Inc.

Congressional Quarterly Almanac. 1982. 97th Congress, 2nd sess., vol. V. Washington, DC: Congressional Quarterly Inc.

Congressional Quarterly Almanac. 1984. Major Crime Package Cleared by the House. 98th Congress, 2nd sess., vol. VI, 40:215–46.

Congressional Record. 1968. 90th Congress, 2nd sess., vol. 114, pts. 2–5. Washington, DC: Government Printing Office.

Congressional Record. 1984a. *Comprehensive Crime Control Act of 1984.* 98th Cong., 2nd sess., vol. 130, Title II of H.J. Res. 648, pp. 1–224.

Congressional Record. 1984b. H10094. 98th Cong., 2nd sess., vol. 130, pt. H.R. 10094.

Congressional Record. 1984c. S. 1762. 98th Cong., 2nd Sess., S.R. 1762, vol. 130, pt. S741–812.

Congressional Record. 1996. *Bill Tracking Report for H.R. 2202:* Immigration and the National Interest Act of 1995. 104th Cong., 2nd sess., Roll Call No. 76, 21 March, vol. 142, pt. H 2589. Washington, DC: Government Printing Office.

Conover, Pamela Johnston. 1988. The Role of Social Groups in Political Thinking. *British Journal of Political Science* 18:51–75.

Conrad, Peter, and Joseph W. Schneider. 1980. *Deviance and Medicalization.* St Louis, MO: C.V. Mosby.

Conyers, John. 1996. *Congressional Record.* Immigration in the National Interest Act of 1995. 104th Cong., 2nd sess., 20 March, vol. 142, pt. H 2475. Washington, DC: Government Printing Office.

Coombs, F. Alan. 1991. Congressional Opinion and War Relocation, 1943. Pp. 88–91 in *Japanese Americans: From Relocation to Redress,* edited by Roger Daniels, Sandra C. Taylor, and Harry H. L. Kitano, rev. ed. Seattle, WA: University of Washington Press.

Courtwright, David T. 2001. *Dark Paradise: A History of Opiate Addiction in America,* 2nd ed. Cambridge, MA: Harvard University Press.

Crawford, Alan. 1980. *Thunder on the Right: The "New Right" and the Politics of Resentment.* New York: Pantheon Books.

Crenson, Matthew. 1983. *Neighborhood Politics.* Cambridge, MA: Harvard University Press.

Cress, Lawrence Delbert. 1982. *Citizens in Arms: The Army and the Militia in American Society to the War of 1812.* Chapel Hill: University of North Carolina Press.

Cruikshank, Barbara. 1999. *The Will to Empower: Democratic Citizens and Other Subjects.* Ithaca, NY; London, UK: Cornell University Press.

Cunningham, Noble E., Jr. 1996. *The Presidency of James Monroe.* Lawrence: University Press of Kansas.

Dain, Norman. 1964. *Concepts of Insanity in the United States, 1789–1865.* New Brunswick, NJ: Rutgers University Press.

Daniels, Roger. 1977. *The Politics of Prejudice: The Anti-Japanese Movement in California and the Struggle for Japanese Exclusion.* Berkeley, CA: University of California Press.

Danziger, Sandra K., Ariel Kalil, and Nathaniel J. Anderson. 2000. Human Capital, Physical Health, and Mental Health of Welfare Recipients: Co-occurrences and Correlates. *Journal of Social Issues* 56 (4):635–54.

Danziger, Sheldon H., and Daniel H. Weinberg. 1994. The Historical Record: Trends in Family Income, Inequality, and Poverty. Pp. 18–50 in *Confronting Poverty Prescriptions for Change,* edited by Sheldon H. Danziger, Gary D. Sandefur, and Daniel H. Weinberg. Cambridge, MA: Harvard University Press.

Davies, Stanley Powell. 1959. *The Mentally Retarded in Society.* New York: Columbia University Press.

Deal, Nathan. 1996. *Congressional Record. Providing for Consideration of H.R. 2202,* Immigration in the National Interest Act of 1995. 104th Cong., 2nd sess., 19 March, vol. 142, pt. H 2361. Washington, DC: Government Printing Office.

de la Vina, Gus. 1997. *Congressional Record.* Subcommittee on Government Management, Information and Technology. *U.S. Border Patrol's Implementation of Operation Gatekeeper.* Y4.G74/7:B64/2. Washington, DC: Government Printing Office.

deLeon, Peter. 1997. *Democracy and the Policy Sciences.* Albany: State University of New York Press.

de Man, Paul. 1986. *Resistance to Theory.* Minneapolis: University of Minnesota Press.

Dean, John. 2001. *The Rehnquist Choice: The Untold Story of the Nixon Appointment that Redefined the Supreme Court.* New York: Free Press.

Desan, Christine A. 1998a. The Constitutional Commitment to Legislative Adjudication in the Early American Tradition. *Harvard Law Review* 111:1381–1503.

———. 1998b. Remaking Constitutional Tradition at the Margin of the Empire: The Creation of Legislative Adjudication in Colonial New York. *Law and History Review* 16:257–317.

Deutsch, Albert. 1949. *The Mentally Ill in America: A History of Their Care and Treatment from Colonial Times.* New York: Columbia University Press.

Dewey, Davis Rich. 1915. *Financial History of the United States,* 5th ed. New York: Longmans, Green, and Co.

DiMaggio, Paul J., and Walter W. Powell. 1983. The Iron Cage Revisited: Institutional Isomorphism and Collective Rationality in Organizational Fields. *American Sociological Review* 48:147–60.

DiMaggio, Paul J., and Walter W. Powell. 1991. Introduction. Pp. 1–38 in *The New Institutionalism in Organizational Analysis: A Biographical Perspective on Entrepreneurs in Government,* edited by Walter W. Powell and Paul J. DiMaggio. Baltimore, MD: Johns Hopkins University Press.

DiNitto, Diana. 1995. *Social Welfare: Politics and Public Policy,* 4th ed. Boston, MA: Allyn and Bacon.

Dobie, Charles C. 1936. *San Francisco's Chinatown.* New York: Appleton Century Co.

Doig, Jameson, and Erwin Hargrove. 1987. *Leadership and Innovation: A Biographical Perspective on Entrepreneurs in Government.* Baltimore: Johns Hopkins University Press.

Donovan, Mark C. 1994. Social Constructions of People with AIDS: Target Populations and United States Policy, 1981–1990. *Policy Studies Review* 12:3–29.

———. 2001. *Taking Aim: Target Populations and the Wars on AIDS and Drugs.* Washington, DC: Georgetown University Press.

Downs, Anthony. 1972. Up and Down with Ecology—The Issue Attention Cycle. *Public Interest* 28:38–50.

Dreier, David. 1996. *Congressional Record. Providing for Consideration of H.R. 2202,* Immigration in the National Interest Act of 1995. 104th Cong., 2nd sess., 19 March, vol. 142, pt. H 2361. Washington, DC: Government Printing Office.

Duncan, Greg J., and Saul Hoffman. 1995. The Effect of Incomes, Wages, and AFDC Benefits on Marital Disruption. *Journal of Human Resources* 30:19–42.

Duncan, Greg J., Kathleen Mullan Harris, and Johanne Boisjoly. 2000. Time Limits and Welfare Reform: New Estimates of the Number and Characteristics of Affected Families. *Social Service Review* 74 (March):55–75.

Durand, Jorge, Douglas S. Massey, and Emilio A. Parrado. 1999. The New Era of Mexican Migration to the United States. *The Journal of American History* 86 (2):518–36.

Eagly, Alice H., and Shelly Chaiken. 1993. *The Psychology of Attitudes.* Fort Worth, TX: Harcourt Brace Jovanovich College Pubs.

Easton, David 1965. *A Systems Analysis of Political Life.* New York: John Wiley and Sons.

Edelman, Murray J. 1964. *The Symbolic Uses of Politics.* Urbana: University of Illinois Press.

———. 1971. *Politics as Symbolic Action.* New York: Academic Press.

———. 1977. *Political Language: Words that Succeed and Policies that Fail.* New York: Academic Press.

———. 1988. *Constructing the Political Spectacle.* Chicago, IL: University of Chicago Press.

Edgcomb, Elaine, Joyce Klein, and Peggy Clark. 1996. *The Practice of Microenterprise in the U.S.: Strategies, Costs and Effectiveness.* Washington, DC: The Aspen Institute

Edin, Kathryn, and Laura Lein. 1997. *Making Ends Meet: How Single Mothers Survive Welfare and Low-wage Work.* New York: Russell Sage Foundation.

Edin, Kathryn, and Kathleen Mullan Harris. 1999. Getting Off and Staying Off: Racial Differences in the Work Route Off Welfare. Pp. 270–301 in *Latinas and African American Women at Work,* edited by Irene Browne. New York: Russell Sage Foundation

Ehlers, Tracy, and Karen Main. 1998. Women and the False Promise of Micro-enterprise. *Gender and Society* 12 (4):424–40.

Ehrenreich, Barbara. 2001. *Nickel-and-Dimed: On (Not) Getting By in America.* New York: Metropolitan Books.

Else, John, and Salome Raheim. 1992. AFDC Clients as Entrepreneurs: Self-employment Offers an Important Option. *Public Welfare* 50 (4):36–38.

Epstein, Lee. 1995. *Contemplating Courts.* Washington, DC: CQ Press.

Epstein, Lee, and Thomas G. Walker. 1996. *Constitutional Law for a Changing America: A Short Course.* Washington, DC: CQ Press.

———. 1998. *Constitutional Law for a Changing America: Rights, Liberties, and Justice.* Washington, DC: CQ Press.

Evans, M. Stanton, and Margaret Moore. 1968. *The Lawbreakers: America's Number One Domestic Problem.* New York: Arlington House.

Fainstein, Susan. 1987. The Rationale for Neighborhood Planning. *Policy Studies Journal* 16, (2):384–91.

Ferguson, E. James. 1961. *The Power of the Purse.* Chapel Hill: University of North Carolina Press.

Fisher, Robert. 1996. Neighborhood Organizing: The Importance of Historical Context. Pp. 39–49 in *Revitalizing Urban Neighborhoods,* edited by Dennis Keating, Norman Krumholz, and Philip Star. Lawrence: University of Kansas Press.

Fiske, John. 1987. *Television Culture.* New York: Routledge.

Fitzgerald, John, Peter Gottschalk, and Robert Moffitt. 1998. An Analysis of Sample Attrition in Panel Data. *Journal of Human Resources* 33:251–99.

Fitzpatrick, John C., ed. 1931–1944. *The Writings of George Washington,* vol. 26. Washington, DC: Government Printing Office.

Fix, Michael, and Jeffrey S. Passel. 1994. *Immigration and Immigrants: Setting the Record Straight.* Washington, DC: Urban Institute.

Ford, Worthington Chauncey, Gaillard Hunt, John C. Fitzpatrick, and Roscoe Hill, ed. 1904. *Journals of the Continental Congress, 1774–1789,* 34 vols. Washington, DC: Government Printing Office.

Fording, Richard C. 2003. "Laboratories of Democracy" or Symbolic Politics? The Political Origins of Welfare Reform. Pp. 1–29 in *Race, Welfare, and the Politics of Reform,* edited by Sanford F. Schram, Joe Soss, and Richard C. Fording. Ann Arbor: University of Michigan Press.

Foucault, Michel. 1973. *The Order of Things: An Archeology of Knowledge.* New York: Vintage.

Fowler, Tille K. 1996. *Congressional Record. Bill Tracking Report for H.R. 2202:* Immigration and the National Interest Act of 1995. 104th Cong., 2nd sess., 21 March, vol. 142, pt. H 2589. Washington, DC: Government Printing Office.

Fox, Richard W. 1978. *So Far Disordered in Mind: Insanity in California, 1870–1930.* Berkeley: University of California Press.

Frankenberg, Ruth. 1993. *White Women, Race Matters: The Social Construction of Whiteness.* Minneapolis: University of Minnesota Press.

Fraser, Nancy. 1987 Women, Welfare, and The Politics of Need Interpretation. *Hypatia* 2 (1):103–21.

Fraser, Nancy, and Linda Gordon. 1993. Contract versus Charity: Why Is There No Social Citizenship in the United States? *Socialist Review* 22 (3):45–68.

———. 1994. A Genealogy of Dependency: Tracing a Keyword of the U.S. Welfare State. *Signs: Journal of Women in Culture and Society* 19 (2):309–36.

Freedman, Estelle. 1996. *Maternal Justice: Miriam Van Waters and the Female Reform Tradition.* Chicago: University of Chicago Press.

Fullinwider, Robert K. 1988. Citizenship and Welfare. Pp. 261–79 in *Democracy and the Welfare State,* edited by Amy Gutmann. Princeton, NJ: Princeton University Press.

Gallup, George. 1950–1983. *Gallup Public Opinion Polls.* Wilmington, DE: Scholarly Resources.

Gamson, William A., David Croteau, William Hoynes, and Theodore Sasson. 1992. Media Images and the Social Construction of Reality. *Annual Review of Sociology* 18:373–93.

Ganske, Greg. 1996. *Congressional Record. Providing for Consideration of H.R. 2202,* Immigration in the National Interest Act of 1995. 104th Cong., 2nd sess., 19 March, vol. 142, pt. H 2361. Washington, DC: Government Printing Office.

Gaventa, John. 1980. *Power and Powerlessness: Quiescence and Rebellion in an Appalachian Valley.* Urbana: University of Illinois Press.

Gest, Ted. 2001. *Crime and Politics: Big Government's Erratic Campaign for Law and Order.* New York: Oxford University Press.

Giddens, Anthony. 1998. *The Third Way: The Renewal of Social Democracy.* Oxford, UK: Blackwell Publishing.

Giddings, Paula. 1984. *When and Where I Enter: The Impact of Black Women on Race and Sex in America.* New York: William Morrow.

Gilens, Martin. 1999. *Why Americans Hate Welfare: Race, Media, and the Politics of Antipoverty Policy.* Chicago: University of Chicago Press.

Gilroy, Paul. 2000. *Against Race: Imagining Political Culture Beyond the Color Line.* Cambridge, MA: The Belknap Press of Harvard University Press.

Glasson, William H. 1918. *Federal Military Pensions in the United States,* edited by David Kinley. New York: Oxford University Press.

Goetz, Ed. 1997. Sandtown–Winchester, Baltimore: Housing as Community Development. Pp. 187–209 in *Affordable Housing and Urban Redevelopment in the United States,* edited by Willem Van Vliet. Thousand Oaks, CA: Sage Publications.

Goffman, Erving. 1963. *The Presentation of Self in Everyday Life.* New York: Anchor Books.

Goldberg, David Theo. 2001. *The Racial State.* Oxford, UK: Blackwell Publishing.

Goodban, Nancy. 1985. The Psychological Impact of Being on Welfare. *Social Service Review* 59:403–22.

Goode, Erich, and Nachman Ben-Yehuda. 1994. *Moral Panic: The Social Construction of Deviance.* Oxford, UK: Blackwell Publishing.

Goodsell, Charles T. 1984. Welfare Waiting Rooms. *Urban Life* 12 (4):467–77.

Gordon, Diane. 1994. *The Return of the Dangerous Classes: Drug Prohibition and Policy Politics.* New York: Norton.

Gordon, Linda. 1988. *Heroes of Their Own Lives: The History and Politics of Family Violence.* New York: Viking.

——— . 1994. *Pitied But Not Entitled: Single Mothers and the History of Welfare.* New York: Free Press.

——— . 1995. *Pitied But Not Entitled,* paperback ed. Cambridge, MA: Harvard University Press.

Graber, Doris. 1980. *Crime News and the Public.* Westport, CT: Greenwood Press.

Graham, Hugh Davis. 1990. *The Civil Rights Era: Origins and Development of National Policy 1960–1972.* New York: Oxford University Press.

Grieco, Elizabeth M., and Rachel C. Cassidy. 2001. *Overview of Race and Hispanic Origin* [online]. Census 2000 Brief, C2KBR/01–1. (Washington, DC: U.S. Bureau of the Census [dated March 2001; cited 18 March 2003]). Available from http://www.census.gov/prod/2001pubs/c2kbr01–1.pdf.

Grob, Gerald N. 1994. *The Mad among Us: A History of the Care of America's Mentally Ill.* New York: The Free Press.

Grodzins, Morton. 1949. *Americans Betrayed: Politics and the Japanese Evacuation.* Chicago: The University of Chicago Press.

Gross, Bertram. 1983. Reagan's Criminal Anti-Crime Fix. Pp. 87–108 in *What Reagan Is Doing to Us,* edited by Alan Gartner, Colin Greer, and Frank Riessman. New York: Harper and Row Publishers.

Grzywinski, Ronald. 1977. *Community Credit Needs: Hearings before the Committee on Banking, Housing, and Urban Affairs.* 95th Cong., 1st sess. (23–25 March), S. 406. Washington, DC: Government Printing Office.

Gulli, Hege. 1998. *Microfinance and Poverty: Questioning the Conventional Wisdom.* Washington, DC: Inter-American Development Bank.

Gusfield, Joseph R. 1955. Social Structure of Moral Reform: A Study of the Women's Christian Temperance Union. *American Journal of Sociology* 61:221–32.

Hajer, Maarten A. 1995. *The Politics of Environmental Discourse: Ecological Modernization and the Policy Process,* Chapter 2. New York : Oxford University Press.

Handler, Joel F. 1992. Discretion: Power, Quiescence, and Trust. Pp. 331–60 in *The Uses of Discretion,* edited by Keith Hawkins. Oxford, UK: Clarendon Press.

Handler, Joel F., and Yeheskel Hasenfeld. 1991. *The Moral Construction of Poverty: Welfare Reform in America.* Newbury Park, CA: Sage Publications.

Haney López, Ian F. 1995. White by Law. Pp. 542–50 in *Critical Race Theory: The Cutting Edge,* edited by Richard Delgado. Philadelphia, PA: Temple University Press.

Harding, D. W. 1937. General Conceptions in the Study of the Press and Public Opinion. *Sociological Review* 29:370–390.

Harrison, John, and Harry Stein. 1973. *Muckraking: Past, Present, and Future.* University Park: Pennsylvania State University Press.

Hartmann, Edward G. 1948. *The Movement to Americanize the Immigrant.* New York: Columbus University Press.

Hasenfeld, Yeheskel. 1992. The Nature of Human Service Organizations. Pp. 3–23 in *Human Service as Complex Organizations,* edited by Yeheskel Hasenfeld. Newbury Park, CA: Sage Publications.

Head Start Bureau. 1992. *Head Start Program Performance Standards.* 45–CFR 1304. Washington, DC: U.S. Department of Health and Human Services.

Higginson, Stephen A. 1986. A Short History of the Right to Petition Government for the Redress of Grievances. *Yale Law Journal* 96:142–66.

Hilgartner, Stephen, and Charles Bosk. 1988. The Rise and Fall of Social Problems: A Public Arenas Model. *American Journal of Sociology* 94 (1):53–78.

Hills, Stuart L. 1980. *Demystifying Social Deviance.* New York: McGraw Hill.

Hochschild, Jennifer L. 1995. *Facing up to the American Dream: Race, Class, and the Soul of the Nation.* Princeton, NJ: Princeton University Press.

Hoffman, Saul D., and Greg J. Duncan. 1991. Teenage Underclass Behavior and Subsequent Poverty: Have the Rules Changed? Pp. 155–74 in *The Urban Underclass,* edited by Christopher Jencks and Paul E. Peterson. Washington, DC: The Brookings Institution.

Holstein, James, and Gale Miller. 1996. *Dispute Domains and Welfare Claims: Conflict and Law in Public Bureaucracies.* Greenwich, CT: JAI Press.

Holzner, Burkhart. 1968. *Reality Construction in Society.* Cambridge, MA: Schenkman Publishing Company.

Horn, Stephen. 1997. *Congressional Record.* Subcommittee on Government Management, Information and Technology. *U.S. Border Patrol's Implementation of Operation Gatekeeper.* Y4.G74/7:B64/2. Washington, DC: Government Printing Office.

Howells, Louise A. 2000. The Dimensions of Microenterprise: A Critical Look at Microenterprise as a Tool to Alleviate Poverty. *Journal of Affordable Housing and Community Development* 9:161–82.

Hunter, Duncan. 1997. *Field Hearing on Public Benefits, Employment and Immigration Reform.* 22 February 1996. Washington, DC: Government Printing Office.

Hutchinson, William T., and William M. E. Rachal, ed. 1962. *The Papers of James Madison.* Chicago, IL: University of Chicago Press.

Ignatiev, Noel. 1995. *How the Irish Became White.* New York: Routledge.

Ingram, Helen, and Anne L. Schneider. 1990. Improving Implementation through Framing Smarter Statutes. *Journal of Public Policy* 10 (1):66–87.

———. 1991. The Choice of Target Populations. *Administration and Society* 23 (3):333–56.

———. 1993. Constructing Citizenship: The Subtle Messages of Policy Design. Pp. 68–93 in *Public Policy for Democracy,* edited by Helen Ingram and Steven R. Smith. Washington, DC: Brookings Institution Press.

Ingram, Helen, and Steven R. Smith. 1993. *Public Policy for Democracy.* Washington, DC: Brookings Institution Press.

Irons, Peter. 1989. *Justice Delayed: The Record of the Japanese American Internment Cases.* Middletown, CT: Wesleyan University Press.

Janowitz, Morris. 1978. *The Last Half Century.* Chicago: University of Chicago Press.

Jencks, Christopher. 1965. The Moynihan Report. *New York Review of Books,* 14 October.

Jensen, Laura S. 1996. The Early American Origins of Entitlements. *Studies in American Political Development* 10:360–404.

———. 2003. *Patriots, Settlers, and the Origins of American Social Policy.* Cambridge, UK: Cambridge University Press.

Jimenez, Mary Ann. 1987. *Changing Faces of Madness: Early American Attitudes and Treatment of the Insane.* Hanover, NH: University Press of New England.

Joankin, Jon, and Laura Enriquez. 1999. The Nontraditional Financial Sector in Nicaragua: A Response to Rural Credit Market Exclusion. *Development Policy Review* 17:141–69.

Johnson, Lyndon B. 1965. *To Fulfill These Rights: Remarks of The President at Howard University, June 4.* Washington, DC: Government Printing Office.

Johnson, Richard. 1817–18. *Annals of the Congress of the United States, 1817–1818.* Washington, DC: Privately published.

Joint Center for Housing Studies. 2002. *The 25th Anniversary of the* Community Reinvestment Act*: Access to Capital in an Evolving Financial Services System* [online]. Prepared for the Ford Foundation. (Cambridge, MA: Joint Center for Housing Studies [updated March 2002; cited 18 March 2003]). Available from http://www.jchs.harvard.edu/publications/govprograms/cra02–1.pdf.

Jurik, Nancy C. 1998. Getting by and Getting away: The Experiences of Men and Women Home Based Workers. *Work and Occupations* 25:7–35.

Jurik, Nancy C., and Julie Cowgill. 1998. Women and Microenterprise: Empowerment or Hegemony? Welfare and Microenterprise. Pp. 321–24 in *Women's Progress, Perspectives on the Past, Blueprint for the Future.* Proceedings from the 5th Women's Policy Research Conference. Washington, DC: Institute for Women's Policy Research.

Kane, H. 1881. *Drugs that Enslave: The Opium, Morphine, Chloral, and Hashish Habits.* Philadelphia, PA: Presely Blakiston.

Kaplan, Sidney. 1951. Pay, Pension, and Power: Economic Grievances of the Massachusetts Officers of the Revolution. *Boston Public Library Quarterly* 3:27–29.

———. 1952. Veteran Officers and Politics in Massachusetts, 1783–1787. *William and Mary Quarterly,* 3rd. ser. 9:34–41.

Katz, Michael B. 1986. *In the Shadow of the Poorhouse: A Social History of Welfare in America.* New York: Basic Books.

———. 1989. *The Undeserving Poor: From the War on Poverty to the War on Welfare.* New York: Pantheon.

———. 1995. *Improving Poor People: The Welfare State, the "Underclass," and Urban Schools as History.* Princeton, NJ: Princeton University Press.

———. 2001. *The Price of Citizenship: Redefining the American Welfare State.* New York: Metropolitan Books.

Kerber, Linda K. 1980. *Women of the Republic: Intellect and Ideology in Revolutionary America.* Chapel Hill: University of North Carolina Press.

———. 1990. May All Our Citizens Be Soldiers and All Our Soldiers Citizens: The Ambiguities of Female Citizenship in the New Nation. Pp. 89–103 in *Women, Militarism, and War: Essays in History, Politics, and Social Theory,* edited by Jean Bethke Elshtain and Sheila Tobias. Savage, MD: Rowman & Littlefield.

Kerber, Linda K., and Jane Sherron De Hart, eds. 1991. *Women's America: Refocusing the Past,* 3rd ed. New York: Oxford University Press.

Kerber, Linda K., Alice Kessler-Harris, and Katherine Sklar, eds. 1995. *U.S. History as Women's History: New Feminist Essays.* Chapel Hill: University of North Carolina Press.

Keyssar, Alexander. 2000. *The Right to Vote: The Contested History of Democracy in the United States.* New York: Basic Books.

Khademian, Anne M. 1996. *Checking on Banks: Autonomy and Accountability in Three Federal Agencies.* Washington, DC: Brookings Institution Press.

Kim, Claire Jean. 1999. The Racial Triangulation of Asian Americans. *Politics and Society* 27 (1):105–38.

Kingdon, John. 1984. *Agendas, Alternatives, and Public Policies.* Boston: Little, Brown.

———. 1995. *Agendas, Alternatives, and Public Policies,* 2nd ed. New York: Harper Collins.

Kitano, Harry H. L. 1969. *Japanese Americans: The Evolution of a Subculture.* Englewood Cliffs, NJ: Prentice-Hall Inc.

————. 1986. The Effects of Evacuation on the Japanese Americans. Pp. 151–59 in *Japanese Americans, from Relocation to Redress,* edited by Roger Daniels, Sandra C. Taylor, and Harry H. L. Kitano. Salt Lake City: University of Utah Press.

Kohn, Richard H. 1975. *Eagle and Sword: The Federalists and the Creation of the Military Establishment in America, 1783–1802.* New York: Free Press.

Ladner, Joyce, ed. 1973. *The Death of White Sociology.* New York: Random House.

Landy, Mark. 1993. Public Policy and Citizenship. Pp. 19–44 in *Public Policy for Democracy,* edited by Helen Ingram and Steven R. Smith. Washington, DC: Brookings Institution Press.

Langer, Jennifer A., Jackie A. Orwick, and Amy J. Kays (ed). 1999. *1999 Directory of U.S. Microenterprise Programs.* Washington, DC: The Aspen Institute.

Laswell, Harold. 1936. *Who Gets What, When, and How?* New York: McGraw Hill.

Latham, Tom. 1997. *Congressional Record.* Subcommittee on Government Management, Information and Technology. *U.S. Border Patrol's Implementation of Operation Gatekeeper.* Y4.G74/7:B64/2. Washington, DC: Government Printing Office.

Lawless, Jennifer, and Richard Fox. 2001. Political Participation and the Urban Poor. *Social Problems* 48 (3):341–61.

Le Pore, Herbert P. 1994. Prelude to Prejudice: Hiram Johnson, Woodrow Wilson, and the California Alien Land Law Controversy of 1913. Pp. 265–76 in *Japanese Immigrants and American Law: The Alien Land Laws and Other Issues,* edited by Charles McClain. New York: Garland Publishing, Inc. First published in *Southern California Quarterly* 61 (1979):99–110.

Lee, Bill Lann. 1999. An Issue of Public Importance: The Justice Department's Enforcement of the *Fair Housing Act. Cityscape* 4 (3):35–56.

Lemann, Nicholas. 1991. *The Promised Land: The Great Black Migration and How It Changed America.* New York: Knopf.

Leonard, Kevin Allen. 1990. "Is That What We Fought For?" Japanese Americans and Racism in California, the Impact of World War II. *The Western Historical Quarterly* 21 (4):463–82.

Levin-Epstein, Jodie. 1998. *The IRA: Individual Responsibility Agreements and TANF Family Life Obligations.* Washington, DC: Center for Law and Social Policy.

Lieberman, Robert C., Anne L. Schneider, and Helen Ingram. 1995. Social Construction (Continued). *American Political Science Review* 89 (2):437–46.

Light, Ivan. 1998. Microcredit & Informal Credit in the USA: Introduction. *Journal of Developmental Entrepreneurship* 3:1–4.

Light, Ivan, and Michelle Pham. 1998. Beyond Creditworthy: Microcredit and Informal Credit in the United States. *Journal of Developmental Entrepreneurship* 3:35–51.

Liou, Y. Thomas, and Robert Stroh. 1998. Community Development Intermediary Systems in the United States: Origins, Evolution, and Functions. *Housing Policy Debate* 9 (3):575–94.

Lipsitz, George. 1995. The Possessive Investment in Whiteness: Racialized Social Democracy and the "White" Problem in American Studies. *American Quarterly* 47:369–87.

Lipsky, Michael. 1980. *Street-level Bureaucracy: Dilemmas of the Individual in Public Services.* New York: Russell Sage Foundation.

Locke, John. 1962. An Essay Concerning the True Original, Extent and End of Civil Government: Second Treatise on Civil Government. Pp. 3–143 in *Social Contract: Essays by Locke, Hume, and Rousseau,* edited by Sir Ernest Barker. London, UK: Oxford University Press.

Loury, Glenn. 2002. *The Anatomy of Racial Inequality.* Cambridge, MA: Harvard University Press.

Lower-Basch, Elizabeth. 2000. *"Leavers" and Diversion Studies: Preliminary Analysis of Racial Differences in Caseload Trends and Leaver Outcomes* [online]. (Washington, DC: U.S. Department of Health and Human Services [updated December 2000; cited 18 March 2003]). Available from http://www.aspe.hhs.gov/hsp/leavers99/race.htm.

Lowi, Theodore J. 1964. American Business, Public Policy, Case Studies, and Political Theory. *World Politics* 16 (4):677–715.

Lowney, Kathleen S., and Joel Best. 1995. Stalking Strangers and Lovers: Changing the Media Typifications of a New Crime Problem. Pp. 33–57 in *Images of Issues: Typifying Contemporary Social Problems,* edited by Joel Best. New York: Aldine De Gruyter.

Lubiano, Wahneema. 1992. Black Ladies, Welfare Queens, and State Minstrels: Ideological War by Narrative Means. Pp. 323–63 in *Race-ing Justice, En-gendering Power: Essays on Anita Hill, Clarence Thomas, and the Construction of Social Reality,* edited by Toni Morrison. New York: Pantheon Books.

MacGillis, Donald. 1983. *Crime in America: The ABC Report.* Radnor, PA: Chilton Book Company.

MacLeod, Laurie, Darrel Montero, and Alan Speer. 1999. America's Changing Attitudes toward Welfare and Welfare Recipients, 1938–1995. *Journal of Sociology and Social Welfare* XXVL:175–86.

Maier, Pauline 1997. *American Scripture: Making the Declaration of Independence.* New York: Alfred A. Knopf.

March, James G., and Johan P. Olsen. 1989. *Rediscovering Institutions.* New York: The Free Press.

Mark, Gregory A. 1998. The Vestigial Constitution: The History and Significance of the Right to Petition. *Fordham Law Review* 66:2153–2231.

Marshall, Thomas H. 1964 [1949]. Citizenship and Social Class. Pp. 71–135 in *Class, Citizenship, and Social Development: Essays by T. H. Marshall,* edited by Seymour Martin Lipset. Chicago, IL: University of Chicago Press.

———. 1964. *Class Citizenship and Social Development.* Garden City, NY: Doubleday.

Marston, Sallie A. 1993. Citizen Action Programs and Participatory Politics in Tucson. Pp. 119–135 in *Public Policy for Democracy,* edited by Helen Ingram and Steven R. Smith. Washington, DC: Brookings Institution.

Martinez, Oscar J. 1994. *Border People: Life and Society in the U.S.-Mexico Borderlands.* Tucson: The University of Arizona Press.

Mashaw, Jerry L. 1997. Findings of the Disability Policy Panel. Pp. 17–27 in *Disability: Challenges for Social Insurance, Health Care Financing, and Labor Market Policy,* edited by Virginia P. Reno, Jerry L. Mashaw, and Bill Gradison. Washington, DC: National Academy of Social Insurance.

Mather, Lynn. 1995. The Fired Football Coach (Or, How Trial Courts Make Policy). Pp. 170–202 in *Contemplating Courts,* edited by Lee Epstein. Washington, DC: CQ Press.

Matthews, Jean V. 1991. *Toward a New Society: American Thought and Culture, 1800–1830.* Boston, MA: Twayne Publishers.

Mazmanian, Daniel, and Paul Sabatier. 1983. Policy Implementation. Pp. 143–169 in *Encyclopedia of Policy Studies,* edited by Stuart S. Nagel. New York: Marcel Dekker.

McAdam, Doug. 1982. *Political Process and the Development of Black Insurgency, 1930–1970.* Chicago, IL: University of Chicago Press.

McClatchy, Valentine S. 1978. THE GERMANY OF ASIA: Japan's Policy in the Far East; Her "Peaceful Penetration" of the United States; How American Commercial and National Interests Are Affected, Sacramento, California, April, 1919. Pp. 1–46 in *Four Anti-Japanese Pamphlets: An Original Anthology,* edited by Valentine S. McClatchy. New York: Arno Press.

McDougall, Harold. 1993. *Black Baltimore: A New Theory of Community.* Philadelphia, PA: Temple University Press.

McGovern, Constance M. 1985. *Masters of Madness: Social Origins of the American Psychiatric Profession.* Hanover, NH: University Press of New England.

Mead, Lawrence M., ed. 1997a. *The New Paternalism: Supervisory Approaches to Poverty.* Washington, DC: Brookings Institution Press.

———. 1997b. Citizenship and Social Policy: T. H. Marshall and Poverty. *Social Philosophy and Policy* 14 (2):197–230.

———. 1998. Telling the Poor What to Do. *The Public Interest* 132 (summer):97–112.

Meier, Kenneth. 1994. *The Politics of Sin: Drugs, Alcohol, and Public Policy.* London: M.E. Sharpe.

Mendelberg, Tali. 1997. Executing Hortons: Racial Crime in the 1988 Presidential Campaign. *Public Opinion Quarterly* 61 (1):134–58.

Meriwether, Robert L., and W. Edwin Hemphill et al., eds. 1959. *The Papers of John C. Calhoun.* Columbia: University of South Carolina Press.

Mettler, Suzanne. 1998. *Dividing Citizens: Gender and Federalism in New Deal Public Policy.* Ithaca, NY: Cornell University Press.

———. 2002a. Bringing the State Back into Civic Engagement: Policy Feedback Effects of the G.I. Bill for World War II Veterans. *American Political Science Review* 96 (2):351–66.

———. 2002b. Citizen Soldiers in Civic Life: Effects of Public Policy for Veterans on Participation in Social Movements and Conventional Politics. Paper presented at the Conference on Social Movements, Public Policy and Democracy, 11–13 January, Laguna Beach, CA.

Meyer, David S. 2002. Social Movements and Public Policy: Eggs, Chicken, and Theory. Presented at the Social Movements, Public Policy, and Democracy Conference, 11–13 January, Irvine, CA.

Microcredit Summit. 1997. *The Microcredit Summit Report* [online]. (Washington, DC: RESULTS Educational Fund [no date; cited 18 March 2003].) Available from www.microcreditsummit.org.

Miller, Gale. 1989. Defining Proper Work Performance: Complaint-making and Negotiation in a Work Incentive Program. *Journal of Contemporary Ethnography* 18:30–49.

Mink, Gwendolyn. 1990. The Lady and the Tramp: Gender, Race, and the Origins of the American Welfare State. Pp. 92–122 in *Women, the State, and Welfare,* ed Linda Gordon. Madison: University of Wisconsin Press

Mintrom, Michael. 2000. *Policy Entrepreneurs and School Choice.* Washington, DC: Georgetown University Press.

Mitchell, W. J. Thomas. 1994. *Picture Theory: Essays on Verbal and Visual Representation.* Chicago, IL: The University of Chicago Press.

Moffitt, Robert. 1992. Incentive Effects in the U.S. Welfare System: A Review. *Journal of Economic Literature* 30 (1):1–61

Mollenkopf, John H. 1983. *The Contested City.* Princeton, NJ: Princeton University Press.

Monroe, Kristen Renwick, James Hanking, and Renee Bukovchik Van Vechten. 2000. The Psychology Foundations of Identity Politics. *Annual Review of Politics* 3:419–47.

Morgan, H. Wayne. 1981. *Drugs in America: A Social History, 1800–1980.* Syracuse, NY: Syracuse University Press.

Morris, Lydia. 1994. *Dangerous Classes: The Underclass and Social Citizenship.* New York: Routledge.

Moynihan, Daniel Patrick. 1965. *The Negro Family: The Case for National Action.* Washington, DC: U.S. Department of Labor, Office of Policy Planning and Research.

———. 1968. *The Politics of a Guaranteed Income: The Nixon Administration and the Family Assistance Plan.* New York: Random House.

———. 1985. We Can't Avoid Family Policy Much Longer. Interview. *Challenge* (September–October):11.

Mucciaroni, Gary. 1995. *Reversal of Fortune: Public Policy and Private Interests.* Washington, DC: Brookings Institution Press.

Musto, David. 1999. *The American Disease: Origins of Narcotics Control,* 3rd ed. New York; Oxford, UK: Oxford University Press.

Myer, Dillon S. 1971. *Uprooted Americans: The Japanese Americans and the War Relocation Authority During World War II.* Tucson: The University of Arizona Press.

Nader, Ralph. 1977. *Community Credit Needs: Hearings before the Committee on Banking, Housing, and Urban Affairs.* 95th Cong., 1st sess. (23–25 March), S. 406. Washington, DC: Government Printing Office.

Naples, Nancy, A. 1997. The "New Consensus" on the Gendered Social Contract: The 1987–1988 U.S. Congressional Hearings on Welfare Reform. *Signs* 22:907–45.

Nash, Gary, and Richard Weiss. 1970. *The Great Fear: Race in the Mind of America.* New York: Holt, Rinehart, and Winston.

Nebraska State Historical Society. 1871. *Official Report of the Debates and Proceedings in the Nebraska Constitutional Convention,* vol. 3. Omaha: Author.

Nelson, Barbara J. 1990. The Origins of the Two-channel Welfare State: Workmen's Compensation and Mothers' Aid. Pp. 123–51 in *Women, the State and Welfare,* edited by Linda Gordon. Madison: University of Wisconsin Press.

Neubeck, Kenneth J., and Noel A. Cazenave. 2001. *Welfare Racism: Playing the Race Card against America's Poor.* New York: Routledge.

The New York Times Index for the Published News. 1889–1909. New York: R.R. Bower Co.

Niemi, Richard G., and Mary A. Hepburn. 1995. The Rebirth of Political Socialization. *Perspectives on Political Science* 24 (1):7–16.

Oakes, Penelope. 1996. The Categorization Process: Cognition and the Group in the Social Psychology of Stereotyping. Pp. 95–119 in *Social Groups and Identities: Developing the Legacy of Henri Tajfel,* edited by W. Peter Robinson. Boston, MA: Butterworth-Heinemann.

O'Connor, Alice. 2001. *Poverty Knowledge: Social Science, Social Policy, and the Poor in Twentieth-century U.S. History.* Princeton, NJ: Princeton University Press.

Odem, Mary E. 1995. *Delinquent Daughters: Protecting and Policing Adolescent Female Sexuality in the United States, 1885–1920.* Chapel Hill: University of North Carolina Press.

Ogawa, Dennis M. 1971. *From Japs to Japanese: An Evolution of Japanese-American Stereotypes.* Berkeley, CA: McCutchan Publishing Corporation.

Okamura, Raymond Y. 1982. The American Concentration Camps: A Cover-up through Euphemistic Terminology. *Journal of Ethnic Studies* 10 (3):95–115.

Olson, Alison G. 1992. Eighteenth-century Colonial Legislatures and Their Constituents. *Journal of American History* 79:554–59.

Omi, Michael. 1987. *We Shall Overturn: Race and the Contemporary American Right.* Unpublished Ph.D. diss., University of California, Santa Cruz.

Omi, Michael, and Howard Winant. 1994. *Racial Formation in the United States from the 1960s to the 1990s.* New York: Routledge.

Pate, Kim. 2000. The State TANF-Microenterprise Initiative. *AEO Exchange* (Association for Enterprise Opportunity Newsletter), November/December, 1.

Pateman, Carol. 1970. *Participation and Democratic Theory.* Cambridge, UK: Cambridge University Press.

Perdue, Charles W., John F. Dovidio, Michael B. Gurtman, and R. B. Tyler. 1990. Us and Them: Social Categorization and the Process of Intergroup Bias. *Journal of Personality and Social Psychology* 59:475–86.

Pierson, Paul. 1993. When Effect Becomes Cause: Policy Feedback and Political Change. *World Politics* 45:595–628.

———. 2000a. Increasing Returns, Path Dependence, and the Study of Politics. *American Political Science Review* 94:251–67.

———. 2000b. Not Just What, but When: Timing and Sequence in Political Processes. *Studies in American Political Development* 14 (Spring):72–92.

Piven, Frances Fox, and Richard A. Cloward. 1982. *The New Class War: Reagan's Attack on the Welfare State and Its Consequences.* New York: Pantheon Books.

———. 1993 [1971]. *Regulating the Poor: The Functions of Public Welfare.* New York: Vintage Books.

———. 1997. *The Breaking of the American Social Compact.* New York: The New Press.

———. 2000. *Why Americans Still Don't Vote: And Why Politicians Want It That Way.* Boston, MA: Houghton Mifflin.

Porter, Kirk H. 1918. *A History of Suffrage in the United States.* Chicago, IL: University of Chicago Press.

Posner, Paul. 2002. Accountability Challenges of Third Party Government. Pp. 523–28 in *The Tools of Government: A Guide to New Governance,* edited by Lester Solomon. Oxford, UK: Oxford University Press.

President's Commission on Law Enforcement and the Administration of Justice. 1967. *The Challenge of Crime in a Free Society.* Washington, DC: U.S. Government Printing Office.

Pressman, Jeffrey L., and Aaron Wildavsky. 1973. *Implementation: How Great Expectations in Washington are Dashed in Oakland.* Berkeley: University of California Press.

Putnam, Robert D. 2000. *Bowling Alone: The Collapse and Revival of American Community.* New York: Simon & Schuster.

Quadagno, Jill. 1999. Creating a Capital Investment Welfare State: The New American Exceptionalism. *American Sociological Review* 64:1–11.

Quadagno, Jill, and Catherine Fobes. 1995. The Welfare State and the Cultural Reproduction of Gender: Making Good Boys and Girls in the Job Corps. *Social Problems* 42:171–90.

Rainwater, Lee, and William L. Yancey. 1967. *The Moynihan Report and the Politics of Controversy.* Cambridge, MA: MIT Press.

Rank, Mark R. 1994. *Living on the Edge: The Realities of Welfare in America.* New York: Columbia University Press.

Raphael, Jody. 2000. *Saving Bernice: Battered Women, Welfare, and Poverty.* Boston, MA: Northeastern University Press.

Ray, Isaac. 1838. *A Treatise on the Medical Jurisprudence of Insanity.* Boston, MA: Charles C. Little and James Brown.

Readers' Guide to Periodic Literature. 1890–1909. Minneapolis, MN: H.W. Wilson.

Reagan, Ronald. 1983. *State of the Union Address* [online]. (Washington, DC: ThisNation.com [updated 25 January 1983; cited 18 March 2003]). Available from http://www.thisnation.com/library/sotu/1983rr.html.

————. 1985. Remarks at the Annual Conference of the National Sheriff's Association in Hartford, CT [online]. P. 886 in *Public Papers of the President of the United States, 1984.* (Washington, DC: U.S. Government Printing Office [updated 20 June 1984; cited 18 March 2003.]) Available from http://www.reagan.utexas.edu/resource/speeches/1984/62084c.htm.

Reed, Adolph, Jr. 1999. *Stirrings in the Jug: Black Politics in the Post-segregation Era.* Minneapolis: University of Minnesota.

Reinarman, Craig, and Harry G. Levine. 1995. The Crack Attack: Politics and Media in America's Latest Drug Scare. Pp. 147–96 in *Images of Issues: Typifying Contemporary Social Problems,* edited by Joel Best. New York: Aldine De Gruyter.

Resch, John. 2000. *Suffering Soldiers: Revolutionary War Veterans, Moral Sentiment, and Political Culture in the Early Republic.* Amherst: University of Massachusetts Press.

Rieder, Jonathan. 1989. The Rise of the Silent Majority. Pp. 242–67 in *The Rise and Fall of the New Deal Order, 1930–1980,* edited by Steve Fraser and Gary Gerstle. Princeton, NJ: Princeton University Press.

Richardson, Bill. 1996. *Congressional Record.* Immigration in the National Interest Act of 1995. 104th Cong., 2nd sess., 20 March, vol. 142, pt. H 2475. Washington, DC: Government Printing Office.

Riis, Jacob. 1970. *How the Other Half Lives: Studies Among the Tenements of New York.* Cambridge, MA: Belknap Press of Harvard University Press. [Reprint of the 1890 ed.]

Riker, William. 1986. *The Art of Political Manipulation.* New Haven, CT: Yale University Press.

Rodriguez, Nestor P. 1997. The Social Construction of the U.S.-Mexico Border. Pp. 223–43 in *Immigrants Out! The New Nativism in the Late Twentieth Century,* edited by Juan Parea. New York: New York University Press.

Roe, Emery. 1994. *Narrative Policy Analysis: Theory and Practice.* Durham, NC: Duke University Press.

Roediger, David R. 1991. *The Wages of Whiteness: Race and the Making of the American Working Class.* New York: Verso Press.

Rogers-Dillon, Robin. 1995. The Dynamics of Welfare Stigma. *Qualitative Sociology* 18:437–56.

Rogin, Michael. 1996. *Blackface, White Noise: Jewish Immigrants in the Hollywood Melting Pot.* Berkeley: University of California Press.

Rohrabacher, Dana. 1997. *Congressional Record.* Subcommittee on Government Management, Information and Technology. *U.S. Border Patrol's Implementation of Operation Gatekeeper.* Y4.G74/7:B64/2. Washington, DC: Government Printing Office.

Ros-Lehitinen, Ileana. 1996. *Congressional Record. Immigration in the* National Interest Act of 1995. 104th Cong., 2nd sess., 20 March, vol. 142, pt. H 2475. Washington, DC: Government Printing Office.

Rosenstone, Steven J., and John Mark Hansen. 1993. *Mobilization, Participation, and Democracy in America.* New York: Macmillan.

Rostow, Eugene V. 1945. Our Worst Wartime Mistake. *Harper's Magazine* 191 (1144):193–201.

Roybal-Allard, Lucille. 1996. *Congressional Record. Immigration in the* National Interest Act of 1995. 104th Cong., 2nd sess., 20 March, vol. 142, pt. H 2475. Washington, DC: Government Printing Office.

Royster, Charles 1979. *A Revolutionary People at War: The Continental Army and American Character, 1775–1783.* Chapel Hill: University of North Carolina Press.

Rubin, Herbert J., and Irene S. Rubin. 1995. *Qualitative Interviewing: The Art of Hearing Data.* Thousand Oaks, CA: Sage Publications.

Rush, Benjamin. 1830. *Medical Inquiries and Observations upon the Diseases of the Mind,* 4th ed. Philadelphia, PA: John Grigg.

Ryan, William. 1971. *Blaming the Victim.* New York: Random House.

Sabatier, Paul, and Hank Jenkins-Smith. 1993. *Policy Change and Learning: An Advocacy Coalition Approach.* Boulder, CO: Westview Press.

Santiago, Senator Nellie R., Thomas T. Holyoke, and Ross D. Levi. 1998. Turning David and Goliath into the Odd Couple: How the New *Community Reinvestment Act* Promotes Community Development Financial Institutions. *Journal of Law & Policy* 6:571–651.

Sapiro, Virginia. 1993. "Private" Coercion and Democratic Theory: The Case of Gender-based Violence. Pp. 432–445 in *Reconsidering the Democratic Public,* edited by George Marcus and Russell Hansen. University Park: Pennsylvania State University.

———. 1994. Political Socialization During Adulthood: Clarifying the Political Time of Our Lives. *Research in Micropolitics* 4:197–223.

Sarat, Austin. 1990. ". . . The Law Is All Over": Power, Resistance and the Legal Consciousness of the Welfare Poor. *Yale Journal of Law and the Humanities* 2:343–79.

Scheingold, Stuart. 1991. *The Politics of Street Crime: Criminal Process and Cultural Obsession.* Philadelphia, PA: Temple University Press.

Schlozman, Kay Lehman, and Sidney Verba. 1979. *Injury to Insult: Unemployment, Class, and Political Response.* Cambridge, MA: Harvard University Press.

Schneider, Anne, and Helen Ingram. 1993. The Social Construction of Target Populations: Implications for Politics and Policy. *American Political Science Review* 87 (2):334–47.

———. 1997. *Policy Design for Democracy.* Lawrence: University Press of Kansas.

———. 1999. What Is "Good" Public Policy. Pp. 11–38 in *Current Public Policy Issues,* edited by Rosalyn Y. Carter and Khi V. Thai. Philadelphia, PA: PrAcademics Press.

Schneider, Mark, and Paul Teske. 1992. Toward a Theory of the Political Entrepreneur: Evidence From Local Government. *American Political Science Review* 86:737–47.

Schrager, Laura, and James Short, Jr. 1980. How Serious a Crime? Perceptions of Organizational and Common Crimes. Pp. 14–31 in *White Collar Crime: Theory and Research,* edited by Gilbert Gees and Ezra Scotland. London, UK: Sage Publications.

Schram, Sanford F. 1993. Postmodern Policy Analysis: Discourse and Identity in Welfare Policy. *Policy Sciences* 26:249–70.

———. 1995. *Words of Welfare: The Poverty of Social Science and the Social Science of Poverty.* Minneapolis: University of Minnesota Press.

———. 2000. *After Welfare: The Culture of Postindustrial Social Policy.* New York: New York University Press.

Schreiner, Mark. 1999. Self-employment, Microenterprise and the Poorest of the Poor in the U.S. Unpublished manuscript. Washington University, St. Louis, Missouri.

Schriek, Bertram J. O. 1936. *Alien Americans: A Study of Race Relations.* New York: Viking Press.

Schriner, Kay, and Lisa Ochs. 2000. *"No Right Is More Precious": Voting Rights for Persons with Developmental Disabilities.* Policy Research Brief. Minneapolis: University of Minnesota, Institute on Community Integration.

———. 2001. Creating the Disabled Citizen: How Massachusetts Disenfranchised People under Guardianship. *Ohio State Law Journal* 62 (1):481–533.

Schriner, Kay, Lisa Ochs, and Todd Shields. 1997. The Last Suffrage Movement: Voting Rights for People with Cognitive and Emotional Disabilities. *Publius* 27 (3):75–96.

———. 2000. Democratic Dilemmas: Notes on the ADA and Voting Rights of People with Disabilities. *Berkeley Journal of Employment and Labor Law* 21 (1):437–72.

Schuman, Howard, Charlotte Steed, and Lawrence Bobo. 1988. *Racial Attitudes in America: Trends and Interpretations.* Cambridge, MA: Harvard University Press.

Schur, Edwin M. 1980. *The Politics of Deviance.* Englewood Cliffs, NJ: Prentice Hall.

Scull, Andrew. 1989. *Social Order/Mental Disorder: Anglo-American Psychiatry in Historical Perspective.* Berkeley: University of California Press.

Sears, David O. 1990. Whither Political Socialization Research? The Question of Persistence. Pp. 69–97 in *Political Socialization, Citizenship Education, and Democracy,* edited by Orit Ichilov. New York: Teachers College Press.

Sears, David O., and Carolyn Funk. 1990. Self-interest in Americans' Political Opinions. Pp. 147–70 in *Beyond Self-interest,* edited by Jane J. Mansbridge. Chicago, IL: University of Chicago Press.

Seccombe, Karen. 1999. *So You Think I Drive a Cadillac? Welfare Recipients' Perspectives on the System and Its Reform.* Boston, MA: Allyn and Bacon.

Servon, Lisa. 1999. *Bootstrap Capital: Microenterprises and the Poor.* New York: Brookings Institute.

Servon, Lisa, and Timothy Bates. 1998. Microenterprise as an Exit Route from Poverty. *Journal of Urban Affairs* 20:419–41.

Severens, C. Alexander, and Amy Kays. 1997. *1996 Directory of U.S. Microenterprise Programs.* Washington, DC: The Aspen Institute.

Shinomura, Floyd D. 1985. The History of Claims Against the United States: The Evolution from a Legislative toward a Judicial Model of Payment. *Louisiana Law Review* 45:625–700.

Shklar, Judith N. 1991. *American Citizenship: The Quest for Inclusion.* Cambridge, MA: Harvard University Press.

Sidney, Mara S. 2001. The Origin of U.S. Fair Housing Policy: Images of Race, Class, and Markets. *Journal of Policy History* 13 (2):181–214.

Sigel, Roberta S. 1989. *Political Learning in Adulthood: A Sourcebook of Theory and Research.* Chicago, IL: University of Chicago Press.

Simon, Jonathan. 1993. *Poor Discipline.* Chicago, IL: University of Chicago Press.

Skocpol, Theda. 1992. *Protecting Soldiers and Mothers: The Political Origins of Social Policy in the United States.* Cambridge, MA: Harvard University Press.

Skowronek, Stephen. 1982. *Building a New American State: The Expansion of National Administrative Capacities, 1877–1920.* Cambridge, MA: Cambridge University Press.

Smith, Geoffrey S. 1991. Racial Nativism and Origins of Japanese American Relocation. Pp. 79–87 in *Japanese Americans: From Relocation to Redress,* edited by Roger Daniels, Sandra C. Taylor, and Harry H.L. Kitano (rev. ed.). Seattle: University of Washington Press.

Smith, Page. 1995. *Democracy on Trial: The Japanese American Evacuation and Relocation in World War II.* New York: Simon and Schuster.

Smith, Rogers. 1997. *Civic Ideals: Conflicting Visions of Citizenship in U.S. History.* New Haven, CT: Yale University Press.

Smith, Steven R., and Helen Ingram. 2002. Policy Tools and Democracy. Pp. 565–84 in *The Tools of Government: A Guide to New Governance,* edited by Lester Solomon. Oxford, UK; New York: Oxford University Press.

Smith, Steven, and Michael Lipsky. 1993. *Nonprofits for Hire: The Welfare State in the Age of Contracting.* Cambridge, MA: Harvard University Press.

Solomon, Gerald. 1996a. *Congressional Record. Providing for Consideration of H.R. 2202,* Immigration in the National Interest Act of 1995. 104th Cong., 2nd sess., 19 March, vol. 142, pt. H 2361. Washington, DC: Government Printing Office.

Somkin, Fred. 1967. *Unquiet Eagle: Memory and Desire in the Idea of American Freedom, 1815–1860.* Ithaca, NY: Cornell University Press.

Soss, Joe. n.d. Spoiled Identity and Collective Action: Social and Political Consequences of Welfare Stigma. Unpublished typescript available from the author.

——— . 2000. *Unwanted Claims: Politics, Participation, and the U.S. Welfare System.* Ann Arbor: University of Michigan Press.

Squires, Gregory D. (Ed.). 1992. *From Redlining to Reinvestment: Community Responses to Urban Disinvestment*. Philadelphia, PA: Temple University Press.

State of Louisiana. 1845. *Proceedings and Debates of the Convention of Louisiana*. New Orleans: Author.

State of Massachusetts. 1853. *Official Report of the Debates and Proceedings in the State Convention Assembled May 4, 1853, to Revise and Amend the Constitution of the Commonwealth of Massachusetts*, vol. 2. Boston: Author.

Stearns, Cliff. 1996. *Congressional Record. Authorizing States to Deny Public Education Benefits to Certain Aliens Not Lawfully Present in the United States*. 104th Congress, 2nd sess., 25 September, vol., 142, pt. H 11091. Washington, DC: Government Printing Office.

Stedman-Jones, Gary. 1971. *Outcast London*. London, UK: Penguin Books.

Steinfeld, Robert J. 1989. Property and Suffrage in the Early American Republic. *Stanford Law Review* 41:335–76.

Stickley, Julia Ward. 1972. The Records of Deborah Sampson Gannett, Woman Soldier of the Revolution. *Prologue* 4 (Winter):233–41

Stoesz, David, and David Saunders. 1999. Welfare Capitalism: A New Approach to Poverty Policy? *Social Service Review* 73 (3):380–400.

Stone, Deborah A. 1984. *The Disabled State*. Philadelphia, PA: Temple University Press.

———. 1989. Causal Stories and the Formation of Policy Agendas. *Political Science Quarterly* 104:281–300.

———. 1993. Clinical Authority in the Construction of Citizenship. Pp. 45–67 in *Public Policy for Democracy*, edited by Helen Ingram and Steven R. Smith. Washington, DC: The Brookings Institution.

———. 1997. *Policy Paradox: The Art of Political Decision Making*. New York: W.W. Norton.

Strother, George. 1818–1819. *Annals of the Congress of the United States, 1818–1819*. Washington, DC: Privately printed.

Sundquist, James L. 1968. *Politics and Policy: The Eisenhower, Kennedy, and Johnson Years*. Washington, DC: Brookings Institution.

Surette, Ray. 1998. *Media, Crime, and Criminal Justice: Images and Realities*, 2nd ed. Boston, MA: West/Wadsworth.

Sutherland, Edwin H. 1950a. The Sexual Psychopath Laws. *American Journal of Sociology* 56:534–54.

———. 1950b. The Diffusion of Sexual Psychopath Laws. *American Journal of Sociology* 56:142–8.

Tajfel, Henri. 1970. Experiments in Intergroup Discrimination. *Scientific American* 223:96–102.

———. 1981. *Human Groups and Social Categories: Studies in Social Psychology*. Cambridge, MA: Cambridge University Press.

Tarrow, Sidney. 1998. *Power in Movement: Social Movements and Contentious Politics.* Cambridge, UK; New York: Cambridge University Press.

Taylor, Arnold. 1969. *American Diplomacy and the Narcotics Traffic, 1900–1939.* Durham, NC: Duke University Press.

Tolman, Richard M., and Jody Raphael. 2000. A Review of Research on Domestic Violence. *Journal of Social Issues* 56 (4):655–82.

Tomes, Nancy. 1984. *A Generous Confidence: Thomas Story Kirkbride and the Art of Asylum-keeping, 1840–1883.* Cambridge, MA: Cambridge University Press.

Tonry, Michael. 1993. Sentencing Commissions. Pp. 137–96 in *Crime and Justice: A Review of Research,* vol. 17, edited by Michael Tonry. Chicago, IL: The University of Chicago Press.

———. 1995. *Malign Neglect: Race, Crime, and Punishment.* New York: Oxford University Press.

Trattner, Walter. 1984. *From Poor Law to Welfare State: A History of Social Welfare in America,* 3rd ed. New York: Free Press.

———. 1999. *From Poor Law to Welfare State: A History of Social Welfare in America,* 6th ed. New York: The Free Press.

Trent, James W., Jr. 1994. *Inventing the Feeble Mind: A History of Mental Retardation in the United States.* Berkeley: University of California Press.

Trethewey, Angela. 1997. Resistance, Identity, and Empowerment: A Postmodern Feminist Analysis of Clients in a Human Service Organization. *Communication Monographs* 64:281–301.

Tryneski, John. 2001. Executive editor, University of Chicago Press. Personal interview by Sanford F. Schram, April 20.

Turner, John C. 1987. A Self-categorization Theory. Pp. 43–67 in *Rediscovering the Social Group,* edited by John C. Turner, Michael A. Hogg, Penelope J. Oakes, S. D. Riecher, and Margaret S. Wetherell. Oxford, UK: Basil Blackwell.

Turner, Margery Austin, Stephen L. Ross, George Galster, and John Yinger. 2002. *Discrimination in Metropolitan Housing Markets: National Results from Phase I HDS 2000* [online]. (Washington, DC: U.S. Department of Housing and Urban Development [updated 7 November 2002; cited 18 March 2003]). Available from www.huduser. org/publications/hsgfin/phase1.html.

U.S. Congress. 1967. Fair Housing Act of 1967. *Hearings before the Subcommittee on Housing and Urban Affairs of the Committee of Banking and Currency.* 90th Congress, 1st sess. on S. 1358, S. 2114, and S. 2280 Relating to Civil Rights and Housing (21, 22, and 23 August). Washington, DC: Government Printing Office.

U.S. Department of Health and Human Services. 1995. *Welfare Reform Fact Sheet.* Washington, DC: U.S. Department of Health and Human Services.

U.S. Department of Health and Human Services. 1998. Characteristics and Financial Circumstances of TANF Recipients [online]. (Washington, DC: U.S. Department of Health and Human Services [updated 1999; cited 18 March 2003]). Available from http://www.acf.dhhs.gov/programs/opre/characteristics/fy99/analysis.htm#list.

U.S. General Accounting Office. 1995. *Illegal Aliens: National Net cost Estimates Vary Widely.* Washington, DC: Government Printing Office.

U.S. House. 1964. A Bill to Provide for Certain Surviving Officers and Soldiers of the Revolutionary Army. Pp. 446, (15/1), 1817–1818; *AC* (15/1), H.R. 8, 12 December 1817, in *Bills and Resolutions of the House of Representatives and the Senate.* Washington, DC: Library of Congress.

U.S. House. 1977. Committee on Banking, Finance and Urban Affairs. *Compilation of the Housing and Community Development Act of 1977.* Washington, DC: Government Printing Office.

U.S. House. 1986. Committee on Energy and Commerce. Petitions, Memorials and Other Documents Submitted for the Consideration of Congress: 4 March 1789 to 14 December 1795. 99th Cong., 2nd sess., Comm. Print 99–AA. Washington, DC: Government Printing Office.

U.S. House. 1998. Committee on Ways and Means. *The Green Book.* Washington, DC: Government Printing Office.

U.S. Senate. 1977. *Community Credit Needs: Hearings before the Committee on Banking, Housing, and Urban Affairs.* 95th Cong., 1st sess. (23–25 March), S. 406. Washington, DC: Government Printing Office.

Van Auken, Howard. 1999. Obstacles to Business Launch. *Journal of Developmental Entrepreneurship* 4:175–87.

van Dijk, Teun A. 1993. *Elite Discourse and Racism.* Newbury Park, CA: Sage Publications.

Velazquez, Nydia. 1996. *Congressional Record. Immigration in the* National Interest Act of 1995. 104th Cong., 2nd sess., 20 March, vol. 142, pt. H 2475. Washington, DC: Government Printing Office.

Verba, Sidney, Kay Lehman Schlozman, and Henry E. Brady. 1995. *Voice and Equality: Civic Voluntarism in American Politics.* Cambridge, MA: Harvard University Press.

Verba, Sidney, Kay Lehman Schlozman, Henry Brady, and Norman Nie. 1993. Citizen Activity: Who Participates? What Do They Say? *American Political Science Review* 87 (2):303–19.

Von Hoffman, Alexander. 2001. *Fuel Lines for the Urban Revival Engine: Neighborhoods, Community Development Corporations, and Financial Intermediaries.* Washington, DC: Fannie Mae Foundation.

Walzer, M., 1992. *What It Means to Be an American.* New York: Marsilio Publishers Corporation.

Weaver, R. Kent, 2000. *Ending Welfare As We Know It.* Washington, DC: Brookings Institution Press.

Wedeen, Lisa. 2002. Conceptualizing Culture: Possibilities for Political Science. *American Political Science Review* 96 (4):713–28.

Weiler, Conrad. 1977. *Community Credit Needs: Hearings before the Committee on Banking, Housing, and Urban Affairs.* 95th Cong., 1st sess. (23–25 March), S. 406. Washington, DC: Government Printing Office.

Welfare Law Center. 1996. *Welfare Myths: Fact or Fiction? Exploring the Truth about Welfare.* New York: Author.

Wellman, David. 1997. Minstrel Shows, Affirmative Action, Talk and Angry White Men: Marking Racial Otherness in the 1990s. Pp. 333–48 in *Displacing Whiteness: Essays in Social and Cultural Criticism,* edited by Ruth Frankenberg. Durham, NC: Duke University Press.

Wildavsky, Aaron B. 1979. *Speaking Truth to Power: The Art and Craft of Policy Analysis.* Boston, MA: Little, Brown.

———. 1987. *Speaking Truth to Power: The Art and Craft of Policy Analysis.* New Brunswick, NJ: Transaction Books.

Williams, Allen. 1883. *The Demon of the Orient and his Satellite Friends of the Joints: Our Opium Smokers as They Are in Tartar Hells and American Paradises.* New York: Author.

Williams, Linda. 2001. *Playing the Race Card: Melodramas of Black and White from Uncle Tom to O. J. Simpson.* Princeton, NJ: Princeton University Press.

Williamson, Chilton. 1960. *American Suffrage from Property to Democracy.* Princeton, NJ: Princeton University Press.

Wilson, James Q. 1973. The Sick Sixties. *Atlantic Monthly* (October), 91–98.

———. 1975. *Thinking about Crime.* New York: Basic Books.

———. 1983. *Thinking about Crime,* 2nd ed. New York: Basic Books.

———. 1985. *Thinking about Crime,* Rev. ed. New York: Vintage Books.

Wilson, James Q., and Richard Hernstein. 1985. *Crime and Human Nature.* New York: Simon and Schuster.

Wilson, William Julius. 1987. *The Truly Disadvantaged: The Inner City, the Underclass, and Public Policy.* Chicago, IL: The University of Chicago Press.

———. 1999. *The Bridge over the Racial Divide: Rising Inequality and Coalition Politics.* Berkeley: University of California Press.

Wilson, William Julius, and Katherine M. Neckerman. 1984. Poverty and Family Structure: The Widening Gap between Evidence and Public Policy Issues. Conference Paper. Madison: University of Wisconsin-Madison, Institute for Research on Poverty, December, Williamsburg, Virginia.

Woerner, John G. 1897. *A Treatise on the American Law of Guardianship of Minors and Persons of Unsound Mind.* Boston: Little, Brown, and Company.

Wood, Gordon S. 1987. Interests and Disinterestedness in the Making of the Constitution. Pp. 69–109 in *Beyond Confederation: Origins of the Constitution and American National Identity,* edited by Richard Beeman, Stephen Botein, and Edward C. Carter II. Chapel Hill: University of North Carolina Press.

Wright, Hamilton. 1910. Report on the International Opium Commission. 61st Cong., 2nd sess., *Opium Problem: A Message from the President of the United States,* Senate doc. 377, 47.

Wu, Cheng-Tsu. 1972. *Chink! A Documentary History of Anti-Chinese Prejudice in America.* New York: World Pub.

Yoo, David. 1993. "Read All About It": Race, Generation, and the Japanese American Ethnic Press, 1925–1941. *Amerasia Journal* 19 (1):69–92.

Young, Iris. 1990. *Justice and the Politics of Difference.* Trenton, NJ: Princeton University Press.

Yung, Judy. 1999. *Unbound Voices: A Documentary History of Chinese Women in San Francisco.* Berkeley: University of California Press.

Zabriskie, Alexander. 1948. *Bishop Brent: Crusader for Christian Unity.* Philadelphia, PA: Westminster Press.

Zimiring, Franklin, and Gordon Hawkins. 1992. *The Search for a Rational Drug Control Policy.* Cambridge, MA: Cambridge University Press.

Zrzek, Slavoj. 1997. Multiculturalism, Or, the Cultural Logic of Multinational Capitalism. *New Left Review* 225 (September/October):28–51.

Contributors

Dionne Bensonsmith currently attends the Maxwell School of Citizenship and Public Affairs at Syracuse University, where she is completing her dissertation on the same topic as her chapter. Portions of this chapter were completed while on fellowship at Cornell University and also appear in the dissertation.

Michelle Camou is a Ph.D. Candidate in the department of Political Science at the University of Colorado at Boulder. Her research interests center on the impact of economic globalization on labor relations, governance, and grassroots collective action in U.S., Canadian, and Latin American cities. Her dissertation compares the rise of community-based governance strategies to combat labor exploitation related to employment in Baltimore, Denver, and Guadalajara, Mexico.

Julie Cowgill is a Ph.D. candidate in the School of Justice Studies at Arizona State University. Her interests focus on domestic violence, gender and identity, violence, and urban youth. She is interested in all aspects of justice theory, including institutional settings, especially nonprofits, and community contexts.

Stephanie J. DiAlto is a Ph.D. candidate in the Department of Political Science at the University of California, Irvine. An earlier draft of this chapter received the Charles Redd Award for Best Paper on the Politics of the American West jointly awarded by the Western Political Science Association and the Charles Redd Center for Western Studies of Brigham Young University. Her dissertation analyzes the competition between official frames produced by the U.S. government and collective action frames produced by social movement organizations in the Native Hawaiian sovereignty movement.

Helen M. Ingram holds the Warmington Endowed Chair in the School of Social Ecology and is a professor in the Department of Society and Politics at the University of California, Irvine. She is coauthor of *Policy Design for Democracy,*

Divided Waters: Bridging the U.S.-Mexico Border, Public Policy and Democracy, and a number of other books. Her research interests focus on public participation and the ways in which public policies affect democracy, policy design and implementation, water resources and equity issues, and transboundary natural resource issues, especially along the U.S.-Mexican border. Her Ph.D. is in political science from Columbia University. She has previously taught at the University of Arizona and the University of New Mexico.

Laura S. Jensen is associate professor of political science and a faculty associate of the Center for Public Policy and Administration at the University of Massachusetts, Amherst. Her work, tracing the rise of U.S. Federal social policy, has been recognized by the National Endowment for the Humanities and the American Political Science Association. In addition to *Patriots, Settlers, and the Origins of American Social Policy* (Cambridge University Press, 2003), Dr. Jensen has published articles in *The Review of Politics, Public Administration Review, Polity, and Studies in American Political Development.*

Nancy Jurik is a Professor of Justice Studies at Arizona State University. Her course offerings include "Women and Work" and "Economic Justice." Her publications focus on gender and work organizations. She has published a book, entitled *Doing Justice, Doing Gender: Women in Law and Criminal Justice Occupations* (Sage 1996), and numerous articles on gender and work issues. She is completing a book on U.S. microenterprise development programs, entitled *Credit for Whom? U.S. Microenterprise Development in an Era of Welfare Reform.* She is the 2002–2003 President of the Society for the Study of Social Problems.

Kenneth J. Meier is the Charles Puryear Professor of Liberal Arts in the Department of Political Science. He also holds the Sara Lindsey Chair in Government in the George Bush School of Government at Texas A&M University. He is interested in virtually every topic in public policy and administration. Currently he is investigating questions of race, ethnicity, and gender in educational politics, the Equal Employment Opportunity Commission, healthcare policy, and local law enforcement policies.

Lina Newton is an assistant professor of political science at Hunter College, CUNY. Her specialty is U.S. immigration policy and minority politics. Her most recent article in *Social Science Quarterly* focused on reaction in the Latino community to California's Proposition 187. Her doctoral dissertation, "Constructing the Immigrant Ideal," was completed at the University of California, Irvine in 2002.

Sean Nicholson-Crotty is a visiting assistant professor in the Department of Political Science at Texas A&M University, from which he received his

Ph.D. in 2003. His research interests include public policy, fiscal federalism and intergovernmental relations, and public management. He has published in the *American Journal of Political Science, Political Research Quarterly,* the *Journal of Public Administration Research and Theory,* and the *Journal of Policy Analysis and Management.*

Anne L. Schneider is the Dean of the College of Public Programs and a Professor of Justice Studies at Arizona State University. She is the coauthor of *Policy Design for Democracy* and *Deterrence and Juvenile Crime.* Her areas of interest include public policy, democracy, policy design, implementation, social justice, citizenship, privatization, women and politics, and specific policy areas such as juvenile and criminal justice. Professor Schneider's Ph.D. is in political science from Indiana University. Previously, she has taught at Yale University and Oklahoma State University. She also directed the private, nonprofit research institute, Institute for Policy Analysis, in Eugene, Oregon.

Sanford F. Schram teaches social policy and social theory in the Graduate School of Social Work and Social Research at Bryn Mawr College. Active in policy deliberations regarding U.S. social welfare policy, he has testified before Congress on welfare reform reauthorization and his research has been used before the Supreme Court in the landmark case *Saenz v. Roe,* which struck down state residency requirements for receipt of welfare. He authored *Praxis for the Poor: Piven and Cloward and the Future of Social Science in Social Welfare* (New York University Press, 2002), *After Welfare: The Culture of Postindustrial Social Policy* (New York University Press, 2000), and *Words of Welfare: The Poverty of Social Science and the Social Science of Poverty* (University of Minnesota Press, 1995)—which won the Michael Harrington Award from the American Political Science Association. He also coedited with Joe Soss and Richard C. Fording, *Race and the Politics of Welfare Reform* (University of Michigan Press, 2003), with Samuel H. Beer, *Welfare Reform: A Race to the Bottom?* (Johns Hopkins University Press, 1999), and with Philip Neisser, *Tales of the State: Narrative in U.S. Politics and Public Policy* (Rowman & Littlefield, 1997). Schram has published research articles on the politics of welfare in the *American Sociological Review, American Journal of Political Science, Polity, Rethinking MARXISM, Social Text,* and other journals.

Kay Schriner, Ph.D., is research professor and assistant director of the School of Social Work at the University of Arkansas. She is the founding editor of the *Journal of Disability Policy Studies,* which she edited for ten years. She has received research honors from the American Rehabilitation Counseling Association and from the University of Arkansas. She was a presidential appointee to the President's Committee on the Employment of People with Disabilities and was designated a Mary E. Switzer Scholar by the National Rehabilitation

Association in 1995. In 1998 and again in 2002, she was awarded Distinguished Switzer Fellowships by the National Institute on Disability and Rehabilitation Research. Dr. Schriner has published extensively on the subjects of disability policy and the political participation of people with disabilities.

Mara S. Sidney is an assistant professor of political science at Rutgers University-Newark. She studies public policy and advocacy against racial inequality, particularly with regard to housing and education. She is the author of *Unfair Housing: How National Policy Shapes Local Action* (University Press of Kansas, 2003) and her work has appeared in the *Urban Affairs Review,* the *Journal of Urban Affairs,* and the *Journal of Policy History.*

Joe Soss is Associate Professor of Political Science and Public Affairs at the University of Wisconsin-Madison. He also serves as an affiliate of the Institute for Research on Poverty. His primary areas of teaching and research include the politics of poverty and social policy, political psychology, public opinion, political behavior, and empirical theory and research methodology. He is the author of *Unwanted Claims: The Politics of Participation in the U.S. Welfare System* (University of Michigan Press, 2000), a study that investigates welfare institutions as sites of political action and learning for citizens. He is also co-editor of *Race and the Politics of Welfare Reform* (University of Michigan Press, 2003), a volume that explores the historical and contemporary role of race in U.S. welfare politics. His current research projects focus on the racial politics of public policy, the consequences of policy feedback for poverty politics, and the relationship between welfare state development and citizen politics in the United States.

Index